ROCK CLIMBING NEW MEXICO

Help Us Keep This Guide Up to Date

Every effort has been made by the author and editors to make this guide as accurate and useful as possible. However, many things can change after a guide is published— trails are rerouted, regulations change, techniques evolve, facilities come under new management, and so forth.

We would love to hear from you concerning your experiences with this guide and how you feel it could be improved and kept up to date. While we may not be able to respond to all comments and suggestions, we'll take them to heart and we'll also make certain to share them with the author. Please send your comments and suggestions to the following address:

The Globe Pequot Press
Reader Response/Editorial Department
P.O. Box 480
Guilford, CT 06437

Or you may e-mail us at:

editorial@GlobePequot.com

Thanks for your input, and happy travels!

A **FALCON** GUIDE ®

ROCK CLIMBING
NEW MEXICO

Dennis R. Jackson

FALCON GUIDE ®

GUILFORD, CONNECTICUT
HELENA, MONTANA
AN IMPRINT OF THE GLOBE PEQUOT PRESS

A FALCON GUIDE®

Spine photo © Brand X Pictures
Text design by Casey Shain
Maps by Volker Schniepp Geographisches Institute © Morris Book Publishing, LLC
Topos on pages 81, 130, 284, 286, 296, 298, 300, 303, 402, 407, 411, and 416 by Martha Morris © Morris Book Publishing, LLC

ISSN: 1558-2175
ISBN-13: 978-0-7627-3132-9
ISBN-10: 0-7627-3132-X

Manufactured in the United States of America
First Edition/Second Printing

WARNING:

Climbing is a sport where you may be seriously injured or die. Read this before you use this book.

This guidebook is a compilation of unverified information gathered from many different climbers. The author cannot assure the accuracy of any of the information in this book, including the topos and route descriptions, the difficulty ratings, and the protection ratings. These may be incorrect or misleading, as ratings of climbing difficulty and danger are always subjective and depend on the physical characteristics (for example, height), experience, technical ability, confidence, and physical fitness of the climber who supplied the rating. Additionally, climbers who achieve first ascents sometimes underrate the difficulty or danger of the climbing route. Therefore, be warned that you must exercise your own judgment on where a climbing route goes, its difficulty, and your ability to safely protect yourself from the risks of rock climbing. Examples of some of these risks are: falling due to technical difficulty or due to natural hazards such as holds breaking, falling rock, climbing equipment dropped by other climbers, hazards of weather and lightning, your own equipment failure, and failure or absence of fixed protection.

You should not depend on any information gleaned from this book for your personal safety; your safety depends on your own good judgment, based on experience and a realistic assessment of your climbing ability. If you have any doubt as to your ability to safely climb a route described in this book, do not attempt it.

The following are some ways to make your use of this book safer:

1. Consultation: You should consult with other climbers about the difficulty and danger of a particular climb prior to attempting it. Most local climbers are glad to give advice on routes in their area; we suggest that you contact locals to confirm ratings and safety of particular routes and to obtain firsthand information about a route chosen from this book.

2. Instruction: Most climbing areas have local climbing instructors and guides available. We recommend that you engage an instructor or guide to learn safety techniques and to become familiar with the routes and hazards of the areas described in this book. Even after you are proficient in climbing safely, occasional use of a guide is a safe way to raise your climbing standard and learn advanced techniques.

3. Fixed Protection: Some of the routes in this book may use bolts and pitons that are permanently placed in the rock. Because of variances in the manner of placement, weathering, metal fatigue, the quality of the metal used, and many other factors, these fixed protection pieces should always be considered suspect and should always be backed up by equipment that you place yourself. Never depend on a single piece of fixed protection for your safety, because you never can tell whether it will hold weight.

In some cases, fixed protection may have been removed or is now missing. However, climbers should not always add new pieces of protection unless existing protection is faulty. Existing protection can be tested by an experienced climber and its strength determined. Climbers are strongly encouraged not to add bolts and drilled pitons to a route. They need to climb the route in the style of the first ascent party (or better) or choose a route within their ability—a route to which they do not have to add additional fixed anchors.

Be aware of the following specific potential hazards that could arise in using this book:

1. Incorrect Descriptions of Routes: If you climb a route and you have a doubt as to where it goes, you should not continue unless you are sure that you can go that way safely. Route descriptions and topos in this book could be inaccurate or misleading.

2. Incorrect Difficulty Rating: A route might be more difficult than the rating indicates. Do not be lulled into a false sense of security by the difficulty rating.

3. Incorrect Protection Rating: If you climb a route and you are unable to arrange adequate protection from the risk of falling through the use of fixed pitons or bolts and by placing your own protection devices, do not assume that there is adequate protection available higher just because the route protection rating indicates the route does not have an X or an R rating. Every route is potentially an X (a fall may be deadly) due to the inherent hazards of climbing—including, for example, failure or absence of fixed protection, your own equipment's failure, or improper use of climbing equipment.

There are no warranties, whether expressed or implied, that this guidebook is accurate or that the information contained in it is reliable. There are no warranties of fitness for a particular purpose or that this guide is merchantable. Your use of this book indicates your assumption of the risk that it may contain errors and is an acknowledgment of your own sole responsibility for your climbing safety.

CONTENTS

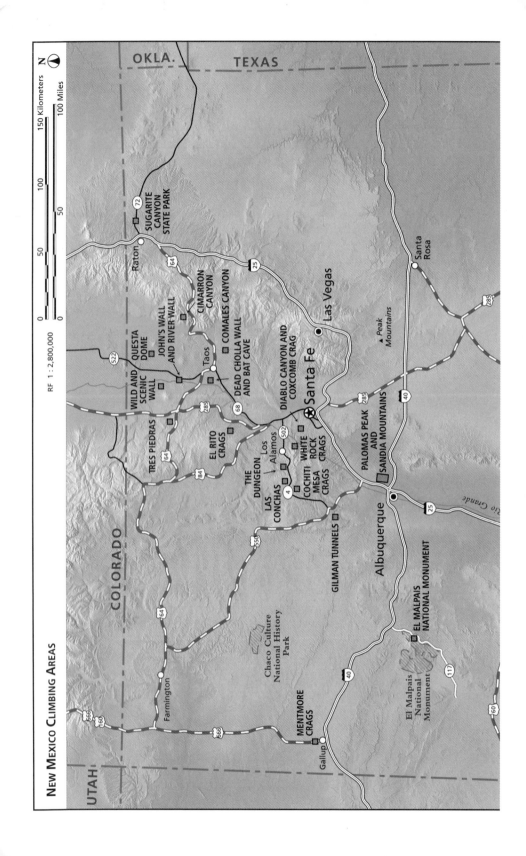

NEW MEXICO CLIMBING AREAS

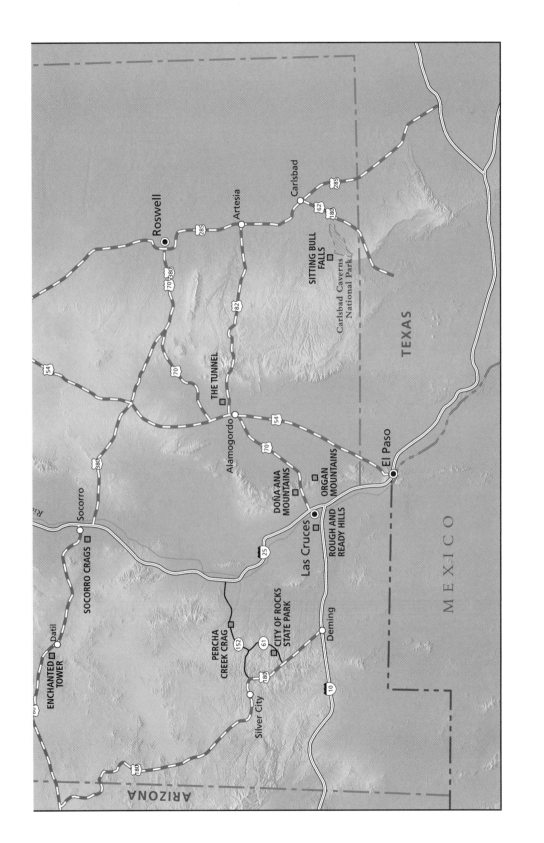

ACKNOWLEDGMENTS

Rock Climbing New Mexico was only possible with the help of many New Mexico climbers. My sincere thanks to all the climbers who aided on an earlier version, including Doug Bridgers, Doug Couleur, Jean Delatalaide, Paul Drakos, Jim Graham, Ed Jaramillo, Dave Pegg, Peter Prandoni, Lee Sheftel, Ken Sims, and Mark Thomas. Their invaluable advice, beta, corrections, and input laid the groundwork for this book.

The following climbers gave freely of their time and knowledge to ensure the accuracy and completeness of this book: Jeff Amato, Dave Baltz, Marc Beverly, Rick Bradshaw, Doug Bridgers, Lee Brinckerhoff, Paul Drakos, Jay Foley, Jim Graham, Lance Hadfield, Scott Halliday, Luke Hanley, Mickey Hazelwood, Trennis Hindoe, John Hymer, John Kear, Karl Kiser, Charley Koehler, Aaron Miller, Bryan Pletta, Rick Smith, Mark Thomas, Kurt Vollbrect, Tom Wezwick, and Vibeka Wilberg. Also muchas gracias to Dr. Ken Sims, my longtime climbing partner and friend, who supplied much information and wrote the comprehensive geology section.

Stewart Green, my editor, and graphic artist Martha Morris were involved with *Rock Climbing New Mexico* from start to finish, providing editorial guidance, corrections, topos, and photographs. This book is as much theirs as it is mine. My heartfelt thanks to these two. Lastly a special thanks to my wife, Carol Jackson, who provided love, support, encouragement, camper time, editing, and home.

MAP LEGEND

Borders

International Border — - -

State Border ─── ─ ─

National, State Park / Forest

Private enclave

Reservation

Fence ················

Transportation

Interstate ⟨10⟩

State highway ⟨54⟩

Paved roads ⟨86⟩

Dirt road = = = = =

Established trail - - - - - - - -

Informal trail - - - - - - - -

Railroad ┠┼┼┼┼┼┼┨

Hydrology

Lake

Stream

Intermittent Stream

Dry Stream (Ephemeral)

Physiography

Cliff / scarp

Peak ▲

Spire/pinnacle/needle ׀

Boulders ●

Symbols

Backcountry campsite ▲

Bridge

Campground ⋀

Climbing site ▣

Dam ─

Gate ●─●

Overlook / viewpoint ◉

Parking 🅿

Picnic area 🅰

Point of interest ■

Toilet 🚻

Visitor Center ❓

Population

Capital ✪

City ◉

Town ○

KEY TO TOPOS

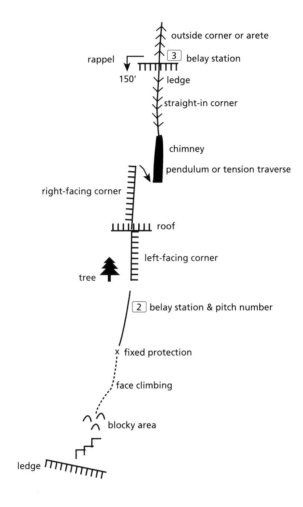

outside corner or arete

rappel 3 belay station

150' ledge

straight-in corner

chimney

pendulum or tension traverse

right-facing corner

roof

left-facing corner

tree

2 belay station & pitch number

x fixed protection

face climbing

blocky area

ledge

INTRODUCTION

Welcome to New Mexico, the "Land of Enchantment." New Mexico, the nation's fifth-largest state with 121,599 square miles, offers excellent rock climbing areas on a variety of rocks including basalt, granite, sandstone, and limestone. Visiting climbers from around the world discover what local climbers have always known—New Mexico has great rock climbing. The state's stunning natural beauty, quality, and quantity of rock, lack of crowds, and friendly scene make for a rich climbing experience.

Those unfamiliar with New Mexico usually envision a hot desert landscape with cacti and shimmering heat. Although the state has a dry, warm climate, this myth is simply not true. Visiting climbers are treated to pristine scenery in the Sangre de Cristo Mountains in northern New Mexico and to arid basins and ranges in the state's southern half. New Mexico's average July temperature is 74 degrees while the average January temperature is 34 degrees. The state's southern areas are much warmer in both summer and winter, although the mountain ranges that tower over the desert basins offer relief from summer heat. With thoughtful pre-planning, it's possible to climb year-round in New Mexico.

New Mexico's climbing scene is alive and flourishing. A lot of new areas were developed in New Mexico since the release of *Rock Climbing New Mexico & Texas* in 1996. This new guide covers thirty-four separate climbing areas including more than eighty crags. This book offers 780 new routes in 18 new areas and expanded coverage of crags covered in *Rock Climbing New Mexico & Texas*. Climbers of all abilities will enjoy these additions to the New Mexico climbing scene. New areas include Bat Cave, Cimarron Canyon State Park, Diablo Canyon, El Rito Crags, Gallow's Edge, Gilman Tunnels, Comales Canyon, Percha Creek Crag, Rough and Ready Hills, Wild and Scenic Wall, Sugarite Canyon State Park, Mentmore Crags, and The Tunnel.

There have also been closures since the 1996 book came out. Heart of Stone Rock near Taos and portions of the Doña Ana Mountains near Las Cruces have been closed to climbing. Fortunately these closures are not the result of climber misbehavior, and the areas may reopen if access issues are resolved. Tres Piedras Rocks, once vulnerable to closure, remains open as a testament that climbers can do it right.

Please continue to exercise good judgment whenever you visit Tres Piedras and other New Mexico areas. Chipping, gluing, hold manufacturing, and other rock-defacing tactics are also less of a problem now. The problem, however, has not disappeared. A "tool kit" with a chisel and glue that belonged to someone "creating" boulder problems was found below Questa Dome in 2003. The U.S. Forest Service removed the trail on maps to Questa Dome and is actively "discouraging visitation" to the area. We can only hope it is not because of an unthinking climber's actions.

Grassroots stewardship of crags has significantly improved relations between climbers and land managers. The Access Fund and New Mexico CRAG lead this effort. Mentmore Crags near Gallup demonstrates what happens when climbers and

A climber cranks the finishing moves of *Apple Cobbler* (5.10a) at El Rito. PHOTO BY
STEWART M. GREEN

local citizens join together to solve access problems. The area, once a private dump, was
purchased by the city and cleaned up for use as a park and a terrific climbing venue.

NEW MEXICO'S CRAGS

The state has historically offered lots of traditional climbing adventures on its many
basalt crags and high mountain cliffs. Now, however, bolted sport climbing is the focus
at most of the state's climbing areas.

North-central New Mexico offers a wealth of climbing in a variety of settings. The
granite cliffs at Tres Piedras and Questa Dome yield brilliant face and crack routes.
Numerous basalt crags, many above the Rio Grande, have superb traditional crack
climbs as well as bolted face routes. They include Dead Cholla Wall, John's Wall, Sugarite
Canyon, Diablo Canyon, and the many superb cliffs at White Rock. Conglomerate is
the climber's medium at El Rito, one of the best new areas. Cimarron Canyon and
Comales Canyon both yield fine cragging on compact sandstone, while Cochiti Mesa,
Las Conchas, and The Dungeon are composed of soft rhyolite.

Central New Mexico's climbing venues near Albuquerque include the big granite
walls on the Sandia Mountains, granite crags at Gilman Tunnels along the Rio

Brett Green laybacks up *Hageemoto* (5.11d) at Dead Cholla Wall.
PHOTO BY STEWART M. GREEN

Guadalupe, and excellent limestone at Palomas Peak. Farther south are the popular Socorro Crags and excellent pocket-pulling at Enchanted Tower.

Western New Mexico offers Mentmore Crags, a good climbing area just west of Gallup. This small island of climbing is one of the few legal climbing areas on New Mexico's Colorado Plateau. Other western New Mexico rock is either on Navajo Nation land, Pueblo lands, or is privately owned. South of Grants is the superb *Crack of Heraclitus* in El Malpais National Monument. Shiprock, in New Mexico's far northwestern corner, remains officially closed to climbers, so detailed information on it is omitted from this book.

Southern New Mexico offers great winter climbing areas. Grand climbing adventures are found in the rugged Organ Mountains above Las Cruces, including some outstanding long new routes on Organ Needle and Minerva's Temple. Percha Creek Crag offers crack climbing on a quiet andesite cliff. The Rough and Ready Hills, northwest of Las Cruces, is a sunny arena for sport climbing. The Tunnel, just east of Alamogordo, is a perfect area for hard winter cranking on steep limestone cliffs.

OTHER NEW MEXICO CLIFFS

This guide covers almost every developed crag in New Mexico but does not include any routes or cliffs on Indian lands or on private property that prohibits climbing. Climbers wishing to climb on Indian reservation land should request permission from the different tribal councils. This is a time-consuming and frustrating process, so plan accordingly. Be advised that Navajo tribal law prohibits rock climbing on their reservation. Climbing Shiprock or any other formation without permission is a serious mistake. Both Cochiti Pueblo and Zuni Pueblo have excellent climbing areas, but both ban climbing. Unauthorized climbing does occur, but neither pueblo currently welcomes climbers.

The Brazos Cliffs, with some of New Mexico's most beautiful and largest cliffs, is privately owned and closed to climbing. The Los Alamos Mountaineers have a historic but unofficial presence here. They are a good resource to contact about access issues and route information.

Philmont Scout Ranch, a 144,000-acre private preserve in northeastern New Mexico, has been mentioned in other guidebooks as having climbing opportunities. This is definitely not true. The Tooth of Time, a miniature El Capitan, is the focal point of the ranch. It begs to be climbed, but don't even ask. The answer will be no.

EQUIPMENT

Many of New Mexico's classic routes were put up in the pre-Friends era, so almost any piece of protection works on most routes. Camming units, referred to in the route descriptions as TCUs, Friends, and camming units, are carried on most traditional routes.

Javier Manrique on *Melanoma* (5.12d) at Sunny Side Wall, The Tunnel.
PHOTO BY STEWART M. GREEN

A double set of Friends or equivalent-size cams, a set of Stoppers, RPs or similar small wired nuts, extra slings, quickdraws, and a 165-foot rope is sufficient for most routes. Refer to area and route descriptions for more specific gear information. Whenever you are in doubt about the possible protection, be sure to carry extra gear to ensure your safety.

A windshirt, rain gear, wool cap, and descent shoes are optional but desirable on mountain routes in the Sangre de Cristo Mountains, Sandias, or Organs. Wearing a helmet is always recommended, especially on mountain cliffs and when belaying below the shorter crags. New Mexico's cliffs are particularly vulnerable to rock fall from climbers setting up topropes or walking along the cliff top. Carrying water can be a hassle when climbing but is recommended on all long routes. Camel up, that is, drink a lot, before you leave the ground. Also carry plenty of water on your route, and have extra water waiting in your pack and car. This is particularly important in summer and at the remote cliffs in southern New Mexico.

Sport routes require only quickdraws to clip bolts for protection. Some routes, usually sparsely bolted, are protected with both bolts and gear. This is especially true at Cochiti Mesa and Socorro Crags. For these climbs, bring a small rack that includes TCUs, Stoppers, and a range of Friends for extra protection between bolts. A single 165-foot rope is sufficient for most sport routes, although a 200-foot rope is needed on a few.

CLIMBING DANGERS AND SAFETY

Have you lost a friend in a climbing accident? Many of us know someone who was killed while climbing. Climbing is dangerous. Don't ever think of it as a safe and sanitized experience. Once you leave the ground and enter the vertical world, all sorts of errors can occur.

Newer climbers, nurtured in a friendly climbing gym, are especially vulnerable to making mistakes. Experience gained in a gym falls short of equipping a climber for the real world of outside rock. It's best to learn outdoors under the supervision of experienced climbers. Newcomers should avail themselves of all the instruction and mentoring they can find. Experienced climbers will make each outing a learning experience so you can continue to climb safely.

The following are some suggestions to make your New Mexico climbing days more fun and safe.

- Make it a rule to never hit the deck (fall to the ground). This is always important near the start of a climb. Ask yourself: Is the first protection placed so I will not hit the ground when I climb above it? Always climb within your ability. Be bold but not foolish.
- Before you weight the rope at any rappel or lowering situation, check your entire system. This relates to above—never fall to the ground. Are the anchors good? Is the

Ian Spencer-Green crimps pockets on *Double Jeopardy* (5.12b/c R) at Cochiti Mesa.
Photo by Stewart M. Green

rope through the anchors? Am I tied in? Is my harness doubled back? Is my belayer ready? Put full weight on the system while still clipped into your daisy chain before unclipping it from the anchors.

- Before you leave the ground, check through your system and your partner's system. Are both harnesses doubled back? Are you both tied in? Does the belayer need an anchor? Do you have what you need to lead and belay? Do you have descent information? Can you get off the route if you need to retreat?
- Avoid climbing beneath other parties. If someone chooses to climb below you, be aware and extra careful not to drop anything on them. Always wear a helmet to protect your head in case of rock fall caused by careless climbers above.
- Place lots of protection, particularly near the bottom of routes and in soft rock where gear can pull out. This relates back to the first rule—don't hit the ground.
- Always tie a secure knot at the loose end of each rope before you rappel, especially if you are unsure if the ropes reach the ground or are making multiple rappels. Climbers die every year after rappelling off the end of the rope. These fatalities are easily prevented by tying knots in the rope ends.
- Insist that your belayer tie off the loose end of your rope when you are lowering from a sport climb's anchors, or insist that he is tied into that end. This keeps the rope from passing through the belay device if your rope is not long enough. Again, folks die every year after the rope slips through the belay device.
- Always insist that your belayer is attentive to you while you are climbing and that he never takes you off belay until you are safely on the ground. Many fatal accidents happen when the belayer takes the lead climber off belay while he is threading the anchor. The leader assumes he is still on belay, leans back, and plunges to the ground. Be responsible for both your own safety and that of your partner.

OBJECTIVE DANGERS

Stuff happens at the cliff that you have no control over. These objective dangers occur despite all your precautions. It's best to recognize and prepare for dangerous situations. Be vigilant about your safety on the way to the cliff, on the climb, and on the descent. Consider yourself vulnerable to injury or death until you safely return to your car.

Use all fixed protection with caution. Always be suspect about bolts and other fixed gear found on routes. Older ¼-inch bolts are particularly suspect. Weathering and rusting, repeated falls, and poor placements all contribute to their danger. Visual inspection cannot always tell you how good these bolts are. Back them up whenever possible and do not fall on them. Never rappel, lower, or toprope from a single piece of gear. Build redundancy into your life support system so that the failure of one part is not catastrophic to the whole system.

Martha Morris belays Dennis Jackson on *Miami Vice* (5.10b) at Sugarite Canyon State Park. PHOTO BY STEWART M. GREEN

Ian Spencer-Green on *Bad Moon Rising* (5.10c) at Sugarite Canyon State Park. Photo by
Stewart M. Green

Rocks falling from above represent one of the biggest climbing dangers. These are
dislodged by weather conditions, yourself, your partner, other climbers, and animals. Stay
out of the fall-line at the bottom of cliffs when you're belaying, and make sure others
are safe under overhangs or away from the cliff base. Make it a practice at the cliff top to
not dislodge rocks, even if you think no one is below. When climbing, test any suspect-
looking holds and warn your belayer before you climb past loose rock. Set up belays to
the side of the line of ascent whenever possible.

Learn to identify and avoid poison oak and poison ivy. These are common plants at
many New Mexico crags. Wasps, bees, ticks, and rattlesnakes are also common at many
areas. Look for wasp and bees' nests on routes. If you see one, select another route. Ticks,
active in late spring and early summer, are usually found in brushy areas or dense woods.
Check your clothing and body for these bloodsuckers and remove them immediately.

Two types of rattlesnakes, prairie rattlesnakes and western diamondbacks, inhabit
New Mexico. You have a good chance of encountering these pit vipers, the only poi-
sonous ones in the state, at most New Mexico crags. Watch where you walk and sit. Use
caution crossing talus fields and hiking along the cliff base or in brushy country. Do not
kill the snakes. If you encounter a rattlesnake, step back and leave it alone. They know
you are too big for prey and usually will only bite if surprised or handled. After the rare
rattlesnake bite, venom is injected in about half the bites. If someone is bitten, treat the
area as a broken bone by splinting and immobilizing it, evacuate him quickly, and seek
medical attention at a hospital.

Weather and climate present objective dangers for climbers. New Mexico's weather is controlled by its complex terrain and large land area. The state ranges in elevation from 13,161 feet atop Wheeler Peak in the Sangre de Cristo Mountains to 2,817 feet where the Pecos River empties into Texas. Expect hot summer temperatures up to 100 degrees throughout the state, with cooler temperatures in the mountains. Drink lots of water to stay hydrated. This helps you avoid heat exhaustion and heatstroke. Seek shade whenever possible in hot weather, particularly during midday. Wear a hat, use sunscreen, and limit your climbing to mornings, evenings, and shaded crags. The threat of heavy thunderstorms with dangerous lightning strikes and flash floods is as dangerous as heat exhaustion and sunstroke. Watch for storms from June through August.

Climbing activity slows in winter except at southern areas. It is possible, however, to climb at most crags in this guide except Questa Dome and the Sandia Mountains on warm winter days. Winter normally brings snowstorms and cold temperatures to central and northern New Mexico. The southern part of the state is mild and often warm with cold nights. It almost never snows there except on the higher elevations.

ACCESS AND ENVIRONMENTAL CONSIDERATIONS

New Mexico's climbing crags, like elsewhere in the United States, have many environmental problems and access concerns. How climbers act at the cliffs dictates the future of climbing at some New Mexico areas. Climbers need to work to preserve and protect these important climbing areas.

Beginning in the 1990s, climbing has undergone a paradigm shift. The old-time maverick mentality of doing whatever you want wherever you want was long part of climbing lore and legend. Now, however, climbers simply cannot do whatever they want. Everyone's actions at the crags have the potential of negatively affecting all climbers.

Climbers need to realize that land managers treat them like every other user group. They have to jump through the same bureaucratic hoops and comply with the same regulations as mountain bikers, hikers, ATV riders, and river rafters. Governmental land managers are willing to work with climbers to develop access trails and management plans for rock climbing on public lands. They are, however, disturbed by the cavalier attitude of some climbers who take it upon themselves to develop new climbing areas by placing bolts and permanent anchors, and by creating social trails to the cliffs, without prior consultation with land managers and with no regard for existing management plans and current regulations. Many areas like Sugarite Canyon State Park were unprepared to deal with a sudden increase in climbing.

Climbers should not see regulations and management plans as an impediment to cliff and route development, but rather as an opportunity to work with governmental land stewards to both protect and utilize public lands. We can ensure continued access to climb on public lands everywhere in New Mexico by cooperating with land managers.

Land managers feel that climbers are no different from the rest of the population when it comes to tending the natural environment. A large influx of new climbers

without a strict environmental consciousness has led to an astonishing disregard for some of New Mexico's cliffs. Climbers have left much behind, including trash, cigarette butts, used tape, and Mylar wrappers at the base of popular routes. Other areas are dotted with chalked holds, laced with unnecessary trails, and have chipped, filled, drilled, and manufactured handholds.

Every climber needs to become a better steward of our crags to ensure continued access and to be able to continue climbing without excessive restrictions. Climbers need to use lots of common sense, have acceptable outdoor behavior, and realize a spiritual connection to the natural world.

Always walk with small footprints wherever you go, whether hiking to the cliff base or climbing a route. Respect the climbing area and its natural environment so everyone who visits after you will also have an enjoyable experience. Try to leave the crags better and cleaner than when you came. The following are some general suggestions that can help.

1. Carry out everything you carry in. Pick up any trash you find and pack it out.
2. Use existing approach and descent trails. Avoid shortcutting trails, which causes extra erosion. Soil erosion destroys plants and groundcover, leading to degradation of the area. Try to belay from a boulder instead of a grass ledge at the crag base. Do not chop down trees or tear off limbs that might interfere with the first few feet of a route. Use a longer approach or descent route if necessary to protect sensitive ecological areas.
3. Be prepared to deal with crapping in the outdoors. Shit happens, but yours doesn't have to happen for everybody else. Carry toilet paper, matches, and a small trowel. If you do not have a trowel, use a stick. Select an area away from where other humans visit, dig a "cat-hole" into the humus layer of soil, do your business, and pack your toilet paper out in a ziplock baggie. Some still advocate burning tissue, but there is always the possibility of starting a forest fire. It's best to always pack it out and dispose of it properly back in civilization.
4. Practice low-impact camping techniques. Use campsites that show signs of previous use. If you have a fire, use existing fire rings. Don't tear down local trees for firewood; anticipate your needs and bring your own. Let the fire burn down to white ashes and cover with a thin layer of dirt before leaving. If there are more fire rings than needed, dismantle the unnecessary ones. Cook with a stove. Crumbs and other food particles attract ants; take care in preparation, when eating, and cleaning up. Construct a small sump hole and screen out particles of food when washing dishes. Be considerate of other campers by limiting noise and other distractions.
5. Respect wildlife and all other special closures.
6. Teach dogs how to behave at climbing areas, keep them under control, and clean up after them.

Superb bouldering is found on volcanic blocks at City of Rocks State Park in southern New Mexico. PHOTO BY STEWART M. GREEN

7. Join and contribute your energies and financial support to national organizations such as the Access Fund and local organizations such as New Mexico CRAG and Rocky Mountain Field Institute. Become involved in any way you can to protect and preserve the natural environment.

CLIMBING ETHICS

Climbers debate ethics, which usually is a debate about style—the manner a route is established and how it is climbed. Traditional climbers who climb from the ground up using natural protection and placed gear to protect routes are sometimes at odds with sport climbers who preplace permanent bolts for protection and use European climbing methods and styles to establish and climb routes.

These two seemingly opposite climbing styles have led to some ugly and highly charged debates between the opposing factions, resulting in bolt wars, character assassination, and punches being thrown. Climbers, whatever their style, need to be civil and remember that the rock is an innocent victim in wars over style. Chopping bolts is harmful to the rock and can lead to land managers closing areas. The existence of climbing at some areas can be threatened by the actions of thoughtless individuals in both camps. Climbers need to leave petty grievances behind and try to find a common ground. It doesn't matter if you are a sport climber or a trad climber; we are all climbers. We need to unite to make sure our wonderful climbing areas are around for future generations of climbers to enjoy.

The style in which a climb is accomplished is a personal choice. There is purity and beauty in the ground-up tradition, of accepting only what the rock offers for protection and technique. The strength, power, and training required to crank difficult gymnastic moves on a sport climb is an equally valid way to climb. Both are different expressions of the same game. Climbing is only enriched by its diversity. Sport climbing techniques have led to the creation of harder traditional climbs, while some sport climbers have adopted trad protection for new hard lines.

At the heart of climbing style are the issues of bolting, rock alteration, and environmental impact to the crags. Cliffs should only be bolted at areas where this is allowed and in accord with local traditions. Climbers who place bolts should seriously consider each and every placement. This should only be done *after* consulting with land managers. This avoids possible area closures and acrimony. Choose a natural line that ends at a natural stance, then toprope the line to assess its quality and to locate bolt placements. Placing bolts next to a protectable crack is never acceptable. Important considerations are the worthiness of the route and the reliability and safety of fixed protection. Don't let the easy rappel-down style lead to overbolting a route or for additional bolts to be added to existing lines.

It is simply unacceptable behavior for climbers to alter the rock in any way, including chipping and manufacturing holds or gear placements. Placing permanent bolts is

Timmy Fairfield pulls through the crux of *White Queen* (5.13b/c) at The Frog Prince in The Enchanted Tower climbing area. Photo by Stewart M. Green

considered alteration by land managers and is cited as a reason to close areas or establish stringent restrictions. If more crags come under scrutiny by land managers, they will discover glued flakes, chipped handholds, drilled pockets, and other rock alterations. This could lead to area closures. Remember that it is a punishable crime to alter any rock on public land. Don't destroy hard climbs for future climbers. This guide omits any route that is obviously altered or has known manufactured holds. Some routes with chipped holds may unknowingly have been included here, but their inclusion doesn't validate this style.

Both visiting and resident climbers need to be on their best behavior at New Mexico's cliffs. It would be tragic if climber misbehavior led to any crag closures. Honor each area's specific rules and regulations, especially those with delicate access issues including Tres Piedras and Questa Dome. Please read and follow information found in the Restrictions and access issues section for all the crags.

A guidebook is a tacit invitation to visit an area. Come on down and climb in New Mexico. Enjoy yourself but please bring your manners, leave your chisels, and while you are here, respect our crags.

USING THIS GUIDE

Rock Climbing New Mexico is a complete guide to New Mexico's crags. More than 1,500 routes are described with text, maps, photographs, and topos. A locator map at the front of the book shows the general locations of the main climbing areas.

Each area's chapter includes an **Overview,** which includes a written description of the area, a brief summary of the area's climbing history, and recommendations for equipment and descent.

Next is **Trip planning information,** which includes condensed summaries of specific information on each area in most of the following categories:

Area description: A brief summary of the area.

Location: A description of the area's location relative to the nearest town or geographical feature.

Camping: Information on developed federal, state, and local campgrounds and suggestions for camping at undeveloped areas.

Climbing season: Description of when is the best time of year to visit an area.

Restrictions and access issues: Important issues to be aware of, such as private land, parking, safety, and land use.

Guidebooks: Published sources of information for the area.

Services: A brief description of where to find local food, gas, and lodging.

Emergency services: Contact information for nearby medical or rescue services in case of emergency.

Nearby climbing areas and **Nearby attractions:** Lists to direct you to other climbing and recreational opportunities in the vicinity.

Finding the crags: A brief but complete set of driving and hiking directions to the crag or crags.

The route descriptions in each chapter identify each route numerically and list the routes in either left-to-right or right-to-left order, whichever sequence is appropriate for clarity. Generally the routes are listed in the order in which they would be encountered along the normal approach trail. Each description gives the route name and rating followed by a brief discussion of the location and nature of the climb, special equipment recommendations, length, and descent information. An overview map of each climbing area and photos—showing cliffs and route locations—accompany the descriptions.

Appendices offer historical information about Heart of Stone Rock (**Appendix A**), further reading (**Appendix B**), a rating system comparison chart (**Appendix C**), and a listing of government agencies and climbing associations (**Appendix D**).

There is a routes by rating index at the back of the book, as well as a general index that provides page references for all routes, formations, and climbing areas, listed alphabetically.

A book of this magnitude offers a wide selection of routes of all difficulties and lengths. Errors will creep into route descriptions due simply to the sheer diversity and number of routes detailed here. The area and crag descriptions have been carefully checked and double-checked by a wide range of active New Mexico climbers to maximize the book's accuracy. Be forewarned, however, that things on paper aren't always as they are in reality. This book is not intended to get you up any rock route. It will get you to the base of the cliff and point you in the right direction, but the rest is up to you and your sound decisions. This book is not a substitute for your own experience and judgment.

Almost all the routes included in this guide are worth climbing. Routes not worth climbing have usually been omitted or described as "not recommended." If a route is especially good, words like "quality" and "excellent" may be included in the route description. Star ratings have been deliberately omitted in an effort to avoid queues and a diminished experience for everyone. These are generally subjective opinions that may or may not be true for every climber. Every climber has their own unique experience on every route. There are many fine routes in this guide to choose from. You are invited to decide for yourself what looks right and feels best on any given day.

RATING SYSTEMS

This book uses the Yosemite Decimal System (YDS), the usual American grading scale, to identify the technical difficulty of the routes. Remember that ratings are totally subjective and vary from area to area. This book has tried to bring a consensus to the grades, but previously listed grades for routes usually have been carried forward. Small rating variances are found in each area. Taos and Organ Mountain climbs, for instance, seem to be more conservative (read harder) than other areas. Easier sport climbs (5.8 to 5.11) are harder to translate to the YDS scale, although the standard of difficulty on the higher end of the scale is comparable to European grades.

Older traditional routes conform to early Colorado and California ratings established at the same time. The current sticky rubber and better protection might make them slightly easier, but climbers will still find them solidly rated. Many of the older bolted climbs have been retrobolted, which can make them seem slightly easier. But 5.9 starts feeling like 5.10 if you're 40 feet out! Use all the ratings as a starting point in each area and expect a one to two letter grade or even a full grade difference from grading at your home area.

Some listed routes also have protection or danger ratings. These routes generally have little or no protection, and a climber who falls could sustain serious injuries or death. R-rated climbs have serious injury potential. X-rated climbs have groundfall and death potential. Remember, however, that every route is a possible R- or X-rated climb.

Mountain travel, as defined by the Yosemite Decimal System, is classified as follows:

- **Class 1**—Trail hiking.
- **Class 2**—Hiking over rough ground such as scree and talus; may include the use of hands for stability.
- **Class 3**—Scrambling that requires the use of hands and careful foot placement.
- **Class 4**—Scrambling over steep and exposed terrain; climbing difficulty is relatively easy, but a long fall could result in injury because of exposure. The lead climber trails a rope, uses natural formations for protection if available, and is on belay.
- **Class 5**—Climbing on steep and exposed terrain where a fall would definitely result in injury or death. Hands and feet only are used for upward progress; no direct or artificial aid is employed. Ropes, belays, running belays (protection), and related techniques are used.

The Yosemite Decimal System (YDS) used to rate Class 5 climbing fails to follow mathematical logic. It is an open-ended scale where the 5 denotes the class and the difficulty rating is tacked on behind the decimal point, with 5.0 being the easiest and 5.15 (read five-fifteen) being the hardest (to date). When it was developed, 5.9 was the upper end of the scale. When routes were climbed that were obviously harder than 5.9, new numbers were invented to denote the difficulty. When a route has had too few ascents for a consensus grade or the estimated difficulty rating is unclear, a plus (+) or minus (-) subgrade may be employed (5.9+ or 5.12- for example). Where there is a consensus of opinion, additional subgrades of a, b, c, and d are used on climbs rated 5.10 and above. Occasionally two letters may be used such as 5.12b/c. This is because the grade still requires consensus or is height-dependent or has some other qualifier.

As originally intended, routes are rated according to the most difficult move. Some climbs may be continuously difficult, seeming harder than other routes rated the same but with only one or two hard moves. In some instances, routes will be described as "sustained" or "pumpy" to give an indication of the continuous nature of the climbing. Also, differences in strength and reach as well as distance between protection points may be factors contributing to rating variations. Where these factors seem significant, they may be pointed out in the written descriptions.

Aid climbing—using artificial means to progress up the rock—has a different set of ratings.

Pete Takeda jams pumpy *S & M Crack* (5.11a) at Sugarite Canyon State Park. PHOTO BY STEWART M. GREEN

- **Class 6**—Aid climbing; climbing equipment is used for progress, balance, or rest; denoted with a capital letter A followed by numbers progressing from 0.

  A0—Equipment may have been placed to rest on or to pull on for upward progress.

  A1—Solid gear placements and aid slings (etriers) are used for progress because the climbing is too difficult to be free climbed.

  A2—Gear placements are more difficult to install and support less weight than an A1 placement.

  A3—Progressively weaker placements, more difficult to install; may not hold a short fall.

  A4—Placements can support body weight only; long falls can occur.

  A5—Enough A4 placements that result in falls of 50 feet or longer.

A pitch or rope-length of technical climbing may have a combination Class 5 and Class 6 rating such as 5.9 A4, meaning the free-climbing difficulties are up to 5.9 with an aid section of A4 difficulty. On the route drawings or marked photos in this guide, the crux (most difficult section) often is marked with the difficulty rating.

An additional grade denoted by Roman numerals I through VI is given to longer routes. This refers to the commitment in terms of length and time requirements for the climb. Climbers should consider other factors such as technical difficulties, weather, logistics, and the approach and descent. Typically a Grade I takes a few hours to complete; Grade II up to half a day; Grade III most of the day; Grade IV all day; Grade V usually requires a bivouac; and Grade VI takes two or more days. One-pitch sport climbs are all Grade I routes.

An additional danger rating may be tacked on to some ratings. Where protection may not hold and a fall could result in injury or death, an R or X is added. A route rated 5.9 R may mean that the protection is sparse or runout or that some gear placements may not hold a fall. X-rated routes have a fall potential that can be fatal, unless one has the confidence and ability to solo a route safely with absolutely no protection and without falling.

See Appendix C for a table comparing the American system (Yosemite Decimal System) to the British, French, and Australian systems.

Injuries sustained from falls are always possible, even on routes that can be well protected. This guide does not give a protection rating, nor does it provide detailed information on how, when, or where to place protective hardware. Suggested standard gear racks are described in the overview for each area, and some recommendations are made on types and sizes of protection that may be useful on some climbs. But safety and the level of risk assumed are the responsibility of the climber.

Sport climbers should also eye their prospective route and count the number of bolts. Bolt counts are given for many routes, but things change on the real rock. Some bolts may be hidden, added, subtracted, or miscounted. Also note that not all bolts are shown on the topos included in this book. Always carry extra quickdraws in case the count is wrong or you drop one. Remember to consider what you need for the anchors and for lowering. Again, it's always really up to you to provide your own safety. Climb safe, climb smart, and have fun!

NEW MEXICO GEOLOGY

The rocks in New Mexico are diverse and offer a range of climbing from multipitch traditional routes on granite domes and sandstone spires to single-pitch sport climbs up pocketed faces and cracks on volcanic lava flows. The rocks we see and climb on today are a product of both regional tectonic forces and local geologic processes that have been operating in this area since Earth's early history, the Proterozoic era of the Precambrian approximately two billion years ago.

In New Mexico most of the climbing is represented by three different categories of rock type: granites, sedimentary rocks (predominantly limestones and sandstones), and volcanic rocks (i.e., basalts, andesites, and rhyolites).

The granitic rocks, particularly those in the Sangre de Cristo Range and Sandia Mountains, represent the oldest rocks. These crystallized deep in the crust during Earth's early history and during previous episodes of mountain building. The sedimentary rocks, such as the limestones in the Lincoln Mountains around Alamogordo or the sandstones in western New Mexico, represent a time in Earth's middle history when inland seas and sandy deserts moved back and forth across this area. The volcanic rocks such as the welded tuffs on Cochiti Mesa or the basalts at Sugarite Canyon State Park near Raton and White Rock are a result of recent extensional forces that thinned the crust and fragmented this region of the North America continent as well as forming large-scale topographic features such as the Rio Grande Rift and the Basin and Range region.

Although a variety of tectonic forces and geologic processes have played a role in forming the different rock types in this region, the Rio Grande Rift is the geological feature most responsible for exposing much of its climbable rock. This rift runs roughly north-south from southern Colorado to western Texas and is a result of recent crustal thinning and extension occurring in this area. This extension resulted in large-scale normal faulting that exposed a number of older plutonic and sedimentary rocks along the margins of the rift and created extensive magmatism within and just outside the rift.

GRANITIC ROCKS

Granitic rocks represent large intrusive bodies of silicic magma that crystallized deep in the earth's crust and were subsequently exposed by uplifting and faulting typically associated with mountain building. Although the term *granite* refers to a very specific composition, for most climbers the classification is much broader, referring instead to almost all varieties of silicic intrusive rocks. This classification, which is both adequate and accurate, is based on the rock's climbing texture—a coarse, granular texture often studded with large knobs or crystals of feldspar—and its color and appearance—generally pinkish to grayish-colored rocks containing quartz, feldspars (plagioclase and alkali feldspars), mica (biotite or muscovite), and other less abundant minerals (e.g., amphibole or iron-titanium oxides).

For those interested in pursuing more detailed classification, it is not always easy with the unaided eye to distinguish differences in the chemical compositions and relative abundances of the minerals that make up this broader category of granitic rocks. These variations are, however, quite substantial and provide earth scientists with important insight into basic issues (e.g., the formation of mountain chains, the differentiation of the earth's crust, etc.). The most generally accepted classification scheme comes from the International Union of Geological Sciences, which divides granitic rocks into fifteen separate categories according to their relative abundances of quartz, plagioclase feldspar, and alkali feldspar. In this scheme, granite is a plutonic rock in which quartz makes up 10 to 50 percent of the silicic components and there is roughly twice as much alkali feldspar as plagioclase feldspar. A diorite is a plutonic rock in which plagioclase makes up more than 90 percent of the silicic components. A syenite contains very little quartz (less than 5 percent), almost equal amounts of plagioclase feldspar and alkali feldspar, and so forth.

The coarse, granular, and sometimes knobby texture, typically associated with climbing granites, is a result of its slow cooling rate at great depths and the different crystallization times for the minerals that make up these rocks. Slow cooling allows larger equilibrium-shaped crystals to grow into a network of interconnected crystals, giving the rock its granular texture. Because different crystals begin growing at different temperatures, there is also often a range of crystal sizes—the larger knobby crystals are generally the minerals that nucleated early in the rock's crystallization sequence (e.g., feldspar) and thus crystallized over the longest period of time.

In New Mexico the majority of the granitic rocks occur along the mountain ranges on the eastern margin of the Rio Grande Rift. Exceptions to this are the Precambrian (1.7 billion years old) granites and quartz monzonites of Tres Piedras found along the western margin of the rift at the foot of the Tusas Mountains. The granitic rocks of the Sangre de Cristo Range and Sandia Mountains exposed along the rift's northern section are Precambrian in age.

SEDIMENTARY ROCKS

Sedimentary rocks are a record of ancient landscapes and times. When complete, this memory can record, in explicit detail, natural events such as the transgression and regression of inland seas that inundated this area during the Pennsylvanian and Permian and left behind large limestone reefs; the large sandy deserts that swept across in the Mesozoic Era, leaving behind sandstones that later eroded into sheer cliffs, desert towers, and petrified sand dunes; or the interlayered sand and shale deposits of ancient tidal mud flats and shallow lakes that recorded the footprints of dinosaurs.

New Mexico offers a sedimentary sequence that ranges from the Cambrian Period (approximately 560 million years ago) up through the present Quaternary. Of the many sedimentary rocks exposed, only a few are climbable. Most of the climbing is on the Pennsylvanian age limestones of the Madera Formation, which caps the Sandia Mountains. This is part of the El Capitan reef system and includes the

Guadalupe Mountains and the caves of Carlsbad Caverns. Western New Mexico's numerous sandstones, including the Zuni and Entrada sandstones, are exposed as cliffs and towers within and along the margin of the Colorado Plateau. Most of these cliffs, however, are on tribal lands and therefore not accessible to climbers.

VOLCANIC ROCKS

Volcanic rocks represent magmas from deep inside the earth and, as such, are important probes into the composition of the earth's otherwise inaccessible interior. For example, basaltic lavas are melts originating down in the earth's mantle, whereas rhyolitic tuffs are generally believed to originate from the melting of shallower, crustal rocks. It has also been recently proposed that slow chemical differentiation of basaltic melts in large steady-state magma chambers can also generate rhyolitic melts.

Because volcanic lava flows are extrusive rocks, meaning that they were deposited and crystallized on the earth's surface, they have cooled relatively quickly and formed a climbing texture different from that of intrusive rocks (i.e., granitic rocks). Extrusive rocks differ from intrusive rocks in several ways. Their crystal sizes are significantly smaller, giving the rock a finer-grained, less granular texture (aphanitic); crystallization at lower pressures enabled the volcanic gases to exsolve into discrete bubbles creating vesicles or pockets; and contraction of the rock during the cooling, particularly at the top and bottom of the flow, caused fracturing in polygonal patterns. When exposed in cross section, these fractures give the cliff faces of lava flows their characteristic columnar appearance and, of course, make for lots of good crack climbing.

Finally, differences in the processes by which volcanic rocks are extruded and then deposited impart a big difference in the feel of the rock and the character of the climbing. In general, volcanic eruptions occur as either lava flows or as explosively erupted deposits. Lava flows, which are typical of the basalts in New Mexico, are generally massive, compact rocks with stretched vesicles and abundant cracks. In explosively erupted deposits such as the welded flow deposits in the Bandelier Tuff on Cochiti Mesa, large volumes avalanched down the side of the volcano. With ash flow tuffs, the degree of welding is critical in determining the climbability of the rock. In general, it is the center part of the rock unit, which cooled slowly and is the most welded, that we climb on. In contrast, the less welded, softer parts of the Bandelier Tuff are the areas where the Anasazi chose to carve out homes at nearby Bandelier National Monument.

In these regions, most of the volcanic rocks are relatively recent (mid–Miocene to Quaternary) and are associated with the extensional tectonics and crustal thinning that created the Rio Grande Rift and the Basin and Range topography. The volcanic centers from which the basalts and welded tuffs were erupted lie either within the rift or along a lineation of volcanoes that run from the Mount Taylor Volcano near Grants through the Jemez Volcanic Field and out to the Raton-Clayton Volcanic Field in northeastern New Mexico. The Jemez Volcanic Field, which produced the largest volume of erupted material, is actually at the intersection of the volcanic centers, which is often referred to as the Jemez lineament. The Cerros del Rio Basalts at White Rock and the Bandelier Tuffs of Cochiti Mesa are from the Jemez Volcanic Field and are relatively recent in age. One can see from the overlying position of the welded tuffs just outside the town of White Rock that these basalts were laid down earlier (about two million years ago). The Bandelier Tuff was deposited from two distinct volcanic episodes, which left large calderas. The lower Bandelier Tuff or Otowi member (approximately 1.5 million years old) created the Toledo Caldera. The upper Bandelier Tuff or Tshirege member (approximately 1.2 million years ago) created the Valles Caldera. While most of the basalt climbing in the Jemez Volcanic Field and throughout New Mexico is consistently good, climbing on the Bandelier Tuff is restricted to the areas that are most densely welded. In many places the climbing character of the Bandelier Tuff has been improved by an iron-manganese oxide desert varnish surface. While this surface can significantly improve the climbing quality of the rock, it also deceives by making the quality of the rock appear better than it actually is. There are many other basalt flow crags such as John's Wall and Dead Cholla Wall that come from small volcanic centers within the rift, as well as basaltic cliffs associated with the volcanics of the Jemez lineament outside the rift, including Sugarite Canyon State Park in the Raton-Clayton Volcanic Field. Other welded tuffs and volcanoclastic rocks that offer climbing in New Mexico include Socorro's Box Canyon and the Enchanted Tower near Datil.

—Ken Sims, Ph.D.

Ken Sims is a longtime New Mexico climber and a geologist currently working at Woods Hole Oceanographic Institute in Massachusetts.

QUESTA DOME

■ OVERVIEW

Questa Dome, overlooking the Rio Grande's deep gorge and broad valley, lies on the western flank of the Sangre de Cristo Range in the Latir Peak Wilderness Area north of the village of Questa. The 500-foot-high, southwest-facing granite cliff offers excellent crack and face climbing in a pristine mountain setting. The routes on Questa Dome range from two to five pitches in length with the brilliant *Question of Balance* unquestionably one of the best in New Mexico.

Questa Dome is a traditional climbing area. Bolting and power drills are banned in Latir Peak Wilderness Area and on the cliff. Visiting climbers should be aware that long runouts are encountered on many routes, some with serious fall and injury potential. Help is a long way off from this remote crag. Use your best judgment and don't climb beyond your abilities. Climbers attempting any lines on the dome should be competent at placing gear and setting up belays, and prepared for thin face climbing, long runouts on hard climbing, and devious route-finding.

Good cragging is found on all of the dome's routes, making Questa Dome worthy of many visits. It's rarely crowded, with only occasional parties encountered on weekends. Climbers can expect quiet weekday visits.

The boulders in the canyon below the cliff are a popular bouldering area.

If the weather turns bad or if the dome is too crowded for your taste, consider visiting the Nutcracker Rocks, aka the Legs, directly west of the Questa Dome. These granite crags, reaching heights of 200 feet, receive little attention from most climbers. The rocks offer fine one- and two-pitch crack lines. Climbing here is a satisfying experience of solitude and discovery.

Climbing History

Bold routes were established on the Questa Dome's excellent rock in the 1970s and 1980s. Paul Horak was the first to test Questa's steep, complicated faces. Ken Trout, Peter Prandoni, and Mike Roybal all lent their considerable talents to connect the discontinuous crack systems and intricate face moves necessary to summit this fine crag. The crag's classic route is *Question of Balance*. This five-pitch line, established in 1970 by Paul Horak, Mark Dalen, Glen Banks, and Dave Balz, is a bold statement up the dome's obvious line. Its only rival in New Mexico for quality of climbing, experience, and position is *Tooth or Consequences* in the Organ Mountains.

Questa Dome experienced a resurgence in popularity in the 1990s with some new route activity and the replacement of the

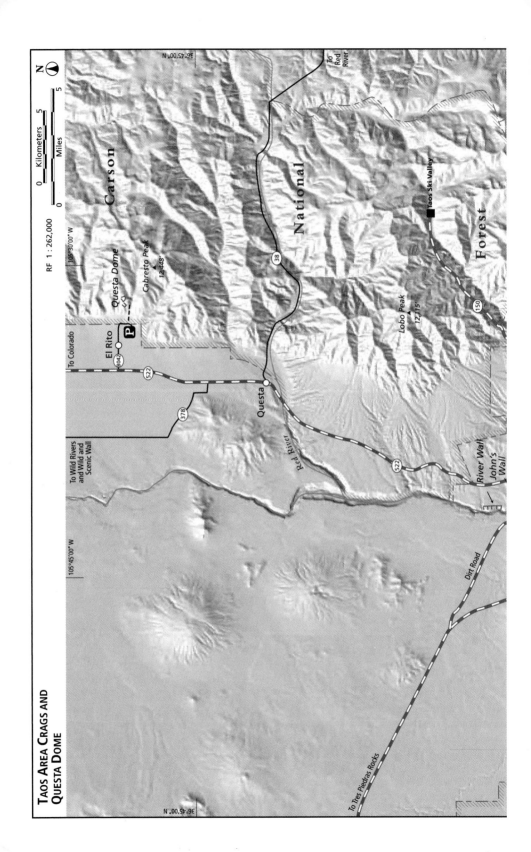

TAOS AREA CRAGS AND
QUESTA DOME

RF 1 : 262,000

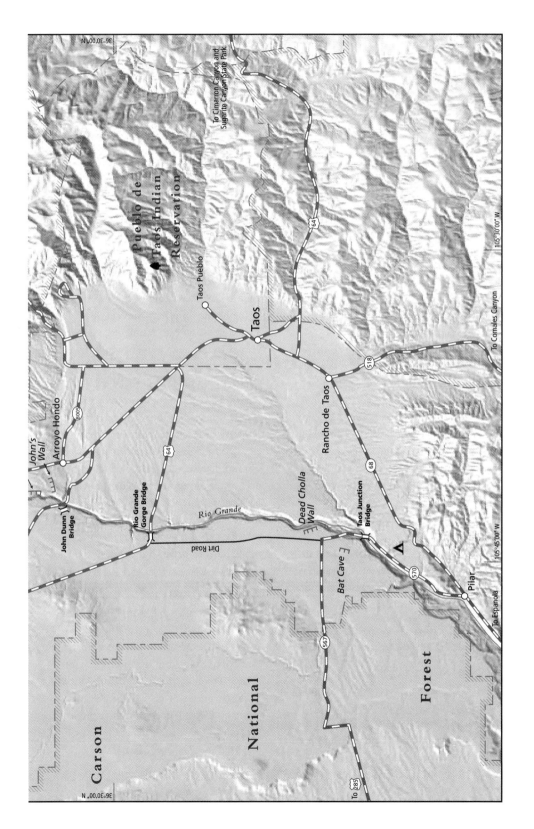

original ¼-inch bolts on some enduring classic lines. Dan Parks, Doug Coleur, and others led this new development. Greg Swift, Sharon Dogruel, and Rick Smith were also active. Greg and Sharon are responsible for Questa's newest route, *Questando la via sin Arboles,* completed in 2002.

Rack and Descent

Bring a full rack of Friends, wired Stoppers, RPs, a dozen quickdraws, extra runners, and a 165-foot rope. An extra rope is helpful if retreat is necessary. Many of the routes still rely on old bolts for protection. Use these with extreme caution and always back them up with gear whenever possible, especially at belay stances.

Descent from the summit is to the east or right side of the dome. Walk east from the summit, pass over the top of a gully, and follow a faint trail trending down and left through trees. Watch for another trail cutting right down a steep, tree-covered slope from this initial faint trail. Follow this trail to the base of the Dome's east flank near the rock's base. Allow thirty minutes for the descent.

Trip Planning Information

Area description: Questa Dome, a south-facing, 500-foot-high granite dome, offers some excellent multipitch traditional routes in a spectacular mountain setting.

Location: Northern New Mexico. In the Latir Peak Wilderness Area north of Taos.

Camping: No established campgrounds in the area. Good camping is available approximately 13 miles from Questa Dome at the BLM Wild Rivers Recreation Area on the rim of the Rio Grande Gorge. Head north from the town of Questa a few miles to Highway 378. Turn west onto Highway 378 and follow signs to the recreation area. The area offers twenty-one campsites in five campgrounds on the rim.

Climbing season: Late May to late October, depending on snow conditions. July through September are the best months. Expect afternoon thunderstorms during the summer months.

Restrictions and access issues: Questa Dome lies in Carson National Forest within the Latir Peak Wilderness Area. An endangered species has recently been identified by the Fish and Wildlife Service, prompting them to ask the U.S. Forest Service to "discourage use" of the Dome from May through September. Although no official closure order is in effect, visitors to the area should be respectful of all wildlife and generally keep a low profile. Contact the Questa Ranger District (505–758–6230) for updated information.

It is necessary to pass through private property to reach the trailhead. Please exercise good judgment when driving through. No motorized equipment, including power drills, are allowed in the wilderness area. Parking is limited at the trailhead. Lock your car because this is New Mexico—break-ins can occur. A four-wheel-drive vehicle is recommended to drive all the way to the parking area.

Guidebooks: *Rock Climbing New Mexico & Texas* by Dennis R. Jackson, Falcon Press, 1996. *Taos Rock: Climbs and Boulders of Northern New Mexico* by Jay Foley, Sharp End Publishing, 2005. Route descriptions for Questa Dome routes were included in *Taos Rock III,* an out-of-print, self-published guide by Cayce Weber and Ed Jaramillo. An account of the first ascent of the route appeared in *Climbing Magazine* #44.

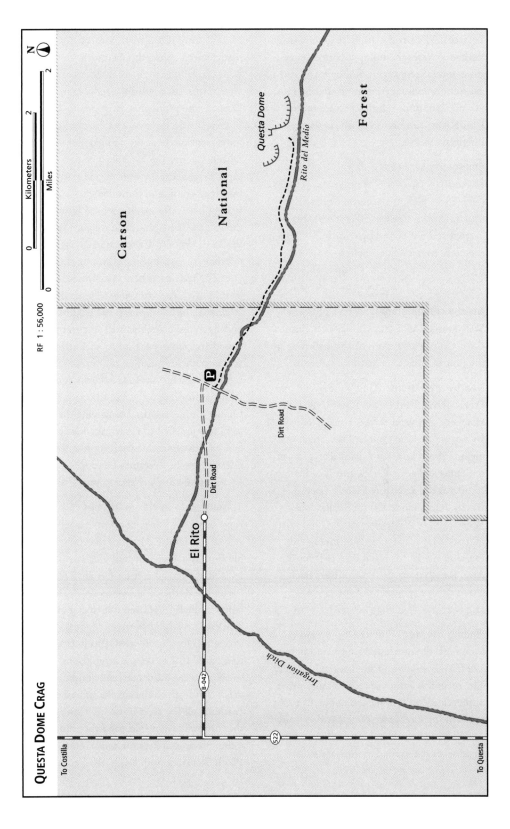

QUESTA DOME CRAG

RF 1 : 56,000

Kilometers
0   2

Miles
0   2

N

Carson

National

Forest

Questa Dome

Rito del Medio

El Rito

Dirt Road

Dirt Road

P

Irrigation Ditch

B-042

522

To Costilla

To Questa

Services: The small village of Questa offers limited services including a convenience store, several restaurants, liquor store, and a gas station. Full services are found in Taos, 20 miles south on Highway 522, and in Red River, 15 miles east of Questa on Highway 38.

Emergency services: Call 911. Holy Cross Hospital, in Taos, 1397 Weimer Road (505–758–8883), is the nearest hospital. Questa Health Center (505–586–0315) is located at 2573 State Highway 522. Contact the New Mexico State Police (505–758–8878) or Taos County Sheriff (505–758–3361) for emergency assistance.

Nearby climbing areas: Wild and Scenic Wall, John's Wall, Dead Cholla Wall, Bat Cave, Comales Canyon, and Tres Piedras are the nearest areas.

Nearby attractions: Rio Grande Wild and Scenic River, Red River, Red River Fish Hatchery, and Wild Rivers Back Country Byway are all near Questa. Taos attractions include Taos Plaza, Kit Carson Park, lots of museums and art galleries, and Taos Pueblo. Nearby is the Enchanted Circle Scenic Byway, Rio Grande Gorge Bridge, and Wheeler Peak Wilderness Area. Good boating, fishing, backpacking, and hiking are found in the BLM's Wild Rivers Recreation Area. Reach it via the Wild Rivers Back Country Byway north of Questa via Highway 378 and Highway 522.

Finding the crag: Questa Dome is accessed from both the north and south via Highway 522 between Taos and the Colorado border. The turnoff is approximately 6 miles north of the village of Questa and about 13 miles south of the Colorado–New Mexico border. Turn east at a sign announcing El Rito (right from the south, left from the north) onto County Road B042, a narrow paved road. Don't confuse this El Rito with the El Rito Crags, which are about 80 miles southwest. Drive east toward the mountains. Questa Dome is the prominent, large granite buttress in view as you drive in. The trailhead is 2.1 miles from the highway and requires four-wheel drive for the last mile. The pavement turns to gravel at 0.9 mile, where it is joined by a road coming in from the left. Continue straight here. After passing a large house on the left, the road gets much rougher. When the road comes to a T junction, go right for 0.2 mile to a small parking area on the left.

The trail starts here and climbs steadily up El Rito Creek to Questa Dome. In an attempt to discourage use and to protect an endangered species, this trail is currently closed and removed from official maps. As you near the dome, the trail travels beside the creek. To reach Nutcracker Rocks, look for a faint trail forking off left in this area. For Questa Dome, continue following the creek until it is possible to easily hike left to the base of the dome. Allow thirty-five to forty minutes for the approach hike.

Routes are described from left to right.

1. Questando la via sin Arboles (5.10+) No topo. 6 pitches. Located on the far left (west) side of the Dome. Much of the route is visible from the approach trail. The start is located about 150 feet up the slope from the toe of the dome on its west side. Begin below a small left-facing dihedral about 50 feet left of a large left-facing dihedral, both about 100 feet up the cliff. **Pitch 1:** Climb to a piton 10 feet off the ground, cross some small rounded overhangs, and continue up a crack that leads to the smaller dihedral. Avoiding all the trees in the dihedral, go up the dihedral's right side, following ramps and a thin crack to a 2-piton belay. 160 feet. (5.9) **Pitch 2:** Friction up a face, then continue up small cracks. After a wide section, go up and gradually left, passing 3 bolts, to a good belay from 2 pitons. 160 feet. (5.10) **Pitch 3:** Climb past a bolt, then up and slightly right to the base of a dramatic vertical crack equipped with pitons. At the top, belay from 1 bolt and a slinged horn on a small ledge. 100 feet. (5.10+) **Pitch 4:** Traverse left via a thin crack, then climb past 2 bolts to a short but strenuous overhang. Belay 20 feet higher on a sloping ledge with 1 bolt. 80 feet. (5.10) **Pitch 5:** Walk left to a tree and jam a finger crack splitting the smooth face above. Climb past 2 bolts above the crack and belay on a good ledge. You can see this crack from the approach trail. 110 feet. (5.10) **Pitch 6:** Follow the left arête to the top of the ridge. **Descent:** Scramble right (northeast) to the walk-off used by all routes reaching the summit of Questa Dome.

2. Que Wasted (aka Sequestered) (III 5.12-)

6 pitches. From the toe of the southwest prow of the formation, walk uphill 50 feet to a prominent dihedral that reaches the ground. At this point the dihedral is a groove. The first 2 pitches are not shown on the topo. **Pitch 1:** Climb easy slabs and the groove up and right until you can do a balance traverse around a bulge to the right. This puts you on the slabs right of the prominent left-facing corner. Climb to a belay below a flake roof. 150 feet. **Pitch 2:** Climb over the flake roof (5.10) and continue up slabs and cracks to a belay from gear in a shallow pod. 150 feet. **Pitch 3:** Difficult face climbing (5.11) is protected by small nuts to easier terrain above. Belay on a large sloping ledge. 100 feet. **Pitch 4:** Climb up left to a hand crack behind some short pillars. Jam the crack to a ledge on top of the pillars. The crux slab is next. Move up then right to a difficult mantle protected by bolts. Belay 50 feet higher from gear at the base of

a water groove/crack. **Pitches 5 and 6:** Follow cracks and grooves up right for 2 slightly runout pitches to the top (5.8–5.9). **Descent:** Scramble right (northeast) to the walk-off used by all routes reaching the summit of Questa Dome.

3. Question Of Balance (III 5.11a) This

excellent route, one of New Mexico's very best, offers 5 long pitches on excellent granite. The route, wandering up disconnected crack systems on the main face, is high-quality, sustained, and very enjoyable climbing. Begin the route a little left of the rock's center and directly below a 2-bolt chained belay stance 150 feet above. **Pitch 1:** Begin climbing by aiming for a short right-curving flake. Jam a 2-inch crack up the flake. At the flake top, continue up left across a slab (5.9) under a roof. Climb back right to a fixed piton under the roof. (The original route traversed left here to a mantle [5.10+] then back right on easy climbing.) Pull over the roof (5.11a crux) and continue up right in a thin crack to some difficult face moves (5.10) End at the 2-bolt belay. 150 feet. **Pitch 2:** Jam a right-angling finger crack past a fixed piton. Go right where the crack pinches down, passing an overlap, then left to another right-trending, fingers to small-hands crack to a 1-bolt and 1-piton belay stance. Gear placements are also available at the belay. 150 feet. **Pitch 3:** Drop down several feet and traverse right 12 feet across a dike. Work up right via thin cracks and face climbing (5.9 and 5.10) to a bolt where it is possible to traverse 35 feet to 40 feet left, passing a large roof with a 2-bolt anchor (the 5.11 roof used by *Questa Dome Direct*). Belay at a 3-bolt hanging belay near the shorter left side of the roof. This is almost directly above the second belay stance and below a notch in a roof. 140 feet. **Pitch 4:** Step left from the belay and face climb to the roof. Jam over the roof

(5.10b) to easier climbing above. Run the rope out by climbing and traversing up right (sparse protection) and belay below a small grove of trees. **Pitch 5:** A short 4th-class pitch to a small grove of trees about 150 feet below the summit. 3rd class up easy rock to the right. **Rack:** Bring a standard rack with sets of Friends, TCUs, and wired Stoppers, some runners, and a 165-foot rope. **Descent:** Climb easy rock to the large trees near the east or right side of the summit. Angling up and right from the end of pitch 4 is the quickest way. When you reach easy rock, walk right (east) above the top of a gully and turn down a slope through the trees by following a faint trail down and contouring right or west. The trail ends at the base of the east flank of Questa Dome and near the rock base. Allow twenty minutes for the descent.

4. Aero Questa (5.12a) 3 pitches. **Pitch 1:** Climb the first pitch of *Question of Balance*. **Pitch 2:** Move left past 2 bolts to a belay at bottom of obvious water streak. **Pitch 3:** Climb a water streak to a horizontal dike and move left on the dike past natural pockets. Climb over a bulge onto another dike and belay. The direct route climbs two 5.12 cruxes directly up the water groove. **Descent:** Multiple rappels from the end of pitch 3 or traverse right and go to the summit via *Question of Balance.*

5. Another Pretty Face (5.11) This route is 2 pitches of thin face climbing to the second belay on *Question of Balance*. Rope up at the same place as *Tostados con Questa.* **Pitch 1:** Climb slabs to the left of a dihedral. Difficult climbing leads to better protection in cracks. Climb corners to the top of two large flakes. Belay on a ledge at the top of the second flake. **Pitch 2:** Difficult face climbing protected by ¼-inch bolts leads up and left to join the second pitch of *Question of Balance.* Continue to the anchors and belay. 120 feet. **Descent:** Multiple rappels to the ground.

6. Questa Dome Direct (5.11) This climb follows the 2 pitches of *Another Pretty Face* and the first part of pitch 3 on *Question of Balance* but belays at a 2-bolt belay anchor below the first and largest roof. Pitch 4 jams over the difficult (5.11) roof, then wanders up easy rock to the summit.

7. Tostados con Questa (5.10) Route follows the major right-facing dihedral on the right side of the cliff. **Pitch 1:** Easy climbing on the face right of the dihedral leads to a sling belay below a roof. **Pitch 2:** Either stay in the crack or move right (5.9 either way) for enjoyable climbing over the roof. Above jam a crack and then face climb to a 2-bolt belay. These 2 pitches can be done as one but require a 165-foot rope and some simul-climbing. **Pitch 3:** Crux pitch. Climb straight up past 2 bolts into the main crack system to a belay stance. **Pitch 4:** Moderate and then easy climbing leads straight to the top.

8. Octoberquest (5.11d A2) This former project may yet live up to its 5.12 projection. Climb *Tostados con Questa* to the end of the third pitch, then up and left through the huge roof system.

JOHN'S WALL AND THE RIVER WALL

■ OVERVIEW

John's Wall, also known as Hondo Cliffs, is the original and oldest Taos climbing area. The south-facing, 70-foot-high basalt cliff tucks into a narrow side-canyon just east of the John Dunn Bridge at the bottom of the 650-foot-deep Rio Grande Gorge. A selection of fine crack and face routes ascend the roadside cliff, offering good, easily accessible climbing. The emphasis is on traditional-style crack climbing with a sprinkling of bolted faces. When attempting the trad routes, carry a substantial rack and be ready for some steep, strenuous jamming. Do not be cavalier in your attitude to any route on this relatively unimposing cliff. The area retains its original traditional values with some routes redefining "dicey" and "bold." Whether trad or sport, nearly every route is runout near the bottom.

Two further inducements to visit are the development of a couple additional areas in the immediate area. The best of these is west-facing River Wall, a compact, bolted sport crag situated on the lower east side of the Rio Grande Gorge. The climbing is mostly up steep bolted faces in the 5.10 and 5.12 range plus a few moderate crack climbs. The other area is Old Stage Coach Road Crag, a small cliff located on the west side of the gorge. This area features short, moderate cracks with bolted anchors to facilitate descending and toproping. Find this area by walking or driving across the John Dunn Bridge and turning right into the BLM boat launch area. The cliff is above and upriver from the northern end of the launching area.

Cliff vandalism detracts from the pleasant surroundings and climbing experience. The area has been the attention of a large cleanup effort, with hideous oil splatters on the base of John's Wall hosed off with a high-pressure hose by the local volunteer fire department. Graffiti has been removed or painted over, and although much still remains, the crag's appearance is much improved.

Climbing History

Convenient access and a pleasant setting deep in the scenic Rio Grande Gorge attracted area climbers to John's Wall in the early 1970s. Skills developed here allowed climbers to turn their attention to other area challenges, including the granite faces of El Salto and Questa Dome and the less intimidating but bold climbs at Tres Piedras. John's Wall, named for nearby John Dunn Bridge, has suffered vandalism dating back to 1910. Taos climber Jay Foley developed the River Wall in more recent times, adding a new dimension to this old-time area.

Rack and Descent

A standard rack here includes quickdraws, wired Stoppers, and camming units or nuts up to #4 Friend. Many older routes are protected by old ¼-inch bolts, which should be used cautiously. Back up all bolts whenever possible with gear.

Descend from John's Wall by walking off the west end (toward the river) or east end of the cliff. Some routes have fixed lowering stations with chains. Most routes on the River Wall are equipped with bolt lowering anchors. Rock fall danger, difficulty in getting to anchors below the cliff top, and lack of anchor placements above the cliff make setting up topropes problematic and should

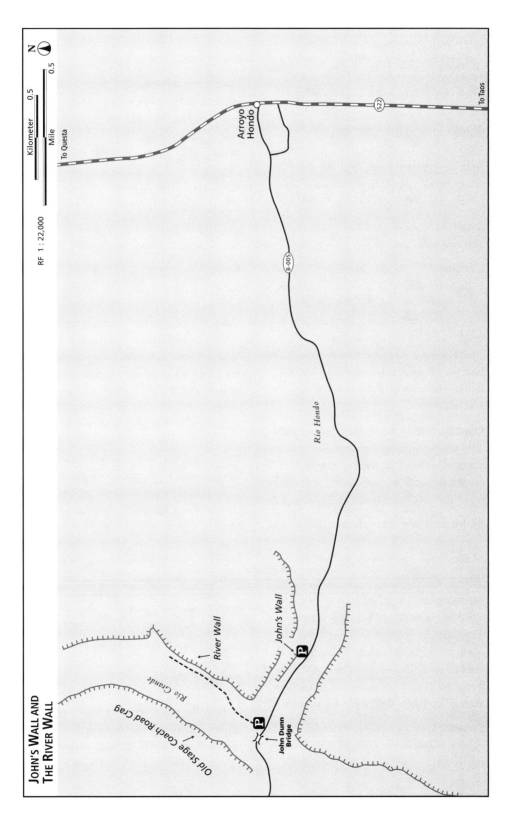

be carefully considered. Use caution whenever walking along the cliff top to avoid knocking loose blocks and boulders onto belayers, climbers, and onlookers below.

Trip Planning Information

Area description: John's Wall offers face and crack climbs on a 70-foot-high basalt cliff in the bottom of the Rio Grande Gorge.

Location: North-central New Mexico. Northwest of Taos.

Camping: Camping opportunities are limited in the immediate area. The road that veers left at the bridge over the Rio Hondo goes downstream on the river's east side. This is a heavily used fishing area and generally occupied. Camping is not permitted at the BLM boat launch site. Primitive and established camping sites are plentiful in Carson National Forest.

Climbing season: Year-round. Spring and fall offer the best weather. Frequent cold temperatures in winter limit the number of climbable days. The south-facing wall can be uncomfortably hot during the summer.

Restrictions and access issues: The crag is administered by the Bureau of Land Management. There are no current restrictions on climbing.

Guidebooks: *Rock Climbing New Mexico & Texas* by Dennis R. Jackson, Falcon Press, 1996. *Taos Rock: Climbs and Boulders of Northern New Mexico* by Jay Foley, Sharp End Publishing, 2005. The area is partially covered in the nonbound, self-published guide *Taos Rock III* by Cayce Weber and Ed Jaramillo.

Services: Limited services in Arroyo Hondo. Nearby Taos is better with a full range of tourist services, including gas, food, and lodging. Taos is known for excellent cuisine, entertainment, and hospitality.

Emergency services: Call 911. The nearest phone is at Herb's Lounge on Highway 522 at Arroyo Hondo. Ambulance service and Holy Cross Hospital, (505) 758–8883. New Mexico State Police, (505) 758–8878. Taos County Sheriff, (505) 758–3361. Taos City Police, (505) 758–2216.

Nearby climbing areas: Bat Cave, Dead Cholla Wall, Tres Piedras, Wild and Scenic Wall, Comales Canyon, and Questa Dome.

Nearby attractions: A popular natural hot spring is located downstream on the west bank of the Rio Grande. Drive across John Dunn Bridge, continue west a short distance to the first switchback, and locate a trail heading down to the river. At peak runoff, the spring is underwater. Another hot spring, Mamby Hot Spring, is located downriver on the east bank. The hot spring is a rough hike about 3 miles downriver. Other attractions include D.H. Lawrence Ranch, Taos Plaza, Kit Carson Park, Taos Pueblo, Enchanted Circle Scenic Byway, San Francisco de Assisi Church in Ranchos de Taos, Rio Grande Gorge Bridge, Picuris Pueblo, Carson National Forest, and Wheeler Peak Wilderness Area. Good boating, fishing, and swimming are found in the Rio Grande Gorge area. Mountain biking on dirt roads and hiking trails can also be found. Wild Rivers Back Country Byway is west of Questa. Check with locals shops for beta on the area's excellent bouldering.

John's Wall

Finding the crag: There are three options to reach John's Wall from Highway 522. From the south, proceed north from the traffic light at the junction of U.S. Highway 64 on the north end of Taos about 7 miles to Arroyo Hondo. From the north, drive south on Highway 522 to the village of Arroyo Hondo. At Arroyo Hondo, just north of Herb's Lounge and gas station, turn west onto Taos County Road B-002 (left turn from the south, right turn from the north) or alternately B-005, just north of the bridge over Rio Hondo. Both roads begin as pavement, then turn to dirt after crossing a short narrow bridge over Rio Hondo. John's Wall is a little more than 2 miles from Arroyo Hondo on the right or north side of the road where it crosses a second small bridge over Rio Hondo. The John Dunn Bridge crosses the Rio Grande a short distance past the cliff.

An alternate, and perhaps preferable, route is to turn west (left from the south, right from the north) onto County Road B-007 5.2 miles north of the traffic light at US 64 and about 2 miles south of Arroyo Hondo. This route avoids driving through the small village of Arroyo Hondo. Stay on the main road, first bending left when the road reaches the Rio Hondo's cliff top, and proceed to the small parking area under the crag just past a short bridge over Rio Hondo.

Routes are described from left to right. Descend from lowering anchors or walk off the west end (preferable) or east end.

1. Awkward Chimney (5.8) Climb through broken rock to a ledge, then up a chimney. Gear route, no bolts, no anchor.

2. Rope-a-Dope (5.7) Start at blocks on the left end of a ledge; climb the face between #1 and #3. Gear route, no bolts, no anchor.

3. Deception (5.8) Start on right side of broken rocks with bushes and a cholla cactus, then up a dihedral to the top. Gear route, no bolts, no anchor.

4. The Trapeze (5.11) A serious undertaking. Start from a large ledge 10 feet off the ground just below a dark gouged-out section with a steep, attractive crack. Gear route, no bolts, no anchor.

5. Heaven Above (5.11) Another serious undertaking. Start on the right side of the upper part of the ledge. Up an overhang to a flake and crack to the top. Difficult and poorly protected at the bottom. Gear route, no bolts. Shares anchor with *Nice Guy Syndrome.*

6. Nice Guy Syndrome (5.12) Difficult and sustained. Seldom led, usually toproped. Start at ground level, then up an attractive face to *Heaven Above* anchors. 3 bolts, fixed pins. Shares anchor with *Heaven Above.*

7. The Bulges (5.10+) Classic. Same start as *Nice Guy Syndrome,* then right to an attractive curving crack system, over bulges, and up a steep, thin crack to the cliff top. Strenuous near top, difficult for its grade. Gear route, no bolts, 2-bolt anchor.

8. The Nose (5.10d) One of the crag's most popular lines. Difficult climbing to a large ledge atop a bulbous nose formation. Face climb up the quality blunt arête above to chain anchors. The grade eases a bit when traversing in from *The Bulges* at the top of the nose. 6 bolts to 2-bolt anchor.

9. Memory Lane (5.8) Same start as *The Nose.* The large dihedral right of *The Nose.* Named in memory of Lane McMurry. Somewhat loose. Gear route, no bolts, shares anchors with *The Nose.*

10. Alberta (5.10+) Very popular. Same start as *The Nose,* then climb up right onto a steep face right of arête. 6 bolts to 2-bolt anchor.

11. Route 66 (5.8) Start right of *The Nose*. Up tricky runout face climbing, then up the obvious left–facing dihedral. Gear route, no bolts, shares anchors with #10.

12. Houston "5" (5.9+) The first bolt has been removed so the start is runout. Most parties start on *Amazon*. Climb up left at *Amazon's* first (and only) bolt onto a slabby face between arêtes. Waltz upward on great

holds and pockets to a 2-bolt lowering anchor. 5 bolts to 2-bolt anchor.

13. Amazon (5.9) Begin on the far right side of cliff. Pick the easiest way through choss rock to a bolt and pull into a classic right-facing corner. Jam and stem the corner (5.8) to a blocky roof. Turn the crux roof (5.9) on the left. Belay from gear and bolts on the cliff top.

The River Wall

The west-facing River Wall is a long basalt cliff on the east side of the Rio Grande Gorge just upriver from John Dunn Bridge. Most of the cliff's routes are bolted and worth climbing. The cliff is shaded in morning, making it a good summer crag.

Finding the cliff: To reach this area, walk down the road from the parking area to an old metal gate located above the road on the right (north) just before reaching the east end of the John Dunn Bridge. Hike 450 feet north on a good path along the base of the cliff to the first routes. Routes are listed from right to left.

1. Unnamed (5.9) No topo. Good route, deserves some bolts. Hand jams up a crack. Runout and dangerous at the bottom. Anchors set well back from cliff top.

2. Black Book (5.8+) Steep climbing past bolts to a good corner. Shares anchors with #3 and #4.

3. Pale Face (5.11) Start 30 feet left of a small cross stuck behind a flake about 10 feet up the cliff. Two bolts protect climbing through good but unattractive rock at the bottom. From a large loose ledge, climb a stratified face left of a crack. Using the crack on the right (*Black Book*) reduces the grade considerably. 8 bolts to 2-bolt anchor.

4. Shake and Bake (5.12a) Excellent. Climb to the large ledge then left. Climb the face between a short crack on the left and arête on the right. 8 bolts to 2-bolt anchor shared with #3.

5. Arora's Diving Board (5.7 R/X) Two starts—directly up past 1 bolt or same start as #4 to the large loose ledge. Move left on the ledge and climb blocky rock to a wide crack.

This crack can be dirty after storms. Gear required. 2-bolt anchor.

6. Unnamed (5.10+) Work up through unattractive rock to a hand and finger crack. No bolts, no anchor. Better than it looks but could use some bolts and anchors.

7. Unnamed (5.10+) Start about 60 feet left of #6. This climb is equipped with welded cold shut hangers. Can also start on *Put in Pump*. 6 bolts to 2-bolt anchor.

8. Unnamed (5.9) The crack between #7 and #9. Start right of #7 on runout climbing to keep the grade at 5.9. Using the bolts for #9 amps the grade to 5.11. Gear required. Slings at anchor.

9. Put in Pump (5.11+) Start 6 feet left of #8. Climb through unattractive but good rock, then move right below an arête onto the face. 8 bolts to 2-bolt anchor.

10. Swallow Your Karma (5.12) The crag's classic climb. Climb straight up a spectacular arête with bolts on the left side. 8 bolts to 2-bolt anchor.

11. Dogie Style (5.10) The crack left of #10. Slings at anchor.

12. False Consciousness (5.12) Classic crimpfest. Start behind a large juniper tree. Climb past some hollow, unattractive, dark rock to a steep red and white face.

DEAD CHOLLA WALL AND BAT CAVE

■ OVERVIEW

Dead Cholla Wall, offering marvelous views that complement great climbing, sits along the west rim cliffs of the 600-foot-deep Rio Grande Gorge. The Rio Grande rushes silently through the steep, rocky canyon far below the cliff. To the east spreads the Taos Valley and the high peaks of the Sangre de Cristo Mountains, including Wheeler Peak, New Mexico's highest point. The 60-foot-high cliff, composed of vertical and over-hanging red and black basalt, is just one of many crags in the immediate area that invite exploration. Dead Cholla Wall is popular with area climbers because of its short five-minute approach, excellent routes on solid rock, and the ample opportunities for solitude and silence in this beautiful area.

More than twenty bolted sport routes are established at Dead Cholla Wall. All are equipped with ⅜-inch bolts. Several good crack climbs that readily accept gear also scale the escarpment. Most of the routes offer steep face climbing on small, positive, in-cut holds. Toproping is possible, although many of the lowering anchors are located well below the top of the cliff. The ledges atop this, as well as most of New Mexico's basalt cliffs, are stacked with loose, precarious rocks and boulders. Take extra care to protect yourself and those below from falling rocks when approaching the crag and when setting up an anchor on the rim. Also watch for rattlesnakes in the area boulder fields during summer and fall.

Climbing History

Ed Jaramillo and Cayce Weber, longtime Taos climbers, found Dead Cholla Wall while searching out sport climbing possibilities in the Taos area in 1989. The crag, named after a large dead cholla cactus found on the approach to the area, is also locally known as "Pilar." Cayce and Ed were amazed at the quality of the rock, the views, and the climbing possibilities. After this initial foray, many routes were established, mostly in the 5.10 to 5.11 range. Several good cracks have been added to the mix in recent years, but by and large the cliff is nearly fully developed now.

Another nearby cliff is Bat Cave. This newly developed crag offers the steepest sport climbing in the Taos area and is sure to please visiting hardmen.

Many fine boulder problems are found on boulders scattered across the wide terrace below Dead Cholla Wall. Access these via the La Vista Trail east of the crag.

Rack and Descent

For Dead Cholla Wall bring ten to twelve quickdraws for the sport climbing routes. Small gear placements (TCUs, RPs, and wired Stoppers) can be factored in for extra security on some of the sport routes. The crack climbs are all easily protected with a standard rack of camming units and wired Stoppers. A 150-foot rope suffices for all routes. Descent from all routes is by lowering from anchors, rappelling, or walking off to the south.

Trip Planning Information

Area description: Dead Cholla Wall, a 60-foot-high basalt cliff, and nearby Bat Cave offer many sport routes on the west rim of the Rio Grande Gorge.

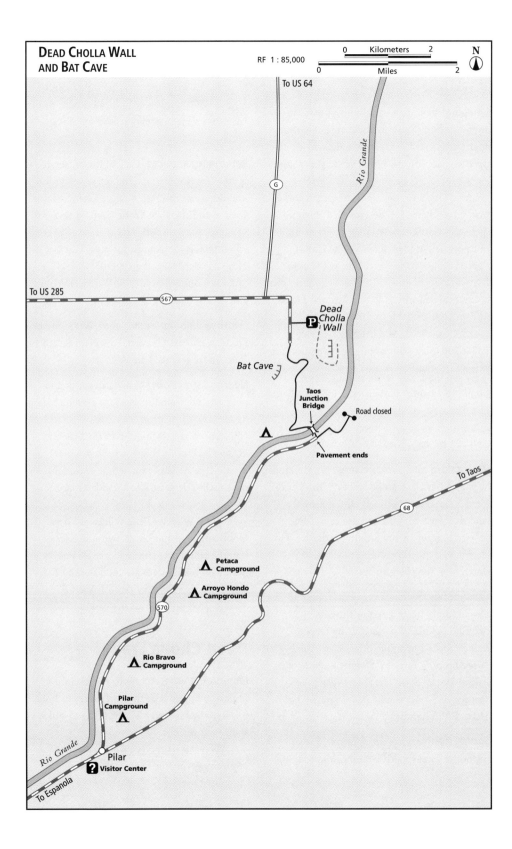

Location: North-central New Mexico. Dead Cholla Wall and Bat Cave are approximately 24 miles southwest of Taos.

Camping: Primitive camping opportunities are limited in the immediate area. A good alternative is a short distance away in developed fee sites in the Orilla Verde Recreation Area, (505–758–4060), along the Rio Grande. This area, operated on a first-come, first-served basis, can be crowded during spring and summer. Advance reservations are not possible, so plan accordingly. Coin-operated showers are available at the Rio Bravo Campground. Additional camping can be found in nearby Carson National Forest; information available at 208 Cruz Alta Road, Box 558, Taos, NM 87571, (505) 758–6200. Also see camping information for other Taos climbing sites.

Climbing season: Early spring to late fall are best. The east-facing cliff provides early morning sun and afternoon shade. Summer days can be very hot.

Restrictions and access issues: Dead Cholla Wall and Bat Cave are located on Bureau of Land Management (BLM) land. All public land management agencies are reviewing their management of climbing activities. The residents of Pilar appreciate that you drive slowly through their village.

Guidebooks: Some of the early routes at Dead Cholla are covered in the self-published guide *Taos Rock III* by Cayce Weber and Ed Jaramillo. Also *Rock Climbing New Mexico & Texas* by Dennis R. Jackson, Falcon Press, 1996. *Taos Rock: Climbs and Boulders of Northern New Mexico* by Jay Foley, Sharp End Publishing, 2005.

Services: All services are found in Taos, including gas, groceries, dining, and lodging.

The small village of Pilar has a restaurant, the Yacht Club, and a bed-and-breakfast inn. Historic Embudo Station, 10 miles south on Highway 68, is pleasantly located next to the river and serves excellent food and local brews.

Emergency services: Call 911. Cell service is spotty but worth a try. The nearest pay phones are at the Rio Grande Gorge Visitor Center and the Pilar Yacht Club. Holy Cross Hospital, on the south end of Taos, (505) 758–8883, is the nearest hospital. Contact the New Mexico State Police, (505) 758–8878, or Taos County Sheriff, (505) 758–3361, for emergency assistance.

Nearby climbing areas: John's Wall, Questa Dome, Comales Canyon, Tres Piedras, and El Rito Sport and Trad areas.

Nearby attractions: Many attractions and museums are found in the Taos area, including Taos Plaza, Kit Carson Park, Taos Pueblo, Millicent Rogers Museum, Padre Martinez Hacienda, Taos Pueblo Enchanted Circle Scenic Byway, San Francisco de Assisi Church in Ranchos de Taos, Rio Grande Gorge Bridge, Picuris Pueblo, Carson National Forest, and Wheeler Peak Wilderness Area. Good rafting, fishing, and swimming are found in the Rio Grande Gorge. Many mountain biking trails are found in the Taos area, including the very popular West Rim Trail located just west of the parking area.

Dead Cholla Wall

Finding the crag: Access to the area from Highway 68, from both north and south, is possible via Highway 570 at Pilar, 15 miles southwest of Taos.

To reach the crag, turn north from Highway 68 at Pilar onto paved Highway

570. Drive along the Rio Grande through
Orilla Verde Recreation Area for about 6 miles
to the Taos Junction Bridge. Cross the bridge
(the road becomes Highway 567) and continue up the winding dirt road approximately
1.6 miles until the road becomes paved again.
Go 0.4 mile on the pavement and take the
second dirt track on the right. A sign here
points to the West Rim Trailhead. The parking
area lies 0.3 mile on this level road just past
the West Rim Trailhead parking area above the
gorge's western rim. At this point you are
north (upriver) of the crag, which is only a
five-minute walk away. The crag trail is visible
on the cliff top just below and to the south
(downriver) as you look east toward the gorge.
The trail leads across the cliff's top, then drops
down and around the crag's southern end.
Routes are listed left to right.

1. Where are the Bolts (5.11a) No topo. 140
feet left of *Jam Time*. Primo climb. Jam a short
40-foot finger crack. Gear route. No anchors.

2. Kissing Fish (5.9) 25 feet left of *Jam Time*.
Gear route, hand and finger crack. 2-bolt
anchor.

3. Jam Time (5.10b) Deceptively difficult.
One of the best crack climbs on the crag.
Classic finger and small hands crack requir-
ing gear. 2-bolt anchor.

4. Blind Faith (5.10+) Place gear before the
first bolt. Excellent stemming up white dihedral to anchors. 3 bolts to 2-bolt anchor.

5. Queso's Delight (5.12-) Just right of
white dihedral. Runout and difficult. Jam the
thin finger crack on a steep, left-facing wall.
Bring small gear. 2-bolt anchor.

6. Lava Flows (5.11a) One of the crag's best
climbs. Up face and arête. Small cam in horizontal crack down low protects first 20 feet.
5 bolts to 2-bolt anchor.

7. Open Season (5.10c) Difficult and committing start. Start up a left-trending finger
crack and then continue up the corner on

the right side of the prow. Gear plus 2 bolts to 2-bolt anchor.

8. Cholla Backstep (5.11) Seldom climbed. Climbs an obvious corner system. Gear route. Gets wide at the top. 2-bolt anchor.

9. Hageemoto (5.11d) Steep face route right of #8's corner. After bolt 5, layback a steep section, then traverse left. 5 bolts to 2-bolt anchor.

10. Merge Left (5.11) Start right of a low roof. Shares the first bolt with *Gorge Yourself*, then move left and follow 4 more bolts up a steep red face to shared anchors. 5 bolts to 2-bolt anchor.

11. Gorge Yourself (5.10d). Wires and TCUs protect the thin corner system after 2 bolts. 2 bolts to 2-bolt anchor.

12. Just Arose (5.11) Climb a red streak with difficult balance moves just right of a dihedral. 4 bolts to 2-bolt anchor.

13. After the Pillar Came Down (5.10b/c) Just right of the pillar that fell down. Face climb up right to a thin crack up a left-facing dihedral. Gear route, no anchors. Belay on cliff top. **Rack:** TCUs and Stoppers.

14. Toxic Socks (5.12) Delicate, steep face climbing up a beautiful red wall. 6 bolts to 2-bolt anchor.

15. Special Ed (5.11+) Thin crack and corner route right of *Toxic Socks*. Crux is pulling the roof near top. 5 bolts to 2-bolt anchor.

16. Fun (5.7) The easiest line on the crag and well named. Face climb right wall of large obvious corner past 2 bolts, then up the crack above. **Rack:** Bring small and medium Friends for optional pro between bolts. 2 bolts to 2-bolt anchor.

17. Games (5.10+) Work up right around an arête onto a steep wall. Small holds lead to smears near the top. 5 bolts and 2-bolt anchor.

18. One for the Book (5.8+) Another good crack climb. Jam a hand crack in a right-facing corner. Gear required. 2-bolt anchor.

19. Corrido Del Norte (5.11) "Story of the North." Work up a beautiful pale face right of a right-facing corner. 4 bolts to 2-bolt anchor.

20. No Lines (5.10+) Face moves lead past bolts right of a wide crack. **Rack:** Small to medium pro to augment the bolts. 3 bolts to 2-bolt anchor (shared with #21).

21. No Waiting (5.11) Thin face climbing up a white-streaked face. 5 bolts to a 2-bolt shared anchor.

22. Festival sin Peliculas (5.10b) Good hand jamming, good pro. Climb an attractive, right-slanting hand crack to a thinner crack up higher. No bolts, no anchor.

23. Twisted Feet (5.11a) No topo. Steep, varied, and fun climbing. Begin right of a large right-facing dihedral. Long reaches and lots of stemming up a white face. 5 bolts to a 2-bolt anchor.

24. Doc's Dangle (5.10b/c) Clip the first 2 bolts of #25, then work up and left up a steep face with thin, crisp edges. 3 bolts to 2-bolt anchor.

25. Somebody Loaned Me a Bosch (5.11a) The route is somewhat contrived, and it's almost impossible not to use many of #24's holds. Start up *Doc's Dangle,* but move up right after first bolt. 4 bolts to 2-bolt anchor.

26. Either Or (5.11) Quality climbing up the nice face right of thin crack system. 4 bolts to 2-bolt anchor.

27. Esmerelda (5.11) An exciting start makes this route one of Dead Cholla's best lines. Face climb up a steep face right of a blunt arête and left-leaning corner on the far right side of the cliff. 5 bolts to 2-bolt anchor.

Bat Cave

Bat Cave is one of New Mexico's new sport areas and offers the steepest climbing in the Taos area. The overhanging cavelike formation sits on the west rim of the Rio Grande Gorge below and south of Dead Cholla Wall. Routes are 45 to 60 feet long and feature technical, difficult climbing. The crag is still a little loose in sections, so climb and belay with extra care. A stick clip is mandatory for all routes as the first bolt is way up there. Most of the routes are very steep at the bottom and usually involve heal hooking and very sharp holds. The crag is not fully developed but only a few choice lines remain. Farther left along the rim top are several quality crack climbs that are worth visiting. The crag gets a direct sun hit in the morning and is shady in the afternoon.

Finding the crag: Follow directions to Dead Cholla Wall. After crossing the river, drive up the dirt road and park at mile marker 11 at the parking area for Vista Verde Trail. Bat Cave, at the bottom of a prominent pour-over on the rim, is visible left of the road to the west well below the rim. Walk back to the road and turn right toward the rim.

About 50 feet past a small bridge, leave the road to the left and follow a very faint trail in the drainage, around a small rock outcrop, then up the slope aiming for the right-hand end of the cavelike formation. Allow five to ten minutes for the approach. Routes are described from left to right.

1. Subaru Nation
(5.11b/c) Highly recommended.

2. Tacoma Man (5.11d) Highly recommended.

3. Unfinished (5.12a)

4. Guillotine (5.13a) This fine route was inexplicably chopped. Look for it to reappear in the future.

5. Feng Shui (5.12) Terrific route.

6. Unnamed (5.13) Great route.

Fixed wire

7. Path to Enlightenment (5.12) First bolt is very high.

8. Horror Scope (5.12+) Potential ground fall at second bolt. Using holds on *Crystal Therapy* lowers the grade.

9. Crystal Therapy (5.12a) Potential ground fall at the second bolt.

10. Holistic Healing (5.11b) Good warm-up.

11. Palm Reader (5.11b) No topo. An inferior route. Hard at the start, 5.9 the rest of the way.

12. Molten Magma (5.11c) No topo. Clipping the fourth bolt is very difficult (and increases the grade) without a fixed draw.

TRES PIEDRAS

■ OVERVIEW

The Tres Piedras crags, Spanish for "Three Rocks," rise above a high mesa that overlooks the Rio Grande Gorge, the historic town of Taos, and the lofty Sangre de Cristo Mountains to the east. Tres Piedras is one of two (Gilman Tunnels is the other) granite climbing areas on the west side of the Rio Grande Rift in New Mexico. This remarkable feature is a series of fault-bound basins trending north-south from Colorado to Mexico. The basins are down-dropped blocks between mountain ranges, and the rift is one of only two continental rift zones on Earth, the other being the East Africa Rift.

The area's excellent climbing, compact granite, pristine mountain setting, and pine-scented forest offer a welcome summer alternative to the hot cliffs at lower basalt areas like Dead Cholla Wall and John's Wall above the Rio Grande. The Tres Piedras granite differs from Questa Dome and El Salto in the mountains north of Taos in both color and texture but is of equal quality and hardness. The area offers six major rock formations along with several smaller cliffs and slabs. Most routes are single-pitch, face climbing lines up slabs and vertical to slightly overhanging faces. Several fine crack climbs are found as well. Climbing holds include crimps, edges, knobs, and small to huge chickenheads. Friction and smearing techniques as well as crack jamming skills are required on many routes.

Climbers of all abilities enjoy the superb routes at Tres Piedras. Most lines range between 5.9 and 5.11, although lots of easier fifth-class climbing is found on low-angle slabs. These routes usually require placing anchors with gear. Setting up topropes is generally difficult to impossible without leading routes.

The area's best and most popular cliff is south-facing Mosaic Rock. This steep face yields the largest concentration of difficult face routes. Sample the 5.10 grade on brilliant classics like *Better Red than Dead* (5.10b/c) and *Serpent Face* (5.10c/d) or ratchet it up on the steep and difficult *Techweenie* (5.11+/5.12). The hardest climbs at Tres Piedras are 5.12. Another excellent crag is the Sundeck Wall above Aspen Alley at the northwest corner of the area. Several quality routes ascend this quiet cliff. Tres Piedras is rarely crowded with climbers, not even on weekends. For a solitary experience, come during the week and your only company will be soaring hawks and raucous ravens.

This older climbing area possesses a strong traditional background and ethic, even though many routes are protected by bolts or both bolts and gear. Most area climbs were established in a traditional ground-up style with bolts drilled on the lead. The newer sport routes are identified by plentiful ⅜-inch bolts and chain lowering anchors at the top. In the early 1990s local climbers removed most of the ¼-inch bolts on Mosaic Rock and replaced them with new beefy bolts. Be watchful, however, for the occasional one that escaped their attention. Some of those bolts are more than thirty years old and should be used with caution.

Expect long runouts between bolts on older routes. It's a good idea to carry a small rack to back up or augment fixed protection, especially at belays on these climbs. Some routes are protected only by gear, requiring competency at placing good cams and nuts as well as setting up safe, equalized belay anchors.

Climbing History

A talented group of Taos climbers began exploring Tres Piedras in the early 1970s. Ed Jaramillo, Cayce Weber, and Bruce Holthouse led this strong group and established most of the area classics. Many of these older climbs are nerve-racking adventures requiring a laser-like focus to edge upward between widely spaced and often dubious pieces of protection.

Since then, development has slowed with an emphasis on establishing bolted lines on slabs and steeper faces without natural protection. Only six new routes were done in the last several years. Although there are still some routes to be done, it can be safely said that the best lines have been climbed. Currently, bolting is disallowed on the area's privately owned rocks and discouraged by the Forest Service on all other cliffs.

Access has long been the key issue at Tres Piedras. The U.S. Forest Service and a private landowner share area management. The former is moderately receptive to climbing activities, but the latter is less so. Visiting climbers should hold themselves to a strict code of conduct while at the area. Doing anything less will surely cancel out our current climbing privileges at this wonderful cragging area. Locals would not be amused if this climbing jewel was closed due to climber misbehavior. Remember that climbing here as well as at all other areas in this guide is a privilege, not a right.

Some Tres Piedras rock formations are on private property with the remainder being located on public land, although the exact boundaries are in question. The Forest Service visitor center, 0.5 mile west of the village of Tres Piedras and on the way to the crag, provides climbers with a map that details public areas and access. Increased climber visitation to the site will undoubtedly affect the future of climbing here. Conduct yourself responsibly by staying on access trails, picking up all trash you encounter, not disturbing plants and animals, and by keeping a low profile.

Rack and Descent

A standard rack for most Tres Piedras routes includes a good selection of Stoppers and TCUs, Friends up to 3 inches, quickdraws, slings, and a 165-foot rope. A 200-foot rope is often helpful, especially on Mosaic Rock. Carry a few extra runners to tie off chickenheads, which on some routes is the best protection. It's not a good idea to leave the ground without a rack on most Tres Piedras routes.

Descent off of these routes is by walking off from the cliff top or lowering and rappelling from fixed anchors. Routes that require a walk-off descent, such as from the top of Mosaic Rock, often involve some moderate downclimbing. Some of these descents are difficult to find the first time, so you might want to locate the downclimb route prior to your ascent.

Not all bolts are shown on the topos.

Trip Planning Information

Area description: Tres Piedras offers traditional and sport routes on quality granite slabs, cracks, and steep faces.

Location: North-central New Mexico. Tres Piedras is 30 miles northwest of Taos.

Camping: Camping is allowed in undeveloped sites along the access road just before the T junction south of the cliffs and just south of the parking area. Because of delicate access issues at the area, climbers should consider alternative camping sites away from the

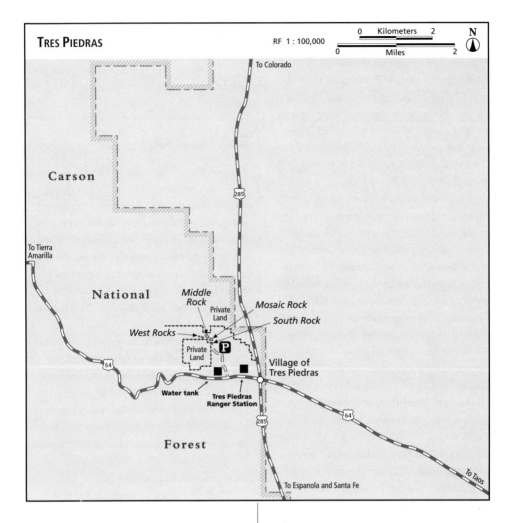

RF 1 : 100,000

0　Kilometers　2

0　Miles　2

N

To Colorado

Carson

National

Forest

285

To Tierra Amarilla

64

285

64

Middle Rock

Private Land

Mosaic Rock

South Rock

West Rocks

Private Land

P

Water tank

Tres Piedras Ranger Station

Village of Tres Piedras

To Espanola and Santa Fe

To Taos

crags. Ask at the U.S. Forest Service ranger station on the west side of the village of Tres Piedras for other camping areas. Be vigilant about leaving a clean campsite and do not camp on private land. Water and sanitation facilities are not available. Fires are not recommended. Developed campsites can be found at Hopewell Lake, approximately 15 miles west on U.S. Highway 64.

Climbing season: Late April to early November is the prime season at Tres Piedras. Expect cooler conditions in early spring and late fall. Summer is excellent, with

generally cool days. Sometimes it can be hot, but shaded routes are easily found. Regular afternoon thundershowers are guaranteed during the summer, especially in July and August when monsoon moisture drifts across the southwest. Snow and cold temperatures are the norm from late November to early March.

Restrictions and access issues: Access to Tres Piedras is a volatile and dynamic issue. Some rocks are on private property with the remainder on U.S. Forest Service land. A ranger station, located 0.5 mile west of the village of Tres Piedras en route to the rocks, provides climbers with a map detailing the public areas. All visitors should use this information. The facility is closed on weekends.

The private landowner, Mr. Gus Foster, has been moderately receptive to requests to climb on his land and should be consulted to have total rock access, although it is doubtful he will appreciate an increase in requests. Increased visitation to the area will undoubtedly affect the future of climbing in this special area. Please conduct yourself in a responsible manner. Additional new route activity is limited and bolting is disallowed on private property and discouraged by the Forest Service.

Guidebooks: *Rock Climbing New Mexico & Texas* by Dennis R. Jackson, Falcon Press, 1996, was the first widely available guidebook to Tres Piedras. Another guide is *Taos Rock: Climbs and Boulders of Northern New Mexico* by Jay Foley, Sharp End Publishing, 2005. A classic, unbound, self-published guidebook by Cayce Weber and Ed Jaramillo was published in 1981. Cayce and Ed are Taos locals responsible for many climbs at Tres Piedras.

Services: Limited services are available in Tres Piedras. A gas station complete with a convenience store is at the corner of U.S. Highway 285 and US 64 West. The Diner, next door, offers moderately priced breakfast and lunch entrees. Taos, 30 miles to the east, offers all services.

Emergency services: Dial 911. Cell service may be spotty at Tres Piedras. Contact the ranger station for emergencies on Forest Service land. If closed, the nearest public phone is in the village of Tres Piedras. Holy Cross Hospital (505–758–8883) is the nearest hospital. Contact the New Mexico State Police (505–758–8878) or Taos County Sheriff (505–758–3361 or 758–2216) for emergency assistance.

Nearby climbing areas: John's Wall, Dead Cholla Wall, Bat Cave, Questa Dome, and Comales Canyon are all within an hour's drive. El Rito Sport and Trad areas are an hour to the south. Another good venue is Penitente Canyon in the San Luis Valley in southern Colorado a couple hours' drive to the north.

Nearby attractions: Taos, one of New Mexico's most historic towns, lies at the base of the Sangre de Cristo Mountains 30 miles to the east. Many excellent museums and attractions are here, including Taos Pueblo, Millicent Rogers Museum, Padre Martinez Hacienda, D.H. Lawrence Ranch, Kit Carson Museum, and Harwood Museum of Art. San Francisco de Assisi Church in Ranchos de Taos is one of the most beautiful and most famous New Mexican churches.

Many Native American and Anasazi sites are found nearby. These include the eight living Pueblos—Taos, Santa Clara, San Juan, San Ildefonso, Tesuque, Pojoaque, Nambe, and Picuris. Bandelier National Monument with many excellent ruins is near Los Alamos to the south.

Besides climbing, there are lots of other outdoor activities. Mountain bikers enjoy the 27-mile South Boundary Trail and the scenic West Rim Trail above the Rio Grande. Great rafting is found on the Class IV rapids of the Taos Box. The Rio Grande offers trout fishing at Orilla Verde Recreation Area. Hikers and backpackers find lots of adventure in nearby Wheeler Peak Wilderness Area. Good wildlife-watching places are along US 285 north of Tres Piedras.

Ojo Caliente Mineral Springs, 30 miles south of Tres Piedras, offers relaxing hot arsenic soaks complemented by herbal wraps and optional massage. A bed-and-breakfast with soak option plus hotel and kitchenette accommodations are also available for plush rest days.

Finding the crags: The small village of Tres Piedras is at the junction of US 285 and US 64, approximately 25 miles south of the New Mexico–Colorado border, 30 miles west of Taos, and 80 miles north of Santa Fe. If approaching from Taos, access US 64 north of town and drive approximately 30 miles west on US 64 to the junction of US 285.

When approaching from Santa Fe, drive north on US 84/285 and be alert for signs near the south end of Espanola that direct you around the town to US 84/285. At the first stop light in Espanola just past Dandy's Burgers, turn left (west) across the Rio Grande. At the next light turn right following signs to Abiquiu, Tierra Amarilla, and Chama, then bend left at the next light. Continue to where US 84 and US 285 divide, and make a right turn onto US 285. Stay on this highway, passing through Ojo Caliente, to the village of Tres Piedras.

Access from the north is via US 285 from Antonito, Colorado. Turn right onto US 64 in the village of Tres Piedras about 25 miles south of the New Mexico–Colorado border.

From the junction of US 285 and US 64 in Tres Piedras at the blinking light, travel west on US 64. Drive 0.5 mile to the ranger station (open Monday through Friday, 8:00 A.M.–4:30 P.M.); stop for local information and a map of the climbing area. Continue west past the ranger station for 0.2 mile and look for an unmarked dirt road on the right. Turn here, go right past a graffiti-covered water tower, and continue 0.5 mile to a T junction where you turn left; stay left at the Y in the road and go a short distance to a

parking area next to a fence and gate. The rock immediately north is South Rock.

The Tres Piedras crags are made up of six distinct rocks from 70 feet to 200 feet in height. Access all cliffs by a climber's path that begins at a narrow gate near an information kiosk provided by the Forest Service. This path parallels a fence on its east side, is cairn marked, and ends on the east end of Mosiac Rock near *Clean Green Dream*. From the parking area, South Rock is the large cliff about 100 yards to the north. Behind and north is Mosaic Rock, the area's most popular climbing sector. Around the west end of Mosaic Rock, turn northeast or right to reach the North Face of Mosaic Rock and Middle Rock. Directly north of Middle Rock is North Rock. Access by going around the right end (east) of Middle Rock. Access West Rock by going left (west) from Middle Rock. Continue west past West Rock to Sundeck Wall.

Lookout Shelf

Lookout Shelf is a long, low, east-facing cliff below the east face of Mosaic Rock. The cliff top is a wide granite ledge that offers stunning views eastward across the Rio Grande Rift to the Sangre de Cristo Range.

Finding the cliff: Approach Lookout Shelf from the parking area by crossing the fence in a Forest Service gate to the right of the private gate. Walk north and slightly east along a cairned trail toward the east end of South Rock. The trail is still evolving but easy to follow. Trend slightly east, then turn north, eventually passing the left turn to the base of Mosaic Rock, then a little farther to the base of Lookout Shelf. Routes are described from left to right.

1. Unnamed (5.9) Trad route. Start under a large triangular roof near the south end of the cliff. Climb to the left side of the roof, then up a short, steep finger crack. No bolts, no anchor, large tree at the top.

2. Unnamed (5.10c/d) Start under the large triangular roof near the south end of the cliff. Difficult climbing up right leads to a traverse that gains a finger and hand crack. Jam to the top. No bolts, no anchor.

3. Unnamed (5.11c) Thin face climbing on positive holds lead straight up to the summit of a rounded block. 5 bolts, no anchors. Toprope possibilities are found continuing right (north) down the cliff.

South Rock

South Rock is the first rock encountered walking due north from the parking area. It is necessary to duck under the fence near its end when approaching on the Forest Service trail. Eleven quality routes are found on the west face and south faces of the formation. Most are sparsely protected face climbs or routes that require gear placements. All of the routes are well worth climbing.

All or part of this rock is on private property. Be respectful and tread lightly.

Routes in the middle of the rock have fixed anchors for descent. Routes on either side of the face require a downclimb on the northeast side. Routes are described left to right.

4. Zig Zag Man (5.9) Trad route. Start on a small pointed boulder below a right-trending arch system. Climb the arch for about 25 feet until it is possible to exit left on large holds. Continue up and slightly right to the summit. A direct start (5.10) is located 20 feet right. No bolts, no anchors. **Descent:** From the summit, walk right (east) to the northeast side of the rock. Tricky and exposed in spots.

5. Airy Scary (5.11-) Start below the apex of a small arch near the ground. Supplemental gear protects moderate climbing to the first bolt, then thin climbing leads to a crack followed by a fixed piton and one more bolt. Climb slightly right at the bolt, then back left to join the upper part of *Zig Zag Man*.

6. Agent Orange (5.9+) Trad route. Start on top of a huge flake that has slipped from the main face. Trend up right to a thin crack that leads to a long ledge. Install a belay here and climb to the summit, or traverse right to bolted anchors.

7. Unknown (5.10+) Start right of the top of the flake. Pull onto the face and clip 3 bolts while going straight up through a series of roofs. 3 bolts, gear to 2-bolt anchor.

8. Unknown (5.9) Start on top of a block directly under the arch's right side. Thin face climbing leads straight up past a shallow right-facing corner. 3 bolts to 2-bolt anchor.

9. Unknown (5.9) Difficult for its grade. Start just left of *Eagle Nest*. Thin face moves lead straight up to anchors. 4 bolts to 2-bolt anchor.

10. Eagle Nest (5.10-) Gear route. Good crack climbing with the crux at the top. **Descent:** Gain the summit and downclimb the northeast side of the formation.

11. Alias the Martian (5.10-) Located 120 feet right of *Eagle Nest*. Start on the right side of a narrow, white triangular face directly under a large roof about 12 feet up. Climb a crack to the right side of the roof, then up right along a steep, thin crack.

12. Static Cling

(5.11-) Climb a slightly overhanging face just right of *Alias the Martian* to a hueco- and chicken-head-studded arête above.

South Rock West Face

The slabby West Face is the west (left) side of South Rock. Hike left a short distance from *Zig Zag Man* for the start of *Yikes Dikes.* Gear required on both routes. Routes are described from right to left.

13. Yikes Dikes (5.8)

2 pitches. Start near the left edge of the slabby west face between an aspen tree and a small pine growing on a slab. **Pitch 1:** Climb straight up, staying left of the prominent crack that bisects the short buttress above. Belay below the left side of the bisected buttress. **Pitch 2:** Climb straight up past 3 bolts. Can be done in one pitch with a 200-foot (60-meter) rope. No anchors.

14. Surface Tension (5.11-) 2 pitches. Start about 90 feet up a shallow gully left of the slabs. **Pitch 1:** Gear and a bolt protect the

initial moves (5.10). Continue left up a series of short discontinuous cracks to a spacious belay ledge left of a bulbous orange formation. **Pitch 2:** Climb the slab left of the crack above the belay, passing 2 fixed pitons and 3 bolts on a smooth slab below the anchors. Rope drag can be a problem on pitch 2, so it's sometimes done in 3 pitches.

Mosaic Rock Area

Raven's Wall

The north side of Mosaic Rock is a complex arrangement of slabs, faces, and buttresses. Raven's Wall is a north-facing wall of the freestanding formation north of Beastie Alley and on the north flank of Mosaic Rock. A large raven's nest, used for many years, perches high in a horizontal crack on the right side of the face. A single sport route, established in 2002, ascends the far left edge of the wall.

Finding the cliff: Follow directions to Mosaic Rock's east end. Walk along the base of the South Face, turn right around the West End, and turn right again in the broad area just past *Danger Mouse* and *Thunder Toad*. Locate the well-used raven's nest of twigs and shredded rope high on the cliff to the left. *Jaws* is to the left.

15. Jaws (5.12b) Superb, airy sport line up the left edge. Established by Bryan Pletta in 2002 and first ascended by Jay Foley. Begin below a bolted face beside a large boulder. Face climb up moderate rock past 3 bolts to a sloping ledge. Swing up the overhanging wall above with thin face moves on edges and pebbles to anchors at the cliff top edge. 9 bolts to 2-bolt chain anchor.

West End

The West End of Mosaic Rock is a couple slabs divided by Beastie Alley, a deep slot canyon. One route, *Pony Express,* is found on the right slab. Beastie Alley harbors three sport routes on steep, excellent rock and a couple trad routes. The two routes on the right (south) wall use *Pony Express* anchors for topropes or leading. Additional routes are in the Alley, some old gear routes that may interest the adventurous. Beastie Alley is a great place to hang on hot days since it's always in the shade.

Finding the cliff: The easiest way to reach the cliff is to walk north from the parking area around the west (left) side of South Rock and continue north to the far west end of Mosaic Rock and Beastie Alley. This necessitates walking on private land, so the legal, though less direct, route is to go through the gate next to the information kiosk and follow it to the east end of Mosaic Rock. A faint trail traveling west along the base of Mosaic leads to its West End and Raven's Wall.

16. Danger Mouse (5.11a).
Dicey face moves and underclings lead up left on the steep slab. 4 bolts to 2-bolt chain anchor (same as *Thunder Toad*). **Descent:** Rappel the route.

17. Thunder Toad
(5.10a/b) First route on the slab left of Beastie Alley. Boulder up moderate moves, then move left to the first bolt. Mantel onto a small sloping ledge (crux), then up thin but easier climbing to the

anchors. TCU placements possible. 3 bolts to 2-bolt chain anchor. **Descent:** Rappel the route.

18. Pony Express (5.9)
No topo. The only route right of Beastie Alley. Edge up a fine slab with several crux bulges for 100 feet. 4 bolts to a 2-bolt anchor. **Descent:** Rappel north into Beastie Alley.

Beastie Alley

Beastie Alley is a narrow slot canyon that splits the west end of Mosaic Rock. It offers several trad routes and some newer sport lines. All the climbs are worth doing, especially on hot summer days when the Alley is naturally refrigerated. The rappel anchors for *Pony Express* can be used to toprope routes beneath them.

The two bolted routes on the south side of the chasm are both fun and worth climbing. The right one is 5.10b and the left one is 5.11. End at the *Pony Express* anchors and lower off. Farther left is a trad route with a fixed piton. On the opposite wall are several routes, including *Inner Sanctum,* a good 5.11 bolted route with a 2-bolt anchor. Not illustrated.

Independence Gully

This developing area is near the southwest end of Mosaic Rock. The south-facing alcovelike area saw limited activity in the early days on the lower angle faces. It is now the focus of more difficult routes on its steeper west (left) side. Look for the area just before turning the southwest end of Mosaic Rock. All routes are on the left (west) wall of the alcove. Routes are described left to right.

19. Independence Day (5.9) Mixed route up the left margin of the Gully's overhanging left side. Two bolts protect the steep initial moves, then small gear and creative placements for the last 50 feet. Formally an all-gear trad route. 2 bolts plus gear to 2-bolt anchor.

20. Double Your Pleasure (5.11a) Start on a sloping ledge about 20 feet right of *Independence Day* and just to the left of *Dependence.* Steep climbing on small sharp edges past 3 bolts leads to easier gear-protected climbing above. Shares anchors with *Independence Day.* 3 bolts to 2-bolt anchor.

21. Dependence (5.11c) Good climb. Difficult, overhanging face. 4 bolts to 2-bolt anchor.

22. Independence (5.11a) Hone your crack skills on an overhanging right-slanting crack. 2-bolt anchor.

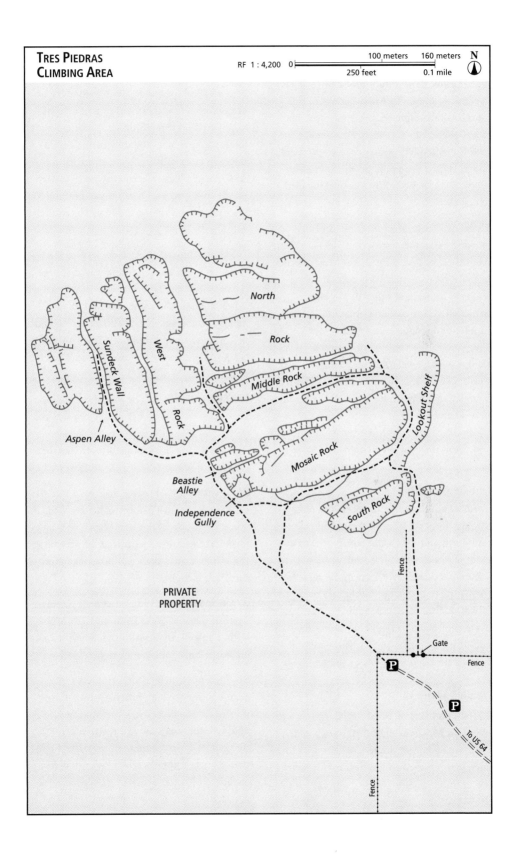

TRES PIEDRAS
CLIMBING AREA

RF 1 : 4,200   0

100 meters   160 meters   N

250 feet   0.1 mile

North

Rock

Sundeck Wall

West

Rock

Middle Rock

Lookout Shelf

Aspen Alley

Mosaic Rock

Beastie
Alley

Independence
Gully

South Rock

PRIVATE
PROPERTY

Fence

Gate

P

Fence

P

To US 64

Fence

Mosaic Rock

The greatest concentration of climbs at Tres Piedras are found on Mosaic Rock's excellent, 200-foot-high, south-facing wall. The face, the area's tallest, offers many brilliant, mostly single-pitch routes protected by bolts and gear. The steep face on the left side of the wall and left of *Dirty Diagonal* is called Mosaic Wall.

Descent: Descent off the cliff top is by walking off to the east or by rappelling from fixed anchors. Some routes on Mosaic Wall's left side are equipped with bolt rappel anchors. To descend other routes not equipped with fixed anchors, climb to the summit and scramble east to easy down-climbing on the east end of the rock. Always trend east to prevent falling off the north or south sides. Carefully wend your way down, negotiating a few tricky spots, to the ground near a large pine tree close to *Raise the Titanic*. First-time visitors may wish to locate and climb this descent route before attempting routes on Mosaic Rock.

Finding the cliff: Mosaic Rock lies directly north of South Rock. To access the cliff, go through the Forest Service gate and follow a trail north and then right around the east flank of South Rock. The trail is faint and sometimes marked with cairns. Be alert for the left turn just before Lookout Shelf, which requires a short scramble up the lower portion of the cliff. The trail reaches the east end of the south face of Mosaic Rock. Routes are listed from left to right.

Mosaic Wall

23. Seaman Girl (5.10b/c) Farthest left climb on Mosaic Wall. Just right of a thin right-facing corner. Third class left up a low-angle ramp system to get to the route start.

Clip a suspect bolt, then edge straight up using the crack for TCU placements. Keep left and climb past the 2-bolt anchor for *Mama Jugs*. For a short and fun exit to the summit, climb straight up, or for a longer and fun exit, move up left and then up a right-trending crack system. Belay at the crack's end. Creative gear placements are necessary on the entire route. Descend by climbing to the summit and then scrambling down the east side.

24. Mama Jugs (5.8) 25 feet right of *Seaman Girl*. Begin off the ramp under a small tree. Runout face climbing leads directly up to a 2-bolt anchor. No bolts; creative gear placements are necessary. Rappel from the anchors or continue straight up or go right on the last pitch of *Seaman Girl* for a good 2-pitch route.

25. T.B.O.L (5.11+ R) Begin off the ramp. Face climb to a large flake and then straight up to 3-bolt anchor shared with *Techtonics, Techweenie,* and *Tech-no-star.* 4 bolts. **Rack:** TCUs and wires helpful.

26. Techtonics (5.11+ R) Sustained and classic. Start by a small 3-foot-high tree at the lower right side of the ramp. Sustained and technical face movements lead directly up to the 3-bolt shared anchor. 4 bolts plus gear. First bolt is high.

27. Techweenie (5.11+/5.12) Start 5 feet right of the small tree. Delicate face climbing with a bulge crux leads to the 3-bolt shared anchor. 5 bolts plus gear to 3-bolt anchor.

28. Tech-no-star (5.12) Classic sport line with continuous and difficult moves. Crimp up a black streak to a tree growing on the cliff. Use the slings around the tree as a directional, then continue up to the 3-bolt shared anchor. 6 bolts plus gear to 3-bolt anchor.

Mosaic Rock: Right Side

29. Dirty Diagonal (5.7) Popular moderate. Follows the diagonal crack that splits the face. Start on the slab above the ground. Work up the crack and adjacent chicken-head-studded face on the right. A 200-foot rope gets you to the top, or you can belay on a spacious ledge below the summit. Gear required for either belay stance. Descend by walking off to the east, or if you choose not to summit, lower from a 2-bolt anchor near the top of the crack.

30. Five Years After (5.7 or 5.9) Start on an attractive green slab (*Chicken Shit* [5.7]) with 1 bolt and climb to a large ledge. Go a little left, then continue straight up the excellent face above (5.7) to a 2-bolt anchor. Ignore the ¼-foot Button Head at the anchor. 80 feet. Belay or lower from here or continue up (5.9) to the summit or the ledge about 30 feet below the summit. 3 bolts, 2-bolt anchor. 200-foot rope necessary to reach summit in 1 pitch. **Rack:** Standard Tres Piedras rack. **Descent:** Walk off to the east.

31. Chickenheads (5.7) Start the same as *Five Years After* by climbing to the large ledge/ramp right of *Dirty Diagonal*. Veer right up the diagonaling crack, climbing on good chickenheads and protecting in the crack. Go left and up when the crack turns left just before it ends. Belay from gear on a large ledge about 30 feet below the summit. Creative pro is necessary. A 200-foot rope is helpful. **Descent:** Walk off to the east.

32. Fried Chickens (5.8) Terrific trad climb. Start up a thin, laid-back crack angling up and right to a small roof. Pull over the crux roof and move up left. Grab giant chickenheads to the cliff top. 200-foot rope required to reach the summit in 1 pitch. Belay from gear. **Rack:** Standard Tres Piedras rack plus an extra 3-inch and 3.5-inch cam for the belay at the summit. **Descent:** Walk off to the east.

33. Better Red than Dead (5.10b/c) Classic Tres Piedras face route. Edge to a slanting crack, then climb up right to bolt 1. Thin, tricky face climbing leads up and right to the second bolt. The climbing above (crux) leads to a short thin crack, then several options to finish. 3 bolts. A 200-foot rope is required to reach the summit from the ground or belay at a lower intermediate stance. Belay from gear. **Rack:** Standard Tres Piedras rack plus an extra 3-inch and 3.5-inch cam for the belay at the summit.

34. Serpent Face (5.10c/d R) Another area classic. Start on a low-angle crack about 15 feet left of *Serpentine Crack*. At the top of the crack, move left to the first bolt then left again to the second bolt. Getting to the third bolt involves hard climbing above protection (characteristic of the route). Difficult and sustained face climbing all the way to the fourth bolt will test your nerves. From here there are three options: go left (easiest), right (harder), or straight up (hardest). It is runout no matter which way is traveled. 4 bolts. Belay from gear. **Rack:** Standard Tres Piedras rack. A 200-foot rope is necessary to reach the summit. **Descent:** Walk off east.

35. Serpentine Crack (5.8) The twisting wide crack up the middle of the wall. Start up a flared chimney. Above it, face climb left onto chickenheads and finish straight up to large belay ledge. **Rack:** Bring a standard rack with some extra large cams. **Descent:** Climb to the summit and walk off the east end. A controversial set of shiny fixed anchors has recently appeared at the top of the crack, making it possible to rappel and not go to the summit.

36. Holthouse to Hell (5.11+) Be cautious. Traverse in from *Serpentine Crack* about 15 feet up or use the *Direct Start*. Difficult climbing goes straight up past 2 bolts to a large ledge below the summit. **Rack:** Standard Tres Piedras rack. **Descent:** Climb to the summit and walk off east.

37. Learn to Forget (5.11a) Climb *Serpentine Crack* for about 20 feet and then traverse right along an unprotected seam (5.9) to the first bolt on the face. Climb straight up past 2 more bolts and then up steep runout rock to a ledge. Move up left to the belay ledge below the summit. **Rack:** Standard Tres Piedras rack. **Descent:** Climb to the summit and walk off east.

38. Direct Start (5.11) Direct start variation. The recommended start. Start on the ground below the face. Climb up left and merge with *Learn to Forget* or *Holthouse to Hell*. To the right of the second bolt are 2 bolts that apparently link up with *Bolts to Nowhere*.

39. Bolts to Nowhere (5.12b) Chris Van Diver climbed this route in the early 1990s, but it sees little traffic now. Start 20 feet right of *Direct Start*. Climb a steep face with crossing horizontal cracks. First bolt is missing a hanger. Belay at a long sloping ledge. **Descent:** Climb to the summit and walk off east.

40. Holthouse in a Haulbag (5.11d) First ascent by Paul Horak and Dave Baltz. A steep face and crack route with 3 fixed pitons and 4 bolts. Belay from gear on a good ledge. **Rack:** Standard Tres Piedras rack. **Descent:** Climb to the summit and walk off east end.

41. Cryin' in the Rain (5.9) Start in a crack. Edge up right and turn the roof above on its left. Work up and left along a crack and slab and finish up *Holthouse in a Haulbag*. **Rack:** Standard Tres Piedras rack. **Descent:** Climb to the summit and walk off east.

42. Dirty Black Nightmare (5.11d) An alternate start to *Black Streak*. Same start as *Cryin' in the Rain*. Climb up right and follow bolts to a prominent black streak. Excellent climbing up the streak leads past 4 bolts to a sloping belay ledge atop the face. 7 bolts. **Rack:** Standard Tres Piedras rack. **Descent:** Climb to the summit and scramble off east.

43. Black Streak (5.10b) Quintessential Tres Piedras climbing. Begin on top of a large block. Committing opening moves lead over three bulges protected by a bolt. Climb an attractive crack then straight up to the black streak. Crimp edges and crystals up the streak to a sloping belay ledge. 5 bolts. **Rack:** Carry a standard TP rack. **Descent:** Climb to the summit and walk off east.

44. Clean Green Dream (5.9) Great route. Start the same as *Black Streak*. At the top of

the crack, execute committing moves right, then up to a bolt. Climb the steep face above past 2 bolts and gear placements to a belay ledge just below the summit. **Rack:** Standard Tres Piedras rack. **Descent:** Climb to the summit and walk off east.

45. Walking Dread (5.10c) Excellent and well-protected. Face route up the far right side of the wall. The easier start is to traverse from right to left to bolt 1. The harder start goes straight up to the first bolt above the overhangs. Continue up the steep slab to a bolted belay ledge. 6 bolts to 2-bolt belay anchor. **Rack:** Standard Tres Piedras rack. **Descent:** Rappel from anchors or walk off east.

46. Bienvenidos (5.10a/b) Excellent. Just right of *Walking Dread*. Work up the prominent crack behind a large pine tree. Crux at the second bolt. 2 bolts to 2-bolt belay anchor. **Rack:** Standard Tres Piedras rack. **Descent:** Rappel from anchors or climb to the summit and walk off east.

47. Baby Cakes (5.8) No topo. Recommended. Climb through two large overhangs. Gear route. **Rack:** Standard Tres Piedras rack. **Descent:** Climb to the summit and walk off east.

48. Raise the Titanic (5.12) No topo. Rarely climbed short crack. Just downhill and left of the descent route. Climb an overhanging crack protected by fixed pins, bolts, and gear. **Descent:** Walk off east.

49. Summer Dreams (5.7) No topo. Seldom climbed; some suspect rock. North and around the corner from the descent route. Start in a crack behind a small pine tree growing on the cliff's northeast side. Above the crack, face climb on large "boiler plates" to a 2-bolt anchor 100 feet up.

Middle Rock

Middle Rock is the long, east-west trending formation immediately north of Mosaic Rock. Its south face is characterized by sweeping slabs capped by diagonaling crack systems and steeper headwalls and overhangs. Several excellent routes ascend the left side of the face. The three difficult sport routes on the right side see less action.

Descent off all the routes is by scrambling down the west or east ends of the formation.

Finding the cliff: Follow directions to Mosaic Rock's West End. Walk around the northwest corner of the formation and hike up a trail along a dry wash to the base of the long south face of Middle Rock on your left (north). Routes are listed from left to right. Not all bolts shown.

50. Cowboy Bob's Chicken Head Delight (5.10) Committing, seldom climbed, but an area classic. Scramble up the rounded west ridge of Middle Rock to a depression under a hole that tunnels through the entire rock. Start by climbing right and along a finger crack on the right side of a small face covered with chickenheads. Traverse right to a row of chickenheads slanting up right below a horizontal finger crack. Use knobs for footholds to the end of the crack and then move up right using large chickenheads to *Fingerfest.* Continue up, keeping left of a final huge chickenhead. Easy climbing leads up right to a belay stance from gear. Keep the rope left of the final chickenhead to protect the second. **Rack:** Wires, TCUs, and extra slings to tie off chickenheads.

51. Fingerfest (5.10d/11a) Sustained and committing climb. Start the same place as *Cowboy Bob's,* then climb up and right to

gain a long slanting finger crack. Continue to end of the crack, crossing *Cowboy Bob's,* then edge directly to the summit. **Rack:** Wires, extra TCUs, and small Friends. Gear required for the belay.

52. Bats in the Belfry (5.8) Good crack climbing. From the base of the south face, climb easy rock up low-angle slabs and set up a belay below a hand crack. Jam the hand crack over a bulge to the summit. **Descent:** Walk east to the end of Middle Rock (several dicey moves) or work down into the next grotto north, then back west to the west end of Middle Rock.

53. Cowgirl Pump (5.11aR) Seldom climbed. Begin about 10 feet right of *Bats in*

the Belfry. Climb an easy left-slanting crack to its end, then up about 20 feet to a belay, or continue up steeper rock passing several horizontal cracks to a bolt-protected crux move over a bulge.

54. Albuquerque Route (5.8+) Recommended. Start about 50 feet right of *Bats in the Belfry.* Quality steep slab climbing edges past 4 bolts to a 2-bolt anchor. 70 feet. **Descent:** Rappel or lower from anchors.

The next three routes are on the right side of the south face. Hike east along the cliff base to an obvious steep face with three bolted lines. Belay from the ground below the routes.

55. Dragon's Lair

(5.11c/d) Scramble up easy rock and then left up a groove to the base of a thin, steep crack. Difficult moves, protected by RPs, work up the lower section. Above, edge up a green lichen streak past 3 bolts. Run it out above along a diagonaling crack and belay from gear. 3 bolts, no anchor.
Descent: Scramble off east along the crest of the formation.

56. Grandma's Cancer

(5.12-). Scramble up easy rock and then crank small holds on the steep face above. At the crack, angle right into a scoop. Belay above from gear. 5 bolts, no anchor.
Descent: Scramble off east along the crest of the formation.

57. Raging Chicken

(5.11+). Crimp small holds up a short, steep face to a crack. Climb right and belay from gear. 3 bolts, no anchor.
Descent: Scramble off east along the crest of the formation.

West Rock

West Rock is a north-south trending formation just west of Middle Rock. A gully divides West Rock's steep east face from slabs on the west end of Middle Rock. Routes are found on the east face, on steep slabs on the south end, and on long slabs on the west side. Many easy slab routes, not described here, ascend the west face slabs.

Descend by rappelling from fixed anchors or scrambling off.

Finding the cliff:
Follow hiking directions to Mosaic Rock's West End. Continue north along the trail another 50 yards to the base of the south face of West Rock. Routes are described from right to left, beginning with the routes on the right or east side of the formation.

58. Growth Spurt

(5.11-) A new route with suspect rock and widely spaced bolts. Begin below a steep face with bolts on the right side of the east face of the formation. Grab edges up a steep blank face to anchors at the cliff top. 4 bolts to 2-bolt chain anchor.

59. The Alien (5.9+) 20 feet left of *Growth Spurt*. This stellar route follows the central crack system up a detached pillar on the left side of the east face of West Rock. **Rack:** Bring a standard Tres Piedras rack. **Descent:** Rappel from a 2-bolt anchor.

60. The Mad Bolter (5.11a)

Located left and around the corner from *The Alien*. Quality difficult climbing up the slabby south face. Start up a thin crack behind a large tree. Climb past 2 bolts and continue up a headwall to a slab finish. Optional gear plus 4 bolts to 2-bolt cold shut anchor on a ledge.
Descent: Rappel from anchors.

61. How Ed's Mind Was Lost

(5.10) Start left of the same tree as *The Mad Bolter*. Climb a hand crack left of the thin finger crack. Work up right along this gear-protected crack and join *The Mad Bolter* below its third bolt. Climb the right prow of the rock, then back left to a 2-bolt anchor shared with *The Mad Bolter*. **Descent:** Rappel from anchors.

62. Ground Up (5.10b/c) Sort

of contrived and funky. Start just left of *How Ed's Mind Was Lost* at the big trees at the base. Edge up a steep slab. 3 bolts and 1 fixed piton to 2-bolt cold shut anchor.

63. New Rage (5.9+) No topo. Start 30 feet

left of *How Ed's Mind Was Lost*. A short section of thin face climbing, then easier climbing to a belay stance on a ledge or use cold shut anchors to the right. 2 bolts to 2-bolt cold shut anchor. **Descent:** Rappel from anchors or walk off west.

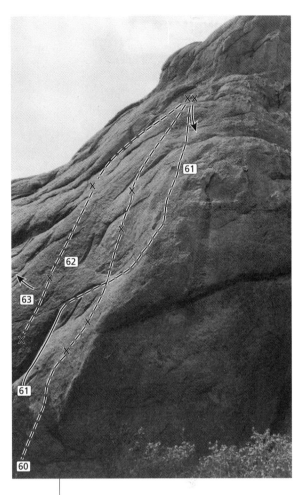

64. Geez Louise (5.8 X) No topo. Seldom

climbed. Be ready to run this one out. Located up the gully on the formation's west side between two dead trees lying against the slab. An old ¼-inch bolt two-thirds of the way up the face protects the route. Delicately friction and edge up the slab between trees to the crest of the formation. **Descent:** Scramble off the top or pick yourself up from the bottom.

Sundeck Wall

The west-facing Sundeck Wall offers excellent face climbing up a beautiful slab above Aspen Alley, an attractive aspen-filled gully that is especially beautiful in late September and early October. All the routes are high quality and highly recommended.

Descend from anchors or scramble off to the north or south.

Finding the cliff: From the base of West Rock's south face, continue walking northwest along the base of the cliffs to the last rocks in the immediate area. Turn right up a wide slot (Aspen Alley) and continue about 50 yards. All routes are located near the north end of the gully. Routes are described from right to left.

65. Zorro (5.10a) Excellent. Pick your way to the first bolt by either angling in from the left along a shallow seam or climbing directly up the slab (harder). Edge up the perfect face above to a thin crack. Work up the crack to a belay atop the face. The climb is slightly easier (and equally fun) if the small chicken-heads to the right of the crack are used. 2 bolts to 2-bolt anchor. **Rack:** Small TCUs protect the crack above bolt 2. **Descent:** Rappel from 2-bolt anchor.

66. Unnamed (5.8) Another good one. Just do it. Face climb up a right-angling crack (protect with small wires) and then work toward a small tree. **Descent:** Rappel from 2-bolt anchor.

67. Gila Monster (5.9+). Excellent. Start left of a groove and between black water streaks. Climb a slab and headwall to anchors below the top. TCUs work in the horizontal crack between bolts 3 and 4. 4 bolts to 2-bolt anchor.

68. Digital Dilemma (5.11a) Quality delicate moves from start to finish. Start up a small flake behind a large ponderosa pine tree. Climb 10 feet past 1 bolt, move left on a bolt-protected difficult move, then edge and smear past 2 more widely spaced bolts. 4 bolts to 2-bolt anchor.

69. Unknown (5.9+/.10) No topo. Good route. Walk north up the gully about 100 feet from *Digital Dilemma* and scramble to the base of a chimney. Face climb up thin holds on the face right of the chimney. Using the chimney reduces the grade. 5 bolts to 2-bolt anchor.

North Rock

All the described routes are found on the north face of North Rock, the large formation immediately north of Middle Rock. Most routes are vintage, sparsely protected face and crack climbs from the 1970s. These routes are seldom climbed because any fall has the potential for serious or fatal injury. A 5.12 route up a beautiful green and yellow lichen streak, one of the more attractive routes at Tres Piedras, had all its hangers removed. The anchors are still in place. Several new routes (not pictured) left of this route are described below. It's difficult to toprope any of the described routes since they lack anchors or the anchors are difficult to access. Ascertain the situation for yourself and decide if you want to go to the effort to climb these lines.

Finding the cliff: The easiest access to the face is to follow directions to Middle Rock. From the base of the south face of Middle Rock, hike east up a gully and the eastern end of the south face. From here, walk northwest below the east slab face of North Rock and go left to the north face.

Descend all routes by scrambling off to the right (west) end. Routes are described from left to right.

70. Unnamed (5.12). Formally a steep face climb up a green and yellow lichen streak. 5 bolts with missing hangers to 2-bolt cold shut anchor.

71. King Crack (5.9 R) The first crack right of *Unnamed* (5.12). Climb the crack, then face climb to 2-bolt cold shut anchor. Protection is difficult and marginal.

72. Queen Crack (5.10 X) Face climb to a fist-size groove offering amorphous jams and marginal protection. Traverse right onto face near the top. No pro after the traverse. Gear required for belay. Both cracks can be toproped by using long extensions at the top or with a 200-foot rope.

73. Unnamed (5.9+ X) Face climb up right side of black streak. Bottom section is sort of protected with TCUs, wires, and small Friends. Top part is protected by a single ¼-inch bolt. Gear required for belay anchors.

Walk off →

All Hangers Missing

74. Unnamed (5.9+ X) Face climb on right side of a thin finlike feature. Two ¼-inch bolts on upper section. Gear required for belay anchors.

75. Back of Jack (5.10- X) A couple old ¼-inch bolts is all your protection. Ground fall potential! Gear required for belay anchors.

76. Eyes that Lie (5.10) Difficult slab climbing up right past 3 ¼-inch bolts. This is the best protected of the slab routes on this side. Gear required for belay anchors.

Three new modern routes are located left of these routes. From right to left they are 5.12 (short crux at the third bolt, then 5.10 the rest of the way), 5.11 (shares last bolt and anchors with the 5.12), and a project on the far left.

COMALES CANYON

■ O V E R V I E W

This small crag tucked in a canyon in the Sangre de Cristo Mountains 18 miles southeast of Taos features a fun mixture of sport and traditional climbs. The area, reached by an easy ten-minute hike, has a peaceful setting complete with a pristine creek running next to the cliff base. The quartzite rock is eminently climbable and features around a dozen 60- to 100-foot routes. Most of the routes are in the 5.8 to 5.10 range with a good mix of sport and traditional offerings. Visiting climbers should be versed in traditional climbing skills since most of the routes require gear placements to supplement bolts or in some cases to protect the entire route. Every route has or shares anchors for lowering or rappelling.

The west-facing cliff is divided into two sections. The lower Water Wall rises directly out of the creek. Some very fine routes ascend this excellent cliff sector. Directly above the Water Wall is the upper cliff, the Fire Wall. The routes on this upper tier are fully bolted and do not require any gear. The crag's three most difficult routes are found here. The Fire Wall is best accessed by climbing a route on the Water Wall, although a rough trail scrambles up steep slopes right of the Water Wall.

Climbing History

All the routes at Comales were installed by Jay Foley with help from his wife, Donna Longo. Shawn Wood and some visiting Australians also contributed.

It's difficult to set up topropes at the Water Wall from the top. The mountain slopes on either side of the cliff are steep and easily eroded, so leading a route is usually the best option. Once a route is led, there are opportunities to toprope other climbs from the anchors.

Comales is a good May-through-October crag. Summer can be very fine with plenty of shade for warm days. Autumn is also excellent and beautiful when the aspens in the canyon change to gold. Winter is difficult unless the weather is unusually mild. Snow blankets the canyon floor most of the winter months.

Camping is available in several U.S. Forest Service campgrounds scattered along Highway 518 below Comales Canyon. Comales Campground, located just across the highway from the parking area, is the most convenient.

Rack and Descent

A rack for Comales should include lots of wires, small camming units, and pieces up to 3 inches. Placing protection here often requires patience, creativity, and a well-stocked rack. A 150-foot rope will get you up and down all routes except for the longer routes on the cliff's left end, where a 200-foot rope is required. Descend all routes by lowering or rappelling from fixed anchors.

Not all bolts are shown on the topos.

Trip Planning Information

Area description: Comales Canyon, an easily accessible and fun crag, offers a good mix of traditional and sport climbs on a 50- to 100-foot creekside cliff.

Location: North-central New Mexico. Comales Canyon is approximately 18 miles southeast of Taos.

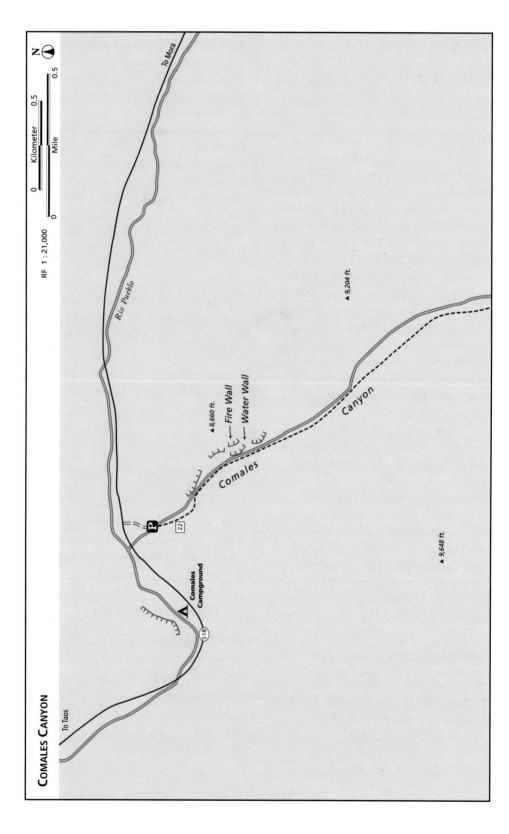

COMALES CANYON

RF 1 : 21,000

N

Kilometer
0   0.5

Mile
0   0.5

To Mora

To Taos

Rio Pueblo

Comales

Canyon

Fire Wall

Water Wall

▲ 8,660 ft.

▲ 9,204 ft.

▲ 9,648 ft.

Comales
Campground

P

22

518

Camping: Good camping is available in the immediate area. A free Forest Service campground is located one-half mile west of the parking area. Primitive camping can be found 100 yards up Trail 22. Additional camping can be found in nearby Carson National Forest (208 Cruz Alta Road, Box 558, Taos, NM 87571; (505) 758–6200). Also see the camping information listed in other Taos climbing sites.

Climbing season: Early spring to late fall are best. The west-facing cliff provides early morning shade and afternoon sun. The crag is an excellent choice for hot summer days.

Restrictions and access issues: Comales Canyon lies within the Carson National Forest.

Guidebooks: *Taos Rock: Climbs and Boulders of Northern New Mexico* by Jay Foley, Sharp End Publishing, 2005.

Services: No services in the immediate area. Sipapu Lodge, about 3 miles east, has limited services. All services are found in Taos, including gas, groceries, dining, and lodging.

Emergency services: Call 911. Cell service is spotty but worth a try. The nearest pay phone is at Sipapu Lodge, about 3 miles east on Highway 518. Holy Cross Hospital (505–758–8883), on the south end of Taos, is the nearest hospital. Contact the New Mexico State Police (505–758–8878) or Taos County Sheriff (505–758–3361) for emergency assistance.

Nearby climbing areas: John's Wall, Dead Cholla Wall, Bat Cave, Wild and Scenic Wall, Questa Dome, Tres Piedras, and El Rito Sport and Trad areas.

Nearby attractions: Many attractions and museums are found in the Taos area, including Taos Plaza, Kit Carson Park, Taos Pueblo, Millicent Rogers Museum, Padre Martinez Hacienda, Taos Pueblo Enchanted Circle Scenic Byway, San Francisco de Assisi Church in Ranchos de Taos, Rio Grande Gorge Bridge, Picuris Pueblo, Carson National Forest, and Wheeler Peak Wilderness Area. Good rafting, fishing, and swimming are found in the Rio Grande Gorge. Lots of terrific mountain biking is available in the canyons and mountains around Taos, including the megaclassic, South Boundary Trail.

Finding the crag: Comales Canyon is located about 18 miles southeast of Taos. From the nearby town of Ranchos de Taos just south of Taos, turn east onto Highway 518. Drive south on Highway 518 and pass a junction where Highway 75 goes west to Vadito. Continue east on Highway 518 and drive a few miles to a right turn onto a dirt road at a sign that reads COMALES CANYON, FOREST TRAIL 22. This turnoff is just past Comales Campground.

Park about 50 yards up this road at the first level spot on the left. The road gets rough and ends a short distance south of the parking area. Hike up the dirt road, which eventually becomes Trail 22. Follow the trail alongside and sometimes through the creek. You pass a long band of vegetated cliffs before arriving at the Comales crag, which rises on the left directly from the creek bottom. Allow ten to fifteen minutes hiking time for the approach.

The Water Wall

The Water Wall is the lower, west-facing cliff sector alongside the creek. All the routes are worth climbing. Routes are described from left to right when facing the cliff.

1. Tranquillo (5.7) No topo. A good introduction to the rock at Comales. Start just right of a short right-facing corner near the left end of the cliff. Optional gear placements available to augment the widely spaced bolts. 3 bolts to 2-bolt anchor.

2. Puro Vida (5.9) No topo. Tricky and sustained. Start 15 feet right of #1. Supplemental gear helps protect you to the first bolt. Climb the white streak above past 2 more bolts. 3 bolts to 2-bolt anchor.

3. Black and Tan (5.10c) No topo. The complete package. Start just right of a large boulder leaning against the cliff. Protect the thin crack with wires and TCUs, move a little left at the top of the crack, then straight up past 2 bolts and 1 suspect fixed pin (at the roof near the top) to 2-bolt anchor. 3 bolts to 2-bolt anchor.

4. Yellow Wall (5.9+ R) No topo. Start about 35 feet right of *Black and Tan* and just left of *Take the Plunge*. Climbs the right edge of the yellow "scoop." Tricky pro. Difficult and runout near the top. 2-bolt belay.

5. Take the Plunge (5.8+) Classic. Start on "cheater stones" in the water about 45 feet right of #3. A #1.5 Friend in the first horizontal crack keeps you out of the creek if you fall, then protect with wires and more cams up to 3 inches. No bolts. 2-bolt anchor.

5.1. Aussie Avalanche (5.9) Start 10 feet right of *Take the Plunge*. Excellent climbing with tricky pro. No bolts. Use *Take the Plunge* anchors.

The area between routes #5.1 and #6 offers many opportunities for ascents. Pick what looks best to you and figure out how to get up and down.

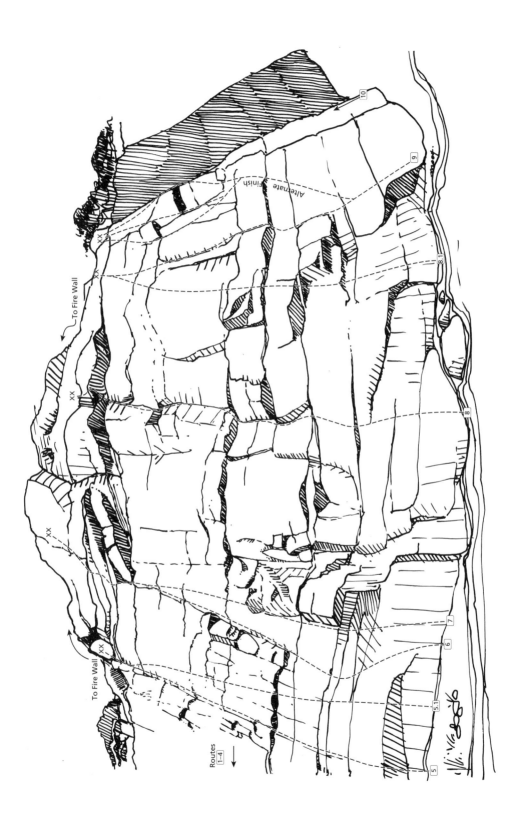

To Fire Wall

To Fire Wall

Alternate Finish

Routes
1-4

10

9

8.1

8

7

6

5.1

5

6. Comale Tamale (5.9+/.10a) A terrific route. Start 55 feet right of #5. Climb straight up into a right-facing dihedral and pull buckets over a triangular-shaped roof at its top to a large ledge. Climb the tiered roofs above (crux) past 2 bolts to easier climbing. A 200-foot rope is required to lower or rappel. 2 bolts to 2-bolt anchor.

7. Tamale con Verde (5.9+/.10a) Good variation to #6. Start 5 feet right of *Comale Tamale* and just left of a large roof about 10 feet off the ground. Climb the short crack above, move right, then up and left to the same bolted finish of *Comale Tamale*. Difficult to protect. Shares anchors with #6. 2 bolts to 2-bolt anchor.

8. Open Book (5.10a) Good route. Start on the right end of a long flat ledge just right of a large roof about 10 feet off the ground. Climb a shallow dihedral system, step right into another dihedral, then up to a large ledge. The pin at the crux bulge doesn't seem loose, but back it up anyway with a #3 Friend. 1 fixed pin to 2-bolt anchor.

8.1. Southern Gothic (5.9+/.10-) Excellent route. Start just left of *Gothic Pillar* and climb up and over the higher of two roofs. Continue straight up the buttress to anchors for *Gothic Pillar*.

9. Gothic Pillar (5.7) Start on the toe of the buttress just where the trail starts uphill on the right end of the crag. Several options exist here, either directly up the prow or coming in from the left. Climb past a small tree to anchors. No bolts to 2-bolt anchor.

10. Dirty Corner (5.6–5.8-) For large crack aficionados. Start 15 feet up the dirt slope on the right side on the cliff. Climb a large right-facing corner, then left and up a gold streak to anchors. Other, slightly more difficult routes are found left of this line on the face of the buttress. At least three options around 5.7 to 5.8 are found here to toprope or lead. No bolts. 2-bolt anchor.

Fire Wall

The Fire Wall, with three hard routes, is the upper sector above the Water Wall. Access the cliff by climbing *Take the Plunge* on the Water Wall or alternately by walking up the slope to the right of route #10. This is not recommended, however, because of impact on the steep, loose slopes.

Some extra toprope anchors are installed and can be reached from any of the bolted lines. Routes are listed from left to right. All routes are well bolted with anchors installed. Not illustrated.

11. Fiyo (5.12a) Start on the left-hand wide black streak. Well bolted to 2-bolt anchor.

12. Burnt (5.11b/c) Start below the next wide black streak to the right of #11. Sustained and pumpy. Well bolted to 2-bolt anchor.

13. Toast (5.12a) Start 5 feet right of #12 on the left side of the next black streak. Well bolted to 2-bolt anchor.

WILD AND SCENIC WALL

■ OVERVIEW

Wild and Scenic Wall, also known as The Candy Store, is a little-known and beautiful crag hidden in the bottom of the Rio Grande Gorge west of Questa in northern New Mexico. The adventurous climber finds excellent, strenuous crack climbs from 80 to 100 feet long on the small cliff's hard basalt. The area is seldom visited except for an occasional angler, guaranteeing a time of solitude and peace. The crag is enjoyed as a day trip, although camping in the gorge opposite the cliff is a great option. The only problem is crossing the Rio Grande, which is often dangerous during spring and early summer

Wild and Scenic Wall

Rio Grande

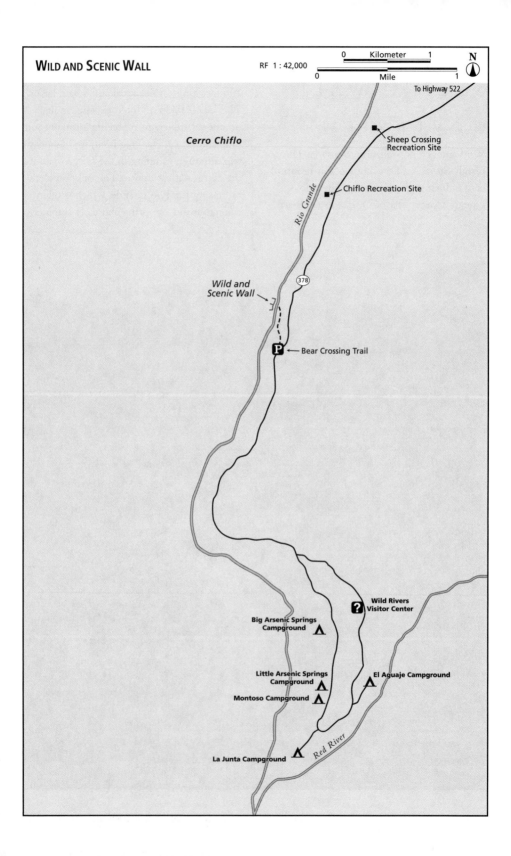

runoff. See below for specifics on this important issue. A poison ivy jungle at the cliff base also poses a significant hazard.

Climbing History

The cliffs along the river in the upper gorge section were visited in the mid-1980s by crack masters Doug Bridgers, Mike Roybal, and Peter Prandoni. The trio visited cliffs at the bottom of the Chiflo Trail, upstream from Bear Crossing. What they climbed that day is unknown, and the area failed to become popular probably because of difficulty crossing the river.

Jay Foley, in his quest to explore climbable Taos area rock, probed the possibilities in the Bear Crossing area in 1994. An attractive crag on the west bank just upriver lured him and partners across, where they felt like kids in a candy store as they sampled the delights of the crag's stellar cracks. *Kids in a Candy Store, Fighting Atrophy,* and *Spearhead* were the first lines ascended.

Rack and Descent

Currently thirteen terrific routes, ranging from 5.10 to 5.12 and equipped with bolt anchors, line the cliff. All routes are traditional affairs requiring varied crack climbing techniques and the ability to place protection. Carry a substantial rack with at least doubles of cams up to 4 inches plus wired nuts and small TCUs. Most routes are 100 feet long, making a 200-foot rope necessary. Descend by lowering or rappelling from fixed anchors.

Trip Planning Information

Area description: The Wild and Scenic Wall, a 100-foot-high basalt cliff located deep within the Rio Grande Gorge, features the best assortment of traditional crack climbs in the Taos area.

Location: Northern New Mexico within the Bureau of Land Management Wild Rivers Recreation Area about 8 miles east of Cerro, New Mexico.

Camping: Some camping possibilities can be found along the riverbank close to the cliff. No facilities. Good camping on the rim of the gorge is available approximately 4 miles south of the Bear Crossing Trailhead at the BLM Wild Rivers Recreation Area on the rim of the Rio Grande Gorge. There are twenty-one campsites in five campgrounds, and this is a U.S. fee area.

Climbing season: Late May to late October, depending on Rio Grande water levels and resources to cross the river. July through September can be uncomfortably warm but are the best months to consider. The crag faces east but receives a late morning sun hit and is shady in the afternoon. Expect afternoon thunderstorms during the summer months.

Restrictions and access issues: Wild and Scenic Wall lies within land administered by the Bureau of Land Management. The crag's remoteness and approach singularities require special safety considerations. Lock your car and leave valuables at home or out of sight.

Guidebooks: *Taos Rock: Climbs and Boulders of Northern New Mexico* by Jay Foley, Sharp End Publishing, 2005.

Services: The small village of Questa offers limited services, including a convenience store, several restaurants, a liquor store, and a gas station. Full services are found in Taos, 20 miles south on Highway 522, and in Red River, 15 miles east of Questa on Highway 38.

Emergency services: Call 911. The nearest phone is at the Phillips 66 station just south of the junctions of Highways 378 and 522. Holy Cross Hospital in Taos is the nearest hospital (1397 Weimer Road; 505–758–8883). Questa Health Center (505–586–0315) is located at 2573 State Highway 522. Contact the New Mexico State Police (505–758–8878) or Taos County Sheriff (505–758–3361) for emergency assistance.

Nearby climbing areas: Questa Dome, John's Wall, Dead Cholla Wall, Bat Cave, Comales Canyon, and Tres Piedras.

Nearby attractions: Rio Grande Wild and Scenic River, Red River, Red River Fish Hatchery, and Wild Rivers Back Country Byway are all near Questa. Taos attractions include Taos Plaza, Kit Carson Park, lots of museums and art galleries, and Taos Pueblo. Nearby is the Enchanted Circle Scenic Byway, Rio Grande Gorge Bridge, and Wheeler Peak Wilderness Area. Good boating, fishing, backpacking, and hiking is found in the BLM's Wild Rivers Recreation Area.

Finding the crag: Drive north from Taos about 32 miles on Highway 522. Just past Questa follow signs to Wild Rivers Recreation Area. The first turn is left (west) onto Highway 378. Drive 8.2 miles to a signed right turn to Bear Crossing Trailhead. Park at the trailhead and locate the trail at the south side of the parking area. The trail is signed. Do not take the trail going directly west which terminates at an overlook a short distance down the slope. Hike down a steep but fairly short trail to the river. The trail is unmaintained and rugged but improves slightly with elevation loss. It takes ten to fifteen minutes to hike to the river. The first rock-hopping and wading possibility is just after the trail reaches the river. At the river hike upstream over boulders for another ten to fifteen minutes to reach the crag and for additional crossing possibilities.

The crag, located at river level, is easy to identify. Depending on river conditions and what you have to assist your crossing, choose to cross opposite either the south or north end of the cliff. The crossing is easier at low water levels (late summer and late winter) and difficult to impossible at high levels (spring to late summer). An inner tube is helpful to get packs across should you decide to wade/swim the large pool beneath the crag. The river flow is determined by mountain snowpack and irrigation demands upstream and varies from year to year. Call the BLM River Flow toll-free number at (888) 882–6188 to check updated river levels. Rock-hopping without getting your feet wet is possible at water flows around 100 cfs (cubic feet per second). Factor in time to figure out your river crossing solutions.

Follow a climber's path that skirts the cliff base to avoid poison ivy. Routes are listed from left to right.

1. Candy Cane Crack (5.10-) Start in a thin crack that goes to hands and fist-size higher. 2-bolt anchor.

2. Pillar Filler (5.12) Start up *Candy Cane Crack* and veer left when the crack makes a short right-angle turn to the right. Delicately climb the left side of a 10-foot flakelike formation, then up the smooth slab above to anchors shared with *Candy Cane Crack*. 6 bolts to 2-bolt anchor. (Note: As of late summer 2005, the holes were drilled but no bolts placed. They should be in place by publication, but make sure before leaving the ground.)

3. Yo W (5.10+) Climb a crack to a large sloping ledge, then up a flared chimney to a chockstone. Belay on a ledge just above. Descend from sling anchors or climb to the top and walk off. Rack a 6-inch piece of pro to ease anxiety on this burly route.

4. Spearhead (5.11) Highly recommended. Named for the shape of a chockstone under the large roof and for the Michael Frantis Band. Start in a corner and follow a thin crack to a ledge. Continue up to the bottom left side of a large roof. Turn the roof on its left side and jam a beautiful off-finger to hand crack to off-width to a 2-bolt anchor.

5. Jolly Rancher (5.10+) Start on the left side of a small roof in a thin crack that leads through a steep section with a fixed pin. Aesthetic climbing above leads to an imposing slot. Large gear protects the crack in the rear of the slot. Your choice of a variety of techniques surmounts the slot to where it narrows, then easier climbing to anchors shared with *More-R-Less.* 2-bolt anchor.

6. More-R-Less (5.10a) Classic climb. Start behind a short detached pillar in a triangular slot. Chimney up, then follow a thin crack to a hand and fingers crack arcing left and up to join the upper part of *Jolly Rancher.* Squirm through a final short slot to hand jams in pods to a 2-bolt anchor.

7. Herb's Lounge (5.10c) This is as good as it gets anywhere. Named after the locally famous watering hole in Arroyo Hondo. Start the same as *More-R-Less* up to the left arcing crack. From this point continue straight up a beautiful and sustained hand to small hands crack in a left-facing dihedral. 2-bolt anchor.

8. Sugar Rust (5.10a/b) Start 20 feet right of *Herb's Lounge.* Climb a crack and corner up right then left across the face to a shallow left-facing dihedral. Large gear is useful on this section. Near the top, exit the crack system via a short crack over a roof. 2 bolts and gear to 2-bolt anchor.

9. Mudd Pie (5.10) Same start as *Sugar Rust,* then right to the left-facing dihedral to a 2-bolt anchor.

10. Poison Ivy (5.11+) Traverse in from the left to avoid poison ivy at the base. Jam a sustained thin splitter to a sloping ledge. Move right to a 2-bolt anchor.

11. Kids in a Candy Store (5.11-) Area classic. Start just right of a large distinct roof located just off the ground. Climb a beautiful, steep hand crack on the cliff's right side to a 2-bolt anchor (same as #10).

12. Fighting Atrophy (5.10+) Excellent. The first route completed on the cliff. Jam a thin vertical crack past two small slanting roofs. A bolt in a scoop above the third and final roof lessens the anxiety, getting to a 2-bolt anchor a short distance up right.

13. Unnamed (5.12) Toprope problem. Climb the beautiful face just right of *Fighting Atrophy.*

SUGARITE CANYON STATE PARK

■ OVERVIEW

Sugarite (pronounced "sugar-reet") Canyon State Park, located just south of the Colorado and New Mexico border near Raton, is an off-the-beaten-track climbing area but well worth a visit. The area is almost fully developed since its brief mention in *Rock Climbing New Mexico & Texas* and now offers more than forty quality established routes. With the exception of one bolted line, all of the routes are traditional affairs that require good protection placement skills and a head for traditional climbing. The excellent climbing here is mostly up vertical faces, using pockets from finger mono-doigts to mailbox-slots and a good assortment of finger and hand cracks. There are climbs for everybody at Sugarite, with routes ranging in difficulty from 5.8 to 5.12. The majority of routes are 5.9 and 5.10.

Crowds are never an issue at Sugarite. Indeed, sightings of bears, wild turkeys, and other wildlife are more common than the rare sightings of other climbers. The absence of crowds allows for a pristine and private climbing experience. Every ascent you do seems like a first ascent since there is little chalk on the rock and almost no bolts.

The cliffs at Sugarite and the surrounding mesas are composed of basalt that resulted from lava flows associated with the Raton-Clayton Lava Field. The higher mesa caps are up to 7.2 million years old, but volcanism occurred in the area about 60,000 years ago, a relatively recent geologic event, with the eruption of Capulin Volcano. A unique feature of the older basalts (including Sugarite) is the abundance of "vesicles," or in climbing parlance, pockets. These vesicles, which make great face holds, are a result of gases that were originally dissolved in the magma. As the magma rose from deep in the earth, the gases were exsolved (released) from the erupting magma to form pockets as the lava flowed and cooled. When climbing with these pockets, note that they are aligned and stretched out in a direction parallel to the flow of the lava, which is generally horizontal in this area.

Climbing History

There is no local climbing community in Raton or northeastern New Mexico to establish routes at Sugarite. The first known climbing here was in the late 1980s when Colorado Springs climber Steve Cheyney and other Colorado climbers visited and established several routes, mostly toprope lines. In 1991 another group of Colorado Springs climbers, including Ric Geiman, Mark Van Horn, and Mike Johnson, installed a half-dozen quality sport routes on the cliff in a few days. These bolted lines were quickly and inexpertly chopped by an unknown person. The chopping was extreme and brutal, leaving bent-over bolt studs and flattened hangers on the cliff.

This vandalism led to the closure of the park to all climbing. In 1992 the park reopened to climbing, although further bolting was disallowed. A developing management plan slated for future adoption may provide for the limited installation of some bolts for lowering anchors and possibly for some limited bolts on new routes that cannot be totally protected by traditional means. The area currently is regarded as a traditional climbing area with a prohibition on all bolting.

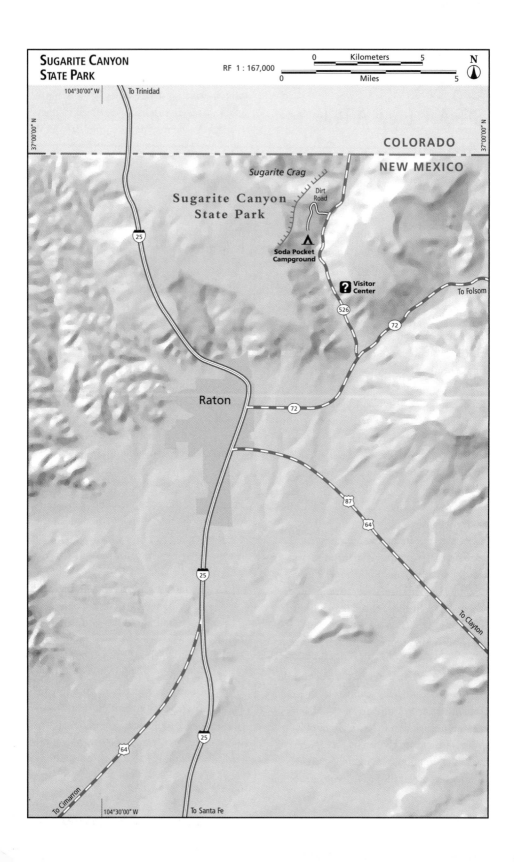

The pocketed face routes included in this guide have all been led in a traditional manner, placing cams and tri-cams in the pockets. Preplaced protection was utilized on several of the more difficult routes, but for the most part routes were led from the ground up. Mark Hesse, Paul Drakos, Stewart Green, Dennis Jackson, and Pete Takeda have led this effort.

Rack and Descent

The local climbing ethic accommodates pre-placed pro if there is the potential for either ground falls or taking long falls onto questionable gear. Visiting climbers should feel free to provide for their safety by preplacing gear or toproping, in view of the prohibition on bolting. Toproping is a valid and safe method of ascent that has always been utilized at Sugarite. The style of the first ascent is usually noted in the written description.

A typical rack for Sugarite includes small to large wires, at least doubles (three is often better) in the small TCUs and #1 to 2.5 Friend sizes. The hand cracks (*Jam your Blues Away, Crack from Hell,* etc.) require multiple #3 and 3.5. Many climbs require belaying from gear at the top, so carry a good variety of nuts and cams. When in doubt, carry extra gear. A 150-foot rope is sufficient for all ascents, lowers, and rappels.

Descent from all routes is by lowering from bolt anchors, rappelling from established rappel stations, or rappelling from gear. Routes with lowering anchors are mentioned in the route descriptions. All other routes require a rappel to descend. Fixed rappel stations are found at the east and west ends of the cliff. Routes not convenient to these anchors require building and removing temporary anchors. The scrub oak and pine trees set back from the cliff rim are often the only option for toprope and rappel anchors. If you use these, you will probably need an extra rope to reach the rim.

Trip Planning Information

Area description: Sugarite Canyon State Park features a south-facing 70-foot-high basalt cliff with more than 40 traditional routes. Routes can be led or toproped.

Location: Northeastern New Mexico. Sugarite is 10 miles northeast of Raton.

Camping: Convenient developed sites at the state park's Soda Pocket Campground are within walking distance to the cliffs. Other developed campgrounds are available along the park access road. Showers (located across from the visitor center) are included in camping fees. Time limits apply. Primitive camping opportunities are nonexistent in the immediate area.

Climbing season: Year-round. Best times are spring and fall. Midsummer days can be uncomfortably warm, although climbing early in the day or in evening shade are good options. Winter climbing is possible only on warmer days. The road to the cliff is closed in winter, so park at the gate and hike just over a mile uphill to the cliff.

Restrictions and access issues: Installation of bolts is prohibited anywhere in the park. A $4.00 day-use fee is required to enter and use the park. The road to Soda Pocket Campground and the trailhead to the climbing area is gated and closed to vehicles from late November to mid-April. Hiking to the crag is permitted year-round. Check with park officials for exact dates of road closures, which vary depending on weather.

Services: All services available in Raton about 10 miles west.

Emergency services: Call 911. Contact a park ranger for assistance. The visitor center is generally staffed seven days a week during normal working hours. A pay phone is located outside the visitor center. The local hospital is Miners Colfax Medical Center (505–445– 3661) located on the south end of Raton.

Nearby climbing areas: None in the immediate area. Maverick Cliff and Probe 1 Cliff in Cimarron Canyon are about 60 miles to the west.

Nearby attractions: Sugarite Canyon State Park (505–445–5607) offers a visitor center with interpretive information about the area. Area attractions include Capulin Volcano National Monument, Folsom Museum, Maxwell National Wildlife Refuge, Raton Museum, and Cimarron Canyon State Park. Other outdoor activities are fishing, hiking, and mountain biking.

Finding the crag: Sugarite Canyon State Park is 10 miles northeast of Raton, the first city encountered in New Mexico when traveling south from Colorado on Interstate 25.

From north and south on I–25, take exit 452 and head east onto Highway 72. This is

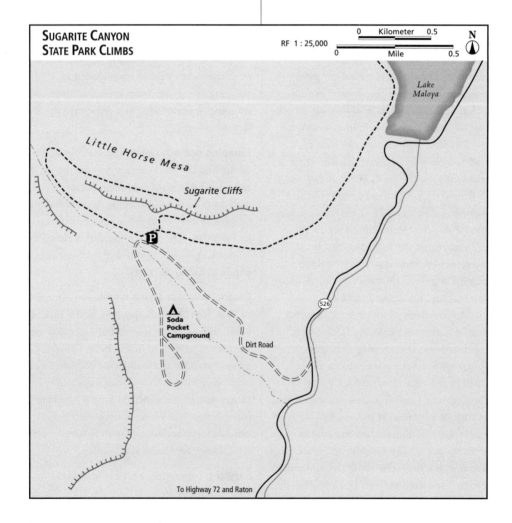

SUGARITE CANYON STATE PARK CLIMBS

RF 1 : 25,000

Kilometer

Mile

N

Lake Maloya

Little Horse Mesa

Sugarite Cliffs

P

Soda Pocket Campground

526

Dirt Road

To Highway 72 and Raton

marked Sugarite Canyon State Park and Folsom. Follow signs to the park, making sure to veer left on Highway 526. Stop at the visitor center to pay the $4.00 day-use fee. Continue 2.4 miles farther north to a left turn to Soda Pocket Campground. This dirt road is generally open from April to November. (Park here and hike the 1.3-mile road if closed in the off-season). Drive 1.3 miles and park in a small pullout on the right, which serves as the trailhead parking for the Lake Maloya and Little Horse Mesa trails. A sign here says NO HORSES OR MULES BEYOND THIS POINT. The cliff is obvious from the parking area.

Two trail options reach the cliffs. The first takes longer but is easier to find and puts you on the cliff top, which requires a rappel to access the cliff base. This may be advantageous for parties wanting to set up topropes. Allow twenty minutes for this approach. The second option takes about ten minutes and accesses the base of the cliff.

1. Top of cliff option. From the parking area follow signs left to Lake Maloya, Segestrom Valley, and Little Horse Mesa. When the trail divides, go right toward Little Horse Mesa. On the mesa top, turn right onto a narrow path and walk for about a half mile to a (usually) dry, small lake. The middle portion of the cliff and Zoid Tower are located below the east (far) end of the lake. Build a rappel here or use established anchors by *S&M Crack, Jam Your Blues Away, Crack Head,* or *Pete's Down Climb* to rappel.

2. Base of cliff option. From the parking area, follow the sign right to LAKE MALOYA 2 MILES. The trail parallels unclimbed cliffs left of the main climbing area. When the trail is just past an obvious jutting buttress that divides the two cliffs, look for a faint path that goes left toward the left end of the

climbing area. This junction is approximately four minutes from the trailhead signs. A small cairn (when people leave it in place) is found here. Follow this faint cairned trail up the slope to some large boulders beneath the cliff. Cairns here direct you left or right. Go left for routes #1 to #20 and right for all other routes.

Routes are described from left to right.

1. Bush Doctor (5.10b/c) No topo. Worth climbing. Start 30 feet left of *Endless Summer.* Climb the left side of an unattractive roof, then up a good crack.

2. Endless Summer (5.9+) Classic. A bolt protects the traversing moves into a demanding and steep finger crack.

3. Up Your Arête (5.10b) Excellent. Led on-sight by Mark Hesse using cam placements in pockets for protection. Veer left near the top to finish on *Endless Summer,* or if you're feeling confident, continue straight up.

4. Pete's Down Climb (5.7/5.8) Off-width crack with 2-bolt anchor on the cliff rim. Good off-size crack but usually done by climbing the face to the right.

5. Salt Mother (5.8) Difficult for its grade. Small hands and tricky climbing down low to easier climbing above. 2-bolt anchor.

6. Sangre Verde (5.10a) Good climb. Sugarite's only sport route. 4 bolts up a blunt arête to the rim. Shares lowering anchors with #7. 4 bolts to 2-bolt anchor.

7. Crack Head (5.8) Excellent. Perfect hand jams with lots of pro. Shares lowering anchors with #6.

8. Great Roof Left (5.9) Recommended. Hand and finger crack.

9. Motengator (5.8) Excellent moderate. Great hand jams, tips, and pockets lead to a steep finish. Ignore the poorly driven and unnecessary piton (placed near the top after the first ascent) if still there.

9.1. Son of Motengator (5.8+) This route veers left to the crack about halfway up from #9.

10. Soma Holiday (5.10b/c) Good climb. The difficulty is at the bottom, then great pocket pulling. Go left at the roof.

11. Lackawanna (5.10b/c) Excellent. Best not to be in this frame of mind for this pocket and thin crack climb. Go for it.

12. Oral Sex in the Whitehouse (5.9+) A statement of the strange times we live in. Good pocket pulling to your choice of thin cracks at the top.

13. Crazy Cams (5.9) Thin crack and pockets yield another moderate classic. Hard at bottom, crux in the middle.

14. Dog Day (5.10c/d) Megaclassic finger crack and pocket pulling. Hard moves at the top.

15. Yo Mamma (5.10b/c) A worthy climb. Preplaced pro was used for the first ascent. Start 4 feet right of *Dog Day,* then climb up and right on good holds. It's runout at the bottom, even with preplaced gear.

16. Taos Lightning (5.10c) Area megaclassic. Named after the famous libation imbibed at the fur trappers rendezvous in the 1840s. Best to have your wits about you on this one. Route was pre-equipped on first ascent. Sequential opening moves lead to slightly easier climbing above. Choose to go straight up or veer right to a lower angle crack or traverse farther right to join *Jam Your Blues Away* at the top. Shares anchors with *Jam Your Blues Away.*

17. Jam Your Blues Away (5.10a) An area classic. You are sure to feel better after finishing this one. Great hand jams to a 2-bolt anchor.

18. Raised by Wolves (5.10d) No topo. Classic. Start 30 feet right of #17. Difficult opening moves up a fingertips crack to good fingers.

19. Bush Pilot (5.10a) No topo. Recommended. Start 15 feet right of #18 in a short off-width with a small chockstone, then crank up pockets and a thin crack.

20. Sweet and Sour (5.8) No topo. Climb around or go through a short chimney to reach a short, low-angle crack.

21. Sapphire Crack (5.8) Worth climbing. A curving hand crack to the right of a perched boulder at the base of the cliff.

22. Carpe Manana (5.10c) Excellent. A striking thin crack on the left side of a large white flake. Crux at the bottom.

23. Get Your Mojo Running (5.11d) A Pete Takeda testpiece. Start in "the pit" (below the boulders at the base of the cliff) and crank burly moves up and around a gray roof to a thin crack.

24. The A-Frame (5.12c) Sugarite's hardest route to date. Established with preplaced pro by Pete Takeda in 1999. Start deep in "the pit" below the cliff. Awkward, thin moves lead up and right past a fixed wire and piton in a thin crack. Pull above to thin but easier climbing.

25. Type O (5.9+) Classic. A single bolt protects the thin opening sequence, then climb a stellar finger crack.

26. Double D Left (5.10b/c) Excellent. Thin face climbing up to a right-facing dihedral. The first ascent avoided the difficult-to-protect section about 10 feet up by moving right to *Double D Right,* climbing about 10 feet, then moving back left. A straight-up ascent has not been done to date.

27. Double D Right (5.10b) Great climb. Gymnastic moves off the ground lead to a beautiful left-facing dihedral.

28. The Pocket Rocket (5.9) An area classic. Start on the right-curving crack or face climb straight up to gain the excellent pocket pulling above. Go left near the top to a 2-bolt lowering anchor.

29. Bad Moon Rising (5.10c) Brilliant route. A stunning splitter over a small roof. One of the original routes at Sugarite.

30. Right on Raton (5.8) Fun classic. Begin off a large boulder wedged against the wall. Awkward jamming at the bottom leads to a perfect hand crack and a 2-bolt lowering anchor just below the rim.

31. Gift of Aliens (5.10b) Classic. The smallest Alien reduces the stress level on this one. The single bolt helps, too. Thin and steep.

32. The Arrowhead (5.9) Good climb. Climb to the top of an arrowhead-shaped flake, then up a finger crack and pockets.

33. The Optimator (5.11d/12a) An improbable looking climb led with preplaced pro by Peter Takeda on his first visit to Sugarite in the fall of 1999. No second ascent to date. Begin off boulders wedged against the wall. Sequential and technical face moves up thin pockets alongside an RP crack lead to an easier finish.

34. Miami Vice (5.10b) Good climb. Step across a narrow chasm to gain a thin flake. Climb a finger crack in a right-facing corner with the occasional welcome pocket to a difficult finish.

35. The Crack from Hell (5.10b) Classic. Start deep in a pit beneath boulders. Hand jam a steep strenuous crack to the top.

36. Primodelic (5.10b/c) Primo! Led first with preplaced pro. Start just right of a striking thin crack and pull down on pockets on a steep face. Go right near the top.

37. Wounded Knee (5.8) Recommended. Step across a gaping chasm above a pit, then work up a crack using good hand and fist jams.

38. Driven to Climbs (5.9+) Superb route. Traverse right on pockets to under a thin crack that splits about a third of the way up. Difficult jams lead straight up. The left crack is slightly easier.

39. March Madness (5.10b/c) A bold classic. Another bold lead that opened up new territory without bolting. Start on a small ledge and climb straight up to a small roof. Turn this on the right, then work up a thin crack.

40. Spoticus (5.9) Recommended. An awkward left-leaning hand and finger crack.

41. Bat Dog (5.10) Another great one. Start 5 feet right of #40. Straight up a thin crack using pockets and face holds. Make a long traverse right on face holds to a slightly

overhanging thin hands crack. Eschew the traverse and climb the left crack near the top for a slightly easier finish.

42. Duke in a Bucket (5.10b) Climb the V-shaped slot to a good finger crack. Better than it looks (or sounds).

43. S & M Crack (5.11a) Strenuous megaclassic crack. This excellent testpiece ascends the cliff's tallest section on the far right side. Most of the climb is out of view from the main cliff area, but it is well worth the effort to find it. Scramble down and right across boulders to the base of the cliff just right of a short, sharp arête. Start by climbing through the shattered rock under a roof. Turn the roof on the left, then jam a pumpy hand crack to a 2-bolt anchor on the rim.

CIMARRON CANYON CRAGS

■ OVERVIEW

Cimarron Canyon slashes through the Sangre de Cristo Range between the towns of Eagle Nest and Cimarron. The Palisades in the central part of the canyon are the biggest cliffs here; unfortunately, park personnel discourage climbing on these beautiful formations because of poor rock quality. But two fine sandstone crags—Maverick Cliff and Probe 1 Cliff—hide just down the canyon near Maverick Campground. These small, fun cliffs are worth a stop if you're traveling through the canyon. The area is quiet, secluded, and low-key since it's somewhat remote. A climbing visit is almost always a solitary experience. Hiking, mountain biking, fishing in the lovely Cimarron River, and bouldering are added inducements to visit.

The cliffs, lying on opposite sides of the canyon, are composed of metamorphosed sandstone, a geologic anomaly in this area, which features lots of softer sandstone and Dacite porphyry, the other main formations in the canyon. Maverick and Probe 1 are the only two climbing sites developed on the sandstones thus far. Other cliffs lie on the higher ridges, but these are on Philmont Scout Ranch property and are off-limits to the general public. A small overhanging cliff with several bolted routes is also on private property just east of Probe 1 above the highway and is generally closed to climbing.

Maverick Cliff is a hidden, south-facing cliff north of Maverick Campground. The climbing area, part of a longer broken cliff band, is a 50-foot-high cliff divided into two sectors with The Block Head, a huge detached block, separating the two. The resistant sandstone is very climbable with lots of jugs and in-cut edges. Slabs with easy beginner routes and steep jug hauls with occasional thin moves characterize the climbing.

Climbing History

The Cimarron Canyon cliffs intrigued climbers since at least the 1970s. The main climbing focus was the large, beguiling cliffs called The Palisades, located a short distance west of Maverick and Probe 1 alongside U.S. Highway 64. These towering ramparts beg to be climbed, but after closer inspection they are less attractive for climbing. The steep crack systems are often loose and discontinuous, and both protection and retreat options are inadequate. Permission to climb on the cliffs may be possible after a permit process that involves a trip to the Fish and Game office in Raton and jumping through more hoops than you care to do.

Since there is a decided lack of climbing possibilities in this part of New Mexico, a few climbers searched for more climbable rock in the fall and winter of 2000–01. Probe 1 Cliff was the first area established, which led to the discovery and subsequent development of Maverick Cliff. Both cliffs were developed by Dennis Jackson and Stewart Green. *Roadblock* (5.11a/b), Maverick's hardest route, was put up by Jay Foley in the summer of 2004. J. B. Haab added *Mickey's Delight* in August 2005. There may be a few lines left to do, but the area is considered fully developed. Today the crags are often visited during the summer by climbing instructors from adjoining Philmont Scout Ranch but languish in obscurity for the rest of the year.

Rack and Descent

Maverick's climbs, ranging in difficulty from 5.4 to 5.11, are well bolted for safety. All the

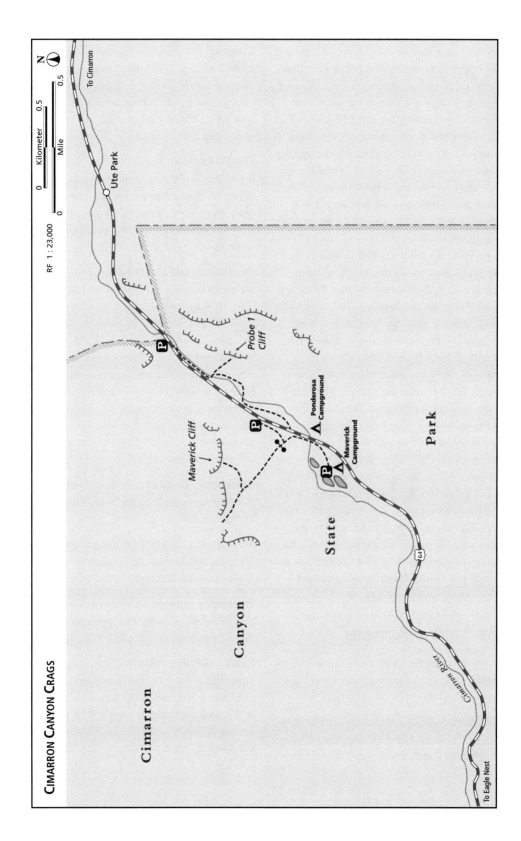

CIMARRON CANYON CRAGS

RF 1 : 23,000

0   Kilometer   0.5

0   Mile   0.5

N

To Cimarron

Ute Park

Cimarron   Canyon

Probe 1
Cliff

Maverick Cliff

P

P

P

Ponderosa
Campground

Maverick
Campground

State   Park

64

Cimarron River

To Eagle Nest

routes either have or share two-bolt lowering or rappel anchors. The first bolt is sometimes high, although the climbing is generally easy getting to it. If you have any doubts about your safety reaching the first bolt, then ask for a spot and climb carefully or turn over that end of the rope to someone else. Setting up topropes from the cliff top is possible, but use extra attention or a belay for safety. The freestanding Block Head must be led, and indeed, this is the best way to set up topropes on all the climbs.

Probe 1 Cliff is the best section of the long cliff band on the south side of the canyon opposite a roadside spring. Probe 1 is a 45-foot-high, north-facing cliff ascended by a selection of moderate sport routes. Small, crisp edges on the vertical face characterize the harder climbs here, while the easier routes have lots of good edges and chicken-heads. All the routes are protected by bolts with two-bolt lowering anchors. The first bolts are above a large ledge 15 feet off the ground. Use caution and climb carefully to the ledge to clip the first bolt. It's best to lead the routes in order to set up topropes.

A simple rack of eight quickdraws and a 150-foot-long rope is sufficient for all routes. A small rack of Stoppers, TCUs, and small Friends is an option for additional protection on some climbs on Maverick Cliff. Descent off all routes is by lowering or rappelling from established anchors.

Trip Planning Information

Area description: Short moderate sport routes on two 50-foot-high metamorphosed sandstone cliffs.

Location: Northern New Mexico. The cliffs are in Cimarron Canyon State Park between Eagle Nest and Cimarron.

Camping: No primitive camping in the immediate area. Developed campsites are found at nearby Maverick and Ponderosa campgrounds. Both are fee areas with time restrictions. Other campgrounds are located in the canyon.

Climbing season: Spring, summer, and fall. It is possible to climb on mild winter days. When it's cooler, Maverick is the best choice since it's sunny for most of the day. Probe 1, with lots of shade, is the crag of choice on warm days.

Restrictions and access issues: The crags are under the joint jurisdiction of Cimarron Canyon State Park and the Collin Neblit Wildlife Area. A permit to climb on The Palisades is required. Check in at the park headquarters in Tolby Campground on the western end of the park to get started on this involved process. These are the first crags in Cimarron Canyon State Park that will see increased climber visitation. Our actions will likely determine any changes in restrictions and access issues.

Guidebook: *Taos Rock: Climbs and Boulders of Northern New Mexico* by Jay Foley, Sharp End Publishing, 2005.

Services: Ute Park, a short distance east, offers limited services. All services are in Eagle Nest and Cimarron.

Emergency services: Call 911 or notify state park personnel at Tolby Campground near the west entrance to the park.

Nearby climbing areas: Sugarite Canyon State Park is 60 miles east near Raton. Lots of climbing is found in the Taos area 35 miles to the west, including Dead Cholla Wall, Bat Cave, John's Wall, and Comales Canyon. Climbing is found at Philmont Scout Ranch, but it's private property and closed to all public use and visitation.

Nearby attractions: Cimarron Canyon offers scenic beauty, fishing, hiking trails, and mountain bike trails. The Pine Ridge store in Ute Park has free maps of the hiking trails in the area. Otherwise Cimarron lies on the old Santa Fe Trail and has a rich history. Taos offers lots of visitor attractions including Taos Pueblo, Ranchos de Taos, and many museums and art galleries.

Maverick Cliff

Maverick is a south-facing cliff on the north side of the canyon near Maverick Campground.

Finding the crag: Maverick Cliff is located in Cimarron Canyon State Park about 12 miles west of the town of Cimarron. From Interstate 25 and Raton to the east, drive west on US 64 through the town of Cimarron to the Cimarron Canyon State Park boundary. A short distance into the park is a park sign and a natural spring on the

right. This is a good place to fill water bottles. Continue 0.3 mile past the spring to a small dirt pullout on the right. Park here and walk up the dirt road paralleling the highway, through a metal gate, then uphill for about 600 yards. Turn right at the first road encountered. A sign here says NO DUMPING. Walk about 100 yards east to a clearing, then turn left (north) into the trees and locate a cairn-marked trail that heads right then up to the hidden cliff. The trail ends below routes #12 to #14. Allow ten minutes for this short approach hike.

If you're coming from Taos and the west on US 64, drive through the canyon, passing The Palisades, to near the park's eastern end and locate the pullout described above, which is about 0.3 mile east of Maverick Campground. You can also park at Maverick Campground and walk along the highway edge to the dirt road.

Routes are described from left to right when facing the cliff.

1. Este Es (5.10b) No topo. Highly recommended but sometimes sandy. This is the farthest left climb at Maverick. Start 90 feet left

of The Block Head next to a large pine tree. Pull up edges on a slight bulge to a slab finish. 3 bolts to 2-bolt anchor.

2. Fred's Friendly Face (5.4) Excellent beginner wall. Find lots of variations from the anchors plus a more difficult toprope problem to the right up a vertical wall on the left side of a deep chimney. 2 bolts to 2-bolt anchor.

3. The Witch (5.6) Located on the slab right of the deep chimney that separates two slabs. Go left at first bolt. 2 bolts to 2-bolt anchor.

4. The Ditch (5.6) Go up and right at the first bolt. 2 bolts to 2-bolt anchor.

5. The Bitch (5.9) Toprope problem on the tricky face left of a fist/off-width crack in a left-facing corner directly behind The Block Head.

6. Reach for the Sky (5.9) Excellent. Located on the west face of The Block Head. Edge up a shallow flake system. 2 bolts to 2-bolt chain anchor.

6.1. Mickey's Delight (5.9+) Pre-clip (or lead up to) the low bolt, then start from the ground to make this route longer and slightly harder. 3 bolts to 2-bolt anchor.

6.2. Roadblock (5.11a/b) The area's hardest route. Located on the narrow south face of The Block Head. 4 bolts to 2-bolt anchor.

7. Block Head (5.9) Highly recommended. The right-hand route on the east face of The Block Head. Perfect face climbing up the short face. 5 bolts to 2-bolt chain anchor.

8. Spinal Tap (5.8) Another good one. The left route on the east face of The Block Head. 2 bolts to 2-bolt anchor.

9. Jugarama #3 (5.7) Recommended. Located on the left side of the main wall. 4 bolts to 2-bolt anchor.

10. Jugarama #2 (5.8) A must-do climb! Edges and jugs up the steep face. A couple cams ease the runouts. 2 bolts to 2-bolt anchor.

11. Jugarama #1 (5.9) Another great climb. The cliff's first route. Start up a thin crack, then over an overhang to easier climbing above. Gear placements possible in upper section. 2 bolts to 2-bolt anchor.

12. A Stiff Upper Lip (5.10b) A muscular route. Start up a short curving crack and pull over the big overhang onto a stance. Finish up some thoughtful climbing above. 3 bolts to 2-bolt anchor.

13. Head 'em Up (5.8) No topo. Excellent. This and the following two climbs are located about 90 feet right of *A Stiff Upper Lip*. Climb jugs up gradually steepening rock to anchors just below the top. 5 bolts to 2-bolt anchor.

14. Move 'em Out (5.10a) No topo. Area classic. Steep jug hauling to a steep difficult finish. 4 bolts to 2-bolt anchor.

15. Rawhide (5.7) No topo. Fun climbing. Climb an attractive laid-back slab right of a large crack. Lots of variations possible. 3 bolts to 2-bolt anchor.

Probe 1 Cliff

Probe 1 is a very good section of north-facing cliff on the band south of the highway and river. All the routes are up to 45 feet long.

Finding the cliff: Probe 1 is on the south side of the canyon. There are two ways to reach the cliff.

The shortest approach is from the parking area opposite the roadside spring near the east end of the canyon. Hike west for about 500 feet along an angler's trail to where it is possible to see a power pole across the river. Cross the river by wading (avoid at high water) and locate a faint trail that angles left up the steep bank just past the power pole. Follow the trail for about 300 feet and then bend right onto a path that heads toward a large gully. Continue up the right side of the gully and a slope to the cliff base. The path is marked with cairns and easy to follow. The important key is finding the power pole. Hiking time is about ten minutes.

Alternately you can park 0.3 mile farther west up the highway at the same parking area as for Maverick Cliff. Cross the road and find a faint path heading south across the grassy flats to the Cimarron River. At the river, find a log jam to cross the water and hike downriver (east) for about 900 feet on an angler's trail to a power pole next to the trail. Turn right about 30 feet before the pole on a faint trail angling left up the riverbank. Follow the directions above to the cliff. Hiking time is about fifteen minutes.

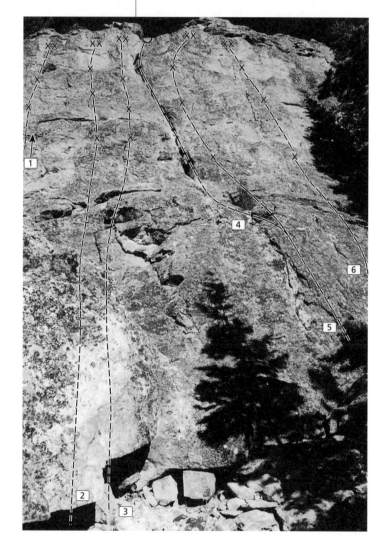

Routes are described from left to right.

1. Circe (5.7) Begin at the far left side of the face. Easy but runout climbing leads to a shelf; continue up fun climbing above. 2 bolts to 2-bolt anchor.

2. Calypso (5.8) Boulder up to the narrow ledge, then edge up the face above. 3 bolts to 2-bolt anchor.

3. Ulysses (5.8+) Fun moves. Climb unprotected up the lower face to a narrow ledge. Continue up the steep face left of a crack that splits the face. 3 bolts to 2-bolt anchor.

4. Dionysus (5.7) Jam the obvious hand and fist crack up the middle of the face to the top. Either toprope it or bring some gear.

5. Priapus (5.10a) Excellent edge climb up the face right of the crack. Gear placements are possible for the start, or you can traverse onto it from the left. 3 bolts to 2-bolt anchor.

6. Gaia (5.10a) Another good route. The direct start is runout and sketchy. It's easier to traverse in from the left. Hidden holds in the crack right of bolt 1 make it easier to clip. 3 bolts to 2-bolt anchor.

EL RITO CRAGS

■ O V E R V I E W

The El Rito Crags are composed of two separate and distinct climbing areas—El Rito Sport, a sport climbing area, and El Rito Trad, a large cliff with many easy to moderate traditional routes.

El Rito Sport, located in Carson National Forest, is considered one of New Mexico's best sport climbing venues. The area, a few miles north of the old farming village of El Rito, is a collection of conglomerate crags scattered across the west flank of a mountain ridge. Although slightly off the beaten path, it is worth an extended visit. Lying at 7,000 feet, the area offers a pristine natural setting, an absence of crowds, great bouldering, and excellent free camping in the valley below.

The climbing at El Rito Sport is on a well-cemented sandstone conglomerate named the El Rito Formation. This coarse rock was deposited during the Eocene Epoch of the Tertiary period about fifty million years ago, just before the formation of the Rio Grande Rift. The conglomerate is composed of both fine sands and large clasts, which are pebble- to boulder-size rocks of quartzite, granite schist, and metavolcanics eroded from the adjacent Sangre de Cristo Mountains. This cobbled rock gives a unique climbing experience since most of the hand and foot holds are either these large clasts or the rounded holes left behind after they fell out.

El Rito Sport, with more than fifty quality routes, offers enjoyment for climbers of all abilities. Most holds tend to be positive edges rather than small and tweaky, keeping the fun in climbing. All routes are liberally bolted with lowering anchors, many of which have received some much-needed (and appreciated) improvement. Most of the routes are graded between 5.11 and 5.13, although a generous mix of moderate routes from 5.8 to 5.10 are also established.

Climbing History

El Rito Trad, the older traditional area, was developed in the 1970s and 1980s by the Los Alamos Mountaineers, who used the area for training and as their annual climbing school site.

Climbers, en route to El Rito Trad, drove by the band of cliffs on the east side of the valley for years but discounted the conglomerate cliff until 1997, when Ed Strang, a Santa Fe hardman, hiked up to the cliffs and quickly recognized the area's potential. Ed's enthusiasm for the cliffs initiated a flurry of route development. Ed and his brother Rich, along with Jean Delataillade, Lance Hadfield, Mark Thomas, and Lee Sheftell, led the effort to establish many of the best lines here. As news of this new area filtered out, climbers from Colorado, Texas, and Arizona joined in the route rush. Interestingly, the initial estimates of "hundreds" of potential routes never materialized, and development has slowed considerably since the original effort. Perhaps the adjoining cliffs to the north, some more than 200 feet high, will fulfill those projections.

Rack and Descent

The only rack you need for El Rito Sport is a dozen quickdraws and a 165-foot rope. A 200-foot rope is necessary to climb and lower off a few routes on the Full Sail (Super Slab). For El Rito Trad bring a rack of gear that includes sets of Stoppers, TCUs, and Friends, along with some quickdraws, extra slings, and a 165-foot rope. If you rappel

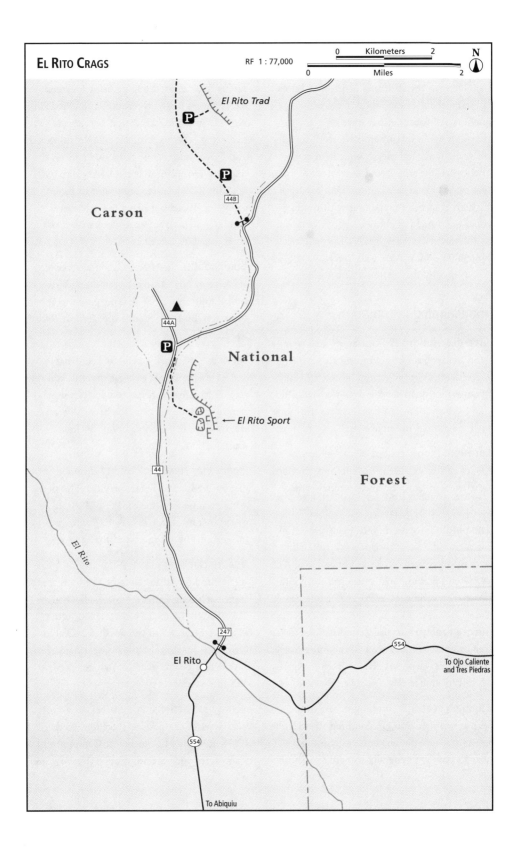

from fixed anchors on the cliff, you'll need two ropes.

Descent for all routes at El Rito Sport is by lowering or rappelling from bolt anchors. All routes either have or share a two-bolt anchor. Remember also to toprope off your own carabiners rather than the anchor hardware to avoid excessive wear and tear on the fixed equipment. Descent from El Rito Trad is by rappelling with double ropes from fixed anchors or by walking off to the north (left) from the cliff top. The preferable option is to walk off.

Not all bolts are shown on the topos.

Trip Planning Information

Area description: El Rito Sport area is an easily accessible sport climbing area with more than fifty routes from 5.8 to 5.13 in a pristine mountain setting. El Rito Trad offers many 5.6 to 5.11 traditional routes from one to three pitches in length.

Location: North-central New Mexico. North of the village of El Rito and 55 miles northwest of Santa Fe and 55 miles southwest of Taos.

Camping: Convenient, free, primitive camping is found a short distance from the cliff parking area. Turn left onto Forest Road 44A at the cliff parking area and select from any number of campsites less than 0.2 mile up the road. El Rito Campground, a U.S. Forest Service facility with toilets and tables, offers free camping 5 miles west of the village of El Rito on Highway 110. It's open from April 15 to November 30.

Climbing season: Climbing is best in the spring, summer, and fall. Summer days can be hot in the sun, but shade is easily found. Winter days are generally too cold to climb.

Restrictions and access issues: El Rito is managed by Carson National Forest. The area suffers from eroded staging areas on steep rocky slopes below the routes and cliffs. The Access Fund and U.S. Forest Service are exploring ways to mitigate climber impact, build more sustainable trails, and address the ongoing erosion problems. A new trail was built in 2003 in partial response to these problems. Typical of many New Mexico climbing areas, it is best to lock your car and keep valuables out of sight.

Guidebooks: *Taos Rock: Climbs and Boulders of Northern New Mexico* by Jay Foley, Sharp End Publishing, 2005. A mini-guide to the sport area by Rich Strang appeared in *Rock and Ice* #84.

Services: Two small, well-stocked grocery and hardware stores, two gas stations, and the terrific El Farolito restaurant are in the village of El Rito south of the area. All services are available in Espanola about 30 miles south.

Emergency services: Call 911. Limited nearby medical or rescue services. The nearest telephone is in the village of El Rito. A medical clinic, Las Clinicas del Norte, is located on the south end of the village.

Nearby climbing areas: No climbing areas are in the immediate vicinity. The Taos area crags, including Dead Cholla Wall, Bat Cave, Tres Piedras, Comales Canyon, and John's Wall, are 50 miles to the northeast. Diablo Canyon is 50 miles southeast near Santa Fe. The White Rock and Los Alamos crags are 45 miles south.

Nearby attractions: Potrero Falls is a short walk west of the parking area. The Red Bluffs are near El Rito Forest Campground. Cano Canyon, a beautiful open meadow, and

Fifteen Springs, the isolated pristine headwaters of El Rito Creek, are local favorite spots. Information on hiking and other recreation opportunities is available from the U.S. Forest Service office in El Rito.

Finding the crags: From the south take U.S. Highway 84/285 to Espanola. In Espanola, turn northwest toward Chama and Abiquiu on US 84/285; keep left onto US 84 where US 285 branches right. Drive approximately 11 miles to a right turn onto Highway 554 heading to the village of El Rito 12 miles away. Drive slowly through the village and turn left onto Rio Arriba County Road 247, also marked Forest Road 44, at a sharp highway curve just after leaving the village.

From the north and the Taos area, access US 285 and drive south to Highway 111, about 30 miles south of Tres Piedras. Turn right (north) and drive about 2 miles to a left turn onto Highway 554. Continue on this road toward the village of El Rito and turn right onto Rio Arriba CR 247, also marked FR 44. Drive 3.7 miles to a small parking area on the left (west) side of the road at the junction of FR 44A.

The trail to the cliffs starts on the east side of the road about 50 feet south of the car parking area. The trail parallels the road for about 300 yards, then turns sharply left (east), crosses an intermittent stream via a wooden bridge, then gradually traverses up and right (south) to enter the climbing area on its left (north) end. Allow ten to fifteen minutes to hike from car to cliffs.

The cliffs are described from left to right (north to south). Unless otherwise noted, all routes have or share a two-bolt lowering/rappel anchor. The access trail from the parking lot leads to the left side of the area, traversing in below The Outsider Wall. Straight ahead is The Beer Block (Cobblisk). Just past The Beer Block on the left is the

Big Pine Wall. Go left through a gap on the right end of the Big Pine Wall to reach Schoolhouse Slab, Rad Wall, and the Gnar Wall. Ed Woody, Pirates Wall, Full Sail (Super Slab), and The Balcony are farther right and reached by a rocky trail below the base of the cliff. About 50 feet below the north end of Pirates Wall is the Training Wall. It may sound confusing, but the area is small and compact, so a quick orientation will set you right.

The El Rito Trad area is located about 1.5 miles north of El Rito Sport. From the Sport area parking lot, drive north another 0.5 mile to the first left turn. A homemade arrow on a ponderosa pine marks the left turn onto Forest Road 44B. This road, leading to the cliff parking, is steep, eroded, and rutted in spots. It's barely passable for a passenger car in dry conditions and difficult to impossible during or after storms. Walking the last mile is advisable in wet or muddy conditions. Drive or hike 0.9 mile from the turnoff and turn right into a small parking area that is west of the obvious west-facing cliffs. Do not drive beyond the parking and through a gate with a private property sign and a NO TRESPASSING sign on a tree. A faint but easy-to-follow trail starts at the east end of the parking area and meanders east and north to the cliff base about a quarter mile away. Allow five minutes for the approach hike.

El Rito Sport Area

The Outsider Wall (aka Walt's Wall)

This large wall is located up and left (north) of the Beer Block near the end of the approach trail. At least five routes and one project are found here. The cliff is relatively unpopular but has some worthwhile routes. Access the cliff by a faint trail just above The

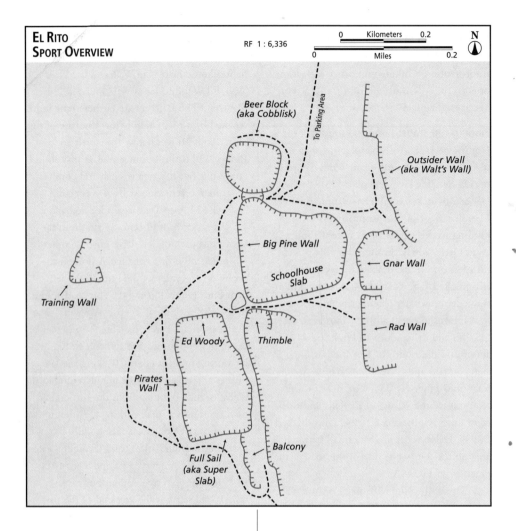

EL RITO SPORT OVERVIEW map showing: Beer Block (aka Cobblisk), To Parking Area, Outsider Wall (aka Walt's Wall), Big Pine Wall, Schoolhouse Slab, Gnar Wall, Training Wall, Rad Wall, Ed Woody, Thimble, Pirates Wall, Full Sail (aka Super Slab), Balcony.

Beer Block. Most of the routes are visible from The Beer Block. Routes are described from left to right. Not illustrated.

1. Unknown (5.12d) Unfinished. This climb takes a little walking being located pretty far left (north). Located near a cave. Short steep and hard route with 4 bolts.

2. Electric Pet Gri (5.11d/.12a) Left of *Walt's Wall Waltz* on a prow. 8 bolts, no anchor.

3. Walt's Wall Waltz (5.9) Recommended. Start on a flake near a right-angling corner.

4. Japs in the NBA (5.9+) Seldom climbed, poorly named, and not recommended. 4 bolts plus gear.

5. Bloodline (5.9) Recommended. Start near the center of the rock. Hard moves at the bottom, then easier above. 7 bolts to 2-bolt anchor.

6. Drive by Genocide (5.10d) An imposing route on the south (right) end of the wall. Located just left of a large ponderosa pine tree. 6 bolts to 2-bolt anchor.

The Beer Block (aka The Cobblisk)

The Beer Block is a massive cobblestone boulder leaning against the north side of Big Pine Wall at the end of the approach trail. The 30-foot-high block has short overhanging faces on almost all of its facets, offering an excellent array of difficult sport climbs. Routes #15 and #16 are on the steep west face. Routes are described from right to left starting on the northwest end of the formation.

7. Little Kings (5.12b)
Good route. 3 bolts to 2-bolt anchor.

8. To Beer or Not to Beer (5.12d)
Good climb. Technical moves on small holds. 4 bolts to 1-bolt anchor.

9. B.Y.O.B. (5.12d/13a)
Good climb on small holds. 4 bolts to 1-bolt anchor. A rather contrived but worth climbing variation named *12 Pack Link Up* (5.13b) starts on *To Beer or Not to Beer.* Do half the crux section, clip the final

bolt, then traverse left to *B.Y.O.B.* Do *B.Y.O.B.*'s crux and continue to anchors.

10. Tecate Two Step (5.12a/b)
Short, steep, and sweet. Arête to an overhanging corner. 3 bolts to 2-bolt anchor.

11. Buddha's Beer Belly (5.12a)
Recommended. Start where trail bends down around rock. 4 bolts to 2-bolt anchor.

12. It's Time to Drink Beer (5.12a) Good climbing. Steep with a difficult slab finish. 4 bolts to 2-bolt anchor shared with #13.

13. Village Cobbler (5.11b) Start at top of gully. 5 bolts to 2-bolt anchor.

14. Texas Whine (5.11c/d) Not recommended. Start in gully. Some homemade hangers. 7 bolts to 2-bolt anchor.

15. The Thing (5.13b) Quality route. Steep climbing out of the cave, then back to finish just right of *Whipper Wonderland*. 5 bolts to 2-bolt widely spaced anchor.

16. Whipper Wonderland (5.12a/b) Good climb. Straight up and over the scallops. 5 bolts to 2-bolt anchor.

14 _____ (11.b)

left of whipper wonderland

Big Pine Wall

The west-facing Big Pine Wall, shaded by a huge ponderosa pine, yields a stunning selection of superb sport routes. All are well protected and easy to work as projects so you can push your redpoint standard. Routes are described from left to right.

17. Cobble Wobble

(5.10c/d) Highly recommended. Start 10 feet right of the big pine tree on the cliff's left side. The upper half climbs the shallow right-facing corner. 7 bolts to 2-bolt anchor.

18. Corn on the Cobble (5.11b)

Good climb. Find the crux in the middle. 6 bolts to 2-bolt anchor.

19. Pocket Rocket

(5.12a) Excellent. Grab good pockets up the center of the wall before pulling over a roof. 6 bolts to 2-bolt anchor.

20. Peach Cobbler

(5.11d) Quality climbing. A must-do El Rito classic up the right side of the wall. 5 bolts to 2-bolt anchor.

21. Apple Cobbler (5.10a) Fun route up the arête on the far right side of the wall with a tricky finish. If you use the face to the right, the grade drops to 5.9. Begin at the slot that leads to Schoolhouse Slab and the Rad Wall. Going straight up to the left of the arête is a contrived 5.10c route. 5 bolts to 2-bolt anchor.

Schoolhouse Slab

The south-facing Schoolhouse Slab rises on the left after you scramble through the slot between Big Pine Wall and The Thimble. The three routes are deceptive for their grade with smooth cobbles and provocative route-finding. Routes are described from left to right.

22. Cobb It (5.7/5.8) 4 bolts to 2-bolt anchor.

23. Toprope (5.7) To set up your toprope, thread the 2-bolt anchor from either #22 or #24.

24. School Daze (5.7/5.8) 3 bolts to 2-bolt anchor.

Gnar Wall and Rad Wall

The Gnar Wall with two good routes is located just left of Rad Wall. The narrow slot between the two rocks also has two routes.

The west-facing Rad Wall, considered "the classic El Rito cliff," hides in a small rock-rimmed amphitheater behind Big Pine Wall and The Thimble. This overhanging wall, offering stout testpieces, is deceptively steep. Bring your A-game to send these technical pumpfests.

Finding the cliff: To reach the cliffs, scramble through the slot right (south) of Big Pine Wall, squeezing under a chockstone between it and The Thimble. Schoolhouse Slab is on the left on the south side of Big Pine Wall, while Rad Wall is the obvious leaning face directly in front. The Gnar Wall is the next small face to the left of Rad Wall. Routes are described from left to right.

Gnar Wall

25. Balls to the Wall

(5.10b) Located just left of *Blackballed*. Angles left. 5 bolts to 2-bolt anchor.

26. Blackballed

(5.10b) A short but stout line. 4 bolts to 2-bolt anchor.

27. Tooth Fairy

(5.10b) No topo. Located in the "Route Canal," the narrow gap between Rad Wall and Gnar Wall. The left-most of two routes. Climb up and over a small bulge. A "belay bolt" on the face behind the climb is helpful to keep the belayer in place on the loose and steep slope. 5 bolts to 2-bolt anchor.

28. Look Ma, No Cavities (5.10c) No topo.

Located just right of *Tooth Fairy*. 4 bolts to 2-bolt anchor.

Rad Wall

29. Procrastination (5.11d) Quality climbing. Finish on left arête. 6 bolts to 2-bolt anchor.

30. Bolting Barbie (5.11d) Highly recommended. Pocket pulling up the steep wall. 6 bolts to 2-bolt anchor.

31. Stroke Me (5.11d) Excellent. Start on top of a boulder at the base. This endurance line is a sustained pocket route. 6 bolts to 2-bolt anchor.

32. Against all Cobbs (5.12c) Quality pumpfest. Difficult all the way to the anchors. 7 bolts to 2-bolt anchor.

33. Crack Attack (5.12a). Great climb. The route with red hangers. Shares anchor with *Against all Cobbs*. 9 bolts to 2-bolt anchor.

34. Stoker (5.12b) Excellent. The crux is the start, then sustained but interesting moves. Difficult clips. 7 bolts to 2-bolt anchor.

35. The Matrix (5.11c) No topo. Climbs the arête on the right end of the face. 6 bolts to 2-bolt anchor.

36. Resurrection (5.10a) No topo. Not recommended. Just right of the arête. Clip first bolt on *The Matrix*, then up right. 7 bolts to 2-bolt anchor.

To Rad Wall

37

The Thimble

This short, north-facing cliff is just right of Big Pine Wall. Begin off narrow ledges below the face. This staging area is on the access path to Rad Wall, so stack your rope and plan for other climbers squeezing through on busy days.

37. El Dorito (5.9+/10a) Short and fun. Climb directly up the middle of the face. 3 bolts to 2-bolt anchor.

Ed Woody

This slightly overhanging, north-facing cliff lies on the north side of Pirates Wall. It offers three excellent and popular routes. Routes are described from left to right.

38. Gridlock (5.10b/c) Quality climbing and very popular route on the left edge of the face. Difficult finishing moves. 4 bolts to 2-bolt anchor.

39. Redline (5.11a) Excellent. Pockets and cobbles to a shallow crack finish. 4 bolts to 2-bolt anchor.

40. Cobbles and Robbers (5.11b) Quality. Pockets straight up the center of the wall. 6 bolts to 2-bolt anchor.

Training Wall

The Training Wall is the short west face of a large boulder located about 50 feet left and downhill from the north end of Pirates Wall.

41. Grits (5.12) Around the corner left of #42. More difficult and shorter than #42. 2 bolts to 2-bolt anchor.

42. Just another Pretty Face (5.11d) No topo. Difficult but mercifully short. 3 bolts to 2-bolt anchor. A 5.11b variation takes the bolt line on the right to the same anchors.

Pirates Wall

Pirates Wall with seven routes is the long west face between Ed Woody and Full Sail. It's a good, shady cliff for summer mornings. Routes are described from left to right.

42.1 Scurvy Dog (5.9) No topo. Located on the far left margin of the wall. Climb up a short face, then onto the arête to a small overhang. The route still needs some additional cleaning, especially near the top.

43. Oxymorons (5.10c/d) Black streak on left side. Loose in places. 6 bolts to 2-bolt anchor. The original name has been changed so the climbing community may not be viewed as racist pigs.

44. Trick or Treat (5.10d) It's a little loose in the black water streak partway up. 10 bolts to 2-bolt anchor.

45. The Buzz aka **Walking the Plank** (5.11c) Long, pumpy, and fun. Start in the center of the wall just left of some large boulders at the base. Watch out for a possible beehive. 10 bolts to 2-bolt anchor.

46. Pirated (5.12a) A former project that was pirated. 6 bolts to 2-bolt anchor.

47. Blackbeard (5.10c/d) An El Rito classic and one of the best routes here. Climb the prominent black streak up the right side of the wall. 8 bolts to 2-bolt anchor.

48. Booty (5.11b/c) Quality steep climbing on good holds. Pumpy and difficult at the top. A 200-foot rope is best for lowering and rappelling. 12 bolts to 2-bolt anchor.

Full Sail (aka Super Slab)

This 90-foot-high, south-facing wall is located on the south side of the Pirates Wall formation. The imposing cliff is visible from the road and reminded Mark Thomas, who did its first ascent, of a sail full of wind, giving the name of the first route and the slab itself. The cliff eventually took the name "Super Slab" in the absence of this information. This attractive face, the tallest at El Rito Sport, is slightly under-vertical and offers five excellent routes. Routes are described from left to right.

49. Super Arête (5.8) Start just right of Full Sail's left edge. Good face climbing leads past 4 widely spaced bolts to a loose crux section. The route originally featured a long runout to the anchors but has since been retrobolted. 8 bolts to 2-bolt anchor.

50. Clast Act (5.9) Highly recommended. A clast is what the cobbles on the faces are called by geologists. Start off the lowest edge of the man-made platform. Delicate opening moves lead to great jug hauling on quality stone. A 200-foot rope is best for safe belaying and lowering. 9 bolts to 2-bolt anchor.

51. Full Sail (5.10a) Another quality route and highly recommended. The cliff's first route. Begin 20 feet right of the slab's left edge. Pocket and cobble

climbing leads to a high crux at a roof. Step left at the crux to keep the grade to 5.10a, or crank straight over the roof (5.11a). A 200-foot rope is best for safe belaying and lowering. 9 bolts to 2-bolt anchor.

52. Boltaneer (5.9) Another recommended and excellent climb. Grab cobbles and pockets straight up the middle of the slab to anchors just below the pointed cliff top. Use a 200-foot rope for belaying and lowering. 85 feet. 10 bolts to 2-bolt anchor.

53. Oreo (5.10a) Start near the top of the dirt slope on the far right end of the cliff.

Full Sail

TR

54

55

56

57

Difficult at bottom, cruising in the middle, then difficult again at the top. A welcome "belay bolt" to help keep the belayer more stable is on the right a little up the slope. 8 bolts to 2-bolt anchor.

The Balcony

The Balcony is a west-facing cliff band located above and right of Full Sail (Super Slab). Access it by scrambling up right of a short cliff to the right of Full Sail. Be careful not to knock any loose rock off the belay ledge above this short cliff onto people below at the base of Full Sail. Routes are described from left to right.

54. Austin Powers, International Man of Mystery (5.9) The farthest climb on the left. The crux is clipping the poorly positioned anchors. 4 bolts to 2-bolt anchor.

55. Gobzilla (5.8) Start left of a green lichen streak. Fun climbing past 4 bolts to Springer lowering anchors. 4 bolts to 2-bolt anchor.

56. Mr. Bigglesworth (5.9/.10a) Height dependent with some inferior bolts. Toprope anchors are to the left. 4 bolts to 2-bolt anchor.

57. Jug-or-naut (5.11a/b)
Pumpy jug haul on the far
right side of The Balcony
between a couple large but
dead ponderosa pine trees.
An overhanging face leads
to the crux bulge between
bolts 3 and 4. 5 bolts to 2-
bolt anchor.

El Rito Boulders

Besides the routes, some
great bouldering is found
on boulders scattered below
the El Rito cliffs. Look
around for chalk and you'll
find the problems.

Several boulders are
near the Training Wall. *Mad
Max Boulder* leans against
the left side of the Training
Wall. *Bozo Boulder* is the
next boulder downhill and
to the left. *Small Boulder* is
the first large boulder
uphill from the Training
Wall, with *Warm-up Boulder*
just below it.

Downhill and to the left of The Beer
Block is *The 45-Degree Boulder* and *Beer
Boulder* just a little farther left. On slopes
below Full Sail are good problems from V1
to V7. Not illustrated.

El Rito Trad

This old-time New Mexico area offers good
beginning to intermediate multipitch climbing in an easily accessible and pleasant setting.
Moderate multipitch routes from 5.2 to 5.9
are found on this cliff in a pristine, remote
setting. The rock, a quartzite intrusion, differs

from the sport area but is equally fun and eminently climbable. The routes require placing your own protection, although some bolts and belay/rappel anchors are found. The area is worth visiting since it is one of New Mexico's few cliffs with easier multipitch routes.

Beginning climbers will find that the easier grades come at the price of some runout climbing, route-finding problems, and the need for creativity in finding and placing protection. Carry an ample rack with a good range of wired nuts, TCUs, camming units up to 4 inches, and a handful of slings. A 165-foot rope gets you up most routes. Two ropes are best for any rappels.

For better or worse, some bolts have appeared. At least two bolt-protected pitches, both second pitches on routes, are now established. Bolt anchors for belaying and rappelling are found on Juniper Ledge, at the top of *Juniper Overhang,* and about 50 feet to the right (rappel from these to anchors on Juniper Ledge). Evaluate the rappels from the top to decide if you can safely reach the lower anchors and easily retrieve your ropes. Two rappels with double ropes are necessary to reach the ground. If you don't rappel, descend by walking back a little from the cliff top and picking up a good easy-to-follow trail north then down forest slopes on the left end of the cliff. This ten-minute hike is the easiest and safest option to get back to the base of the crag. Routes are described from left to right.

1. Commie Pinkkos (5.4) 2 pitches. Hike left up a faint trail along the cliff base toward two large ponderosa pine trees. Start below the upper tree. **Pitch 1:** Climb the rounded

shoulder of the cliff. Belay about 125 feet up. **Pitch 2:** Climb cracks and slabby faces to the cliff top. Descend by walking north on a good trail contouring down the left (west) side of the cliff.

2. Gnarly (5.5) 2 pitches. Start below the lower ponderosa pine. **Pitch 1:** Climb to a large ledge and belay by an ancient gnarled juniper tree. **Pitch 2:** Go right and up a right-facing dihedral to the summit. Going straight up from the belay is also an option although protection is sparse. Descend by walking north on a good trail contouring down the left (west) side of the cliff.

3. Weapons of Mass Construction (5.9) First ascent in 2003. **Pitch 1:** Climb the first pitch of *The Big "E."* **Pitch 2:** Climb left onto an attractive slab, then face climb past 5 bolts and optional gear to the summit. Install your own anchor on the rim. 5 bolts, no anchor. Descend by walking north on a good trail contouring down the left (west) side of the cliff.

4. The Big "E" (5.7) 2 pitches. Start by two small juniper trees just below a rotten log lying next to the cliff. **Pitch 1:** Climb to a small roof, then out right along a seam, passing a small tree to a good ledge, and belay from a 2-bolt anchor. **Pitch 2:** Go up a shallow left-facing corner system left of *Juniper Overhang,* the major roof below the summit, then continue on easier climbing to the summit. Descend by walking north on a good trail contouring down the left (west) side of the cliff.

5. Juniper Overhang (5.9+) Below #3 is another rotting log next to the cliff. Start

near the middle of the log. **Pitch 1:** Climb straight up to a triangular roof, out its left side, then up to the left end of Juniper Ledge. **Pitch 2:** Work up the dihedral that forms the left margin of the overhang, then onto the face above. Belay from a 2-bolt anchor. Carefully consider the descent option and either rappel from these anchors or the anchors on top of *Guillotine,* or walk off to the left down the descent trail.

6. Bring Me a Bucket (5.9+) This is a bolt-protected variation to pitch 2 of *Juniper Overhang.* Climb the bolt-protected face left of the dihedral forming the left margin of the formation. Continue up and over the roof to a bolt-protected (optional gear placements) face above. Belay from a 2-bolt anchor. 6 bolts to 2-bolt anchor. Carefully consider the descent option and either rappel from these anchors or the anchors on top of

Guillotine, or walk off to the left down the descent trail.

7. Juniper Direct (5.6) 1 pitch. Start on the ground directly below the large juniper tree on Juniper Ledge. This poor lead is not recommended.

8. El Faralito (5.4) 1 pitch. Start near the bottom end of a rotting log. Climb 20 feet to a skinny 5-foot-high pine tree. Wander up broken crack systems above and belay from a 2-bolt anchor on the right end of Juniper Ledge. Descend from here or finish up *Juniper Overhang, Bring Me a Bucket,* or *Chili Verde.*

9. Chili Verde (5.6) 2 pitches. **Pitch 1:** Face moves lead to a small gnarled juniper in a left-facing dihedral. Continue to the right end of Juniper Ledge and a 2-bolt belay anchor. **Pitch 2:** Climb a left-facing dihedral

to a roof. Finish up cracks and gullies to the top.

10. Refritos (5.6) 2 pitches. **Pitch 1:** Climb a distinctive black streak, aiming for a small juniper tree on the right side of Juniper Ledge. Belay at a 2-bolt belay on the ledge. **Pitch 2:** Climb the dihedral above or move left and finish on *Juniper Overhang, Bring Me a Bucket,* or *Chili Verde.*

11. Guillotine (5.6+) 3 pitches. Start about 15 feet right of *Refritos.* **Pitch 1:** Grab cobbles up to a smooth slab with an inverted V at its top. Continue up right, passing a brushy crack to a belay ledge. **Pitch 2:** Climb 4th-class rock up left to the base of a final headwall. **Pitch 3:** Finish up the headwall to the summit and a 2-bolt belay. Descend by rappel from here or walk off the descent trail.

12. Techo al Derecho (5.8) 3 pitches. Begin by a large juniper tree growing about 10 feet up the cliff. **Pitch 1:** Wander up 4th-class rock to the left side of a huge roof system on the right side of the cliff and belay. **Pitch 2:** Climb cracks below the main right-angling

dihedral. Turn a big overhang near its left side and belay just above. **Pitch 3:** Three options are available: 1. Continue up the crack (5.0); 2. Go left up a low-angle face (5.2); or 3. The preferable finish. Traverse right from the belay and climb an airy face to the top (5.6 to 5.7 depending on where you go). Option #3 is one of the best pitches on the crag.

13. Moanin' (5.7 R) 2 pitches. Not recommended. **Pitch 1:** Scramble up 4th-class rock to a large black depression below the main overhang. **Pitch 2:** Climb the right side through chossy rock with poor pro to join *Techo al Derecho.*

14. Techo Directo (5.11-) The hardest sustained pitch at El Rito Trad. On-sight first ascent by Rick Smith. Climb directly up the center of the slabs (5.9) and go over the big roof near its center.

15. Packrat Dihedral (5.6) 2 pitches. **Pitch 1:** Climb an attractive left-facing dihedral to a belay under the right end of the large overhang. **Pitch 2:** Turn the overhang, then climb either straight up (best choice) or move right and up a crack system.

DIABLO CANYON AND COXCOMB CRAG

▧ O V E R V I E W

Diablo Canyon and nearby Coxcomb Crag, featuring a mix of quality sport climbs and challenging crack systems, form one of New Mexico's best and most interesting cragging areas. Easy approaches to the cliffs, a variety of routes ranging in difficulty from 5.8 to 5.13, and a beautiful setting characterize the area.

The cliffs, lying northwest of Santa Fe, are composed of hard, dark basalt. The cliffs differ from other climbing areas along White Rock Canyon across the Rio Grande, which are mostly lava flows. The cracks there are the direct result of cooling after eruption. The diverse cliffs in narrow Diablo Canyon are thought to represent a complex volcanic network of lava flows (the upper Grotto walls) and volcanic necks (the Winter Wall) that is similar to Devil's Tower in Wyoming.

Climbing at Diablo Canyon is divided into three separate areas. The Winter Wall, an imposing 300-foot-high sweep of basalt, towers on the north side of the canyon. The megaclassic three-pitch *Sun Devil* ascends this huge cliff. The canyon's south side is rimmed by the Early Wall, named because it receives the day's first hit of sunshine. The compact reddish basalt of this fine cliff harbors more than seventeen routes. The Grotto, with more than thirty sport and crack lines, is a hidden side-canyon at the west end on the Early Wall and high above Diablo Canyon's sandy floor. The routes here, in both sun and shade, climb some of the area's best rock.

Unless noted otherwise, every Diablo Canyon and Coxcomb route is worth climbing. Exceptional climbs are denoted in the description. As is usual with basalt, the climbing is often steep and strenuous. Vertical cliffs, overhanging faces, and arêtes are plentiful. The canyon's many cracks, some with lowering anchors, are equal to the best found at other New Mexico basalt crags. Crack climbers can select routes from 5.8 to 5.12. As a bonus some of the state's best multipitch climbing is found here. These routes demand both sport and traditional expertise on routes as difficult as 5.12. Most of these testpieces are on the East Wall (left side) of The Grotto.

Farther down-canyon sits Coxcomb Crag atop a high ridge overlooking lower Diablo Canyon near its confluence with the Rio Grande. This excellent crag rivals neighboring Diablo Canyon in quality of its routes. See the section below on Coxcomb Crag for directions and route information. Both areas have ample rock that await further development.

Climbing History

Diablo Canyon's cracks have lured climbers since the 1970s. Ken Sims, a strong crack climber in Santa Fe, was active in The Grotto during this time and made a bold first ascent of *Sun Devil Crack* in the early eighties. Other cracks on the Winter Wall and Early Wall were likely climbed during this time, but their names, ascent parties, and dates of ascent were never recorded. The steep, difficult-to-protect faces of the Winter Wall were ignored.

The advent of sport climbing and some aggressive route cleaning ushered in a new climbing era at Diablo Canyon. In 1994 a talented group of Santa Fe and Los Alamos climbers began to develop the steep pocketed faces in The Grotto and Early Wall. Many classic 5.10 and 5.11 lines were established during this time. Rick Bradshaw was, and continues to be, the driving force in the

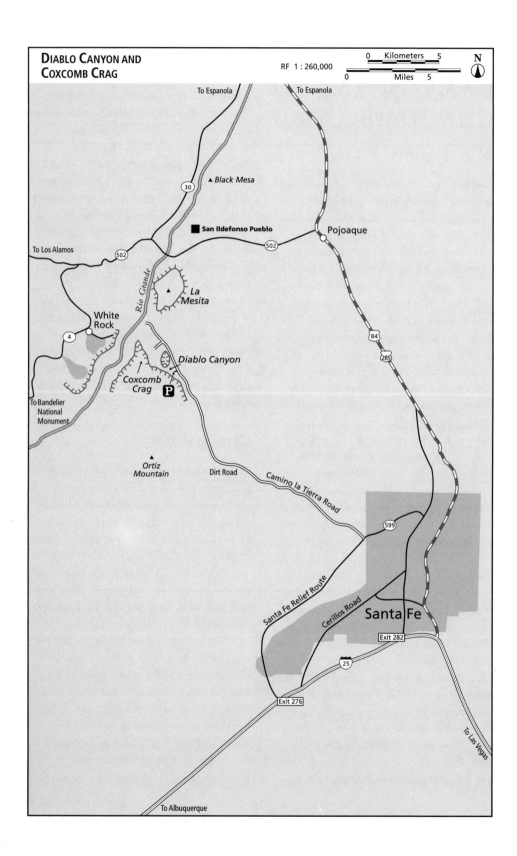

DIABLO CANYON AND COXCOMB CRAG

RF 1 : 260,000

Kilometers 0 — 5

Miles 0 — 5

N

To Espanola

To Espanola

30

▲ Black Mesa

■ San Ildefonso Pueblo

Pojoaque

502

502

To Los Alamos

502

Rio Grande

▲ La Mesita

White Rock

4

Diablo Canyon

84

285

Coxcomb Crag

P

To Bandelier National Monument

▲ Ortiz Mountain

Dirt Road

Camino la Tierra Road

599

Santa Fe Relief Route

Cerillos Road

Santa Fe

Exit 282

25

Exit 276

To Las Vegas

To Albuquerque

canyon's development. Rick Smith, Josh Smith, Denny Newell, Tom Wezwick, Scott Beguin, Mark Thomas, Walt Wehner, Karl Kiser, and Chris Kessler were also active during this time. Boldness was tested on the alluring arêtes as the vision of the possible was expanded.

These successes eventually led Bradshaw, Josh Smith, and Wehner to imagine a steep line up the tallest part of the foreboding western end of the Winter Wall. The trio worked many hours cleaning loose rock and installing bolts over several months in 1999 and then climbed *Sun Devil* (5.11b/c). Development slowed at the turn of the century but jumped again in 2003–04 as climbers started developing The Cave, the imposing formation that defines the Winter Wall's left end. Aaron Miller, Rick Bradshaw, and Peter Steadman contributed to these difficult first-rate climbs. The only comparable climbing on overhanging basalt is Bat Cave in the Taos area.

Rack and Descent

Diablo's routes are well installed, mostly with ⅜-inch bolts. The anchors on the sport routes are hefty ½-inch x 3-inch stainless steel bolts. Many are equipped with Springer Hangers, making a safe and quick lowering system. The development of the area has been thoughtful, resulting in properly installed modern fixed hardware.

All sport routes require quickdraws only. The cracks and belay stations eat up protection, so bring a good rack for any trad route. A 200-foot rope is best for climbing many Diablo Canyon routes. Two ropes are needed for the rappels on many Winter Wall routes. A helmet is definitely recommended because loose rock, even on "cleaned routes," is always a concern.

Not all bolts are shown on the topos.

Trip Planning Information

Area description: Diablo Canyon offers exceptional sport and traditional routes up to three pitches long on basalt cliffs.

Location: North-central New Mexico. The canyon is 15 miles northwest of Santa Fe.

Camping: The immediate area has limited camping opportunities. Primitive camping is available near the parking area, although the area is a popular site for "raves" on some weekends. Other camping is found on the dirt road past the parking area. Avoid camping in the wash because of flash flood danger. The Ski Basin road out of Santa Fe offers several opportunities for primitive and developed camping. A full-service KOA Kampground is in Santa Fe. Many motels are also found in Santa Fe on Cerillos Road if you don't want to rough it.

Climbing season: Year-round. Best seasons are spring and autumn. Summer days can be very hot, but it is possible to find shady routes at The Grotto and Early Wall. The Winter Wall is climbable on all but the coldest winter days.

Restriction and access issues: The area is jointly administered by the Bureau of Land Management (BLM) and the U.S. Forest Service. For safety reasons, visitors should avoid driving, parking, or camping in the wash. Flash floods are common in summer. The trails to the cliffs are primitive and are sometimes hard to locate. Trail erosion is a serious problem on the steeper slopes. The staging areas below many routes are steep and prone to erosion. Tread as lightly as possible until these problems receive the attention they require if climber usage increases.

Guidebooks: None. Rick Bradshaw's Web site, www.vla.com/bradshaw/diablo, and the

Los Alamos Climbing Web page, www
.losalamos.org/climb, are good resources for
updates and local color.

Services: All services are in Santa Fe 15
miles to the southeast.

Emergency services: Dial 911. Cell phone
service is spotty but possible depending on
your carrier and location in the canyon.

Nearby climbing areas: White Rock Crags,
The Dungeon, Cochiti Mesa Crags, and Las
Conchas.

Nearby attractions: The Rio Grande,
Bandelier National Monument, eight
Northern Pueblos, casino gambling, Santa Fe
Opera, dining, and museums and art galleries
in Santa Fe. Skiing, hiking, fishing, mountain
climbing, mountain biking, and backpacking
are in the nearby Santa Fe National Forest.

Finding the crags: From U.S. Highway
85/285, exit onto Highway 599 south about
1.5 miles north of Santa Fe. This road is also
called Santa Fe Relief Route and Veterans
Memorial Highway. If approaching from the
south on Interstate 25, take this route at exit
276B and avoid traveling through Santa Fe.
Continue to Camino La Tierra exit. After
exiting US 85/285, travel 3.4 miles and exit
right onto Camino La Tierra. Take this exit
(left turn) also if approaching from the south.
Stay on Camino La Tierra for about 4 miles
where it becomes a dirt road. This dirt road is
generally passable by passenger cars except
during or after heavy rains, when it turns into
a muddy, impassable quagmire. Avoid the road
in these conditions even in a four-wheel-
drive vehicle. Continue on the dirt road for
approximately 8 miles to a left turn into the
obvious mouth of Diablo Canyon. Plenty of
parking places are just off the main dirt road.
The last and most convenient parking sites

are toward the cliffs just before the road gets
narrow and difficult. Parking past here or
driving in the wash is not advisable. The
Winter Wall is visible on the right (north)
side of the wash and the Early Wall is high
above the left (south) side.

Diablo Canyon

Winter Wall

The Winter Wall is the grand sweep of basalt
on the north (right) side of the canyon.
Much of the lower and upper cliff sections
look loose and unattractive for climbing, but
solid, quality rock is abundant. Many routes
have undergone extensive cleaning, but
always use caution when climbing. Test holds,
stay on route, wear a helmet, and tread
lightly. Place belays and spectators off to the
side to avoid getting hit by falling rocks.
Both sport and traditional routes from one to
three pitches ascend the wall. A 200-foot
rope is best.

Finding the cliff: Hike down the narrow
road from the parking area toward the wash
for about 100 yards. Look for a small gate
through the wire fence on the left to gain
access to the wash. If you miss the gate, cross
through the fence at the next best spot available. Walk down the wash to the only trail to
the right. This is just under *Post Moderate* and
is generally cairned and easy to locate. The
trail goes across a talus slope to the cliff base
and then up the rocky slope below the cliff.
It is usually cairned. The trail accesses routes
#1 to #10. Stay low on the rocky slope to
access routes #14 to #17 in The Cave. The
trail to the Early Wall's east end is almost
directly across the wash. Routes are listed
from right to left.

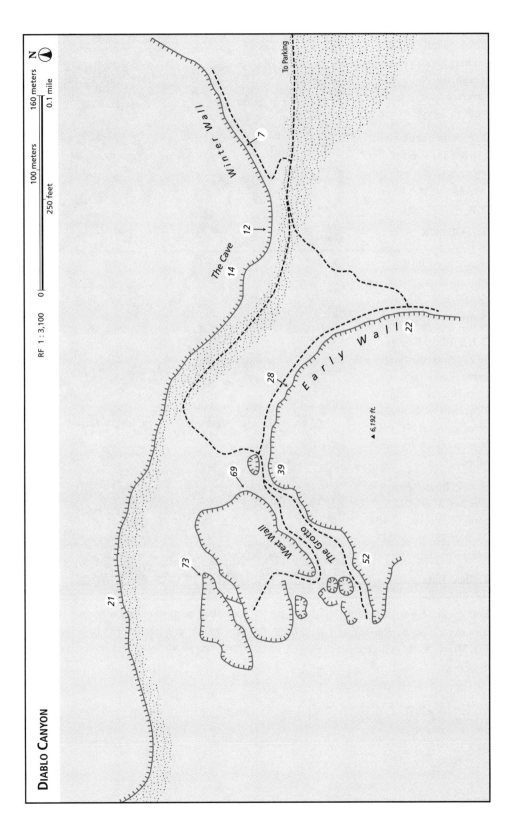

DIABLO CANYON

RF 1 : 3,100

N

1. Sunbaked (5.10a)

Follow 3 bolts up left of a bush, then up a broken face to anchors. 7 bolts to 2-bolt anchor.

2. Protein Supplement

(5.10) Climb straight up on gear, then a little left. 6 bolts plus gear to 2-bolt anchor.

2.1. Vitaman

(5.9+/.10a) Gear route. Aim for a hand crack through a roof. Descend from 2-bolt anchor above the roof.

2.2. 5.8 Trad Route

(5.8) Climb the first crack system right of *Roid Boys* with gear, then descend from *Roid Boys'* anchors. 200-foot rope necessary for the rappel.

3. Roid Boys (5.10a) Up

and over a series of roofs. 7 bolts to 2-bolt anchor. 200-foot rope necessary for the rappel.

4. Blind Faith (5.11a)

No topo. The only bolted route between *Roid Boys* and *Original Face Route*. Lots of exposure and good climbing. Mostly 5.10+ with crux at the top. A long sling helps to reduce rope drag at the first overhang. 2-bolt anchor. Two 200-foot ropes necessary for the rappel.

5. Original Face Route

(5.8) Gear required down low. 3 bolts to 2-bolt anchor.

6. Highway to Hell (5.9)

Gear required. Questionable pro in spots. 2-bolt anchor. Two 200-foot ropes necessary for the rappel.

7. Post Moderate (5.9)

The area's best moderate route and one of the best anywhere. Start next to an old fence post beside the cliff. Pull down on jugs for 155 feet. Be extra careful at bolt 10, where a large detached flake lurks. Two 165-foot ropes are best for the rappel. Anchors for *Highly Caffeinated* can be used to break the climb into 2 pitches or 2 rappels. 17 bolts to 2-bolt anchor.

8. Highly Caffeinated

(5.10-) Gear required. Tricky placements down low. 2-bolt anchor.

9. Grape Ape (5.10c) A stellar, well-protected climb with a difficult crux through the roofs. Two 165-foot ropes required for the rappel. 14 bolts to 2-bolt anchor.

10. Basalt Therapy (5.10-) Bolts in the hard/thin sections supplement gear placements. 2-bolt anchor. Two 200-foot ropes required for the rappel.

11. Kaboom (5.9) 3 pitches. Not the best route but worth climbing. Start right of the toe of the buttress and up the slope right of *Sun Devil*. **Pitch 1:** Climb up left across a face on 5.6 runout climbing to a belay under a small roof located just above and right of a larger roof. **Pitch 2:** Crux pitch. Step right to a good crack. Jam and stem to a belay in a large alcove. **Pitch 3:** Climb right, then up on easy but runout rock to the top. **Descent:** Walk northeast across the top to a descent trail on the east end of Winter Wall.

12. Sun Devil (5.11b/c) 3 pitches. First ascent by Rick Bradshaw, Josh Smith, and Walt Wehner. One of New Mexico's classic basalt routes.

Ascends the tallest cliff in Diablo Canyon. Some loose rock is found, so test handholds, wear a helmet, and tread lightly. **Pitch 1:** Goes up lesser quality rock but is better than it initially appears. Ends on a good ledge with a 2-bolt rap anchor and another bolt to secure the belay. (5.9) **Pitch 2:** The roof is the crux, then 5.10 to belay anchors. (5.11b/c) **Pitch 3:** Quality rock and great exposure on a knife-edge arête. (5.11b) **Descent:** Use anchors at the end of each pitch. 3 rappels with a 200-foot rope. First rappel is 60 feet, second is 50 feet, and the third is 100 feet.

13. Sun Devil Crack (5.10+) 2 pitches. First ascent by Ken Sims in 1980. The opening scene of *All the Pretty Horses* pans directly up this section of Winter Wall. **Pitch 1:** Climb pitch 1 of *Sun Devil* or pick a line to the left. Both ways are 5.9 and pretty spacey. Use *Sun Devil's* bolted anchors or install your own anchor higher in the crack. **Pitch 2:** Straight up the crack using many face holds. Depending on where you set up belays, either climb to the summit or do a third pitch. Be careful on this worthy multipitch route. Descend by walking off to the right (east) to a descent trail on the east end of Winter Wall.

The Cave

This imposing formation is home to wild climbing up its steep sides. Several difficult, well-bolted lines are established. Look for a few more in the future. The Cave received extensive cleaning and is solid if you stay on route. Approach from the *Post Moderate* trail or by a short trail farther down-canyon. **Rack:** Bring at least fourteen quickdraws and a 200-foot rope. Not illustrated.

14. Clovis Hunter (5.12a/b) Start 70 feet left of *Sun Devil* near the right end of the large cave formation. Climb overhanging rock past 9 bolts to the right end of the large horizontal band of roofs 70 feet up. 9 bolts to 2-bolt anchor.

15. Sapian (5.12d/.13a) The Cave's shortest route. Located 15 feet left of *Clovis Hunter.* Bolts 4, 5, and 6 have permanent quickdraws to make climbing, not clipping, the crux. 10 bolts to 2-bolt anchor.

16. Meanderthal
(5.11+/.12-) Requires some long quickdraws to avoid dire rope drag. Go right at fourth bolt. Be ready for runout 5.9 climbing. Crux is on the upper face. 14 bolts to 2-bolt anchor.

17. Cro-Magnon (5.12a) Classic. Shares start and first 4 bolts with #16. Go straight up at fourth bolt. The crux is pulling the roof. 13 bolts to 2-bolt anchor.

Several fun, traditional routes are farther down-canyon on the far left side of Winter Wall. These short, easy-to-find, one-pitch routes ascend crack systems up jointed basalt columns to 2-bolt chain anchors. All are worth climbing and are good for moderate leaders wanting to practice placing gear.

Hike down-canyon past *Sun Devil Crack* about 400 yards to a low-angle section of columnar basalt that rises directly out of the wash floor. Bring a rack of Stoppers, TCUs, and small to medium Friends.

18. Unknown (5.8)

19. Unknown (5.8)

20. Baby Boomers (5.9-) The variation to the left is 5.8.

21. Cold Day in Hell (5.8) A 5.9- variation is just to the left.

Early Wall

The Early Wall is an excellent northeast-facing cliff band on the south side of Diablo Canyon opposite Winter Wall. The cliff offers excellent routes on solid basalt in a relatively quiet setting high above the canyon floor.

Finding the cliff: Hike down a narrow road from the parking area toward the wash for about 100 yards. Look for a small gate through the wire fence on the left to access the wash. If you miss the gate, cross the fence at the next best spot available. Cross the broad wash and walk down to a break in its steep left (south) bank before the canyon narrows down. This is just left of a boulder field on the slope below the left (east) end of the cliff. A faint trail begins here and initially goes a little east, then switchbacks up through large boulders to the cliff's left side. Cairns generally mark the way. Routes on the west (right) end of the cliff are reached from this trail, but the trail from The Grotto to the west is more convenient. Not all bolts shown.

22. Rope Burn in Hell (5.12b) The farthest left (east) climb. Steep, thin, tricky moves and balance characterize this difficult, quality route. 9 bolts to 2-bolt anchor.

23. Airway Arête (5.11b/c) Quality technical route requiring good balance. Bolts to 2-bolt anchor.

24. Project Anchors installed but no bolts.

25. Schmeming (5.12a/b) A Diablo testpiece. Bolts were added to the lower section in 2002, making the route safer. Be ready for stemming, difficult cracks, tenuous arête climbing, and hard traverses. 7 bolts to 2-bolt anchor.

26. Rock 'n' Road (5.11) Gear required. Sustained, quality route. Descend by walking off to the left (east).

27. Early Arête (5.11d) A beautiful and bold line. 9 bolts to 2-bolt anchor.

28. Up to Bat (5.9) Gear required. No anchors. Worth climbing though a little loose at the top. Descend by walking off to the left (east).

29. Humbolt (5.10a) Quality climbing on terrific rock. 9 bolts to 2-bolt anchor.

30. Two Wheel Drive (5.10c)
Recommended. Bolts to 2-bolt anchor.

31. Mocos Locos (5.11b) Excellent.
Originally established to approach *La Naris*
above, but the climbing was compelling
enough to be considered a separate line. 100
feet of sustained climbing. Bolts to 2-bolt
anchor. **Descent:** A 200-foot rope required
to rappel or lower from the anchors.

32. Diablo Standard (5.10b) 2 pitches. First
pitch is runout and hard to protect (5.9).
Second pitch is a quality 5.10b hand crack.
No anchors. Gear required. **Descent:** Walk
off the top to the east.

33. La Naris (5.11b) Quality. Approach the
belay by climbing either *Mocos Locos* or
Diablo Standard. From the top of *Mocos Locos*,
climb up right on broken rock about 50 feet
to a comfortable belay stance on top of a
boulder on a shelf. Currently there is a fixed
line that serves as an anchor. Then traverse
left 50 feet to another ledge just below the
first bolt of *La Naris*. Bolts to 2-bolt anchor.

Descend by lowering down to rap anchors
30 feet below the belay. A 200-foot rope
required for the rappel to the ground.

34. Ergo (5.10c/d) Climbs a pillar to a good
ledge. Can be used to approach #35. Bolts to
2-bolt anchor.

35. You're Scaring the Horses (5.12b) Great
climbing and highly recommended. From the
top of *Ergo*, climb up and right to a 2-bolt
belay anchor below an arête. Start from here
to ensure enough rope to lower the leader
safely. The crux is 20 feet of overhanging
rock near the top of the sharp arête. Bolts to
2-bolt anchor.

36. Drunk Rednecks with Golf Clubs (5.8)
The easiest sport route in the canyon. A fun
climb on its own or can be used to approach
#38. Climb a blocky face to anchors below a
broken terrace. Bolts to 2-bolt anchor.

37. Clip Art (5.11d) Quality. Sustained difficult climbing on vertical to overhanging
rock. Bolts to 2-bolt anchor.

38. Lichening the Serpent (5.11c) Quality climbing on good rock. If approaching from *Clip Art,* go past the belay chains to a stance on top of a pillar below *Lichening the Serpent's* first bolt. A sling here connects 2 bolts that serve as a belay and rappel anchor. Bolts to 2-bolt anchor. One 200-foot rope required for the descent.

The Grotto

East Wall

The Grotto is a narrow side-canyon tucked into the south rim of Diablo Canyon high above the canyon floor. Many excellent climbs are found in this secluded grotto.

To reach The Grotto, walk down the canyon past *Sun Devil* and The Cave. Just past some smooth graffiti-plastered boulders on the south side of the wash, look up left and spot the entrance to The Grotto. The trail begins just past the boulders. Hike up the steep and loose trail, passing many large boulders to the canyon entrance. Uphill hiking is about eight minutes. Cairns sometimes mark the trail's start from the canyon floor.

Routes on the west (right) side of the Early Wall are easily and best reached from the entrance to The Grotto.

Routes are described from left to right. Routes

#39 to #42 are located on the Upper Tier near the left end of the east side of The Grotto. Access these routes by climbing one of the routes below them.

39. Medusa (5.12c) Quality Upper Tier route. Approach from *KSR* (#43). A difficult, long, and tweaky route. Bolts to 2-bolt anchor.

40. Rolling Brown Out (5.11+) Quality. A crack testpiece first ascended in 1989 by Ken Sims. Approach from *KSR* (#43). Gear required. 2-bolt anchor.

41. Mary Poppins (5.12c) This route starts on a spacious ledge about 50 feet above the top of the first 4 bolted routes on the left side of The Grotto. The most convenient and best climbs to access it are *Good* (#46) and *Evil* (#45). Perfect rock featuring slab, arête, face, and overhanging climbing on this spectacular route. One 200-foot rope required both to lower leader back to the start and to rappel to the ground. 9 bolts to 2-bolt anchor.

42. Guillotine Crack (5.10d) Quality Upper Tier route. Perfect hand and fist crack in one of the area's best cracks. Ken Sims made the first ascent the same day he put up *Rolling Brown Out*. Climb a 5.9 crack out of The Grotto to reach the base of the crack. Gear plus 2-bolt anchor.

43. KSR (5.10d) Well worth climbing. 7 bolts to 2-bolt anchor.

44. Chopping Block (5.11a) Loose at the top, not often climbed. 8 bolts to 2-bolt anchor.

45. Evil (5.10c/d) Hard start to easier climbing above. Well worth climbing. 6 bolts to 2-bolt anchor.

46. Good (5.10b) Difficult for its grade. Shares anchors with *Evil*. Recommended. It is about 25 feet of low 5th-class climbing from these anchors to belay anchors for *Mary Poppins* and *Guillotine Crack*. 8 bolts to 2-bolt anchor shared with #45.

47. Bergers Bakeshop (5.10d) Sustained and challenging. Well worth climbing. The grade increases to 5.11a/b when climbing to the left of the arête. 9 bolts to 2-bolt anchor.

48. Affirmative Action (5.10c) The first sport route installed in The Grotto. Difficult at the start and finish. Well worth climbing. Bolts to 2-bolt anchor.

49. Waiting to Procrastinate (5.10b) Very popular. Good rests ease the difficulties. Bolts to 2-bolt anchor.

50. Unnamed (5.10) Crack right of #49. No bolts. 2-bolt anchor.

The next five routes are approximately 75 feet right.

51. Evil Paradise (5.10c) Quality. A terrific route on perfect rock. Start on a sloping ledge with a 2-bolt cold shut anchor. Traverse left, then up via cracks, face, and slabs. 10 bolts to 2-bolt anchor.

52. Hidden Slab (5.10a) Fun low-angle paradise. Start at the 2-bolt cold shut anchors as for #51, then up the attractive slab. Crux near the top. Bolts to 2-bolt anchor.

53. Sunday Bloody Sunday (5.10c) Another crack climber's testpiece. Hard to protect at the bottom; easier to start by traversing in from the left. 2-bolt anchor.

54. Lucifer's Hammer Drill (5.12d) Quality climbing. A difficult crux requiring flexibility and power. 200-foot rope required to lower or rappel. 10 bolts to 2-bolt anchor.

55. Ojo (5.12a) Excellent climb. About 200 feet right of #54 near the right end of the East Wall. Climb a smooth, red, wavy face to a laid-back fractured section, then up a steep face to chain anchors. 200-foot rope required to lower or rappel. 11 bolts to 2-bolt anchor.

Not pictured to the right of #55 is a burly 5.11 crack up a steep corner by a hollow flake and the right side of a roof. Gear 1.5-inch to 3.5-inch. 2-bolt anchor.

West Wall

The West Wall lies on the right side of The Grotto as you enter it from the main canyon. Routes are listed from left (south) to right (north) as you face the wall.

56. Unnamed (5.12b) Quality. Pumpy, continuous, and varied climbing with lots of thin crimps. 7 bolts to 2-bolt anchor.

57. Project (5.13?) The only chipped and glued route at Diablo. Ugly. Likely to disappear in the future.

58. Trailer Park Girls (5.12b) Recommended— one of Diablo's best routes. Steep and sustained. 6 bolts to 2-bolt anchor.

59. Where the Wild Things Aren't (5.11c) Sparse but adequate protection. Well worth climbing. 5 bolts to 2-bolt anchor.

60. Pulling a Tooth (5.11d) Start 20 feet right of *Where the Wild Things Aren't*. A hard start—climb a steep face to an off-width crack. A 4-inch piece optional on the upper crux. 5 bolts to 2-bolt anchor.

61. Winter Solstice (5.10a) Located on the left side of the red face left of *Winter Warm Up*. A #2 Friend augments the last bolt. 6 bolts to 2-bolt anchor.

62. Winter Warm Up (5.8) Good moderate trad route that features a bolt and fixed anchor (bolt installed for *Winter Solstice*). Gear required. 2-bolt anchor.

63. Winter Capacity (5.11a) Has sun for only an hour in winter but worth climbing anytime. Bolts to 2-bolt anchor.

64. Venarete (5.12a/b) Great climbing. Difficult sections separated by good rests. Bolts to 2-bolt anchor.

65. Crack Whores (5.10c) Gear required to 2-bolt anchor. Originally called *Crack Wars* by first ascentionist Ken Sims.

66. Rickety Rock (5.11c) A loose rock at the crux has resisted repeated attempts at removal, so climb with care. Belay to the side. Good climb otherwise. 5 bolts to 2-bolt anchor.

67. Class Act (5.10a) Quality. Good introduction to the 5.10 grade at Diablo. 6 bolts to 2-bolt anchor.

68. Bong Crack (5.10c) A 1979 Ken Sims effort. Gear required. Difficult at the top. 2-bolt anchor.

69. Wodgie's Wild Ride (5.11b) Brilliant climbing with great rest spots. Crux at the bulge. 10 bolts to 2-bolt anchor.

The following routes are located on top of the small flat mesa above and west of The

Grotto. Access is via a climber's path from the south end of The Grotto's West Wall. The short path climbs to the mesa top, passing a cave en route. Route #70 is on the left (south) end of the mesa, and #71 to #75 are straight ahead on the west side of the mesa.

70. Exit Arête (5.11a) Very good. Located on a detached pillar. Difficult at the top. 5 bolts to 2-bolt anchor.

71. Chains for Brains (5.12b) No topo. Located approximately 100 feet right of #70

at the opening to the distinct alcove on the mesa's western side. Very difficult to make the clips without using the crack.

About 75 feet to the right is a high-quality 5.11 crack that is difficult to reach. Gear

route with #1.5 to #3 Friends. No anchor but a good boulder to sling at the top.

72. Walker-Wehner Direct (5.8) No topo. Interesting climbing. Starts in the bottom of the alcove. Gear required. 2-bolt anchor.

73. Larcombe's Lament (5.10c) Good route. 6 bolts to 2-bolt anchor.

74. Slap Happy (5.10d) No topo. Recommended. 6 bolts to 2-bolt anchor.

75. No Name Crack (5.8) No topo. A fine crack route. Around the corner, faces north.

Coxcomb Crag

Coxcomb Crag, located west, or downstream from the main Diablo Canyon climbing area, is a high, northeast-facing cliff band that offers a superb selection of both sport climbs and traditional cracks. The cliff's name derives from a row of distinct small pinnacles at the far west end of the cliff that looks like a rooster's comb.

All the routes are left of the coxcomb and bounded on the far left by a large white scar caused by a massive rock fall. The left-most sector, called Chicken Little for the first route on the crag, starts just right of this scar. The Poultrygeist area is about 400 feet right of the Chicken Little Sector. This crag section features some attractive crack routes that require traditional climbing expertise along with many quality sport routes.

Coxcomb Crag is best in the spring months of April and May and the fall months of September and October. It's also a great cliff for summer afternoons with plentiful shade and cool breezes. Winter is rarely good since the cliff is in the shade all day and the rock stays cold.

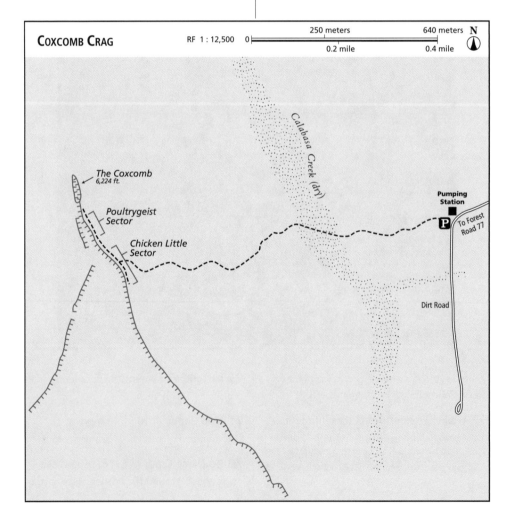

Chicken Little Sector

Poultrygeist Sector

Trail

Climbing History: Coxcomb Crag's development began in the spring of 2001 when Rick Bradshaw, his wife, Leslie Kelch, Jason Smith, Ken Kissel, Rick Smith, Scott Beguin, Walt Wehner, and others cleaned, bolted, and climbed routes. Rick and helpers also sited and constructed the access trail.

Rack: Bring a basic rack with a dozen quickdraws and a 165-foot rope for all the sport routes. These well-bolted climbs also feature Springer quick-clip anchors for lowering. The traditional-style routes require a generous rack of Friends, TCUs, and Stoppers.

Finding the crag: Follow directions to Diablo Canyon and drive to the turnoff to Diablo Canyon's parking area. Continue for another 1.5 miles, turn left at a crossroad, and drive south a short distance to a fenced pumping station. Park on the south side of the fenced building. Follow a barbed fence west to a dry arroyo and duck through the fence. Follow the arroyo south toward the

obvious cliffs until it intersects the wide, sandy drainage of Diablo Canyon. Locate the faint but easy-to-follow climber's trail that begins on the south side of the main drainage and heads through a deep break in the stream bank across and a little downstream. A small cairn marks the start of the trail. The trail meanders up the steep slope and eventually ends near *Chicken Little*. Cairns keep you on the right path. Walk right along the base of the cliff to reach Poultrygeist Sector. A serious thrash through underbrush and over talus is in store if the trail isn't followed. Allow thirty to forty-five minutes for the approach hike.

Chicken Little Sector

All routes are worth climbing. New route possibilities, especially the crack systems, are found along the cliff. Routes are listed from left to right.

1. Chicken on the Wing at the Gates of Evening, Oh! How Glorious is Thy Flight
(5.10a) No topo. Located about 150 feet left of route #2. Trad route. No bolts, no anchor.

2. Left Wing (5.11a) Start at top of a steep scree gully. Climb a rib to a small shelf, then crimp up the smooth face above. 9 bolts to 2-bolt anchor.

3. Little Chicken (5.7) Climb a right-facing corner 25 feet to a ledge. Keep jamming to the top. Trad route, no bolts, no anchors.

4. Chicken Little (5.11d.) Start at an obvious bulging pillar. Come in from the left using laybacks to first bolt or in from the right (5.12b). Climb the arête to a broken section, then up a smooth wall to an overhanging finish. 8 bolts to 2-bolt anchor.

5. Cruisin' for Chicks (5.10c) Start 10 feet right of *Chicken Little* next to a small juniper tree. Climb up a square rib to jugs over a bulge. Edge up the immaculate black face to skyline anchors. 7 bolts to 2-bolt anchor.

6. Casada Noodle Soup (5.10b) Start 40 feet right of *Cruisin' for Chicks* just right of a juniper tree and small pillar. Pull jugs over a bulge and finish up a steep headwall. 5 bolts to 2-bolt anchor.

7. Technical Fowl (5.10d) Scramble onto a ledge, then technical edging up a face left of a black crack. 6 bolts to 2-bolt anchor.

8. The Chicken (5.10a) Start 12 feet right of *Technical Fowl*. Climb easy black rock past 2 bolts, then up a face between 2 cracks. 7 bolts to 2-bolt anchor.

9. The Egg (5.9) Start 10 feet right of *The Chicken*. Face climb black rock, then up to the right side of an arête. 8 bolts to 2-bolt anchor.

10. Chicken Scratch (5.10a) Start 18 feet right of *The Egg* in the middle of a group of juniper trees. Climb broken rock past 3 bolts, then up a laid-back rib/arête. 8 bolts to 2-bolt anchor.

11. Chicken Thief (5.11a) Start 8 feet right of *Chicken Scratch* behind two juniper trees. Climb a short rib, then through a broken band to a shelf. Face climb right of a dull arête. 9 bolts to 2-bolt anchor.

Poultrygeist Sector

Hike the cliff-base trail about 400 feet to the right (west) from *Chicken Thief*. All routes are worth climbing and highly recommended. Routes are listed from left to right.

12. Chicken Cha Cha (5.10d) Climb a beautiful face with edges. 5 bolts to 2-bolt anchor.

13. Cock Star (5.11c) Up left side of a blunt arête. 5 bolts to 2-bolt anchor.

14. Cockwork Orange (5.10d) Begin by scrambling up broken rock for 15 feet. Pockets and edges help on the smooth wall above. 4 bolts to 2-bolt anchor.

15. Finger Lichen Good (5.10a) Face climb up a slabby wall right of a broken arête. 7 bolts to 2-bolt anchor.

16. Stunt Cock (5.12a) Start 5 feet right of *Finger Lichen Good*. Technical face climbing up the wall left of a left-facing corner. 8 bolts to 2-bolt anchor.

17. Chicken Out (5.10c) Start 10 feet right of *Stunt Cock* and just right of a large open corner. Face climb steep slab to a roof. Pull over, assisted by a heel hook, and finish up a steep arête. 8 bolts to 2-bolt anchor.

18. Coca-doodle-do (5.11c) Start 12 feet right of *Chicken Out*. Climb a blunt rib past 3 bolts. Powerful moves required to get up the spectacular overhanging arête above. 7 bolts to 2-bolt anchor.

19. Chicken Fingers (5.10c) Start on *Coca-doodle-do* and exit right onto a large ledge, then up a steep finger crack. Trad route, no bolts. Step left at top to clip anchors for #18.

20. Poultrygeist (5.11a) Steep technical climbing on perfect rock. Climb a rib past 3 bolts to a ledge. Work up a steep face right of an arête. 8 bolts to 2-bolt anchor.

21. Chicks with Ricks (5.10c) Start in a pronounced alcove. Climb steep rock to a technical arête. Finish up thin crack. 9 bolts to 2-bolt anchor.

22. Crack (5.9) Start same as *Cockeyed* or climb left finger crack past 3 bolts to a ledge, then up a pedestal to a good hand crack. 2-bolt anchor.

23. Cockeyed (5.10c) Climb face between double cracks past 3 bolts to a small ledge about 20 feet up. Climb the beautiful blunt arête above. 8 bolts to 2-bolt anchor.

24. Fowl Play (5.11a) Climb the outside of a blunt pillar, then finish up the left side of an arête. 8 bolts to 2-bolt anchor.

WHITE ROCK CRAGS

■ OVERVIEW

The White Rock Crags are a cluster of excellent basalt cliffs scattered along the western rim of deep White Rock Canyon, a sharp defile carved by the Rio Grande between Santa Fe and Los Alamos. The area offers many excellent and classic one-pitch routes up mostly east-facing cliffs that range from 45 to 70 feet high. The clean cliffs are easily accessible, usually sunny and dry, and are peaceful and quiet with a feeling of remoteness even though your car is parked a half mile away in a suburban neighborhood.

Although White Rock is historically a traditional climbing area, sport climbers also find excellent gymnastic climbing up vertical to overhanging faces between crack systems. Lots of quality sport routes, well protected with bolts, lace most of the area's crags. Some crags, however, are strictly off-limits for sport climbing and remain bolt-free bastions for traditional-style climbing by agreement among local climbers.

Crack climbers jam steep, strenuous finger and hand cracks on perfect basalt with plentiful gear placements to protect the routes. The area's many crack routes, ranging from 5.7 to 5.12 in difficulty, will both test and improve every climber's jamming skills. If you can successfully jam some of the area testpieces at The Playground, for instance, you should be able to jam any crack anywhere else. A typical White Rock day sees both trad and sport climbers peacefully playing their vertical game on the same crag.

The easily accessible White Rock Crags are beautifully situated on the west rim of White Rock Canyon near the suburban village of White Rock southeast of Los Alamos. White Rock functions primarily as a bedroom community for Los Alamos. The White Rock Crags include The Overlook, The Underlook, Below The Old New Place, The

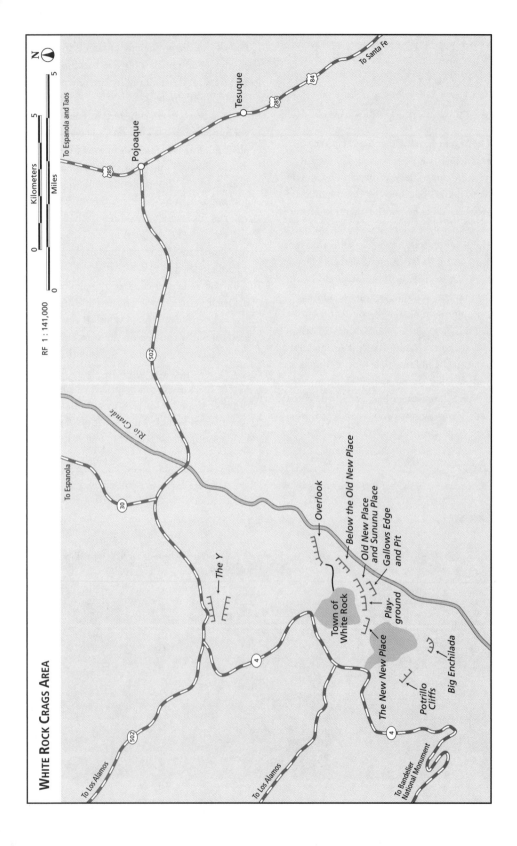

WHITE ROCK CRAGS AREA

RF 1 : 141,000

Kilometers
0   5   5

Miles
0   5

N

To Espanola and Taos

Pojoaque

Tesuque

285

285

84

To Santa Fe

To Espanola

Rio Grande

30

502

To Los Alamos

502

To Los Alamos

4

The Y

Overlook

Below the Old New Place

Old New Place and Sununu Place

Gallows Edge and Pit

Town of White Rock

Playground

The New New Place

Potrillo Cliffs

Big Enchilada

4

To Bandelier National Monument

Old New Place and Sununu Place, Gallows Edge and The Pit, The Playground, The New New Place, The Big Enchilada, Potrillo Cliffs, and The Y. All the cliffs except The Y are clustered within a couple miles of each other along the canyon rim on the east and south side of the village of White Rock. All offer fine views, quality climbing, and easy access. The Y is located 5 miles north of White Rock and below Highway 502.

Only the best White Rock cliffs are described in this guide. Some crags are just not worth the effort since they have funky, dirty routes or had their bolt hangers stripped and stolen. Other cliffs have access issues, including Sewer Crag west of The Overlook, which is lined with many bolted climbs. Later it was discovered that the cliff lies on Pueblo land, and it is now off-limits to climbing.

Good climbing weather occurs year-round at the White Rock Crags. Spring and fall offer the best and most stable weather, with generally warm, mild days. It can be windy on spring afternoons. Conversely many of the crags face east and are out of the usual westerly wind. The sunny orientation of the crags makes them a natural heat sink and perfect on calm winter days. The Overlook, Below The Old New Place, and The Playground are excellent cliffs to ease your winter discontent during the dog days of January and February. Summer days are usually hot in the sun, but afternoon shade is easily found on most of the cliffs. Be sure to bring lots of water and keep a sharp eye out for rattlesnakes, especially in boulder fields and at the base of the cliffs.

Climbing History

White Rock climbing dates back to the early 1950s, with the earliest explorations led by members of the Los Alamos scientific com-munity. George Bell, a member of the 1953 American K2 Expedition, teamed up with a strong and adventuresome group to test the area's steep unrelenting cracks beginning in 1952. The venerable Los Alamos Mountaineers, a club founded in 1952 by Don Monk and Kermith Ross, were active on the smaller cliffs as well as surrounding areas like The Brazos. The Mountaineers continue to be active and bring leadership to local climbing and access issues.

Layton Kor, the prolific 1960s Colorado climber, visited White Rock in 1968, solidify-ing the 5.9 grade with ascents at Potrillo and giving impetus to new exploration. Mike Roybal, a talented young New Mexico climber, honed his skills here as well. The "dis-covery" of The Y in 1970 by Len Margolin and Jim Porter pushed area standards into the then rarefied 5.10 and 5.11 grades. *The Nose,* New Mexico's first 5.12 and perhaps one of the first routes with this rating in the country, was established at The Y by Mike Roybal in 1974. Chances are no matter where you climb in northern New Mexico, Roybal was there first and ticked the best routes. Other basalt pioneers include Bob Taylor, Don Liska, Mike Williams, Carl and Lou Horak, Bill Hendry, Jim Porter, Len Margolin, Larry Campbell, Norbert Ennslin, and Carl Keller.

White Rock's early testpieces were splitter cracks and dihedrals ascended in stark traditional style with hammered pitons for protection. The local practice of toproping the difficult-to-protect faces yielded to rap-bolting in the summer of 1989. *Wailing Banshees* (5.11b/c) at Below The Old New Place owns the distinction of being the first rap-bolted route at the White Rock Crags. The following months saw seventeen more bolted routes established on Below The Old New Place as well as some rappel-bolted lines at the popular Overlook area. This development was led by Tom MacFarlane, Brian Riepe, Peter Gram, Rick Smith, Mike Schillaci, Chris Vandiver, Lee Sheftel, and Bob D'Antonio.

This departure from the long-established area tradition of climbing new routes from the ground to the summit sent shock waves throughout the New Mexico climbing community. Longtime local activists Norbert Ennslin and Rick Smith organized a series of meetings to openly discuss the bolting question and future new route opportunities. The outcome was that several crags were identified as off-limits to bolting. These bolt-free venues are The Playground, The Y, The Old New Place, Potrillo Cliffs, and The New New Place. Bolting is allowed at all the other cliffs. Visiting climbers, however, should leave their drills at home as new route possibilities are very limited since everything worthwhile has already been done.

Rack and Descent

A rack of camming units like Friends or Camalots up to 4 inches, wired Stoppers, and a 150-foot rope are sufficient for most trad routes. All crack routes are one pitch long and generally require setting up belay anchors on the rim or tying off a tree at the top. Most of the sport routes are equipped with sturdy ⅜-inch bolts and double-bolt lowering anchors. Be alert for occasional gear placement opportunities like small Friends or tri-cams in pockets on some routes for additional pro between bolts. It's a good idea to bring and wear a helmet here, especially if you're belaying. The harsh desert climate loosens blocks and boulders, so even a passing rope can dislodge them.

Descent off routes is by lowering off from established bolt anchors or by belaying at the top and walking back to the base to retrieve your pack or to do another route. When you do walk off, be extremely careful on the cliff rim so no loose rocks are knocked onto unsuspecting climbers below.

Not all bolts are shown on the topos.

Trip Planning Information

Area description: The White Rock Crags, perched on the rim of White Rock Canyon near the village of White Rock, are excellent 45- to 70-foot-high basalt cliffs that offer bolted sport routes and traditional crack climbs.

Location: Central New Mexico. Northwest of Santa Fe near Los Alamos.

Camping: No camping in the immediate White Rock area. Overnight camping is not allowed at Overlook Park or anywhere else in White Rock or at The Y. The best nearby public campsite is Juniper Campground at Bandelier National Monument (505–672–3861), 12 miles west of White Rock off Highway 4. The campground, on the rim of Frijoles Canyon, offers pleasant, wooded sites with water and restrooms. The fee area is open year-round on a first-come, first-served basis and quickly fills up in summer. Primitive off-road camping is available farther west in Santa Fe National Forest. A forest map is available by visiting or writing the U.S. Forest Service office in Santa Fe. Avoid camping on private land and nearby Pueblo Indian land.

Climbing season: Year-round. March through October offers the best weather. Morning sun and afternoon shade is found at the east- and south-facing cliffs. Summer days are usually hot, making early morning and late afternoon the best times to climb. Spring days are often windy, but many of the cliffs are sheltered from the wind. Climbing is possible at the White Rock Crags on all but the coldest winter days. The sunny southern exposure of the cliffs combined with the black rock allows for warm enjoyable winter climbing. Sunny and calm winter mornings are ideal.

Restrictions and access issues: The cliffs clustered around White Rock are on Los Alamos County land. The county has not imposed any restrictions on the area crags largely due to the proactive efforts of the local climbing community led by the Los Alamos Mountaineers Club (LAMC). In 1989 climbers met to discuss the proliferation of bolts on all the basalt cliffs west of the Rio Grande and identified which crags could be bolted and which would be bolt-free. Bolting is allowed at The Overlook, Below The Old New Place, The Doughnut Shop, The Underlook, The Sununu Place, The Lounge, and Pajarito Gorge. Bolting is not allowed at The Playground, The Old New Place, The New New Place, Potrillo Cliffs, and The Y. The limited installation of anchors at all White Rock Crags (even ones previously off-limits to bolting) was agreed to in 2004 in response to the die-off of many of the piñon trees often used as anchors caused by extended drought conditions.

The Y is a detached segment of the Bandelier National Monument. There are plans to transfer management of this historic area to the New Mexico Highway Department. A climbing management plan is not developed for this area, although this could change. Visitors should check with locals for the latest information. In the meantime, keep a low profile and be careful not to climb near any petroglyphs or rock drawings.

Visiting climbers should leave their drills at home as new route possibilities on all crags are nearly nonexistent. Stay on existing trails along the rim and en route to the crags to minimize human impact. Please stay on the main trails. Objective dangers include loose rock on the cliff tops, rattlesnakes, cacti, and primitive access trails.

Guidebooks: *Rock Climbing New Mexico & Texas* by Dennis R. Jackson, Falcon Press, 1996. The out-of-print *Sport Climbing in New Mexico* by Randal Jett and Max Samet, 1991. Mini-guides were featured in *Rock and Ice* magazine #36 and #40.

Services: Limited food, fuel, and lodging is found in the village of White Rock. Smiths, a large grocery store located several blocks west on Highway 4, has a good selection of food and brews. Nearby Los Alamos, the "Atomic City," offers more variety and entertainment possibilities. Santa Fe offers complete visitor services including its world-famous, unique northern New Mexico cuisine. You just about can't go wrong at any Mexican restaurant. Try Tomasitas Cafe (the local favorite), Dave's Not Here (hot and a lot), and Maria's New Mexican Kitchen for starters.

Emergency services: Call 911. The nearest public phone is in White Rock at the corner of Highway 4 and Rover Drive. A medical crisis center is available twenty-four hours a day throughout New Mexico; call (800) 432–6866. Search and rescue is conducted by St. John's Search and Rescue and initiated and coordinated by the New Mexico State Police (505–827–9300). The Los Alamos Medical Center (505–662–4201) at the corner of Diamond and Trinity Drives in Los Alamos offers twenty-four-hour emergency care.

Nearby climbing areas: Cochiti Mesa Crags, Las Conchas, The Dungeon, and Diablo Canyon.

Nearby attractions: Bandelier National Monument offers 34,000 acres of designated wilderness with great hiking and exploring

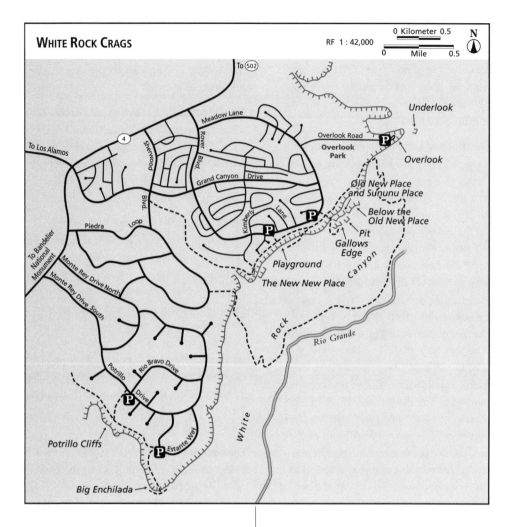

RF 1 : 42,000

0 Kilometer 0.5

0 Mile 0.5

N

To 502

Underlook

Meadow Lane

Overlook Road

Overlook Park

P

Overlook

Sherwood

Rover Blvd.

4

To Los Alamos

Grand Canyon Drive

Old New Place and Sununu Place

Blvd.

Below the Old New Place

Piedra Loop

Kimberly Lane

P

P

Pit

Gallows Edge

To Bandelier National Monument

Monte Rey Drive North

Playground

Rock Canyon

The New New Place

Monte Rey Drive South

Rock

Rio Grande

Rio Bravo Drive

Potrillo

Drive

P

White

Potrillo Cliffs

Estante Way

P

Big Enchilada

possibilities. The area was occupied by the Anasazi Indians from A.D. 1150 to 1500. A visitor center and self-guided tour of the Pueblo ruin Tyuonyi is in Frijoles Canyon. A self-guided hike to the Tsankawi Unit of the monument is a short distance north of White Rock. Park at a designated lot on Highway 4. The Bradbury Science Museum at the Los Alamos National Laboratory displays artifacts from the history of the laboratory and the production of the first atomic bomb along with exhibits of modern nuclear weapons, life sciences, computers,

particle accelerators, and geothermal, fusion, and fission energy sources.

The Rio Grande offers excellent rafting, canoeing, and kayaking opportunities. Private and commercial launches are best in early spring to late summer. Check with the Bureau of Land Management (BLM) for private launch information. Local commercial companies include Santa Fe Rafting and Far Flung Adventures. The nearby Rio Chama, America's first designated Wild & Scenic River, also offers good rafting, kayaking, and canoeing. Check with the BLM for launch information. Excellent fishing is found on both rivers and smaller streams in the area.

There are ample backpacking, mountain biking, and hiking opportunities in Santa Fe National Forest, (505) 438–7840. All the Indian pueblos along the Rio Grande are interesting to visit. Visitors should inquire about special considerations and any required permits by calling the Tourist Division, Eight Northern Pueblos (505–852–4265).

Finding the crags: The village of White Rock is 30 miles northwest of Santa Fe and 10 miles southeast of Los Alamos. Approach the area via U.S. Highway 285 between Santa Fe and Espanola. Turn west from US 285 onto Highway 502 just north of the roadside village of Pojoaque. Signs point west toward Los Alamos and Bandelier National Monument. After 7 miles, the highway crosses the Rio Grande. Continue west past the junction with Highway 30 and head uphill on a four-lane highway. The highway divides about 4 miles later, with Highway 502 going to Los Alamos. Stay on Highway 4 toward White Rock. Drive 4.1 miles to a left turn onto Rover Boulevard into the village of White Rock. Drive 1 block and turn left onto Meadow Lane, then left again onto Overlook Road. After 0.8 mile you reach the Overlook Vista parking lot. To reach the other crags, continue another 0.5 mile on Meadow Lane to the public access trail located on the east side of Meadow Lane between house addresses 719 and 721. Refer to specific directions for each crag for trail access. The New New Place is accessed from Kimberly Lane farther along Meadow Lane. The Big Enchilada and Potrillo Cliffs are accessed farther west from the White Rock turn on Highway 4. Refer to each crag's section for specific directions.

The Overlook

The Overlook, a V-shaped cliff with east and northwest faces, sits directly below a ridge and a popular observation point that overlooks the Rio Grande in White Rock Canyon and the distant Sangre de Cristo Range. The views from the point and the cliff are spectacular and make any visit worthwhile. The 60-foot-high Overlook crag, one of New Mexico's premier basalt areas, offers excellent climbing on more than forty routes that include both bolted sport lines and great cracks.

Climbers of all abilities enjoy this area. Many sport routes are in the moderate 5.10 to 5.11+ range. The east face features steep hand and finger cracks from 5.8 to 5.11. Popular routes include *Bosker Boozeroo, Boy What Assholes (You Guys Turned Out To Be), Paul's Boutique, No Exit, Holy Wall, Sale at Mervyn's,* and *Thorazine Dream. Overture* (5.12b/c) and *On Beyond Zebra* (5.12c/d X) are local testpieces. *Cholla Wall* is a popular toprope problem that the bold leader can ascend using small gear placements in shallow pockets. Local consensus keeps this superb route off-limits to bolting.

Bring a rack of twelve quickdraws and a 165-foot rope for the sport routes. Most have lowering anchors. A rack of Friends or other cams to 3.5 inches along with a set of wired Stoppers and a few TCUs are needed to jam the cracks. TCUs are also useful in small pockets. Bring slings to set belay or toprope anchors atop the cliff. Use extreme caution not to knock any loose rock down on climbers below. Descend by walking around the cliff to the south on the access trail or lowering from bolt anchors.

Finding the cliff: Reach The Overlook from Highway 4 in White Rock by turning left onto Rover Boulevard. Signs direct you to Overlook Park. Go 1 block and turn left onto Meadow Lane. Go 0.8 mile through a residential area and make another left turn onto Overlook Road. Pass sports playing fields and reach a dead-end parking area for the Overlook viewing area. Walk north past the railings at the observation deck onto a narrow rocky ridge. At the end of the rocky ridge, locate a rough trail that drops right or southeast toward the Rio Grande. Follow the trail down and around to the south end of The Overlook crag. The trail leads north along the base of the east face (main climbing area) to the point of the ridge prow. Here it turns sharply west to reach the northwest face. Routes are listed from left to right starting at the southern end of the main southeast-facing cliff.

1. Bosker Boozeroo (5.11a) First climb on the cliff. Up a steep arête. 7 bolts to 2-bolt anchor.

2. Squeeze Chimney (5.10+) No bolts. After a short chimney, a finger and hand crack leads to a dihedral. Belay at the top.

3. Boy, What Assholes (You Guys Turned Out To Be) (5.10b) Excellent face and arête climbing. 5 bolts to 2-bolt anchor.

4. 5.8 Crack (5.8) No bolts. Steep and difficult to protect at the top.

5. Paul's Boutique (5.11b) Steep arête and face climbing. 5 bolts to 2-bolt anchor.

6. Headwall Crack Left (5.8) No bolts. Quality jams up the crack to the top.

7. No Exit (5.12a) Quality climb. Difficult at the top. 5 bolts to 2-bolt anchor.

8. Headwall Crack Right (5.9) No bolts. Great jams to a difficult finish. Step right to the top of #9 and belay off gear or continue to the cliff top.

9. Double Vision/Ream Dream (5.10d or 5.11c) 5.10d if the arête is used. 5 bolts to 2-bolt anchor.

10. Cholla Wall (5.10a) No bolts. An area classic. No bolts by a consensus agreement. It's usually done as a toprope since the gear placements are marginal.

11. Cholla Crack (5.9) No bolts. Classic finger and hand jams to the cliff top. A 3.5-inch cam is useful at the top.

12. Holy Wall (5.10a) A fun pocket route and one of the most popular routes on the crag. 5 bolts to 2-bolt chain anchor.

13. Holy Crack (5.9+) No bolts. Quality lead.

14. Sale at Mervyn's aka **Dave's Face** (5.10c) Popular. Great face and pocket climbing. 5 bolts to 2-bolt anchor.

15. Way Beyond Zebra (5.11b) Popular route with more excellent face and pocket climbing. 5 bolts to 2-bolt anchor.

16. Polly's Crack (5.8) No bolts. Fingers and hands up a crack to the cliff top.

17. Thief in Time (5.12d) Start in a right-facing crack on the right or in *Polly's Crack*. Grab small pockets up an overhanging face. Go right at upper arête. 5 bolts to 2-bolt anchor.

18. Narcissistic Dream (5.11+) Thin and difficult. A former toprope problem with bolts added for leading.

19. Face Off (5.12a) Considered the best route of its grade on the crag. Pockets up a bulging wall. 6 bolts to 2-bolt anchor.

20. M.C. Epic (5.8) No bolts. Start in an overhanging hand and fist crack to easier climbing above. Belay at top.

21. Captain Smarmbag (5.10) No bolts. A difficult finger crack leads around a roof to easier climbing above. Belay at the top.

22. Box Overhang Left (5.8+) Classic climb. No bolts. Fingers and hand jams on the left side of the large roof to a 2-bolt lowering anchor.

23. Len's Roof (5.11a) No bolts. Carefully climb choss rock just right of the center crack. Strenuous hand jams up the center crack lead to easier climbing above.

24. Overture (5.12b/c) Missing its bolt hangers. Seldom done.

25. Box Overhang Right (5.8) No bolts. Hand and fist jams lead to easier climbing above. Belay at top.

26. On Beyond Zebra (5.12c/d X) Just to the right of #25. You have the potential for a ground fall while getting to the second bolt. 4 bolts to 2-bolt anchor.

27. 5.9 Crack (5.9) No topo.

28. Thorazine Dream (5.11d) Quality route. Difficult moves over a small roof to a slab with 2 bolts, then past a horizontal crack (TCU placement possible). 5 bolts to 2-bolt anchor.

The following routes are located around the northern prow of the crag on the northwest face.

29. View With a Room (5.11b) Scramble up to a short steep face, then climb past 3 bolts to a 2-bolt anchor.

30. Overlord (5.11a) 4 bolts up a face/arête to 2-bolt anchor with chains.

31. Overlard (5.10c) On the right side of a roof. Joins *Overlord* and shares a 2-bolt anchor.

32. Over-Ripe Fresh-Squeezed California Females (5.11b) 4 bolts and 2 tied-off holes to a 2-bolt anchor. Be cautious of any in-situ old webbing.

33. The D'Antonio Approach (5.12a) Climb the face left of a wide crack. Shares anchors with #32. 4 bolts to 2-bolt anchor.

34. Huecos Rancheros (5.10c) Located about 60 feet right of #33. The most popular route at this cliff sector. Climb large pockets up a vertical face left of a chimney. 4 bolts to 2-bolt anchor.

35. Unknown (5.11d) Climb a steep face with a chimney on the left and a finger crack on the right. 3 bolts to 2-bolt anchor.

36. Just Say No To Jugs (5.11a) Large pockets and jugs up an overhanging face right of a blunt prow. 4 bolts to 2-bolt anchor.

37. Overlichen (5.11a) Climb to the arête, then more right and finish up a face. 4 bolts to 2-bolt anchor.

38. Chocolate Thunder (5.11d) Edge up a black arête to anchors. 4 bolts to 2-bolt anchor.

39. Hammertime (5.12a) Start on top of a blocky shelf, then pull small holds up an arête. 4 bolts to a shared 2-bolt anchor.

40. Citizen Of Time (5.11d/.12a) Thin edging up a black face. 4 bolts to 2-bolt anchor.

41. Crisis In Utopia (5.11a/b) A finger crack in a left-facing corner. No bolts, gear required.

42. Primal Scream (5.12a) Climb past 1 bolt, then left up a steep face and arête to anchors. 4 bolts to 2-bolt anchor.

43. Overkill (5.11a) Move right at first bolt of *Primal Scream* and climb a black pocketed face. 4 bolts to 2-bolt anchor.

The following three routes are right of #43. Not illustrated.

44. Lubme (5.12a/b) Poor quality. Start up chossy rock to 2 bolts, then left up more looseness to a steep face. 1-bolt lowering anchor.

45. Unknown (No rating) Contrived route and seldom climbed. Clip the first 2 bolts of *Lubme,* then up an arête/prow.

46. Putterman Gully Jump (5.9+) Another contrived route. Go right at bolt 1 of *Lubme,* then 6 feet right and past 4 bolts on a black face.

The Underlook

The Underlook, a shady north-facing cliff, is located a short distance below the north end of The Overlook. This fun 35-foot-high crag offers four short routes, shade on hot days, and some boulder problems.

Finding the cliff: To reach The Underlook, hike down a faint trail on a ridge that starts below the north prow of The Overlook. The hidden cliff is a few hundred feet down the path. Anchors at the top of the cliff are visible from the left as you near it.

Routes are listed from left to right.

1. Thunder and Lichen

(5.9-) Begin at the toe of a buttress. Climb pockets up a slabby prow. 4 bolts to a 2-bolt chain anchor.

2. Simon Bar Sinister (5.11a) Begin 5 feet

right of #1. Climb pockets and edges up a slightly overhanging face. 4 bolts to a 2-bolt anchor.

3. Under the Weather (5.10d) Begin 3 feet

right of #2. Climb a rounded overhanging arête. 4 bolts to a 2-bolt chain anchor.

4. Little Miss Polly (5.10a) Start on the face

6 feet right of #3. Best to stick-clip the high first bolt. Using the crack on the left makes things a little easier and safer. Gear placements ease the stress on the long runout to the anchors. 2 bolts to a 2-bolt anchor.

The Old New Place

The Old New Place, a 60-foot-high, east-facing basalt crag, is a longtime local toprope area. Most climbs can be led. At least eight high-quality hand and finger cracks, ranging from 5.8 to 5.11+, ascend the cliff. A rack of camming units up to 3 inches plus a good assortment of wired nuts or Stoppers is sufficient to lead most routes. Toprope and belay anchor placements are plentiful on top. Long runners are often necessary. The Old New Place is a no-bolt area by local agreement. Please respect the local traditions. Watch, as

always, for loose rocks on the cliff top when setting up your anchors.

None of the routes have names, which follows a long area tradition that allows each visitor to ascribe their own name and rating. Be forewarned that the cracks are as difficult as others in the White Rock area. Not illustrated.

Finding the crag: Follow the directions provided in the Overview section of the White Rock Crags. Drive through White Rock's residential area east of Highway 4 and reach the public access trail on the east side of Meadow Lane between house addresses 719 and 721. Follow the concrete trail through a fence. Once on dirt, walk toward the rim and turn left or north onto the trail closest to the rim. Follow the trail northeast along the rim for about 150 yards to the top of a small knoll on the rim. This is the top of The Old New Place. Walk a short distance left (north)

and descend the north side of a gully down through rock bands on the north flank of The Old New Place. Turn right or south to the cliff base.

A standard rack complete with sets of wired nuts, TCUs, and camming units is necessary to lead the crack routes. It's helpful to carry doubles in most sizes. Long extension runners for setting up toprope anchors are often necessary. To descend walk back down the approach trail.

The Sununu Place

The Sununu Place is a small 45-foot cliff sitting directly below The Old New Place. The rock quality here is not as good as the upper wall but may be worth a visit because of its easy access. Not illustrated.

Finding the cliff: Walk a short distance down from the north end of The Old New Place.

The small cliff is tucked away amid large boulders on the right.

Routes are listed from left to right.

1. Barbara's Midnight Missile (5.10c/d) Begin off a large boulder at the base. Face climb up pockets and edges past 3 bolts with homemade hangers to a 2-bolt lowering anchor.

2. Bush Whacker (5.9) Begin 15 feet right of #1 off a flat boulder. Climb up left to the first bolt. Continue up the face left of a corner past 2 more bolts to a traverse left to #1's anchors.

Below The Old New Place

Below The Old New Place, an excellent 65-foot-high basalt crag, is a superb sport climbing crag with nineteen bolted lines. It also offers quality crack routes that range in difficulty from 5.9 to 5.11. Below The Old New Place is just north and not surprisingly below The Old New Place.

Rack: All the cracks are led with a rack of camming units up to 3 inches and Stoppers. A rack of ten quickdraws suffices for the sport routes. Most routes have two-bolt lowering anchors. Some crack climbs require setting up a belay atop the crag. Watch for loose rock on the cliff edge.

Finding the cliff: To reach the crag, follow the directions to The Old New Place. From the north end of The Old New Place, continue switchbacking downhill a short distance, then go left for about 150 feet to the base of Below The Old New Place. Routes are listed from left to right.

1. Putterman Cracks (5.9) Converging finger cracks to a slightly loose section. Use either or both cracks for varying difficulties.

Belay at the top from gear or from a 2-bolt anchor 10 feet right.

2. Scandinavian Airlines (5.10c) Quality. The arête right of *Putterman Cracks*. 3 bolts to 2-bolt anchor. Difficult clips.

3. In-Flight Movie (5.12a) Difficult moves up a face and arête to *Scandinavian Airlines* anchors.

4. Monsterpiece Theater (5.12a) Quality route. Long steep face with 6 bolts to a 2-bolt anchor.

5. Little Shop of Horrors (5.12a) Climb a crack for 25 feet, then move left to a face. 3 bolts to a 2-bolt anchor.

6. Polyester Terror (5.10a) Jam the right-slanting finger crack to a triangular roof, then left to the top.

7. Ralph's Leisure Suit (5.11c or 5.12a) Steep climbing past 5 bolts to a 2-bolt anchor under a triangular roof. It's 5.12a if you ignore the crack on the right.

8. Ralph's Dilemma (5.10) A thin crack and stemming problem to the apex of the triangular roof. Move right and up to a 2-bolt anchor shared with #9.

9. Flesh Eating Gnats (5.11c) Recommended. Start from ground level and just right of *Ralph's Dilemma*. Climb straight up the arête. 5 bolts to 2-bolt anchor.

10. Ralph's Revenge (5.9) Quality. Climb 10 feet to a ledge and then up a finger crack. Belay at the top or from *Adam Ant's* anchors. Difficult near the top.

11. Adam Ant (5.12a) Quality. Start on the same ledge as *Ralph's Revenge,* but climb the face right of the crack. 4 bolts to 2-bolt anchor.

12. Wailing Banshees (5.11b/c) Excellent. Avoid a ground fall by traversing in from the left. Climb a steep arête to shared anchors with *Adam Ant*.

13. Manic Crack (5.11d) Quality jamming up a difficult steep finger crack.

14. Manic Nirvana (5.12b/c) On the face between *Manic Crack* and *Lost Nerve*. 4 bolts to 2-bolt anchor.

15. Lost Nerve (5.10c) A steep and strenuous finger crack. Shares anchors with #14.

16. L Dopa (5.9+) Follow a finger crack that curves up right to a ledge with a 2-bolt anchor.

17. P.M.S. (5.11c) Edge up a steep face bracketed on the right by an arête. Using the arête lowers the grade to 5.10a. 3 bolts to a 2-bolt shared anchor with *L Dopa*.

18. I Dogged Your Wife and She Is a Doofus (5.11a/b) Start on a large ledge. Face climb past 3 bolts to a 1-bolt anchor.

19. Instant Dogma (5.10c/d) Start on a face between two ledges. Climb a face left of a sharp arête. 3 bolts. No anchors.

20. Fat Boys Don't Fly (5.12b/c) Face climb up a white face, then over a bulge. The climb is 5.12b going right after bolt 3 or 5.12c straight up from the bolt. 4 bolts to 1-bolt anchor.

21. Unknown Up the arête left of a roof. Shares anchors with #22.

22. Unknown Climb an off-vertical face between two cracks. 5-bolts to 2-bolt anchor.

23. Sardonic Smile (5.11d) Thin pocket and face climbing up a steep white face to a 2-bolt anchor. 4 bolts to 2-bolt anchor.

24. Color of My Potion (5.12a) An arête and face climb to *Sardonic Smile*'s anchors.

25. Strong Urge to Fly (5.12b) Start just left of a ledge shaded by a tree. 4 bolts to 2-bolt anchor.

26. Unnamed (5.12b) Start from the ledge. Climb a black face and arête. 5 bolts to 2-bolt anchor.

27. Got a Nightstick, Got a Gun, Got Time on My Hands (5.11c) The farthest right route on the cliff. Start from upper shelf, then up a black arête. 3 bolts to 2-bolt anchor.

Gallows Edge and The Pit

Gallows Edge is a small, fun sport cliff situated three cliff tiers below the rim of White Rock Canyon. The five-minute hiking approach ends at a "tilted block," a laid-back basalt formation. A once-vertical face slumped above and rotated as it slid down the slope, coming to rest at an inviting low angle for moderate climbing.

The routes range from 5.4 to 5.9, making it attractive to many climbers. The routes are safely bolted with bolt-lowering anchors. Many anchors could be improved with the addition of bolt hangers. Most routes are face climbs with a small selection of protectable cracks. The crag's southeast-facing aspect makes the crag a good winter area. Summer time can be uncomfortably warm, especially in the morning.

The Pit is an unusual cliff that features a hidden entrance passage that leads to a walled-in shady room. The crag has four good routes, including the area's best splitter crack.

Gallows Edge

Finding the crag: Follow directions above to the parking area for The Old New Place and The Playground. Walk down the concrete access path between houses 719 and 721 to the main trail. Continue straight ahead and a little left (north) to the canyon rim. The trail down to the cliff starts here. The south end of The Old New Place is visible to the left. The well-defined trail to Gallows Edge scrambles down a cliff band and then heads steeply downhill and slightly right. The lower section of the trail is somewhat difficult to follow as it crosses over rocks, but generally trend to the right when faced with choices. After you descend to the third cliff tier, Gallows Edge is the obvious cliff on your left. Routes are described from left to right.

1. Butler Route (5.5) Good beginner crack climb. Can be led or toproped. No bolts, no anchor.

2. Planet of the Apes (5.8+) Good route just right of an arête. 4 bolts to 2-bolt anchor.

3. Unknown (5.7) No topo. The off-width crack right of *Planet of the Apes*. Gear route, no anchor.

4. Prince Humperdink (5.12a) No topo. Located around the corner left of *The Fire Swamp*. The grade drops slightly by using the right-hand arête. 3 bolts, no anchor.

5. The Fire Swamp (5.6) Excellent. Good edging to perfect pockets. 4 bolts to 2-bolt anchor.

6. Unknown (5.8) Good climb. Starts just left of a bulge, then straight up. 3 bolts to a 2-bolt anchor shared with #5.

7. Princess Buttercup (5.5) Start left of a large chimney. Fun climbing straight up a slabby face. 3 bolts to 2-bolt anchor.

8. 99 Red Balloons (5.7+) Excellent route. Starts just right of a large chimney. Avoiding the arête makes the climb a bit harder. Watch for loose rock at bolt 4. 4 bolts to 2-bolt anchor.

9. Unknown (5.7) Off-width crack. Gear route.

10. Once Were Warriors (5.8-) Good route, easy for its grade. Jugs help at the top crux.

11. Pejo's Route (5.5) 4 bolts to 2-bolt anchor.

12. Giant Killer (5.4) Solo or beginner toprope problem. No bolts, no gear placements, no anchor.

Upper Ledge

These routes are located on the cliff tier above and right of *Giant Killer*. Not illustrated.

13. Dave and Crissa's Route (5.9-) The left-hand route. Oddly bolted. 4 bolts to 2-bolt anchor.

14. Quality Control Be Damned (5.7) The least desirable route here but still okay. Loose near the top. 3 bolts to 2-bolt anchor.

15. Forgotten Crack (5.9) It begins right of a large off-width crack right of *Quality Control be Damned*. Start in an alcove. Short, not much of a problem. Gear route, no bolts, and no anchor.

The Pit

This unique hidden cliff features some good routes and is well worth finding and visiting. It is somewhat difficult to find the first time.

Finding the cliff: Walk to the north for about 250 feet past Gallows Edge on a small but easy-to-follow trail. As you get closer to

a blocky section, look for three sets of bolt anchors on your left about 40 feet up the cliff. These are anchors for several routes in The Pit. Stay well below these and cross above a small talus field. Turn left and climb into a large hole made by tumbled boulders. Worm your way through the tunnel and angle left to a short downclimb to the floor of The Pit. You will know you are in the right place when you see an imposing Thunderbird painting on the west wall.

Routes are described from right to left on the west wall, then circling to the east wall. Not illustrated.

1. Thunder the Bird (5.10a) This route goes up the right side of the Thunderbird. It is generally toproped, but it's probably better that it doesn't get climbed at all. No bolts, no anchor.

2. Unknown (5.9) Excellent finger crack that gets wider near the top. Start just left of the Thunderbird. No bolts, no anchor.

3. Gralisa Leen (5.10c) The best route here. Long and sustained. 4 bolts (2 with homemade hangers) to 2-bolt anchor.

4. Unknown (5.8) Not recommended. Loose rock. The wide crack left of *Gralisa Leen*. No bolts, no anchor.

5. The-Odor Takeda (5.8) The left-hand climb on the west face. 4 bolts to 2-bolt anchor.

6. Fay Drostenson (5.10b) Located on the southeast corner of The Pit. Short with a large ledge halfway up. 3 bolts to 2-bolt anchor.

7. Unknown (5.7) 20 feet of face climbing on the left end of the east wall. No bolts, no anchor.

The Playground

The Playground, a 70-foot basalt cliff, offers the best concentration of crack climbs in the White Rock–Los Alamos area. Only The Overlook up-canyon boasts as much diversity and challenge for crack masters. The thirty routes at The Playground range in difficulty from 5.9 to 5.12. Expect steep, strenuous jamming on solid basalt with generally good gear placements. Great views of the Rio Grande in White Rock Canyon, a short approach, the quality crack climbing, and a friendly local scene make The Playground a superb alternative to the nearby busy sport crags.

No bolts for protection are found on this traditional cliff. Climbers must place gear to protect the many finger and hand cracks. Routes are also toproped. The most popular routes are the strenuous *Unrelenting Nines, First Strike,* a 5.12c with ground fall potential that's usually toproped, *Original Horak Route, The Flying A* up a quality 5.10+ corner, popular *Beginner's Crack,* and *The Blowhole* up a sustained, overhanging dihedral. Many routes are unnamed. This is a local tradition with different names applied as new climbers "discover" the area. All routes and variations, however, are worth jamming.

Bring a rack of Friends or other cams through 3 inches or hand-size, along with a set of wired Stoppers. A few hexes, TCUs, RPs, and tri-cams might prove useful on some cracks. Set up belays on the broken ledge above the cliff to bring up your second. Toprope anchors, using gear and long slings, are also easily constructed on this ledge. Some bolted anchors were installed in 2004 in response to the drought-caused die-off of trees sometimes used for anchors. Be careful not to trundle boulders or loose rock

from the ledge onto unsuspecting innocents below. Good bouldering is found along the cliff base. Descend by rappelling or walking down from either end of the cliff.

Finding the cliff: To reach The Playground from Highway 4 in White Rock, turn left onto Rover Boulevard. Drive 1 block and turn left onto Meadow Lane. Continue past the turnoff to Overlook Park about 0.5 mile and park near a public access trailhead between houses numbered 719 and 721 on the left or east side of Meadow Lane. A sign here says MOTOR VEHICLES PROHIBITED.

Walk east down the cement trail to the main rim trail. Turn right or south onto this trail. It follows the area between the cliff top and a fence on the right. Locate an easy downclimb in a gully on the north end of the crag about 300 yards from the gate. Finding the downclimb is important for easy access. It may be difficult to find the first time. Sometimes there is a wooden playhouse with a colorful roof behind the fence on the right. A broad flat area below the wall's base is visible just before starting down. Scramble down the rough trail between the north edge of the cliff and a detached basalt pillar.

Routes are listed from right to left.

1. Repo Man (5.12b) No topo. A relatively new route. Reachy.

2. The Blowhole (5.10c/d). Thin jams lead up to the "blowhole" about 20 feet up. Continue up and right to the top.

3. Unnamed (5.9+) Five paces to the left of #1. A thin flake leads up to a finger crack in a dihedral. Turn the triangular roof on its left.

4. Battle of the Bulge (5.11b/c) Tips and stemming up a finger crack and past a bulge under the middle roof in a set of three roofs.

5. Barlow's Buttress (5.9) Face, edges, and crack climbing lead up to the middle roof (as in #4). Go right around the upper roof.

6. Fingertip Layback (5.10d/11a) Fingertip crack to a left-curving hand crack, then up a good crack to the left-hand roof. Turn the roof on the right.

7. Upper Left Roof (5.9+) Low-angle face climbing leads to a right-facing dihedral that goes to the left-hand roof. Turn on its left.

8. Advanced Start (5.10c/d) Good hand jams for 10 feet, then hand traverse left to the main crack.

9. Beginner's Crack (5.9) Perfect hand jam crack to a thin hands to fingers crack.

10. Cactus Climb (5.10a/b) Face and crack climb to the right of two cracks.

11. Unnamed (5.10d/lla) Strenuous crack climbing from bottom to top.

12. Black Wall (5.9) Climb the right side of a bulbous nose, then right and up a crack to the top.

13. Mr. Foster's Lead (5.9) Two parallel cracks lead to a crack system to the right of a tree at the top.

14. Vulture Roof (5.11b/c) No topo. Face and crack climb 10 feet to a large orange roof. Difficult moves over the roof lead to a crack system going up right.

15. Unnamed (5.11b/c) No topo. Four paces to the left of *Vulture Roof.* Climb straight up for 20 feet, then right up thin cracks.

16. The Cheeks (5.11a/b) Difficult climbing to a bulbous roof, then right and up an inside dihedral.

17. Unnamed (5.9+/10-) Climb up to the left side of a bulbous roof. Move up right via cracks to a short left-facing corner.

18. Unnamed (5.11) Two paces left of #17. Straight up to a crack system.

19. Unnamed (5.10a) Thin cracks lead 25 feet to a triangular roof. Continue up the crack system on the left side of the roof.

20. The Flying A (5.10d/11-) Start in a 5-foot rectangle, then move up and over two blocks to a left-facing dihedral. The face to the left is a 5.12a toprope problem.

21. Texas (5.8) Easy climbing leads to a flake. Layback around to the right.

22. Zander Zig Zag (5.10d) Same start as *Texas.* Go left at the bottom of the flake.

23. Original Horak Route (5.10a) The right-trending crack system six paces left of *Texas.*

24. First Strike (5.12c X) 10 feet left of *Original Horak Route.* A quality toprope problem.

25. Unnamed (5.10b) Climb the right side of a flake that has a large hole near its top. Continue along a thin right-trending crack.

26. Unrelenting Nines (5.11b/c) 15 feet left of #25. A thin, steep crack from the bottom to cliff top.

27. Unnamed (5.11a) Start up a 10-foot black streak, then climb up right along a thin crack.

28. Unnamed (5.11d) Start uphill of #27. Climb up left.

The New New Place

The New New Place is an attractive 70-foot-high cliff that has lots of good cracks that can be led or toproped. You are on your own here to figure out the routes, which adds a sense of adventure. Many good high-standard routes ascend the cliff. Not illustrated.

Finding the cliff: The area is easily approached from Kimberly Lane, which dead-ends at a cul-de-sac. The left turn onto Kimberly Lane is approximately 0.75 mile past the public access trail for The Playground, Gallows Edge, and Below the Old New Place. From the cul-de-sac, walk north on the trail for a short distance until a spur trail branches right (south). Take this branch and hike to the rim. Find a way down from the rim by following graffiti-covered rock north to the base of the cliff. Allow five minutes for the approach.

The Big Enchilada

The Big Enchilada is a remote cliff that features some fine traditional climbs and two sport routes. Other good qualities are the basalt is generally good to excellent, the approach hike is minimal, and you rarely see another party climbing here. None of the routes are named. Setting up toprope anchors is problematic given the absence of convenient trees or boulders along most of the rim.

Bring a rack with sets of Stoppers and Friends as well as a 150-foot rope. None of the routes are equipped with lowering anchors, so all your belay anchors are from gear and any trees that can be safely used along the cliff top. Extra rope is useful to extend anchors from trees that are located well back from the cliff top. Installing anchors with gear at the top of the routes is usually the best option. Descend via rappel from your anchors or walk back to the base via the approach trail.

Finding the crag: From White Rock drive west on Highway 4 toward Los Alamos and Bandelier National Monument. Turn left onto Monte Rey Drive South. This is one of the last streets in White Rock. Drive to Potrillo Drive and turn right and then go right again on Estante Way. Park on either side of the road between mailbox number 428 and 422.

The trail starts between mailbox 428 and the fire hydrant at power pole #9. After walking a short distance, take the first left fork and hike southeast along a good trail until it ends at the canyon rim above White Rock Canyon. Walk left about 60 feet and locate a short downclimbing section over broken basalt. Scramble down a gully to the cliff base. Go left at the bottom of the gully for routes #1 to #7 and right and around the prow of the cliff for routes #8 to #25. Routes are listed from right to left.

East Cliff

The first seven routes are on a tall, east-facing cliff that is accessed by walking left from the base of the descent gully. The only sport routes at The Big Enchilada are here.

1. Unnamed (5.11b) Start by a large cholla cactus. Climb a short, obvious hand crack between two pillars to a ledge 20 feet up. Work up a steep right-angling seam above. Finish on the left side of a roof.

2. Unnamed (5.10d/.11a) Start by the same large cholla. Scramble up broken corners 15 feet to a pedestal ledge. Work up a steep right-arching finger crack and finish over the left side of a roof.

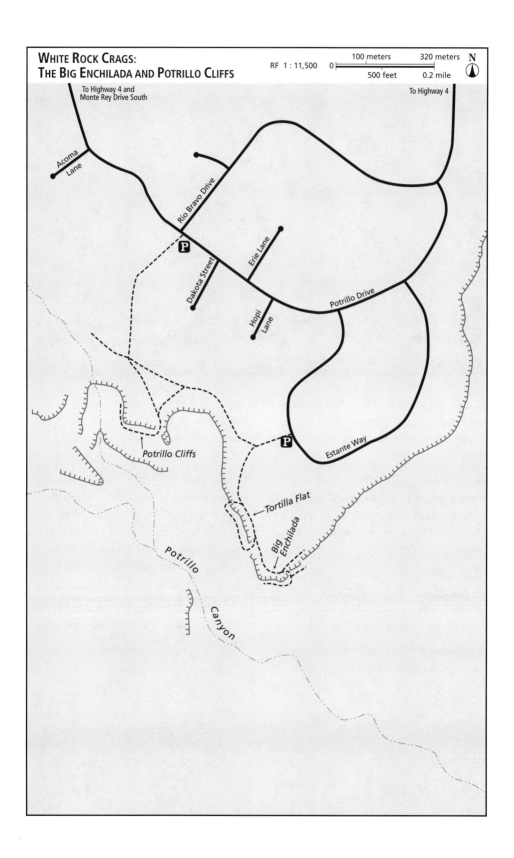

3. Unnamed (5.10b/c) Scramble up easy rock, then jam the obvious splitter up the middle of the face. Keep left where the crack branches.

4. Unnamed (5.11c) Begin 5 feet left of #3. Climb broken rock, then up a thin crack system that ends. Work up the bulge above past 2 bolts and finish up easier rock to a 2-bolt anchor.

5. Unnamed (5.9) Climb the right-hand side of double open corners and work up an imposing chimney. Clip sport anchors on the left to lower or continue to the top.

6. Unnamed (5.12b) Begin below a double open corner system. Climb the right-hand

system 20 feet to a ledge. Swing up the steep rib above on pockets and edges past 3 bolts. Delicately climb over the bulge above to a 2-bolt anchor.

7. Unnamed (5.9+/.10a) Climb a thin crack system just left of double open corners to a large ledge. Jam a crack up right of the left side of ledges to the base of a roof. Hand traverse left under a precarious block to an exciting exit over the roof. Continue up blocks to the cliff top.

The following routes are located right of the downclimb descent gully on a south-facing wall left of the mesa prow.

West Cliff

8. Unnamed (5.9+) Difficult to protect, best to toprope it. Begin below a broken corner left of the nose of the buttress. Climb 20 feet to a shattered ledge. Step left and climb the steep face right of an arête using a crack and edges.

9. Unnamed (5.11a) Begin on a broken block below a large roof. Climb a crack 20 feet to the base of a roof. Angle left and execute a thin fingery layback up a shallow corner to a block roof. Pull over and finish up easier rock.

10. Unnamed (5.10d) Climb a shallow corner 20 feet to a ledge. Climb the corner up left and follow a crack system left of a large roof to the top.

11. Unnamed (5.9) Begin 3 feet left of #10. Climb cracks up a corner to an awkward slot to a large ledge. Finish up the broken dihedral above.

12. Unnamed (5.9) Start off two large blocks and climb a large open corner to the right side of a roof. Exit right and finish up the off-width crack above.

13. Unnamed (5.12a) Toprope problem. Begin off blocks. Swing up steep rock to a ledge left of a large roof. Edge up the face right of the crack to easy rock.

14. Unnamed (5.9+) Start same as #13. Climb a loose left-angling corner and crack. Hand traverse right and mantel onto a large ledge. Jam the hand crack up the obvious corner to an easy finish.

15. Unnamed (5.10a) Start in a shallow open corner. Climb 20 feet to a ledge. Work up the dihedral above to the top of the cliff.

16. Unnamed (5.9+) Start 20 feet left of #15 by a pointed boulder. Climb the crack with the large chockstone. Go right under the roof near the top.

17. Unnamed (5.11b) Start up loose rock to difficult moves into a crack, then up through a slot to a featured face left of the obvious rim-top tree.

18. Unnamed (5.11c/d) Start 10 feet left of #17. Climb a thin crack to a sloping ledge, then up a crack splitting the face above.

19. Unnamed (5.11c) A short, thin left-facing crack leads to difficult moves over a roof. Climb the right-angling crack above to the same finish as #18.

20. Unnamed (5.11b/c) Start below a roof forming an arch. Climb to the base of the arch (crux or alternately come in from the left). Pull through the arched roof, then climb an easier broken corner up right. Finish up a crack to the top.

21. Unnamed (5.11a/b) Tricky layback moves up the crack lead to a small ledge 17 feet up. Climb a broken dihedral up right to the cliff top.

22. Unnamed (5.10d) Stem up a shallow white corner to a roof 12 feet up. Exit left around a block. Climb to a slot above right of a large roof and continue up the big right-facing dihedral.

23. Unnamed (5.10b) Same start as #22. Climb past the slot, step left, and climb a crack on the right side of a fragile pillar. Finish up an easy slab to the top.

24. Unnamed (5.10?) Begin below the left side of a large roof. Climb a good finger crack to the roof. Make awkward moves to the left to a slot, then climb to a small piñon pine tree. Finish up easier rock above.

25. Unnamed (5.10?) Begin 10 feet left of #24. Climb a broken corner system to the small piñon pine tree. Finish up easier rock above.

Potrillo Cliffs

Potrillo Cliffs, an excellent traditional cliff, is one of White Rock's oldest climbing venues. Its climbing is a good mix of easy and moderate cracks. This is a good place to hone your crack climbing skills. The best routes are between 5.7 and 5.10. Almost every route is recommended. The cliff is easily approached and is classically situated overlooking impressive Potrillo Canyon, a deep side canyon of White Rock Canyon.

Potrillo, along with other basalt cliffs in the area, is unique because molten lava flowed up faults through the crust into a surface covered with water. This occurred about four million years ago. The rock quickly cooled in the water, producing both horizontal and vertical curvilinear cracks on pillow-shaped formations. Iceland is supposedly the only other place in the world to have basalt formed in a similar situation.

The cliff is deservedly very popular, with easy access, lots of routes, and a good winter climate. The cliff's south-facing aspect makes it a busy destination in winter and early spring. The south-facing black cliff is an efficient solar collector. Expect shade in the morning and sun for the afternoon. Summer days are often too hot for comfort except in the morning.

This unimposing cliff has a long and storied climbing history that began in 1954. Potrillo Cliffs has the distinction of being the first basalt cliff developed in the White Rock–Los Alamos area. Early climbing icons George Bell, a member of the remarkable 1953 K2 Expedition, and Layton Kor, one of America's great climbers, both did first ascents at Potrillo. Bell, who still lives in the area and is a scientist at Los Alamos National Laboratory, climbed here in the early 1950s while Kor visited in 1968. *Pillars of Hercules*

(5.7/5.8) defined the upper levels of difficulty in the 1950s. Layton established the 5.9 grade in New Mexico with an ascent of the now-classic *Upper Kor's Crack*. Interestingly, that same day he also free climbed a former aid line, now called *Lower Kor's Crack,* and also rated it 5.9. Today this stiff little climb is rated 5.10d.

Several sport routes were established at Potrillo in 1989. These routes had their hangers removed when the local climbing community agreed to honor the crag's long traditional climbing ethic. The crag was identified as a "no-bolt" area. Locals continue to honor this commitment.

Bring a good rack with sets of camming units and wired nuts. By local agreement this is a trad area with no bolting allowed. Toproping climbs is a long-standing Potrillo practice, but be forewarned, setting up anchors on the cliff top is difficult. This situation will likely change in 2004 with the addition of some bolt anchors installed in response to a drought-caused die-off of many of the trees traditionally used as anchors. Descent off the rim is by walking back down the descent trail at the east end of the cliff.

Finding the cliff: Drive west through the village of White Rock on Highway 4 toward Los Alamos and Bandelier National Monument. Go past Monte Rey Drive North and turn left onto Monte Rey Drive South. This is one of the last streets in White Rock. Drive 0.7 mile and turn right onto Potrillo Drive. Drive another 0.7 mile and turn right onto Estante Way. Drive a short distance and park on either side of the road between mailboxes 428 and 422. Make sure your car is all the way off the road.

The access trail begins between the mailbox for 428 and the fire hydrant at power pole #9. To find the cliff, which might be slightly tricky the first time, remember to stay right whenever you are presented with options to go left. The obvious left turn on the main trail takes you southeast to The Big Enchilada. At the sign announcing the government rules for the area, veer left. A short hike across level ground ends at the canyon rim. The descent gully to the cliff base is at the eastern end of the cliff.

Alternately, continue past the sign several hundred yards farther to a large drainage coming in from the right. There is no distinct trail here, but turn sharply left, then trend slightly left to the short path to the rim. You will probably reach the westernmost edge of the crag, in which case walk left or east to find the easy downclimb gully at the eastern end of the crag. Allow ten minutes to approach the cliff. Routes are listed from right to left.

1. Porky's Bad Luck (5.6) No topo. Start 10 feet right of *Ardeidae Arête.* Finish on a low-angle face.

2. Heron's Fissure (5.8+) First ascent in 1968 by Joy Heron, the fiancée and, later,

wife of Layton Kor. Select a way up to a hand and fist crack just left of a face with unusual scoop formations. Work up the crack to the top.

3. Ardeidae Arête (5.8) Start just outside the cave on its right side. Climb a blunt arête right of the huge hueco. Toprope problem.

4. Right Cave Route (5.11c) Climb a series of thin cracks on the right side of the cave. Joins the *Cave Route Center* at the roof before the huge hueco.

5. Cave Route Center (5.9) Start in the rear of the cave and wiggle out, then up and over several roofs to the huge human-size hueco above the cave. Continue to the top from here. It's awkward and difficult for the grade. Can be toproped with special precautions required because the overhang is close to the ground.

6. Left Cave Route (5.10b) Recommended testpiece. Start on the left side of the cave. Jam a difficult fist crack, then up a left-trending crack above.

7. Grandstanding (5.4) Start 5 feet right of #8. Climb up right around a detached pillar. Easy climbing up left from here to the cliff top.

8. Belly Up (5.7) Climb low-angle rock past blocks. Finish up a thin crack right of #9.

9. Belly Flop (5.9-) Start 4 feet right of #11. Climb a thin crack to a low-angle face with a short wide crack at its top. Continue up the crack to the top.

10. Unknown (5.10c) Good climb. Climb a steep, curving hand crack to the face between #11 and #9. Toprope problem.

11. Chuckwalla (5.8) Climb a chimney system just right of *Call of the Crane* to a right-facing dihedral.

12. Call of the Crane (5.10a) Climb the cracks 5 feet right of *Cindy's Chimney* to an overhang and a smooth face above. Finish up a short finger crack. A good toprope problem.

13. Cindy's Chimney (5.7) Classic and fun. Straight up the obvious chimney using an assortment of crack climbing skills.

14. Unknown (5.9) Usually toproped.

15. Pillars of Hercules (5.7 or 5.8) A local favorite since the first ascent by the Los Alamos Mountaineers in 1955. Climb to the top of the large flat-topped boulder from the left (5.7) or the right (5.8). Finish by jamming and stemming up parallel wide cracks to the top.

16. Fool on the Hill (5.12b) No topo. Another former sport route with missing hangers. Can be toproped.

17. Dream of White Gerbils (5.11c) No topo. A former sport problem with missing hangers. Can be toproped.

18. Lower Kor's Crack (5.10d) Excellent and recommended. Start just left of a large juniper tree near the prow of the cliff. Difficult moves off the ground up a finger and hand crack lead to twin cracks directly above.

19. Gymnast (5.8+) Classic route. Use the same start as *Upper Kor's Crack* but go right up to twin cracks.

20. Upper Kor's Crack (5.9) A must-do area classic. Tricky climbing up a thin crack, then left up a long hand crack to the top.

21. Desperate (5.8 or 5.9) Climb the first section of *Kor's Dog,* then choose either the center crack (5.8) or the crack splitting the face (5.9).

22. Kor's Dog (5.8) Climb a wide crack and go right at the Y junction with another crack. Continue up and way left to finish up a short right-facing corner.

23. Fickle Fingers (5.10d) Begin behind a juniper tree and pick a way to the steep left-curving crack above. Jam your way to the top.

24. Shaky Flake (5.10c) Climb a low-angle slab without protection, then left up easier climbing to the top. The route can be protected if you come in from the right.

25. Pieces of Eight (5.8+) Climb a hand crack to a large platform. Finish up an attractive finger crack to the top.

26. Tarzan (5.10d) Same start as *Jane,* then right and up at the roof.

27. Jane (5.9) Start in an alcove about 15 feet right of *Sleeper.* Climb a wide crack and turn the roof above on its left. The crux is a short thin crack above here.

28. Sleeper (5.10d) Climb up loose-looking flakes lodged in a crack to a large shelf. Finish up the attractive left-leaning finger crack.

29. Unknown (5.11a) Another steep, hard problem with the difficult moves close to the ground. Start under the right end of a huge roof.

30. Double Trouble (5.12c) A former bolted route now missing its hangers.

31. Car Camping with the Kids (5.6) Fun climbing up a variety of crack sizes.

32. Unknown (5.11a) Start up a thin crack to more reasonable climbing above.

The Y

The Y, sitting in a shallow canyon below the Y-road junction east of Los Alamos, is a popular basalt crag divided into two sectors—the North Wall and the South Wall. The 60-foot-high cliffs offer more than thirty toprope and lead routes. The area's superb crack climbing, easy access, and friendly scene contribute to its popularity. The Y's steep finger and hand cracks, sharp overhangs, and occasional dicey face moves on pockets and edges give first-time New Mexico visitors a sampling of what awaits them at the other fine basalt crags surrounding White Rock. The Y also serves as the Los Alamos area's usual climbing introduction for beginners. This roadside crag has a quiet, pleasant ambience, with a trickling creek that flows year-round except during the hot summer months. Avoid, however, drinking or splashing in the water because of its suspect upstream origins in the Los Alamos area.

The Y sits near the eastern edge of the Pajarito Plateau, a large sloping mesa composed of river gravels, lava flows, and volcanic ash deposits and deeply dissected by tumbling creeks that rush eastward to the Rio Grande's canyon from snowfields on the Jemez Mountains. The Y's cliffs formed some four million years ago when viscous fluid lava flowed from vents along fissures and faults. The lava blanketed underlying river gravels with an 80-foot-thick layer that slowly cooled into basalt. As lava cools, it generally forms hexagonal columns; here, however, the molten lava flowed into water and created not only columns but also strange rolls and pillow-shaped blobs. These unique and rare formations are found in only a few other world locales, including Iceland. Later erosion from snowmelt and flash floods excavated this abrupt little canyon, leaving today's steep canyon walls for climbers to pursue their vertical craft.

The Y was "discovered" by local climbers Len Margolin and Jim Porter in 1970. That first day they ascended three of today's classics—*Boy Scout, The Ramp,* and *Ratshit Cave.* Other lines were quickly ascended that year, including *Wisconsin,* a route up the North Wall's center that uses both sides of a Wisconsin-shaped flake. *Spiral Staircase,* the area's first 5.11, fell to Margolin in 1973. A less talented and nonthinking climber later chiseled out the initial holds and eased the grade. This route plus *Six Pack Crack* immediately to the left, *Ring Jam,* and *Ratshit Cave* immediately to the right are off-limits to climbing because of their proximity to petroglyphs. The following year Mike Roybal established *The Nose,* a thin face problem rated 5.12a X. Most folks toprope this audacious lead, New Mexico's first 5.12 route.

Toproping with lots of hanging is the normal course of climbing action here, although most routes can be led. Weekends are often crowded with climbers stringing topropes off the more popular routes. The scene is friendly, however, with most climbers willing to share ropes and beta information. School and rescue groups also use the area. If it is too crowded, visit one of the other fine nearby climbing areas at White Rock.

It is possible to climb here all year, although colder winter days can limit opportunities. The best weather is in spring and fall. By alternating routes on the north and south walls, sun can be found or avoided throughout the year. Summer days can be hot.

Management of The Y is by the New Mexico Highway Department. The area went through a state of ownership flux, and fortunately for climbers, San Ildefonso Pueblo and

Bandelier National Monument were not assigned jurisdiction as this would have limited or banned climbing access.

No bolting or power drills are allowed on the cliff by an agreement between officials and local climbing groups. Please avoid climbing on or near the petroglyphs located at the base of the cliff. Any climbing activity can damage these important and precious parts of American prehistory. Other archaeological sites are found in the immediate area. Please do not disturb or pot-hunt. It's against the law. Also watch for rattlesnakes in the warmer months and use caution on the cliff top when setting up topropes. Lots of loose rock is found on the rim and is easily trundled onto others below. The stream at the base of the cliff should be avoided at all costs by man and beast because of possible upstream pollution.

All the routes at The Y are worth climbing. The North Wall (south-facing) offers the greatest concentration of climbs. The more popular routes include *Triple Overhang* (5.10), *Open Book* (5.8+), *Wisconsin* (5.10-), *The Nose* (5.12a), *Beastie Crack* (5.9+), *The Three Mothers* (5.10c/d, 5.10a/b, and 5.11b/c), and *Porter Route* (5.7). The shady South Wall has fewer climbs but more opportunities for moderate routes. *Cavemantle* (5.10a/b), *Twin Cracks* (5.7+), and *Little Roof* (5.7) are the most popular.

Both walls are easy to access for setting up toprope anchors. Easy scrambling just upstream from *Little Roof* reaches the top of the South Wall. Extra-long runners are useful to tie off trees and boulders for anchors above both walls. Exercise caution on the cliff tops to safeguard yourself and others below. There are no bolts at The Y. This is a traditional area. Lead on gear or toprope only please. Placing gear for protection is necessary.

Bring a rack that includes sets of wired Stoppers, TCUs, and Friends. An occasional large cam might be required. Descend from the north cliff top by following a trail west, then left and down into the canyon. Resist the temptation to turn left too early to avoid getting cliffed out.

Finding the crag: The crag lies south of Highway 502, 7 miles east of Los Alamos and 25 miles northwest of Santa Fe. Most climbers will approach from the north (Espanola) or south (Santa Fe) on US 285. Turn west (right from the north and left from the south) onto Highway 502 just north of the roadside village of Pojoaque. Follow signs toward Los Alamos and Bandelier National Monument. After approximately 7 miles, the road crosses the Rio Grande and an exit to Espanola. Proceed up a long hill on a divided highway until the road divides with Highway 502 going to Los Alamos and Highway 4 to White Rock. Drive toward White Rock on Highway 4 for approximately 0.7 mile until it is possible to pull off in a large parking area on the right. Use this area to turn around and head back east toward Santa Fe on Highway 502. This is necessary because it is impossible to cross over the divided highway when approaching from the east. Drive 0.9 mile back and park as soon as possible alongside a fence when the guard rail on the right ends. The cliffs are less than 100 feet away through the fence to the south.

Cross the fence and walk south to the top of the crag's North Wall. A trail goes west (turn right on the cliff top) and drops down into the canyon. Go left or downstream about 50 feet to access the first routes. Hiking time to the cliff base is about five minutes.

To reach The Y from Los Alamos, drive east on Highway 502 to its junction with

Highway 4. Continue east and park approximately 0.9 mile after the exit to Santa Fe.

North Wall

1. Six Pack Crack (5.11b/c) No topo. Thin crack and face climbing through the roof. Closed to climbing.

2. Spiral Staircase (5.11b) No topo. A crack just to the right of #1. Closed to climbing.

3. Ringjam (5.10d/11a) No topo. Up to the right side of the roof, then slightly left and up. Closed to climbing.

4. Ratshit Cave (5.10b/c) No topo. Left around the roof. Closed to climbing.

5. Batshit Roof (5.10+) Go either left or right at the roof system.

6. Triple Overhang (5.10) The hard start can be avoided by entering from the right to make a 5.8 climb.

7. Open Book (5.8+) One of the most popular climbs at The Y. Thin jams at the start defeat many attempts.

8. Broadway (5.8) Start to the right of #8.3 and traverse left at the ledge.

8.1. Hard Start (to Broadway) (5.11+) An arête problem. No protection, best to toprope.

8.2. Less Hard Start (to Broadway) (5.9) The thin vertical crack to the right of the arête.

8.3. Inside Dihedral (5.8) Join *Broadway* after moving right, then back left or join #9.

9. The Notch (5.10c/d). Same start as *Broadway*. Difficult moves straight up from the right side of the ledge.

10. El Queso Grande (5.12d/13a) Difficult moves to the left of the roof to the left of *Wisconsin*.

11. Wisconsin (5.10-) An area classic and highly recommended. Difficult to protect, generally toproped.

12. The Nose (5.12a X) Difficult to protect, missing hangers on face above the roof. It's usually toproped. The direct start is harder.

13. Beastie Crack (5.9+) A thin crack up to a small roof with ground fall potential. Protect the lower part with TCUs, but it's best not to fall. Go left or right after the roof.

14. Herb's Roof (5.9) Excellent route. Up and over the roof to the face above.

15. Original Open Book (5.8) Go right under the roof.

16. The Three Mothers The common start for all the *Mothers*. **16a. Left Mother**

(5.10c/d) Excellent steep jamming. **16b. Middle Mother** (5.10a/b) Fun climbing. The easiest of the *Mothers*. **16c. Right Mother** (5.11b/c) Good practice route. The hardest *Mother* with thin jams.

17. IDBI Wall (5.11b/c X) Best to toprope.

18. The Ramp (5.9) Go straight up through the overhang for a harder finish.

19. Porter Route (5.7) Easy jams on the right side of the roof.

20. Monster (5.10) Seldom led. Good jams to the top.

21. Hessing Route (5.7) An area favorite. Easy to toprope, easy to lead.

22. Lizard Man (5.8 X) Best to toprope.

South Wall

23. Cavemantle (aka Heel Hook and Apeshit) (5.10a/b) Heel hook the roof, then jam the crack above. Hard to protect first moves; easy to install anchors at top for toprope. The climb just to the left is a 5.12+ toprope problem.

24. Black Mantel (5.10 X) Good toprope problem.

25. Twin Cracks (5.7+) Wires and small gear protect two finger cracks. A popular toprope problem.

26. Little Roof (5.7) Hard for its grade under the roof.

THE DUNGEON

■ O V E R V I E W

The Dungeon, tucked into a small canyon just west of Los Alamos, is a small but good climbing area with lots of difficult sport routes on several steep cliffs. The canyon's cool environment with a gurgling stream and enormous ponderosa pines make it a premier summer sport crag—something of a rarity in New Mexico. Routes on the grid-bolted cliffs, a popular venue for locals, offer hard climbing. Most routes are 5.12 and 5.13, with only a handful of easier lines that are of lesser appeal.

The cliffs are composed of rhyolite, a volcanic rock that formed from cooling volcanic ash spewed from a nearby volcano. The soft rock, better than the tuff rock on Pajarito Plateau to the east, is generally hard with plentiful holds. Most routes, established on the best rock, are between 25 and 60 feet long, well bolted, and have or share lowering anchors.

Summer is the best season to climb at The Dungeon. Expect generally cool temperatures, plenty of shade, and afternoon thunderstorms. Autumn is also good, although the crag is chilly in the morning. Spring is variable, depending on snowpack and weather systems. Winter brings snow and cold.

Climbing History

Development at The Dungeon began in 1995. Luke Laeser, Tim Fairfield, Walt Wehner, Peter Gram, Jean Delataillade, Carlo Torres, Rich and Ed Strang, and other climbers were active through the late nineties. Development, except for the installation of some directional bolts on some climbs, has essentially ceased and little rock remains for future first ascents.

Rack and Descent

A Dungeon rack includes twelve to fifteen quickdraws and a 165-foot rope. If you're doing any of the full-length routes on the Main Wall, you might want to use a 200-foot cord. Descent off all routes is by lowering from two-bolt anchors.

Not all bolts are shown on the topos.

Trip Planning Information

Area description: The Dungeon, a collection of small rhyolite cliffs offering a good selection of difficult sport climbs in a pleasant setting.

Location: North-central New Mexico. West of Los Alamos.

Camping: The best public campsites are in Juniper Campground at Bandelier National Monument off Highway 4. The campground offers pleasant sites with water and restrooms. The fee area is open year-round on a first-come, first-served basis and quickly fills in summer. Primitive camping is available on nearby Santa Fe National Forest public lands. Find a forest road like the ski hill road or others and camp off the road in the forest. Fires are definitely not recommended since the area is very dry and susceptible to forest fires.

Climbing season: Spring through fall. Summer offers the best climbing weather with shade and relatively cool temperatures. September and October are also excellent. Spring is variable and winter is almost impossible with snow and cold temperatures.

Restrictions and access issues: The crag lies on land administered by the Santa Fe National Forest.

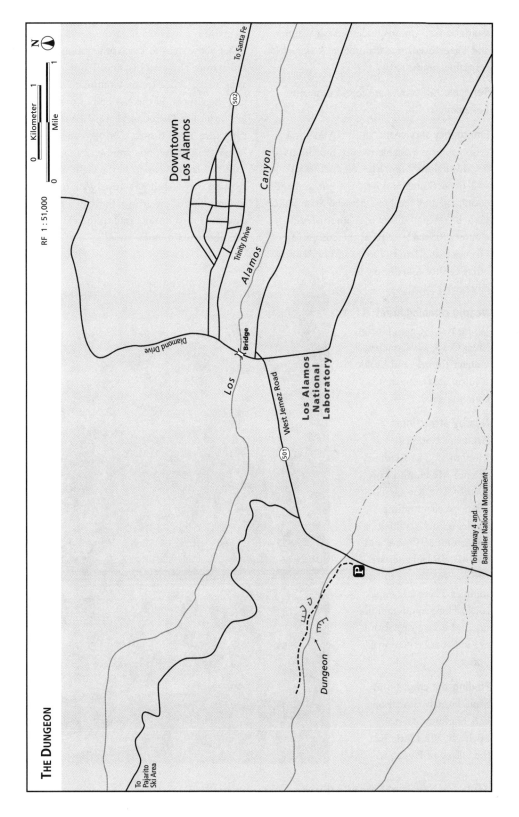

THE DUNGEON

RF 1 : 51,000

Kilometer
0   1

Mile
0   1

N

To
Pajarito
Ski Area

Los

Downtown
Los Alamos

Diamond Drive

Bridge

Trinity Drive

Alamos

Canyon

To Santa Fe

502

501

West Jemez Road

Los Alamos
National
Laboratory

Dungeon

P

To Highway 4 and
Bandelier National Monument

Guidebooks: A mini-guide by Walt Wehner and Theo Takeda was featured in *Rock and Ice* magazine, June 2000.

Services: All services are found in nearby Los Alamos.

Emergency services: Call 911. A medical crisis center is available twenty-four hours a day throughout New Mexico. Call (800) 432–6866. Search and rescue is initiated and coordinated by the New Mexico State Police (505–827–9300). The Los Alamos Medical Center (505–662–4201) at the corner of Diamond and Trinity Drives in Los Alamos offers twenty-four-hour emergency care.

Nearby climbing areas:
White Rock Crags, Cochiti Mesa Crags, Las Conchas, Gilman Tunnels, and Diablo Canyon are the nearest climbing areas.

Nearby attractions:
Bandelier National Monument, The Bradbury Science Museum in Los Alamos. The Rio Grande offers excellent rafting, canoeing, and kayaking opportunities. Private and commercial launches are best in early spring to late summer. There are ample backpacking, mountain biking, and hiking opportunities in Santa Fe National Forest.

Finding the crag: From Santa Fe, drive north on U.S. Highway 285 to Highway 502 a little past the village of Pojoaque.

Access this same turn from the north on US 285. Follow signs to Los Alamos about 35 miles away. The road becomes Trinity Drive as you enter Los Alamos. Continue 2.3 miles past the airport on the east end of town, to a left turn onto Diamond Drive. Take the first right turn after crossing a bridge onto West Jemez Road. Continue another 2 miles and park in a large turnout on the right just after crossing over a shallow arroyo. Walk north toward the shallow arroyo, through a metal gate, then up a distinct trail to the climbing area about ten minutes away.

Trash Tower

Trash Tower is a small semidetached pillar on the right side of the trail just before the main cliff area. It has a few good routes, including some of the easier ones at the area.

1. Court Jester (5.9) No topo. Located a short distance right of Trash Tower. 3 bolts to 2-bolt anchor.

2. Garbageman/Weenies Go Like This (5.11b) Ascend the overhanging west face. 3 bolts to 2-bolt shared anchor.

3. Trash Compactor (5.12b) Shares anchors and last bolt with #2. 4 bolts to 2-bolt anchor.

4. Magic Carpet Ride (5.10a) Not recommended, seldom climbed. 3 bolts to 2-bolt anchor.

5. Trash Disco (5.10b) Recommended. Climb the corner system. 4 bolts to 2-bolt anchor.

6. Garbageboy (5.9) A fun moderate. 3 bolts to 2-bolt anchor.

Fin Wall

This wall is located up the gully right of Black Wall. Not illustrated.

7. Pleasure Cruise (5.10c) A rare low-angle face. 6 bolts to 2-bolt anchor.

Black Wall

Black Wall is the obvious black wall on the right side of the trail and opposite Main Wall. Routes are described from left to right.

8. The Reverend Mr. Black (5.11d) On the far left side of the formation. 7 bolts to 2-bolt anchor.

9. Rampage (5.11a) Up the middle of the face. 6 bolts to 2-bolt anchor.

45-Degree Boulder

East Face

This large overhanging boulder sits in the stream just past Main Wall. Its two short faces have a good assortment of difficult and bouldery routes. Routes are listed from left to right.

10. Xena: Warrior Princess

(5.10d) Climb the water streak, then move right. 4 bolts to 2-bolt anchor.

11. Dragonslayer (5.13c)

Difficult climbing up an overhanging face to a thin slab. 5 bolts to 2-bolt anchor.

12. Honkey Serial Killer

(5.13d) A harder start to *Dragonslayer*. Shares last 3 bolts and anchors. 5 bolts to 2-bolt shared anchor.

13. Beastmaster (5.12c)

Classic climb up the arête on the north end of the boulder. 5 bolts to 2-bolt anchor.

West Face

14. Toss No Moss (5.12a) No topo. Seldom climbed. On the far left side of the boulder. Luke Laeser says this is the worst route he ever put up. 2 bolts to 2-bolt anchor.

15. Tweak Freak (5.12c) Badly bolted and not recommended. 3 bolts to 2-bolt anchor.

16. Slope-a Dope (5.12a) Good route. Has its own anchors, but it's better to clip *The Muscle Hustle* anchor.

17. The Muscle Hustle (5.13a) Using the crack makes the climb 5.12b. 4 bolts to 2-bolt anchor.

18. Tendon Bender (5.12c) Sustained difficulty up a steep face. 4 bolts to 2-bolt anchor.

19. Moon-boot Mission (5.12c) Start on *Tendon Bender,* then right at third bolt to link up with *Crimp Chimp.* The linkup from *Tendon Bender* to *Crimp Chimp* is 5.12b.

20. Crimp Chimp (5.12a) One of the best climbs here. 5 bolts to 2-bolt anchor.

21. Perverse Traverse (5.11c) 3 bolts to 2-bolt anchor.

Main Wall

The area's longest and most popular routes ascend this impressive northeast-facing wall. The climbing is characterized by strenuous pulling on edges on vertical and overhanging stone. High water sometimes limits access to the routes. Routes are listed from left to right.

22. Phrenology (5.11b) No topo. Not recommended. 6 bolts to 2-bolt anchor.

23. Meltdown (5.12d) No topo. Climbs the narrow overhang left of a chimney. 4 bolts to 2-bolt anchor.

24. Battering Ram (5.11c) No topo. On the far left side of the Main Wall. The start traverses right on unattractive rock to *Evil Alchemist*'s last bolt. Shares 2-bolt anchor with *Evil Alchemist*.

25. Evil Alchemist (5.13a) Shares a common start with *Siege Warfare* and *Sissy Warfare*. After second bolt, climb up left. 7 bolts to 2-bolt anchor.

26. Siege Warfare (5.12d) Climb straight up to anchors below the roof. 7 bolts to 2-bolt anchor.

27. Sissy Warfare (5.11d) Short variation to *Siege Warfare*. After 35 feet, lower from a lowering carabiner on the fourth bolt of *Siege Warfare*.

28. Dragon's Lair (5.13b) A 4-bolt extension to *Siege Warfare* that cranks over the upper roof. 2-bolt anchor.

29. Against Nature aka **Peter's Route** (5.12b) Great route. Straight up to anchors below the large upper roof. 6 bolts to 2-bolt anchor.

30. Death Drives a Stick (5.13b/c) This 4-bolt extension route climbs above #29's anchors over the widest part of the upper roof to a 2-bolt anchor.

31. Excalibur (5.12c) Classic. Steep at the start and finish. 6 bolts to 2-bolt anchor.

32. Gangland (5.12c) Classic. Sustained steep climbing to the cliff top. Climb to *Excalibur*'s belay station under the large roof. Traverse right and turn the lip of the roof, then climb a slab to the highest set of anchors. 5 bolts to 2-bolt anchor.

33. Loose Cannon (5.13a/b) Straight up and over the large upper roof near its right-hand end. 9 bolts to 2-bolt anchor. *The Catapult* (5.13a) is an alternate start just right and rejoins *Loose Cannon* at its fifth bolt.

34. Moat Jump (5.12a) A must-do climb and one of the area's best routes. Cross the small stream, then climb the steep overhanging face. 8 bolts to 2-bolt anchor.

35. Moat Pump (5.12b/c) Recommended. 8 bolts to 2-bolt shared anchor.

36. Rogue Warrior (5.12b) Start about 10 feet right of *Moat Pump*. 8 bolts to *Moat Pump* anchors.

37. Couch Warrior (5.12a) Climb the narrow face right of *Rogue Warrior*. 7 bolts to 2-bolt anchor.

38. Castle Greyskull (V4) Pick a direction and traverse the base of the wall.

LAS CONCHAS

■ OVERVIEW

Cool summer temperatures, easily accessible rock, good climbing, and wonderful mountain scenery all make Las Conchas a popular climbing area. The area's cliffs, scattered above a pastoral, grassy valley at 8,400 feet, are composed of rhyolite, a volcanic rock spewed millions of years ago during violent eruptions of the Jemez Caldera immediately to the north. The routes, mostly bolted sport climbs, range from 30 to 60 feet in height and 5.8 to 5.13c in difficulty. Nine different crags spread out for a mile along the East Fork of the Jemez River.

Most of the cliffs are accessed from the parking area for the East Fork Trailhead on the north side of Highway 4. The trail heads northwest into the canyon following the lovely East Fork of the Jemez River. Immediately east of the parking area is Cattle Call Wall, a prominent cliff with ten routes. Several bolted lines also ascend this popular instructional and toprope crag. Roadside Attraction, with a single route, is located just east of Cattle Call Wall. The other crags are encountered by walking northwest or downstream from the main parking area west of Cattle Call Wall and include Gateway Rock, Chilly Willy Wall, Love Shack Area, Gallery Wall, Dream Tower, The Sponge, Botched Rock, and The Leaning Tower.

The area is popular with anglers, day-hikers, mountain bikers, and campers. Climbers should adopt a low-key approach if developing new routes or when climbing in general. Future Forest Service management of the area will certainly be influenced by all of our actions, so please tread lightly in this fragile area.

Climbing History

Most of the area routes were established by numerous local climbers including Bob D'Antonio, Cam Burns, Mike Schillaci, Chris Vandiver, Mike Baker, and Mike McGill in the early 1990s. Juan Lopez is a more recent activist. The area has not seen much new route development in recent years.

Trip Planning Information

Area description: Las Conchas, a small climbing area tucked into the Jemez River's upper canyon, offers many sport routes in the heart of the Jemez Mountains.

Location: North-central New Mexico. In the Jemez Mountains about 15 miles west of Los Alamos.

Camping: Las Conchas Campground, on the north side of Highway 4 just east of the climbing area parking lot, is popular and often crowded. Five additional campgrounds are found in the immediate area. Free primitive campsites are south toward Cochiti Mesa along Forest Road 289 from its junction with Highway 4 about 7 miles east of Las Conchas. Good camping is also found at Bandelier National Monument farther east near Los Alamos.

Climbing season: Spring to fall. Las Conchas, at 8,400 feet elevation, is primarily a May-through-October area. Climbing is best during the warm summer months. The high elevation limits climbing on all but the warmest winter days. Watch for heavy thunderstorms on summer afternoons.

Restrictions and access issues: Las Conchas lies within land administered by the U.S. Forest Service. The area is also popular with anglers, hikers, and campers. Use discretion and good

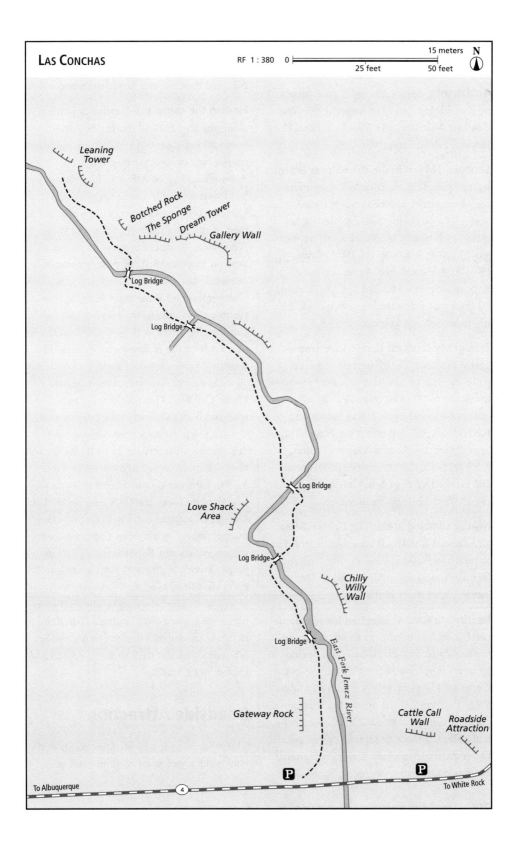

judgment when climbing to favorably represent climbing activities to other user groups.

Guidebooks: *Sport Climbing in New Mexico* by Randall Jett and Matt Samet, 1991. *Rock Climbing New Mexico & Texas* by Dennis R. Jackson, Falcon Press, 1996.

Services: No services in the immediate area. Jemez Springs, 15 miles to the west, offers fuel, a restaurant, and bed-and-breakfast options. Good dining and commercial hot spring bath houses are found there. An excellent choice is Jemez Spring Bath House, (505) 829–3303. A free option and local favorite is Spence Hot Springs. Los Alamos, 20 miles east, offers full services including gas, groceries, and lodging.

Emergency services: Dial 911 for emergency assistance. The nearest phone is in Jemez Springs or Los Alamos, each approximately 15 to 20 miles away. Search and rescue is conducted by St. John's Search and Rescue and coordinated by the New Mexico State Police. Los Alamos Medical Center, (505) 662–4201, at the corner of Diamond and Trinity Drives in Los Alamos, offers twenty-four-hour emergency care.

Nearby climbing areas: The Cochiti Mesa Crags and White Rock Crags are nearby. The Sandias and Palomas Peak are approximately 50 miles southeast by Albuquerque. Gilman Tunnels is 20 miles south.

Nearby attractions: Excellent hiking, mountain biking, and fishing are found in the surrounding area. Popular Spence Hot Springs is located 1.5 miles west from the village of La Cueva off Highway 4. Park near a sign advising NO PARKING AFTER 10:00 P.M., walk down, cross the river on a log, and hike up a steep trail a short distance to three excellent pools. Other attractions include Bandelier National Monument, Indian ruins, Jemez State Monument, Jemez Pueblo, Rio Grande, San Ildefonso Pueblo, Los Alamos, Valles Caldera National Preserve, and Los Alamos attractions.

Finding the crags: Las Conchas is located along the East Fork of the Jemez River about 20 miles west of Los Alamos and 50 miles north of Albuquerque. From Los Alamos take Highway 501 to Highway 4 and head west toward Jemez Springs. The Las Conchas crags parking area is about 12 miles west of this road junction. From the White Rock area, the easiest route is to continue west on Highway 4. After passing through beautiful Valle Grande Caldera, Las Conchas Campground is on the right (north). Continue 0.5 mile to the parking area just past the river. Park in the paved lot on the north side of the highway and walk northwest or downstream on a good trail to access all rocks except Roadside Attraction and Cattle Call Wall. These rocks are north of the road and 0.25 mile east of the parking area.

To reach the area from Albuquerque, drive north on Interstate 25 to Bernalillo and turn northwest onto Highway 44 to San Ysidro. Turn north onto Highway 4 and follow it to the parking lot 0.5 mile before Las Conchas Campground. Las Conchas is also reached from Cochiti Mesa Crags by continuing north on dirt Forest Road 289 to its junction with Highway 4. Las Conchas is 7 miles west from here.

The trail and the convenient river crossings were washed away during a flash flood in 2004. An evolving trail negotiates the last 0.5 mile down the river to the crags and may require some wading.

Roadside Attraction

This 60-foot rock is located just north of the road and has one route. Park in front of

Cattle Call Wall and walk a short distance to the next rock east (right). Not illustrated.

1. Roadside Attraction (5.12a/b) Bring wires, a #2.5 Friend, and clip the bolt. Poor rock and runout after the roof.

Cattle Call Wall

Cattle Call Wall, bordering the highway, is the large rock east of the main parking area and fronted by a level grassy meadow. Park in front of the rock on the wide highway shoulder if this is your destination. This is a good parking alternative if the main lot is full. The wall is a popular instructional toprope area and can be crowded on week-ends. Routes are sport, trad, and toprope. The far left side has some leads plus a set of oddly placed bolts for top anchors. Be circumspect when using these bolts. Routes are described from right to left.

2. Unknown (5.9) One of the cliff's best lines and easy to rig for a toprope. 4 bolts to 2-bolt anchor with Springer hangers.

3. Cowpies for Breakfast (5.10d) One of the original bolted routes on the cliff. Good climb but difficult for its grade. 6 bolts to 2-bolt anchor.

4. Unknown (5.6) Popular moderate sport route. 4 bolts to 2-bolt anchor.

5. Cow Flop Crack (5.8) A longtime favorite. Straight up the crack near the cliff's center.

6. Unknown (5.7) Popular. 3 bolts to 2-bolt anchor.

7. Pie In Your Eye (5.9) Difficult opening moves go straight up. It's easier to get onto the route from either side. 6 bolts to 2-bolt anchor.

8. Cud for Lulu (5.8) Toprope problem.

9. Bovine Inspiration (5.9) Toprope problem. Difficult opening moves, then easier climbing to a ledge below a scooped overhang. The moves to surmount the overhang are challenging but easier if you can reach buckets above.

10. Ow Now (5.11a) Located on the attractive steep slab on the far left side of the cliff. Gear route. 2-bolt anchor. There are multiple possibilities for toproping and leading in this area.

Gateway Rock

Gateway Rock, alongside the riverside trail, is the first cliff encountered when walking north on the trail. The crag offers several fine routes, although the rock is somewhat unattractive.

The best choices are the two long bolted climbs. Toprope anchors are in place for the east ridge.

11. Woof Toof Noof Roof (5.10d) 4 bolts to 2-bolt anchor.

12. Drive by Shooting (5.10a/b) Difficult at the bottom. Just around the corner on the east face. 6 bolts plus a fixed nut to 2-bolt anchor.

13. Road (5.10c/d) Just right of *Drive by Shooting*. Difficult at the bottom. 7 bolts to 2-bolt anchor.

Chilly Willy Wall

Chilly Willy Wall is located on the river's east side about 600 feet from the parking lot. Access usually involves wading. Nestled among the pines, this area is often bypassed on the way to The Sponge area. Several easy-to-locate, good routes and hidden camping spots are found here. Routes are described from right to left. Not illustrated.

14. Turkey Sandwich (5.8) Seldom climbed. Scramble to the top of a detached low-angle rock on the extreme southern (right) edge of the cliff. Climb up and right to a short chimney, then your choice to the top.

15. Tasty Freeze (5.9 R) Start 25 feet left of *Turkey Sandwich*. 3 bolts plus wires and camming units to 3.5 inches protect a steep face and crack.

16, 17, and 18. Unknown These three routes are located on a 30-foot boulder leaning against the main wall left of the cliff's south end. All are moderate routes that share the same anchor.

19. Wet Willies (5.11b/c) Start on the main wall behind the 30-foot boulder's left side. Initial section is mossy and sometimes wet. Camming units through hand-size protect the lower section to a 6-bolt face.

20. Donkey Show (5.10c) Located 150 feet north (left) of *Wet Willies* on the extreme northern edge of the rock. Face climb to a difficult clip, then climb past 2 more bolts that bracket a thin crack to a 2-bolt anchor. TCUs and camming units are helpful.

Love Shack Area

A couple good bouldery routes ascend the overhanging base of a large wall above the left side of the river near the second crossing. These climbs can be difficult to access because of the changing river channel along the base of the cliff. Routes are described from left to right.

21. Happy Entrails (5.12d) Start in the left circular depression and climb up and out toward a bush. Seldom done. 3 bolts to 2-bolt anchor.

22. Unknown (5.12+) Start in the right circular depression. Pull over a roof and climb the short face above. 3 bolts to 2-bolt anchor.

Gallery Wall

Gallery Wall is a pillar high above the river's north bank. After the fifth river crossing, backtrack upriver along the north bank (passing The Sponge and Dream Tower) to the base of a broken wall. Do an easy access pitch to a bushy ledge below the pillar. Routes are described from right to left.

23. Presumed to Be Modern (5.12a/b) 5 bolts to 2-bolt anchor.

24. Across the View (5.11d) Climb a black streak up a blunt prow left of #23. 4 bolts to 2-bolt anchor.

24.1. Unknown (?) No topo. Located on the river's north side about 500 feet east (right) of #24. This is the first rock right of a barbwire fence that crosses the river. The route ascends a short overhanging face. 3 bolts to 2-bolt anchor.

Dream Tower

Dream Tower is a tall buttress looming above the grassy meadows along the river's north

bank. Some fine, long routes ascend the tower to a high anchor.

25. Animal Magnetism (5.11d) On the tower's right side. Loose in spots. 6 bolts to 2-bolt anchor.

26. Sanctuarium (5.12b/c) After climbing past 4 bolts, move left to join #27. 8 bolts to 2-bolt anchor.

27. East Coast Dreams (5.11b/c) Direct line up the tower's left side. Start behind a boulder. 6 bolts to 2-bolt anchor.

28. Hail Dancer (5.9) 60 feet left of *East Coast Dreams.* Start left of a roof. Climb a low-angle face to a bolt, then crank an arête to a 3-bolt anchor. TCUs and gear up to 3 inches. 1 bolt to 3-bolt anchor.

The Sponge

The Sponge, a south-facing cliff with some of the canyon's best rock, is popular and offers some excellent climbing. Expect lots of pockets and steep rock. The cliff sits above the last river crossing about a mile from the parking. Routes are described from right to left.

29. Hollywood Tim (5.9+) Quality climbing up the cliff's right side. Start in a crack or face climb left of the crack to bolt 1. Deceptively difficult pocket climbing and pinches up the steep face. 3 bolts to 2-bolt anchor.

30. Mad Dogs and Englishmen (5.10b) Clip the first 2 bolts of *Hollywood Tim,* then crank up left past a small roof. Continue up right on easier rock to #29's anchors. 4 bolts to 2-bolt anchor.

31. Unknown (5.10+) Start left of *Hollywood Tim.* Pull up steep pocketed rock to a 1-bolt anchor. Lower from here or continue up right to *Hollywood Tim*'s anchors. 4 bolts to 1-bolt anchor.

32. Pumpin' Huecos (5.10d/11a) Excellent and popular. May be the area's best route. A pumpy route up a slightly overhung pocketed buttress in the middle of the crag. Crux is above bolt 2. 4 bolts to a 2-bolt anchor.

33. Unknown (5.11a) Start 30 feet left of the large overhang near the ground left of *Pumpin' Huecos.* Climb a steep face right of a wide crack. 5 bolts to 2-bolt anchor.

34. Sal's Neuroses (5.10d/.11) Located on Botched Rock, a small outcrop 60 feet left of The Sponge. Short (30 feet) with quality moves. 4 bolts to 2-bolt anchor.

The Leaning Tower

The Leaning Tower, the canyon's largest cliff, offers its hardest and longest routes.

Continue 700 feet downstream from The Sponge to a dramatic south-facing outcrop split by a long overhanging crack system.

35. The Mean Leaner

(A2) The central crack that splits the tower. Placing and removing pitons will probably destroy this fragile crack system. If aiding, consider climbing it without pitons.

36. Mainliner (5.13c) A

sustained, pumpy, and technical 100-foot line up the tower's left side. First ascent in 1995 by Jean DeLataillade. Start left of *The Mean Leaner.* Expect hard face climbing, laybacking, and thin jamming. 12 bolts to 2-bolt anchor set back from the top edge. Bring some TCUs for extra protection. **Descent:** Rappel with two ropes.

37. Unknown (5.12b/c)

Left around the corner from *Mainliner.* 5 bolts to 2-bolt anchor.

38. Lichen Attack Crack (5.10b) No topo.

Seldom climbed, though quality. An obvious, attractive right-facing dihedral 40 feet left of The Leaning Tower with 80 feet of hand jams. **Rack:** Wired nuts and cams up to 3.5 inches plus extras for the belay. Go left to rappel down a loose gully off a tree.

39. Project (5.12b/c) No topo. On the arête

left of *Lichen Attack Crack.*

40. Unknown No topo. No information

available. Start 35 feet left of #38. Climb the left side of the buttress. 5 bolts to 2-bolt anchor.

COCHITI MESA CRAGS

■ OVERVIEW

The Cochiti Mesa Crags, a collection of cliff bands rimming Cochiti and Eagle Canyons on the southeast edge of the Jemez Mountains, is one of New Mexico's oldest and most popular sport climbing venues. Besides offering a multitude of excellent bolted routes, the area has easy approaches to the cliffs, stunning views across the Rio Grande valley, and a pleasant setting of canyons and mesas sheathed in a ponderosa pine forest. The most popular crags are Eagle Canyon, Cochiti Mesa, Cacti Cliff, and Disease Wall. Some other lesser known and seldom visited cliffs are also in the area. A smattering of fine crack climbs are also found on the four main crags. The best concentration of these cracks is on The Dihedrals wall at Cochiti Mesa.

Cochiti Mesa is characterized by pocket climbing up vertical faces and steep arêtes on sunny, open cliffs. The routes, ranging in difficulty from 5.8 to 5.13, ascend cliffs up to 80 feet high on good quality rhyolite or welded tuff rock. The bolts on all the Cochiti Mesa Crags come in a variety of sizes and types, with some obviously better than others. Many of the original bolts have been replaced for safer climbing, although you should always use caution when trusting a single bolt and in your route selection. Welded tuff is a very soft rock with a thin, hard surface coating that actually makes climbing feasible. Effective bolts here need to be the largest and longest available sizes and placed in well-drilled holes. Unwelded cold shuts, while being replaced, are still used as lowering anchors for some climbs. Use these for lowering only. On many routes it is possible to back up these anchors. This is especially important for safe toproping.

Chipping, drilling pockets, and other hold enhancement techniques were used at many of the crags on Cochiti Mesa. Some of these created holds were severely botched. This guide attempts to omit any route where such activity has obviously occurred. Erosion problems at Eagle Canyon and Cochiti Mesa are a continuing issue. Please tread lightly in all areas and use existing trails whenever possible.

These horizontal cliff bands are composed of the more densely welded parts of the Bandelier Tuff formation, which were deposited during periodic eruptions of the nearby Jemez Volcano. The immense volcano, roughly the same size as Mount St. Helens before its 1980 eruption, spewed out more than one hundred times more material. The last of this volcanic activity occurred in relatively recent geologic time, when huge eruptions some five million years ago blanketed the Pajarito Plateau, including the Cochiti Mesa area, with deep layers of ash. The beautiful circular bowl of Jemez Caldera or Valle Grande, a basin that formed after the collapse of the volcano, is all that remains of this once-massive stratovolcano.

Some confusion exists regarding the area's name. The early route developers didn't pinpoint the exact location of the various cliffs and applied the name Cochiti Mesa to the area. The climbing is on the rims of Cochiti and Eagle Canyons. The real Cochiti Mesa is identified on USGS maps as a few miles farther west from the climbing area. Don't let this confuse you if you use these maps.

Climbing History

Development of the Cochiti Mesa Crags began in 1987 in response to the closure by the Tribal Council of Cochiti Pueblo of the

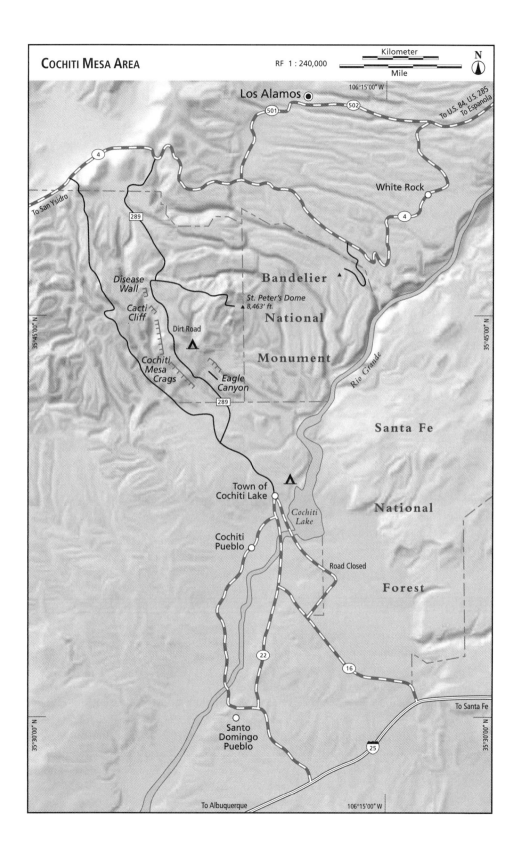

Cochiti Mesa Area

RF 1 : 240,000

Kilometer

Mile

N

106°15'00" W

Los Alamos

501

502

To U.S. 84, U.S. 285
To Espanola

4

To San Ysidro

White Rock

4

289

35°45'00" N

Disease Wall

Cacti Cliff

Dirt Road

Bandelier

St. Peter's Dome
▲ 8,463' ft.

National

Cochiti Mesa Crags

Eagle Canyon

289

Monument

Rio Grande

35°45'00" N

Santa Fe

Town of
Cochiti Lake

Cochiti Lake

National

Cochiti
Pueblo

Road Closed

Forest

22

16

To Santa Fe

Santo
Domingo
Pueblo

25

35°30'00" N

35°30'00" N

To Albuquerque

106°15'00" W

nearby popular Cochiti Canyon climbing area along the Rio Grande. Locals had long enjoyed the vast amount of solid basalt cliffs found there, and with its closure were forced to look elsewhere for vertical adventures. The softer rhyolite rock found in what was to be called the Cochiti Mesa area was first visited in the 1970s, when many of the cracks at The Dihedrals were first climbed, including the classic *Apprentice* by Mark Hesse, Peter Prandoni, and Mike Roybal. Ken Sims and others were active in the area through the 1980s. *Bookworm,* one of New Mexico's hardest sustained crack lines, was completed by Ken Sims in 1989.

The steep, unprotected faces at Cochiti Mesa were largely ignored until rappel-bolting and other sport climbing techniques were introduced to New Mexico. Early pioneers include Todd Skinner, John Duran, Ed Romback, Tom Wezwick, Lee Sheftel, Doug Couleur, Adam Read, Jean DeLataillade, Doug Pandorf, and Tom Kalakay. French climber Jean DeLataillade's ascent of *Touch Monkey* ushered the 5.13 grade into the area in 1989. Since those halcyon days of the late eighties and early nineties, climbing has been at a hiatus here with little new route activity and fewer climbers that visit. Now it's possible to come on a weekend and have the whole area to yourself.

Rack and Descent

A rack of twelve quickdraws, sometimes augmented by wired stoppers and TCUs, is sufficient for most routes. If you want to jam any of the crack routes, bring a trad rack that includes camming units up to 4 inches. Place all your cams as deep as possible in the crack and take the time to put in lots of gear for extra protection in this soft rock area. Pieces have been known to rip out with a fall's

impact. Most crack routes also require gear for the belay anchors and a rappel or walk-off descent. Descent for all sport routes is by lowering from bolt anchors.

Not all bolts are shown on the topos.

Trip Planning Information

Area description: Cochiti Mesa Crags offer excellent sport climbing routes from 5.8 to 5.13c on 30- to 80-foot-high welded tuff cliff bands on the rim of Cochiti and Eagle Canyons.

Location: North-central New Mexico. On the southeast flank of the Jemez Mountains and northwest of Cochiti Lake and Interstate 25.

Camping: Undeveloped campsites are found near the climbing areas along Forest Road 289. Water and facilities are not available. Avoid camping on Cochiti Pueblo land south of the Santa Fe National Forest boundary. Excellent developed sites in scenic Bandelier National Monument are approximately 20 miles to the northeast. Developed sites with water, restrooms, and showers are at Cochiti Dam, administered by the U.S. Army Corps of Engineers.

Climbing season: The Cochiti Mesa Crags are at a 7,000-foot elevation. Climbing is best from spring to late fall. Climbing is possible on warmer winter days, although the road may be impassable due to snow and mud. The south-facing cliffs provide warm afternoons and cool mornings. Eagle Canyon's north-facing cliffs are a good choice on hot summer days.

Restrictions and access issues: All crags lie within Santa Fe National Forest. Eagle Canyon is included in the Dome Wilderness Area, which prohibits motorized vehicles. Limited parking can be problematic on busy days at Cochiti Mesa and Eagle Canyon. Heavy use of the popular North Cliffs at Cochiti Mesa has seriously impacted the area. Please leave little evidence of your visit by picking up all trash, including cigarette butts and mylar wrappers; following existing trails; and not making any fires. Forest Road 289 is closed by gates near its northern entrance off Highway 4 and at the forest boundary on the southern end during and after wet conditions. When open, the road is always rough although generally passable by high-clearance vehicles. Check on current road conditions with the Jemez Ranger District (505–829–3535).

Guidebooks: *Rock Climbing New Mexico & Texas* by Dennis R. Jackson, Falcon Press, 1996. Crags in the Cochiti Mesa area are also covered in the out-of-print *Sport Climbing in New Mexico* by Randal Jett and Matt Samet, 1991. A guide to Cochiti Mesa appeared in *Climbing Magazine* #133. Cacti Cliff is covered in *Rock and Ice* #40 and *Climbing Magazine* #124.

Services: A convenience store with snacks, groceries, liquor, and auto fuel is located in the Town of Cochiti Lake. All services are available in Santa Fe and Albuquerque.

Emergency services: Call 911 for emergency assistance. The nearest phone is located at the convenience store in the Town of Cochiti Lake. Search and rescue services are conducted by the St. John's Search and Rescue and initiated by the State Police, (505) 827–9300. The New Mexico Medical Crisis Center, (800) 432–6866, is available twenty-four hours a day throughout New Mexico. The nearest hospital is St. Vincent Hospital, (505) 983–3361, in Santa Fe.

Nearby climbing areas: White Rock Crags, The Dungeon, Las Conchas, Diablo Canyon, Coxcomb Crag, Sandia Mountains, Gilman Tunnels, and Palomas Peak.

Nearby attractions: Tent Rocks, Cochiti Pueblo, Santo Domingo Pueblo, San Felipe Pueblo, Bandelier National Monument, Jemez State Monument, Jemez Pueblo, Rio Grande, Cochiti Lake, Spence Hot Springs, and good dining and commercial bath houses in Jemez Springs. Santa Fe includes St. Francis Cathedral, San Miguel Mission, Santa Fe Opera, Santa Fe Plaza, and El Rancho de las Golondrinas (preserved Spanish colonial village 15 miles south of Santa Fe). Santa Fe is a world-class destination point with excellent northern New Mexico cuisine, shopping, and museums. Albuquerque attractions include Coronado State Monument, Petroglyphs National Monument, and Sandia Crest and Peak Tram.

Finding the crags: All of the crags are easily reached from the Albuquerque and Santa Fe areas via I–25 or from the north (Los Alamos/White Rock area) via Highway 4 and FR 289. Cochiti Mesa Crags lies within Santa Fe National Forest 20 miles west of Los Alamos and 60 miles north of Albuquerque.

From the south take I–25 north toward Santa Fe and turn north at exit 259 onto Highway 22 toward Santo Domingo Pueblo. Continue approximately 13 miles to the Town of Cochiti Lake.

From the north, take I–25 south toward Albuquerque for about 25 miles and turn right at exit 264 onto Highway 16 toward Cochiti Pueblo. Follow Highway 16 for 8.2 miles to the junction with Highway 22 and turn right toward the Town of Cochiti Lake.

Drive through the Town of Cochiti Lake a short distance to the golf course, then continue 0.9 mile past the golf course to a right onto a dirt road, FR 289. There is a brown wooden building on the left just past the turnoff. This poorly marked road is sometimes signed DOME ROAD TO STATE ROAD 4. Depending on weather conditions, the road can be rough to impassable, although cars with high clearance usually have no problem.

The parking area for Eagle Canyon is approximately 3.4 miles from this turn and 1 mile before the Cochiti Mesa parking area. It is 7.1 miles from the Town of Cochiti Lake to the Cochiti Mesa parking area. Cacti Cliff is located a short distance north of Cochiti Mesa parking lot. Continue a short distance to the Vista Point Overlook; it's not signed, but obvious. A Forest Service gate here is usually locked until mid-April depending on road conditions. Continue 0.5 mile from here to a small parking area on the left or south side of the road by a relatively tall pine tree. Disease Wall parking is located 0.3 mile farther north from the Cacti Cliff parking area. Park here as best you can on either side of the road in small pulloffs. Additional parking, camping, and alternate access to Disease Wall is located a short distance farther north. Refer to each crag's description for specific trail directions to the cliffs from the parking areas.

Eagle Canyon

Eagle Canyon, a smaller version of nearby Cochiti Mesa, offers twenty-eight routes equipped with ⅜-inch bolts and lowering anchors. Many of these routes are now in need of an upgrading retrobolting effort, so select your climbs thoughtfully. Glue-ins would be the best option for this soft rock crag. The routes, up to 80 feet long, ascend vertical welded tuff faces pocked with huecos and pockets. The rock quality here is generally superior to the more popular Cochiti Mesa cliffs. Climbs range in difficulty from 5.9 to 5.13, with many in the 5.10 and 5.11 range. Only limited crack climbing opportunities exist. Most of the lines were established by John Duran, Ed Rombach, and Tom Wezwick in the early 1990s.

Eagle Canyon is Cochiti Mesa's premier summer crag. When all the other area crags are baking under the noon sun, Eagle Canyon's cliffs are cool and shady. The north-facing wall offers welcome relief from the heat-absorbing black basalt at White Rock and the sun-drenched walls farther up the mesa. Expect summer daytime high temperatures in the 70s and 80s with cool nights. Autumn also offers great climbing weather at Eagle Canyon. Winters, however, can be cold and snowy in the shadows. Sunnier south-facing walls on the other crags are better choices on cold days.

A rack of twelve quickdraws and a 165-foot rope is sufficient for most routes. Descent off most routes is from bolt-lowering anchors. If you do top out, it is possible to scramble down the right or west end on the cliff.

Finding the cliff: Follow the above directions to FR 289, which begins on the right 0.9 mile northwest of the Cochiti Golf Course. Drive approximately 3.4 miles on this rough dirt road (high clearance required) to the parking area. Forest Road 289 can also be accessed from the north via Highway 4 approximately 9 miles west of Los Alamos. The parking area is about 9 miles south this way, although on a generally better road.

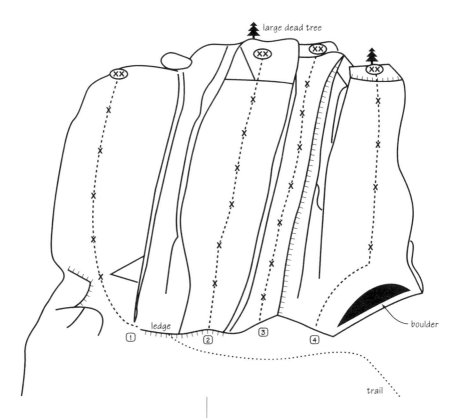

large dead tree

ledge

boulder

trail

From the parking area, which is the trailhead for Dome Wilderness Area, walk northwest or left of Trail 118 to an abandoned flat road overgrown with chamisa plants. This is the original Trail 118 before it was rerouted because of erosion problems. After hiking about 0.3 mile, turn left up Eagle Canyon just before a washed-out area of the trail. An easy-to-follow path leads up through an impressive stand of ponderosa pine to the northeast-facing cliff. The routes are on the left or south side of the canyon. Look for the climber access trail to the base of the routes after about a three-minute hike up the main canyon. Most of the erosion problems in the climbing area are associated with these short spur trails, so use extra care to minimize your impact.

Routes are listed from left (down-canyon) to right (up-canyon) when viewed from the cliff base.

1. Kona (5.12a) The farthest left climb on the cliff. Scramble to end of ledge system about midheight on cliff. Cram your fingers in small pockets up the face. 5 bolts to 2-bolt anchor.

2. Pepto-Dismal (5.11c/d) Excellent pocket climbing up a slightly laid-back face. 6 bolts to 2-bolt anchor.

3. Maalox Moment (5.11a) An area favorite. Small pockets past a large depression. 7 bolts to 2-bolt anchor.

4. Wannabee (5.11c/d) Small pockets and thin face climbing over a small roof. 4 bolts to 2-bolt anchor.

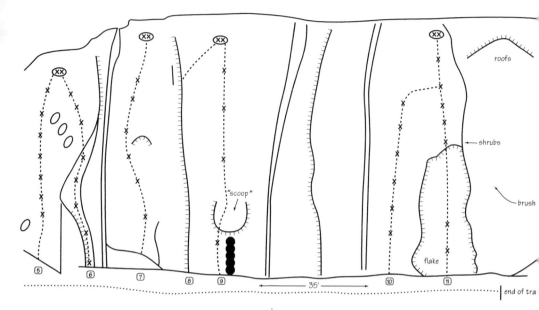

5. Killer Bee (5.9+) The easiest climb in Eagle Canyon. 7 bolts to 2-bolt anchor.

6. Indecent Insertion (5.12b) Start to left of chimney and climb a prow up to an arête. Shares anchors with *Killer Bee.* 8 bolts to 2-bolt anchor.

7. New Wave (5.11c) Start to right of chimney in a scoop, then through several bulges and a steep face. 6 bolts to 2-bolt anchor.

8. Old Wave (5.9) The best of the two crack climbs on the cliff. Perfect hands to the *Tutti Frutti* anchors on the right. Hand-size Friends protect the crack. Use anchors for #9.

9. Tutti Frutti (5.11a) Clip a low bolt and boulder to an hourglass–shaped scoop. Powerful moves up an overhanging arête lead to eyebolt anchors. 4 bolts to 2-bolt anchor.

10. Jug Abuse (5.12a) Start about 35 feet right of *Tutti Frutti* to the right of a chimney and left of a large flake. Shares the last two bolts and anchors with *Turkey Baster.* 8 bolts to 2-bolt anchor.

11. Turkey Baster (5.10c) Start in middle of large flake. Climb past a bush to a 2-bolt anchor. 7 bolts to 2-bolt anchor.

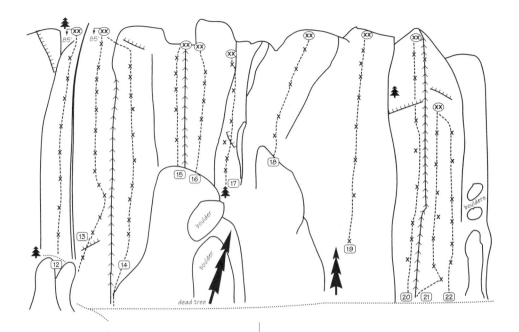

12. Manhattan (5.10c) A popular favorite. If climbing at the previous route area, descend to the access trail going up from the canyon bottom and take the right fork. Scramble up to a sloping ledge and climb a long pitch up the face. A 165-foot rope is required to lower from here. 8 bolts to 2-bolt anchor.

13. Unnamed (5.11b) Quality climbing. 13 bolts to 2-bolt anchor.

14. Unnamed (5.11c) Start at bottom of cliff, then up to a roof and left to anchors for #13. 10 bolts to 2-bolt anchor.

15. The Blade (5.12a/b) Start on a low-angle face to the left of a tree with a dead tree attached to it. 5 bolts to 2-bolt anchor.

16. Unnamed (5.11a) Start on the left wall of an amphitheater. Steep and thin climbing up to the right of an arête. 5 bolts to 2-bolt anchor.

17. Handsome Parish Lady (5.13a) Start high near the upper right side of the amphitheater. 3 bolts protect an upper variation, also 5.13a. 6 bolts to 2-bolt anchor.

18. E Pluribis Cruxi Unum Puripus (5.11b) Excellent. A short face climb right of #17. 5 bolts to 2-bolt anchor.

19. Racist Fantasy (5.12a) Very popular. The black streak protected with 8 bolts to 2-bolt anchor.

20. Accrojovia (5.12b) Recommended. 8 bolts to 2-bolt anchor.

21. Omdulation Fever (5.12c) Recommended. 7 bolts to 2-bolt anchor.

22. Are You Lichen It (5.11c) Recommended. 6 bolts to 2-bolt anchor.

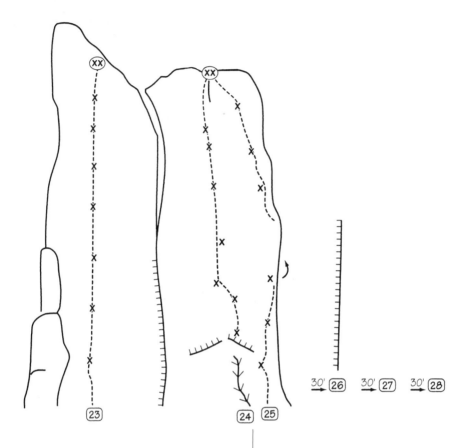

23. Earth Monster (5.11d) Popular and excellent. Sustained thin face climbing over a bulge then up to a 2-bolt anchor. Difficult clips. 7 bolts to 2-bolt anchor.

24. Psycho Thriller (5.11c/d) An area favorite. Difficult between first and third bolt. Sustained climbing but easier up top. 7 bolts to 2-bolt anchor.

25. Banana Rama (5.10c) Very good climbing. First bolt is suspect; #1 Friend in crack adds extra security. Serpentine movements around the arête to a 2-bolt anchor shared with *Psycho Thriller.* 9 bolts to 2-bolt anchor.

26. The Wrong Mr. Wong (5.8) No topo. Located about 40 feet right (west) of *Banana Rama.* Work up the moderately aesthetic hand crack, which offers only mediocre climbing. Belay from gear placements.

27. Ego Maniac (5.11c) No topo. Located about 30 feet right of #26. 6 bolts up a steep face. Gear required for the belay.

28. Mr. Wong's Zipper (5.10b) No topo. Located about 30 feet to the right of #27. A splitter finger crack up to a seam. No bolts on this route. Gear required for the belay.

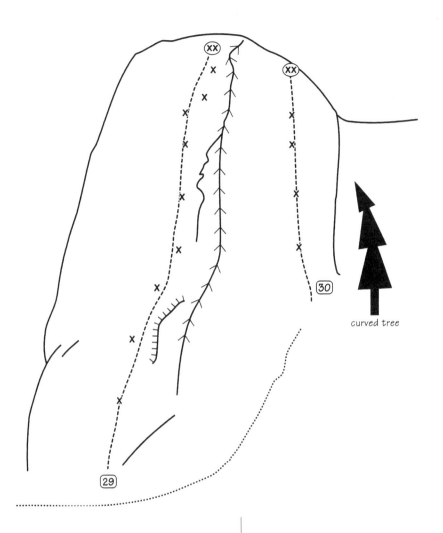

curved tree

29. Bunga Bunga (5.12a) Starts low on the west end of the rock. Quality climbing that angles up right to anchors. 10 bolts to 2-bolt anchor.

30. Didgemaster (5.13c) The area's hardest climb. First ascent by Frenchman Jean DeLataillade in 1991. A short, radically overhanging face left of a curved tree. 4 bolts to 2-bolt anchor.

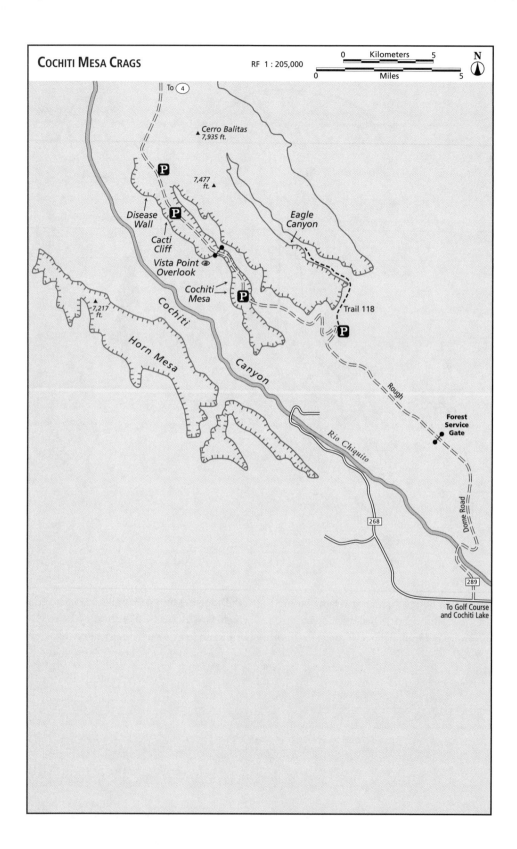

Cochiti Mesa

Cochiti Mesa is the largest, most developed, and most popular of the Cochiti Mesa Crags. It offers more than fifty established routes that range in difficulty from 5.8 to 5.13. Pocket climbing and thin face climbing on steep vertical faces up to 80 feet high is characteristic of the area.

Although the sport routes are the principal attraction at Cochiti Mesa, an excellent assortment of finger and hand cracks are found at The Dihedrals, about 250 yards north or left of the main cliff band. Climbing possibilities were sought here in the late 1970s, when many of the classic lines were ascended. Routes range from 5.8 to 5.11+. Most of the routes require doubles in all sizes of gear.

A rack of quickdraws and 165-foot rope is sufficient for most sport routes. TCUs and larger SLCDs are sometimes necessary. A longer rope can be advantageous on the longer South Cliff routes and The Dihedrals.

Descent from all sport routes is by lowering from bolt anchors, some with unwelded cold shuts. Descent from traditional routes without fixed anchors is by rappel from small trees on the cliff. Use carabiners on the anchors whenever you toprope to alleviate excessive wear on the bolt hangers.

Finding the cliff: Follow directions above to FR 289, accessed 0.9 mile northwest of the Cochiti Golf Course. Drive 4.4 miles on this rough dirt road (high clearance recommended) to parking areas on both sides of the road. The parking area is just past a shallow canyon and just before a sharp right-hand turn. Forest Road 289 can also be accessed from the north via Highway 4 about 9 miles west of Los Alamos. The parking area is 8 miles south from the highway on a generally good dirt road.

The trail to the cliffs starts on the west side of the road and heads gently uphill to the northwest. A short five-minute hike ends atop the cliffs. Locate an easy one-move downclimb below a large dead tree where

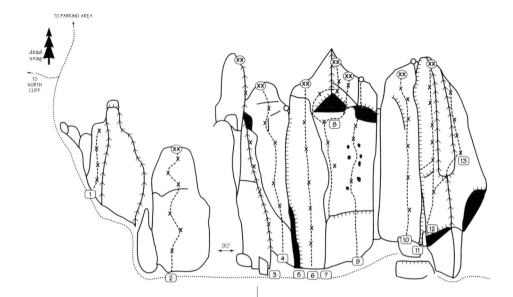

the cliff band thins. This downclimb divides the South and North Cliffs. After the downclimb, turn left or south to access routes #1 to #34 or turn right or north to reach routes #35 to #62 and The Dihedrals area.

Routes #1 to #34 are described left to right. Routes #35 to #62 are described right to left when viewed from the base of the cliffs.

South Cliff

Routes are described from left to right when viewed from the base of the cliff.

1. Leslie's Little Fingers (5.12b) Short, steep, and seldom climbed. Visible to the left from the top of the downclimb. 4 bolts. No anchor.

2. Mononucleosis (5.12c) Located 25 feet right of #1. Mono-doigt pockets and thin face climbing. 6 bolts to 2-bolt anchor.

3. Unknown (5.10b/c) The thin arête left of *Crackerjack*. 5 bolts to 2-bolt anchor.

4. Just Say No To Crack (5.10a/b) An area favorite. Face moves up a low-angle face. 5 bolts to 2-bolt anchor.

5. Crackerjack (5.9+) Quality crack climbing up a thin finger crack to shared anchors with #4.

6. Dinabolic (5.12a) Steep face climbing 3 feet right of #5. 6 bolts to 2-bolt anchor.

7. The Prow (5.11d) One of the area's best classics. Just do it! Edge up a low-angle arête and finish up the juggy overhanging prow above. 6 bolts to 3-bolt anchor.

8. Double Jeopardy (5.12b/c R) Variation. Go right on face above 3rd bolt. 4 bolts to 3-bolt anchor.

9. End of the French Revolution (5.11b) The face right of #7. Runout 5.8 face climbing leads to a small roof split by a fist crack. 3 bolts, no anchor. Gear placements possible at the roof. No anchor.

10. Another Lichen Nightmare (5.11a) Small pockets up a low-angle face lead to a left-angling ramp. 6 bolts to 2-bolt anchor.

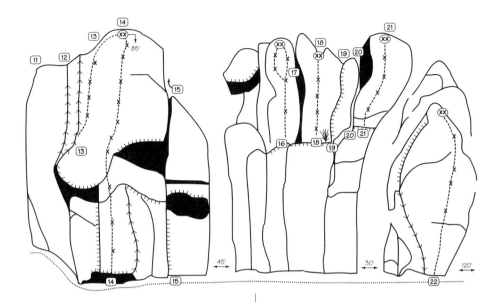

11. Dreamscape (5.11d) An area classic. Start 10 feet right of #10. An attractive left-leaning finger and tips crack up an offset corner on a northwest-facing wall. Trees for anchors. No bolts. **Rack:** TCUs, RPs, and Stoppers.

12. Shadowdancer (5.12c or 5.12d) Excellent technical route that is one of New Mexico's best pocket routes. Matt Samet calls it "the best route on the Cochiti escarpment." High praise indeed! Start up *Dreamscape,* then move right onto a dark, overhanging face and pull down on shallow pockets. The higher traverse onto the face is 5.12d. 6 bolts to 2-bolt anchor.

13. Terminal Ferocity (5.11d) Start in *Dreamscape* crack and climb to the first bolt of *Shadowdancer.* Step around corner to a small sloping stance. Edge up the thin face above right of a prow. 5 bolts, 2 fixed pins to 2-bolt anchor.

14. Velocity Unto Ferocity (5.12a/b) Start in a right-facing corner at the base of the cliff right of *Dreamscape.* Pass a small roof, then

steep face climbing. Shares anchors with *Terminal Ferocity.* 10 bolts to 2-bolt anchor.

15. Crack a Smile (5.10b/c) Start 10 feet right of #14 in a left-facing corner capped by a triangular roof. The off-size crack above the roof ends at a small ledge.

Routes #16 to #21 are accessed by rappelling from a 2-bolt anchor on the cliff top about 50 feet south of the top of the *Dreamscape* area to a large ledge that divides the face.

16. Desert Storm (5.11c) Rappel down from anchors and scramble to a face right of a hanging horn. Edge up a steep face, going left after bolt 2. Continue up the face above, then back right to anchors. 4 bolts to 2-bolt anchor.

17. Desert Shield (5.11a) From the ledge, crank the vertical face to a difficult finish. 4 bolts to 2-bolt anchor (same anchor as #16).

18. Confusion Say (5.11a) Crank up the short, steep face above the big belay ledge. 4 bolts to 2-bolt anchor.

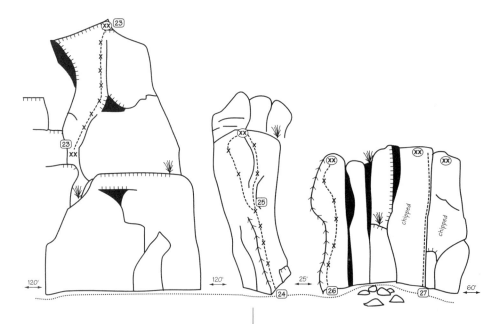

19. Unknown (5.7) Jam the crack up a corner right of #18.

20. Unknown (5.8+) A wide crack.

21. Lumpy Gravy (5.10d/11a) Walk down gully to left (from cliff top) to start route. Edging up a steep featured face. 4 bolts and anchors. The extra anchors are a mystery.

22. Acid Rain (5.10c) Starts 100 feet right of #21 on a lichen-covered slab right of a right-facing corner system. Smears and edges up a licheny slab. Move up left at the top of the slab to anchors. 4 bolts to 2-bolt anchor.

23. Cardinal Sin (5.13a) Brilliant line. Rappel from the cliff top to a chained belay station on a ledge 45 feet above the cliff base. Face climb up right to a steep arête above a triangular roof. 8 bolts to 2-bolt anchor.

24. Rocket in My Pocket (5.11d/.12a) About 120 feet right of #23. Start on the face left of an arête. Pull up the razor arête to a thin face. Go left at fourth bolt. 6 bolts to 2-bolt anchor.

25. Finger in the Socket (5.11b/c) Variation finish to #24. Start the same as #24 but move up right at fourth bolt and crank up a face with 3 bolts. 6 bolts to #24's anchors.

26. Kids in Toyland (5.12c) Start just left of an off-width crack. Climb right of a steep arête, then face climb to anchors. 5 bolts to 2-bolt anchor.

27. Olympian Crack (5.13a) Toprope route up thin crack. Use trees for anchors on cliff top. Routes to the left and right are chipped and drilled and not described here or anywhere.

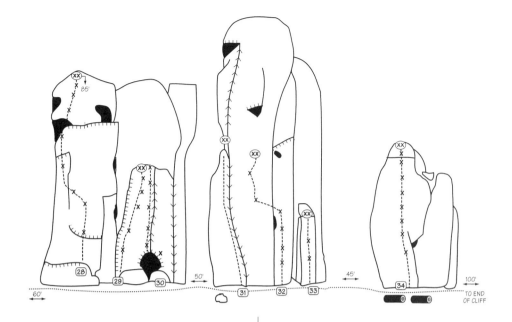

28. Sanadine Dream (5.11b) Route is 60 feet right of #27. Wander up the vertical face through a couple bulges. 9 bolts to 1 eyebolt anchor. If slings are in place, you can rap after 5 bolts.

29. Crystal Suppository (5.11d) Drilled pockets. 5 bolts to 2-bolt anchor.

30. Strange Attractor (5.11c) Located 5 feet right of #29. Difficult climbing up a steep arête. 6 bolts. Lower from the last bolt.

31. Fainting Imam (5.12b/c) Start behind a large juniper tree. Originally rated 5.13a after first ascent by Todd Skinner. This testpiece requires laybacking up a thin crack and edge to a 2-bolt anchor. No bolts. Gear required.

32. Immaculate Deception (5.12c/d) Drilled holds. 6 bolts to 2-bolt anchor.

33. Tolerated and Excused (5.10c) A low-angle slab 5 feet right of #32. 2 bolts plus TCUs in the horizontal crack near top.

34. Illusion Dissolution (5.11c) Drilled pockets. The last climb on this section of the cliff. Starts about 45 feet right of #33. 8 bolts to 2-bolt anchor.

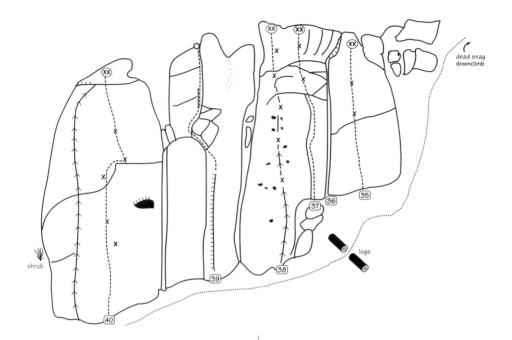

dead snag
downclimb

logs

shrub

North Cliffs

The following routes, located on the North Cliffs, are located to the right (north) after the one move downclimb. Routes are described from right to left when looking at the cliffs.

35. Napoleon Blown-Apart (5.11b) A short, thin face climb. 2 bolts to 2-bolt anchor.

36. Grunge up the Munge (5.9+) A seldom-climbed off-width crack left of *Napoleon Blown-Apart*. Finish up bulging crack to #35's anchors.

37. Proctologist's Fantasy (5.12b) Start 5 feet left of #36. Camming units protect the lower section. Difficult at the bulge. 2 bolts to 2-bolt anchor.

38. Praise the Lunge (5.11b/c) Up a blunt arête. An area favorite. 5 bolts to 2-bolt chained anchor.

39. Unknown (5.11a/b) No bolts. The thin parallel cracks between two off-size cracks. Climb the thin cracks 25 feet, then up left to a finger crack over a bulge.

40. Gunning for the Buddha (5.12a) Good route. Small pockets to a small shelf/crack, then more small pockets to anchors. 5 bolts to 2-bolt anchor.

41. Lainbo (5.12b) Start on top of boulders. Climb a short arête, then left to a steep face. 6 bolts to 2-bolt chained anchor.

42. Holy Wars (5.11a) Finish on #43. 5 bolts and shared anchors.

42.1. Montana Deviate (5.9+) A 2-bolt variation to #43. Climb a large crack to a left-slanting crack, then past 2 bolts to shared anchor.

43. Back to Montana (5.11c/d) Small pockets lead to big pockets and a ledge, then up right. 4 bolts to 2-bolt anchor.

44. Mr. Toad's Wild Ride (5.10c/d) Jam and layback a hollow left-facing flake with a bolt at its top. A steep finger crack leads to 2-bolt open cold shut anchor.

45. Touch Monkey (5.13a) An area classic up a beautiful face. Small pockets up a steep southwest-facing wall on a detached pillar. Sequential and technical. 6 bolts and shared anchors.

46. Digital Pleasures (5.12b) Follow the steep arête just left of *Touch Monkey,* then up right in a thin crack. First bolt is missing. 5 bolts to 2-bolt chained anchor.

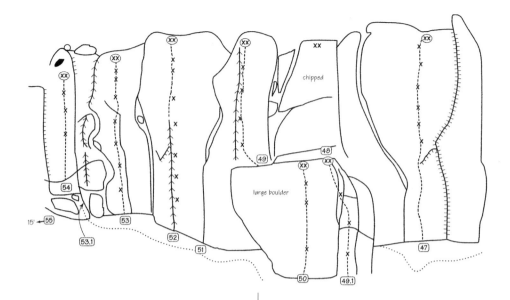

47. Empty and Meaningless (5.12b) Steep face and pocket climbing up a vertical wall. Start just left of a left-facing dihedral. 6 bolts to 2-bolt anchor.

48. Femanist Men (5.12a) Chipped, drilled, and manufactured. Dumb route. Matt Samet described it as "a route brought to you by various individuals with chisels and brain cramps."

49. Monkey Lust (5.9+/10a) Start by gaining the top of a large boulder via an easy chimney next to the cliff. One of the area's best moderates. 4 bolts to 2-bolt anchor.

49.1. Unknown Located on the large boulder down and left of #47. A new, short, moderate route. 3 bolts to 2-bolt anchor.

50. Unknown (5.9) A quality moderate route. On the west face of the large boulder in front of the cliff. 3 bolts to 2-bolt anchor.

51. Cochiti Classic (5.10) No bolts. Start in an attractive hand crack left of the large

boulder at the base of the cliff. Climb up through a wide, loose section to a left-leaning vertical fist crack. **Rack:** Friends to 4 inches.

52. La Espina (5.12a) Quality route. Face and arête climbing 5 feet left of #51. 7 bolts to 2-bolt anchor.

53. Thief in Time (5.12a) Recommended climb. Climbs the vertical face left of an off-width crack. 7 bolts to 2-bolt anchor.

53.1. Unknown (5.9+) Quality crack climb in a left-facing corner.

54. To Catch a Thief (5.11b/c) Chipped route. 3 bolts to 2-bolt anchor.

55. Unknown (5.8 or 5.10a) No topo. Located about 15 feet left of #54 on a short rock behind trees. Twenty-five feet of moderate face climbing. Using the left edge makes the climb about 5.8. 3 bolts to 2-bolt open cold shut anchor.

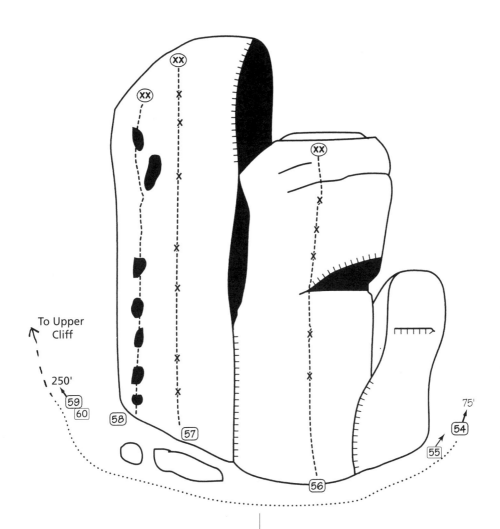

56. Pickpocket (5.11b) Chipped holds. Located on a separate cliff down and left from the main cliff. 5 bolts to 2-bolt anchor.

57. Open Mouth Syndrome (5.11b) Excellent. Located to the left of #56. 7 bolts to 2-bolt anchor.

58. Unknown A former project. On the left side of the cliff. No information available. 7 bolts (not shown) to 2-bolt anchor.

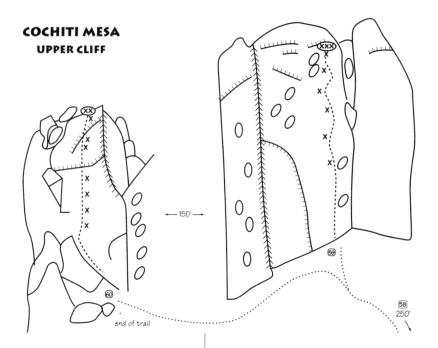

Routes #59 and #60 are located on the cliff band up and left of the main area. Access this area by hiking uphill and slightly left from *Open Mouth Syndrome* on a good trail for about 250 feet to a dark face left of a dihedral.

59. The Boya from La Jolla Who Stepped on a Cholla (5.11a) A popular recommended route. Start left of a dihedral. Ascend a dark brown face. 6 bolts to 3-bolt anchor.

60. New Age Nightmare (5.11c)
Recommended. Start in a loose, slanting off-width crack up a ramp to a 7-bolt face to a 2-bolt anchor.

The following two routes are worth climbing and best approached from the cliff top. From the top of the downclimb that divides the North and South Cliffs, walk right or north along the cliff top, then right and up to the next level. A faint trail eventually reaches anchors for #59 about 200 yards from the top of the downclimb. Past here are two dead snags hanging over the rim. It helps if you

locate these from below before you start. The top of *Shunning Theocracy* is 25 feet past (north of) the first snag, and the top of *Path of the Doughnut Man* is about 65 feet north of the second one. Rappel to base of both routes. Not illustrated.

61. Shunning Theocracy (5.11d) Soft rock. 6 drilled pitons. No anchors.

62. Path of the Doughnut Man (5.12a/b)
Recommended. Rap down a 60-foot face with 6 bolts and a 1-bolt belay anchor on a ledge with a cactus on it. Preclip the first bolt above the belay on the way down. A large Friend can back up the belay. No anchors.

Vista Point

Several established routes lie below the Vista Point Overlook. Some of these routes are worth searching out. The approach is by rappel or by a loose and somewhat dangerous downclimb. At least one serious accident has occurred here. Be cautious, careful, and thoughtful. Ask locals about *Coming of Age* (a 5.6 bolted face), *Adolescent Fantasy* (5.10), *Stridex* (5.11d), *Wasted Youth* (5.11c), and *Fortuitous Circumstance* (5.12a). Not illustrated.

The Dihedrals

In addition to several quality sport routes, this area offers the best crack climbing in the Cochiti Mesa area. Approach via a faint trail heading left or north below the main cliff band from the *Touch Monkey* area. Routes are described from right to left.

63. Inchworm (5.10d/.11a) Located on the left side of an alcove on the right side of the crag. Scramble up the slope a short distance to a hand and off-size crack leading to a ledge with a small oak tree. Belay on this ledge or continue up the attractive thin finger crack (crux). Extra TCUs are helpful here. Belay at

a good stance from some funky anchors. Descend from here or climb the corner above (5.10b/c) and rappel (two ropes) from a tree.

64. Art Gecko (5.12a) Climb first part of *Inchworm* to the ledge with a small oak tree. Climb past 6 bolts up a face with small pockets. **Descent:** Rappel (two ropes) from trees at top of cliff.

65. Bookworm (5.11d) 2 pitches. The longest and most sustained crack climb at Cochiti Mesa. **Pitch 1:** Face and crack climb past 2 fixed pitons to a fist crack through a roof. The first 20 feet is the crux. A 5.8/5.9 hand crack above the roof ends at the ledge below the difficult *Inchworm* fingertip crack. **Pitch 2:** Climb the thin finger crack of *Inchworm,* then the thin corner (5.10b/c) above to the top. Small TCUs and wires protect this seldom-climbed section. Descent is via a two-rope rappel from a tree.

66. The Apprentice (5.11b/c) Classic. Located about 15 feet left of *Bookworm*. Start in a steep chimney capped by a narrow chockstone. Above, continue up a hand and finger crack. Descend via a two-rope rappel from trees at top of cliff. **Rack:** Take at least a double rack of Friends and TCUs and runners for the rappel.

67. Autobahn (5.8+) Start 12 feet left of *The Apprentice*. Moderate crack climbing up a dark corner to a triangular roof, then left up a finger crack. Descend via a two-rope rappel from trees. **Rack:** Carry a hand and fist rack plus runners for the rappel.

68. Eternal Spring (5.10) Excellent crack reminiscent of Indian Creek jamming. Located about 75 feet left of *Autobahn*. Climb a short moderate section up to a spacious ledge with several small oak trees. Belay from here or continue up an awkward left-facing corner that becomes a perfect hand crack. Belay on a good ledge from your own gear. Descend by scrambling left to rap anchors on a tree. Make a 145-foot double-rope rappel. **Rack:** Carry at least a double set of Friends to 3 inches.

69. Indiscipline (5.11a) Located left of *Eternal Spring* past a prominent arête. Start in a corner. Climb onto a wavy face to an arête. Runout on 5.11 climbing near top. Gear placements protect bottom section. Descend via a 145-foot rappel from trees (same as #68).

70. Discipline (5.11d R) Located about 50 feet left of *Eternal Spring*. Jam a finger crack to a roof. Climb the arête to the right past 4 bolts to a tree with slings. Descend via 120-foot two-rope rappel.

71. Wyoming Saw (5.10b/c) Located 7 feet left of *Discipline*. Climb a hand crack past a shrub to a chimney capped by a small roof.

Difficult climbing above the roof in a thin crack to anchor trees. **Descent:** Two-rope rappel from tree anchor.

72. Cactus War (5.10a/b) Recommended. Same start as *Wyoming Saw*. Climb the chimney to the small roof and traverse left into a crack system with shrubs and cactus. The initial moves of the traverse are difficult to protect; be extra careful not to fall here. **Descent:** Rappel from *Wyoming Saw*.

73. Marlboro Country (5.11a) Located left of *Wyoming Saw* and left of the obvious arête. Thin crack climb protected by RPs and TCUs. **Descent:** Rappel from *Wyoming Saw*.

Cacti Cliff

Cacti Cliff, with an excellent selection of sport routes plus a few crack climbs, offers a good alternative to the more popular and often crowded Cochiti Mesa cliff. The southwest-facing crag yields quality sport routes and cracks up vertical 50- to 75-foot-high, welded rhyolite tuff walls. The rock, considered equal or better than Cochiti Mesa, features small huecos and pockets. The pale salmon-colored rock was deposited from violent ash eruptions of the nearby Jemez Volcano.

Difficult, strenuous, and well-protected sport routes ascend this beautifully situated cliff. Cacti Cliff is noted for its excellent arête routes. Almost twenty-five routes grace the crag, including thirteen rated 5.12 and two rated 5.13. Some sculpted and manufactured holds, however, detract from the fine climbing. Four superb crack routes, including the difficult *Crank Addiction* (5.12b/c), are also found here.

A rack for Cacti Cliff should include lots of quickdraws, TCUs, and camming units to 4 inches. Tape may be useful to avoid

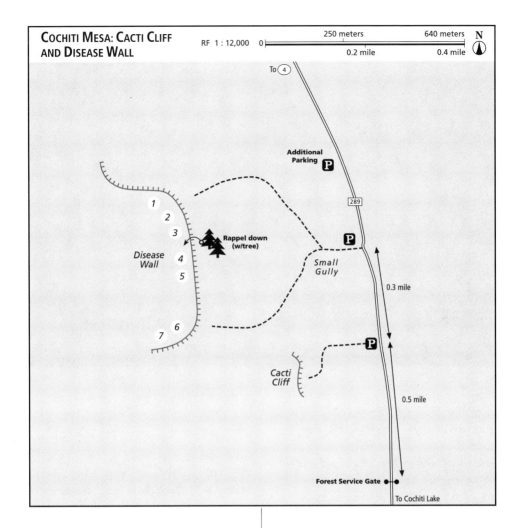

To ④

Additional Parking **P**

289

P

Disease Wall

1
2
3

Rappel down (w/tree)

4
5

6
7

Small Gully

0.3 mile

P

Cacti Cliff

0.5 mile

Forest Service Gate ●—●

To Cochiti Lake

tweaking finger tendons on sharp mono-doigt pockets. As for descent, it is possible to lower from two-bolt anchors on all routes except *Gravity's Angel* and the crack routes. For these, either rappel from nearby trees or walk to the top of the right or south end of the cliff and scramble down.

Finding the cliff: Follow directions above to FR 289, accessed 0.9 of a mile northwest of the Cochiti Golf Course. Drive approximately 4.4 miles on this rough dirt road (high clearance recommended) to the parking area for Cochiti Mesa. Forest Road 289

can also be accessed from the north via Highway 4 approximately 9 miles west of Los Alamos. Continue past the parking area a short distance to Vista Point (not signed, but obvious) and a Forest Service gate. Drive 0.5 mile north of the Forest Service gate to a parking area on the left or west side of the road by a relatively large pine tree. Cacti Cliff is approximately 150 yards below the parking area.

From the parking area, walk out to the canyon rim and locate a faint trail that heads left across the upper cliff's rim. Look for a steep rocky gully on the left that drops down

level with the cliff base to your right. This descent is direct but fairly steep and loose. The trail is rough and hard to follow in spots. Contour right or west to the base of the cliffs. The approach is short and takes about ten minutes. It will be only a little tricky to locate it the first time.

Routes are described from right to left from the cliff base.

1. Cross-eyed and Painless (5.12a) The first arête on the right end of the cliff. Technical moves. 5 bolts to 2-bolt anchor.

2. Reach or Bleach (5.12b) To the left of #1 on the same face. TCUs protect the horizontal crack. Reachy and hard at the bottom, easier above. 4 bolts to anchors. Shares anchors with #1.

3. Technobiscuit (5.12b) Steep slab climbing with 5 bolts. Good rest opportunities. 5 bolts to 2-bolt anchor.

4. Hump Me Dump Me (5.12c) A classic arête climb with exciting moves. 5 bolts to 2-bolt anchor.

5. Premature Infatuation (5.11c) Start in the smaller, short crack system left of a long off-size crack. Face climb (gear placements possible) up to a steep face on the right. 4 bolts to 2-bolt anchor.

6. Pendejo Park (5.10b) Start at ground level and boulder up to a short, curving hand crack. Face climb past 2 bolts near top. Gear placements necessary. Lower from welded cold shuts.

7. Chipped route. No topo. Not described.

8. Cheese Grater (5.10c) Climb up to large ledge to start. Fingers and hand-size crack. Install belay anchors at the top.

9. Slums of Bora Bora (5.12c) Start from the same ledge as *Cheese Grater*. Hard cranks up a face. 6 bolts to 2-bolt anchor.

10. Balance of Terror (5.12a) Classic arête route. Start on #9, then left up the right side of a long, steep arête. 6 bolts to 2-bolt anchor. Shares anchors with #9.

11. Direct Terror (5.12c/d) Up the arête from the left end of ledge. *Action Indirect*, a 5.13a variation, leaves #10 at the roof, then joins *Crank Addiction*. 6 bolts to 2-bolt anchor.

12. Crank Addiction (5.12b/c) Serious climb and seldom attempted. Start on *Izimbra,* then right to a thin crack. Many TCUs and wires required. No anchor.

13. Izimbra (5.13a/b) Long and sustained. Classic. Start just to right of a left-slanting thin crack, then up increasingly difficult face climbing to the left of *Crank Addiction*. 8 bolts to 2-bolt anchor. **Rack:** Bring gear for the bottom section.

14. Anazazi Momma (5.10b) A classic multi-discipline crack route. Fingers, hands, and fists up a right-facing dihedral. Lowering anchors at top. **Rack:** Friends to 4 inches.

15. Funktuation (5.13b) Yet another classic arête. Technical, long, and sustained. 7 bolts to 2-bolt anchor.

16. The Sample (5.12d) Start in a shallow corner, then up a thin finger crack protected by 2 bolts and small gear.

17. Vibrator Dependent (5.12a) A classic short arête climb. 5 bolts to 2-bolt anchor.

The following routes are located 40 feet to the left of #17. Not illustrated.

18. Clandestine Desire (5.11d) Interesting moves up a wavy face to a steep arête (crux). 6 bolts to 2-bolt anchor.

19. Full Cortex Meltdown (5.12) Start in a finger crack and then up a steep face to join #18. **Rack:** Small gear protects the bottom. 3 bolts to 2-bolt anchor

20. Flameout (5.11a) A classic climb diminished by unnecessary chipped face holds. Good climbers can do it without them. Jam the strenuous finger crack up a corner. 1 bolt up high and lowering anchors. **Rack:** Extra TCUs and wires are useful.

21. Gravity's Angel (5.12b/c) Start about 50 feet left of #20. Long reaches up a steep face, then over a 3-foot roof. TCUs helpful after roof. 6 bolts. No anchor.

Disease Wall

The Disease Wall, the farthest north crag in the Cochiti Mesa area, offers a small but excellent selection of hard sport routes on its steep southwest-facing cliff. Five quality routes grace the wall's steep hueco-covered face. The cliff is popular with locals because of its classic hueco and arête routes. Easy access from the nearby road, no other climbers, and stunning views of the Rio Grande valley make this small cliff a worthwhile destination. The crag, composed of welded tuff, lies about 300 yards up-canyon or northwest from Cacti Cliff. The easiest approach is from FR 289. All the routes were put up by Jean DeLataillade and Adam Read, along with several other partners. All are bolted sport lines up to 60 feet high.

Bring a rack of ten quickdraws and long slings for tying off cliff-top trees for rappel and belay anchors. A selection of thin crack pro is needed for one of the routes. The quality rock here invites future development.

Finding the crag: Follow directions above to FR 289, accessed 0.9 of a mile northwest of the Cochiti Golf Course. Drive about 5 miles on this rough dirt road (high clearance recommended) to the Forest Service gate and Vista Point. Forest Road 289 can also be accessed from the north via Highway 4 approximately 9 miles west of Los Alamos. Approximately 0.8 mile north of the Forest Service gate, park as best you can on the left side of the road. Additional parking (and camping) is found 0.2 mile farther on the left.

From the obscure small parking area, walk southwest down and slightly right from the left or west side of the road for about 100 yards to a small drainage that drops down to the left or southeast. Follow this gully down (starts small, gets wider and deeper) for about one-third of a mile to the cliff top. This is near the *Endorphin* route. Traverse right across the cliff top for about 100 yards to reach the top of *Chicken Pox*. Rappel to the base using trees for anchors to reach all routes. The routes are listed from left to right when viewed from the cliff's base. Routes #6 and #7 are about 300 feet right (southeast) of route #5. Access these by rappel or via a faint brushy trail at the base of the cliff heading southeast.

1. Common Cold (5.9) No topo. The cliff's only moderate line. Climb a long hueco face and arête. 8 bolts to 2-bolt anchor.

2. Small Pox (5.12c/d) A hard classic. Face climb a featured face to an overhanging black streak. 5 bolts to a tree belay.

3. Chicken Pox (5.12) Same start as #2 with a hand traverse right onto a bulging face with 2 bolts. 7 bolts. No anchors.

4. Anorexia (5.11a) Climb the off-width crack up to the first bolt. Layback the crack and face climb up bolt-protected huecos to the top. 5 bolts. No anchors.

5. Bulimia (5.11c) Climb an attractive thin corner past 1 bolt to the cliff top. Use a tree for belay anchor. **Rack:** Bring a selection of thin crack pro.

6. Endorphin (5.12a) This quality line starts 300 feet right of #5. Climb a blunt arête with 7 bolts to a 1-bolt anchor.

7. Opiate of the Masses (5.11c) Start 30 feet right of #6 behind a pine tree. Tree-climb to a large limb to clip bolt 1. Work up left along an overhanging dihedral. 5 bolts to a 1-bolt anchor shared with #6.

GILMAN TUNNELS

■ OVERVIEW

The dramatic Guadalupe Box canyon, carved through a band of granite by the Rio Guadalupe on the western flank of the Jemez Mountains, is one of New Mexico's best sport climbing venues. The deep canyon, formerly the exclusive domain of anglers and loggers, offers a great selection of both single-pitch and multipitch routes on walls up to 300 feet high. The routes, mostly between 5.10 and 5.12, are well bolted and equipped with bolt anchors for belaying and descending. The climbing area, called Gilman Tunnels for the canyon's two impressive tunnels, is a developing climbing arena with lots of rock available for new routes. The area has not seen a lot of climbing activity, so tread lightly and expect some loose rock.

The Guadalupe Box and the cliffs are accessed on a narrow, twisting road along the canyon's narrow floor. The canyon's two tunnels, reportedly hand-chiseled by nineteen local residents between 1942 and 1945, allowed logs cut in the Jemez high country to be easily hauled down to sawmills. Now the tunnels are a unique tourist attraction, especially during spring runoff when the normally placid Rio Guadalupe is a raging torrent. They are also seen in *Coyote Waits,* a 2003 PBS mystery movie based on a novel by Albuquerque writer Tony Hillerman.

Climbing History

Juan Lopez is responsible for some of Gilman's original climbs. Old pitons and fixed nuts on the better crack routes probably were placed by Juan or Bob Moor, another early activist. Activists in the 1990s include Tom Wezwick, Ed Romback, and Matt Grey. Most of the sport routes were established in the early 2000s by a cadre of climbers including Lance Hadfield, Chris Eckstein, and Marc Beverly.

Rack and Descent

A dozen quickdraws and a 165-foot rope is sufficient for all routes except the long multi-pitch lines on Spectator Wall, which require two 165-foot ropes for rappels. A small rack of Stoppers, TCUs, and Friends can supplement bolts on some routes.

Not all bolts are shown on the topos.

Trip Planning Information

Area description: Gilman Tunnels offers many excellent bolted sport routes and a few trad climbs on granite cliffs between 40 feet and 300 feet high in a narrow canyon.

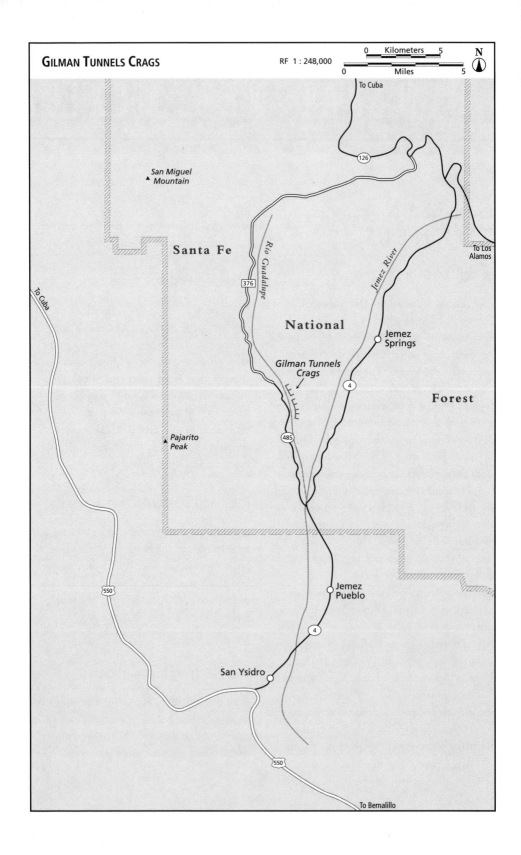

Location: North-central New Mexico. On the west flank of the Jemez Mountains about 50 miles northwest of Albuquerque.

Camping: Many free primitive campsites are found beyond the cliff parking area and through a metal gate. The nearest developed camping is Vista Linda Campground about 4 miles north on Highway 4 from the junction of Highway 485 and Highway 4. Additional fee campsites are plentiful in Santa Fe National Recreation Area along Highway 4 in the Jemez Mountains.

Climbing season: Spring, summer, and fall are the best times to climb. High spring runoff can make crossing the Rio Guadalupe (necessary for most routes) difficult and extremely dangerous. It is possible to climb on warmer winter days, although snow lingers in the canyon shadows.

Restrictions and access issues: Guadalupe Box is administered by Santa Fe National Forest.

Services: Gas and a convenience store at the Walatowa Visitor Center a short distance south of Cañon on Highway 4. More services are found 10 miles north on Highway 4 in Jemez Springs.

Emergency services: Call 911 for search and rescue and emergency medical services. The Jemez Valley Medical Clinic (505–834–0802) is a short distance south on Highway 4 just before Jemez Pueblo.

Nearby climbing areas: Las Conchas crags are 20 miles northeast in the Jemez Mountains. The Cochiti Mesa Crags are on the eastern side of the Jemez. Palomas Peak and the Sandia Mountains are 50 miles southeast near Albuquerque. Cabazon, a volcanic neck ascended by an easy scramble, rises above the Rio Puerco valley south of Cuba.

Nearby attractions: Jemez Pueblo, Zia Pueblo, Jemez State Monument, hot springs at Jemez Springs, Valles Caldera National Preserve, Bandelier National Monument, hiking, fishing, camping, and mountain biking in Santa Fe National Forest.

Finding the crags: It's easiest to access the area from the south. Drive south from Santa Fe or north from Albuquerque on Interstate 25 to Bernalillo and take exit 242 onto U.S. Highway 550. Drive 24 miles to San Ysidro and a right (north) turn onto Highway 4. Drive another 10 miles and turn left onto Highway 485. This turn can be reached from the north by driving from Los Alamos to the Las Conchas climbing area to the junction of Highway 502 and Highway 4. Turn south onto Highway 4 and drive to a right turn onto Highway 485.

Drive slowly through the narrow streets of the small village of Cañones and continue about 5 miles to two narrow tunnels. Drive through the tunnels (passing most of the climbing area on the right) and park at a large pullout on the left just before a metal gate. The first described route is a short distance back down the road on the cliff right of a large gully that bisects two formations.

Routes are listed from left to right. All numbered routes except #14 require crossing the Rio Guadalupe. Use extreme caution in high water.

There are three routes (no topos) that do not require crossing the river. They are on the left just before the first tunnel. The three routes, from left to right, are *Unknown* (5.9), *Racial Tension* (5.10-), and *Roadside Distraction* (5.10). Another three routes are in an alcove left of route #1 including two projects and a 5.10a.

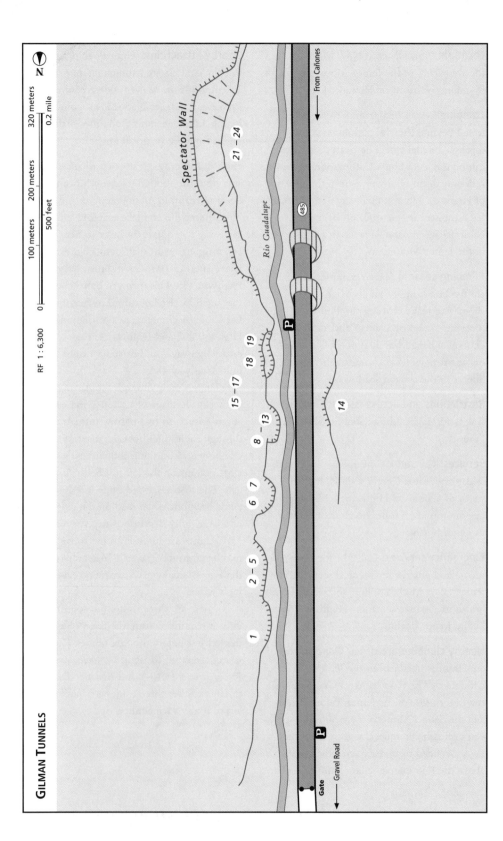

GILMAN TUNNELS

RF 1 : 6,300

100 meters   200 meters   320 meters

0   500 feet   0.2 mile

N

Spectator Wall

21 – 24

Rio Guadalupe

485

From Cañones

P

18 19

15 – 17

8 – 13

6 7

2 – 5

1

14

P

Gate

Gravel Road

1. Rink Rinker Fink (5.12a) Start 60 feet right of a large gully. This route is difficult to reach, or at least, to stay dry getting there because the cliff bottom is usually in the water. Hard initial climbing to easier climbing above. A long route ending at a 2-bolt anchor rigged with slings. 8 bolts to 2-bolt anchor.

Use stepping-stones across the river to access the next four routes.

2. Juan (5.10a) An early Juan Lopez route.

Start 80 feet right of #1 and at the end of the stepping-stones. Angle slightly left and up. 8 bolts to 2-bolt anchor.

3. Wet Feet (5.9+) Another Juan route. Start same as #2, then straight up. Some loose rock. 8 bolts to 2-bolt anchor shared with #2.

4. Straight Away (5.11c) Start 10 feet right

of stepping-stones. 4 bolts to 2-bolt anchor with some ancient carabiners.

5. Leftist Tendencies (5.10) 5 bolts to 2-bolt anchor with ancient carabiners.

6. Entrapment (5.10-) 5 bolts to 2-bolt chain anchor.

At least three projects plus a more direct start to #6 are in progress to the right of #7.

7. Cyber Crime (5.10) 8 bolts to 2-bolt anchor.

8. Ecksteinator (5.12a) 7 bolts to 2-bolt chain anchor.

9. Under Siege (5.11c) Start just right of #8. 9 bolts to 2-bolt chain anchor.

10. Old Punks on Crack (5.10) An old piton and a fixed nut were found on the crack, prompting the name. A little loose rock but a worthy climb.

11. Hostile Takeover (5.11d) A direct start to the *Original Bolted Route.* 9 bolts to 2-bolt anchor.

12. Original Bolted Route (5.11b) Start on #11, then right and up at second bolt. 8 bolts to 2-bolt chain anchor.

13. Lancelot (5.12b) Climbs the right arête of the formation. 8 bolts to 2-bolt anchor.

14. Out of the Shadows (5.10) This route is on the left (west) side of the road opposite #13. Does not require wading the Rio to reach the start. Sunny in the morning. It's currently a 1-pitch climb with most of its original second pitch erased because of poor rock.

15. Project (No rating) No topo. 1 bolt to 2–bolt anchor.

16. Puddy Girl (5.12c) Good climbing. Steeply overhanging route. 7 bolts to 2-bolt anchor. Lowering carabiner on 5th bolt.

17. Dough Boy (5.13b) Steep, attractive climb. 35 feet. 4 bolts to 2-bolt anchor equipped with carabiners.

18. Good Morning America (5.10–) Good trad route. 2-bolt anchor. A project is farther left.

19. Edge of Night (5.10) Attractive route. Located across the river from the end of the guardrail at the parking area after tunnel 2.

Crack and slab to anchors under a large roof. 8 bolts to 2-bolt anchor.

20. Ziggurat (5.10c/d) No topo. Climb a long, easy ramp to a belay that stands alone halfway across the left face from an alcove. A long strenuous trad pitch. One bolt with a rap ring.

The Spectator Wall

The Spectator Wall, an imposing 300-foot-high, east-facing cliff across the river from the first tunnel, offers four impressive two-pitch bolted lines. The routes received liberal cleaning but have seen little traffic, making it best not to stray too far from the bolt line until they clean up better.

Descent off the routes is by rappel. Bring a small rack with an assortment of wired nuts and cams, sixteen to eighteen quickdraws, some extra slings, and two 165-foot ropes.

Finding the cliff: From the entrance to the first tunnel, scramble down a rough, steep trail to the river.

Routes are listed from left to right.

21. Outlander (5.11-) The left route. **Pitch 1:** Climb through a large white scar to a 2-bolt anchor. (5.10+) **Pitch 2:** Straight up on the prow left of a shallow left-facing corner.

22. Vicarious Living (5.10) **Pitch 1:** Straight up to anchors at the left end and over the top of a large diagonal crack system near the center of the wall. **Pitch 2:** Straight up past many bolts to anchors just below the top. (5.10-).

23. Moist Hoist (5.10+) **Pitch 1:** Climb straight up (5.10a) to anchors over the top and near the center of the diagonal crack. **Pitch 2:** Climb straight up to a 2-bolt anchor. Some gear placements optional on this pitch. A little dirty near the top. (5.10+).

24. Stallone's Bone (5.12a) **Pitch 1:** Straight up to anchors near the right-hand end of the diagonal crack and below a large two-tiered roof. (5.11-) **Pitch 2:** Crux pitch. Short pitch. Traverse above the roof, then up a broad, long right-slanting ramp system.

PALOMAS PEAK

■ O V E R V I E W

Palomas Peak, a minor 8,600-foot mountain at the northern end of the Sandia Mountains, is one of New Mexico's best and largest limestone climbing areas with close to one hundred routes that range from 5.6 to 5.14. Most of the climbing is on the upper cliff band, which is composed of a more compact limestone than the looser lower layer. The cliff, averaging 50 feet in height, offers technical face climbing on steep slabs and vertical to overhanging stone. The Slab sector, with some of the cliff's hardest routes like *Snake Dance* (5.13d/14a), overhangs an astounding 20 feet in only 50 vertical feet. Most Palomas routes, however, are characterized by vertical terrain with upward progress defined by edges, crimps, smears, and an occasional jam. Most of the routes are technical, sequential, and fingertip-intensive. The limestone can be painfully sharp. Be prepared by packing some tape and tough fingertips.

The blatant chipping of holds and the total manufacturing of routes has been a major problem at Palomas Peak. Thankfully most of the damage was done by only a handful of climbers when the cliff was first being developed. In the mid-1990s, one section of The Slab was grid-bolted with more than thirty bolts that were placed to accommodate a photo shoot for an artificial hold manufacturer. Kudos to local climbers Lance Hadfield and Bryan Pletta who filled the holes in an attempt to erase this rock debasement. Local ethics frown on chipping holds as well as any other hold enhancements like drilling pockets. The more recent routes at Palomas avoided chipped holds.

Palomas Peak, lying just outside the boundaries of the Sandia Mountain Wilderness Area, is composed of several layers of limestone separated by tree- and shrub-covered shale slopes. The limestone formed in a vast inland sea that flooded much of New Mexico in the Pennsylvanian Period some 200 million years ago. When the Sandia massif thrust upward, the limestone layers were pushed to the top of the mountains. The cliffs on the peak are separated into many 40- to 70-foot-high bands and vary in rock quality. Almost all the climbing is on the upper band, which features the best rock.

Climbing History

Interestingly enough, it was traditional climbers that first visited Palomas Peak, seeking out the crag's quality crack lines. This initial development was led by Dave Whitelaw and John Groth. Later Paul Horak attempted *Turbo Trad* in the mid-1980s before departing to the East Coast. The cliff band was later rediscovered by Lewis Rutherford and Timmy Fairfield in 1993, which led to the crag's development as one of New Mexico's premier sport climbing areas. The divergence in traditional and sport climbing ethics led to a period of acrimony between the opposing views on style of ascent. Now peace reigns at the area with ethical accommodations tacitly agreed on by both trad and sport climbers. The sport climbers concentrated their bolting efforts on the unprotectable faces, while cracks that accept gear were left in the province of the traditionalist. Most of the sport climbs were installed by Mark Thomas and Bryan Pletta. Additional activists include Lance Hadfield, Lewis Rutherford, Joey Tefertiller, Eric Gompper, and Lorne Raney. *Turbo Trad* (5.13a), a superb, bolted, fingers-to-fist crack, was completed by Albuquerque climber Lance Hadfield in 1995, while Dave Pegg, an English climber then residing in

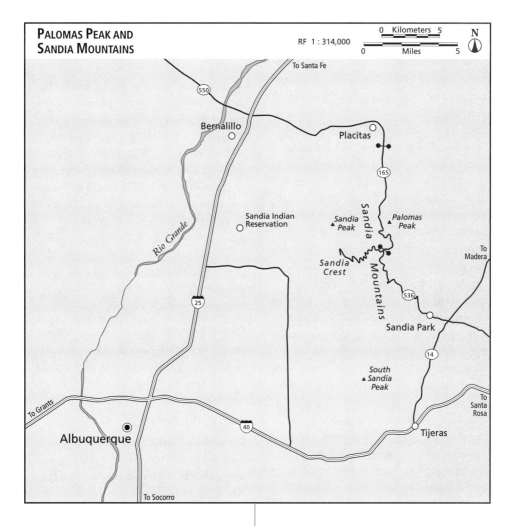

RF 1 : 314,000

Kilometers 5

Miles 5

N

To Santa Fe

550

Bernalillo

Placitas

165

Sandia Indian Reservation

Sandia Peak

Sandia

Palomas Peak

To Madera

Sandia Crest

Mountains

536

Rio Grande

25

Sandia Park

14

South Sandia Peak

To Grants

40

To Santa Rosa

Albuquerque

Tijeras

To Socorro

New Mexico, redpointed *Snake Dance* (5.13d/14a) that same year. Tim Fairfield bolted, chipped, and climbed *Sick Man,* the area's hardest route. Adding their talents to the original batch of developers are Randy Eisler, Steven Hofmeyr, Deborah Evans, Chris Grijalva, Paul May, and Bernard Moret.

Besides the extensive development at Palomas Peak, there is a wealth of nearby limestone cliffs in the immediate area that invite more exploration, with many lying outside the boundaries of Sandia Mountain Wilderness Area. The limestone cliffs within

Sandia Mountain Wilderness Area have not been developed because of a prohibition on motorized drilling and long brushy approaches. Check with local climbers for information and beta on these cliffs since some traditional routes were established in the past. A handful of routes are found on the limestone cliffs just down-canyon from the Sandia Man Cave in the lower canyon. To find these routes, park in a pulloff on the west side of the road directly below and scramble up a steep gully to the base of two cliffs with routes.

Rack and Descent

Most Palomas routes are protected by bolts with lowering anchors including chains, rap hangers, and both welded and open cold shuts. Besides the sport routes, the cliff also offers a good selection of traditional crack lines that require cams and nuts for protection. Few of the route anchors are readily accessible from the cliff top, which is an unconsolidated slope of loose gravel, dirt, and perched boulders. If you want to toprope here, it's best to lead your route of choice rather than try to rig a rope from above since you run the risk of knocking rocks onto climbers below. Also remember, like at all sport areas, that the anchors are for lowering only, not for toproping, which wears the anchors out quickly. Instead thread your rope through a pair of quickdraws with locking carabiners.

A rack of twelve quickdraws and a 165-foot or shorter rope is sufficient for most routes. The occasional intermittent cracks found on the cliff face also accept gear. Bring a standard rack of Friends and Stoppers for the crack climbs. Descent off all routes is from lowering anchors.

Not all bolts are shown on the topos.

Trip Planning Information

Area description: Palomas Peak climbing area, a southwest-facing limestone cliff band, offers more than eighty sport routes on the southern flank of Palomas Peak.

Location: Central New Mexico. Northeast of Albuquerque on the northern edge of the Sandia Mountains in Cibola National Forest.

Camping: None in the immediate area. Although primitive campsites can be found on the road between Placitas and the parking area, it is not recommended. There are no developed campgrounds in the Sandia Mountains. All areas on the range crest are day-use-only picnic sites. The nearest developed sites are in the Mountainair Ranger District, P.O. Box 69, Mountainair, NM 87036 (505–847–2990), approximately 50 miles south of Albuquerque on the east side of the mountains. Two KOA campgrounds are in the Albuquerque vicinity: Albuquerque Central KOA (505–296–2729) and Albuquerque North KOA (505–867–5227). Coronado State Park (505–867–5589), sited next to the Rio Grande in Bernalillo just north of Albuquerque, has showers and is convenient to Highway 165.

Climbing season: Year-round. Best seasons are spring and fall. Winter access can occasionally be a problem because of snow. The cliff is often warm and sunny in winter. Summer days are usually too hot on the sunny south-facing cliff.

Restrictions and access issues: The main problem here is very limited parking, which creates big problems on busy weekends. Park only in the car park and squeeze in so others can also park here. Rangers will ticket any vehicle either on or partly on the road. Access to the Palomas Peak cliff is an easy twenty-five-minute hike on a well-defined climber trail that leads to the right side of the cliffs. Be sure to locate and follow this trail, which begins by barriers at the parking area, as otherwise it's a serious thrash through dense underbrush. Stay on the access trail to avoid damaging vegetation. Remember to pick up all litter, including cigarette butts.

Guidebooks: *Rock Climbing New Mexico & Texas* by Dennis R. Jackson, Falcon Press,

1996. An article on Palomas Peak appeared in *Climbing Magazine* #155. An online guide by Bernard Moret is available at www.cs.unm.edu/~moret/crag.html.

Services: Nearby Placitas offers a convenience store and gasoline. A supermarket and restaurants are 3 miles farther west. Bernalillo, west of Interstate 25, offers more selection. Albuquerque, about forty-five minutes away, offers full services.

Emergency services: Dial 911 for all emergencies. The nearest phone is in Placitas about 7 miles away. Dial 911 for all emergency services in the Albuquerque area. Search and rescue services are initiated by the New Mexico State Police; dial 911 or (505) 841–9256. Albuquerque hospitals with twenty-four-hour emergency care: Lovelace Medical Center, 5400 Gibson Boulevard SE, (505) 262–7000; Presbyterian Hospital, 1100 Central Avenue SE, (505) 841–1234; University of New Mexico Hospital, 2211 Lomas Boulevard NE, (505) 843–2411; and Kindred Hospital, 700 High NE, (505) 242–4444.

Nearby climbing areas: The nearest sport routes are at Sandia Man Cave crag down the road from the Palomas Peak car park. The Sandia Mountains include lots of cliffs including The Shield, The Needle, Muralla Grande, Torreon, and Mexican Breakfast Crag. The Cochiti Mesa Crags to the northwest include Eagle Canyon, Disease Wall, Cacti Cliff, and The Dihedrals. Bouldering areas near Albuquerque are U-Mound, Fat City, and Embudo Spring Boulders. Other small areas are Three Gun Springs; Big Block Wall south of Tijeras off Highway 14; and New Canyon in the Manzano Mountains southeast of Albuquerque. To the north near Santa Fe is Diablo Canyon and the Coxcomb

and the White Rock basalt crags near Los Alamos.

Nearby attractions: Sandia Man Cave, a controversial archaeological site, is about 1.5 miles north of the crag. This registered National Historic Site was excavated from 1936–1940. Artifacts and debris found here radically pushed back previous estimates of early man's occupation of the New World. Albuquerque history and culture, Old Town, the Albuquerque Museum, New Mexico Museum of Natural History, Rio Grande Nature Center State Park, Rio Grande Zoological Park, Petroglyph National Monument, Coronado National Monument, Indian Pueblos, and Indian gaming. The internationally famous Balloon Festival is held annually in October. Many biking trails are found in the foothills east of town, and a wealth of hiking trails are found in the Sandia Mountains.

Finding the crag: Drive north from Albuquerque or south from Santa Fe on I–25 and take exit 242. Go east on Highway 165 toward Placitas. Drive through Placitas about 7 miles east. The road turns to dirt 2.5 miles past Placitas. Drive almost exactly 5 miles on this dirt road to a parking area on the left identified by three large concrete railings. This parking area is 14 miles from I–25.

From the parking area, walk up the road about 25 yards to a good trail that begins just past a large ponderosa pine. This excellent trail contours northeast and down into the upper narrows of the valley below (about ten minutes to the valley). The trail then climbs north out of the valley up a broad ridge. Head gently uphill directly to the base of the cliff's right end. The trail is easy to follow. Allow thirty to forty minutes for the approach hike.

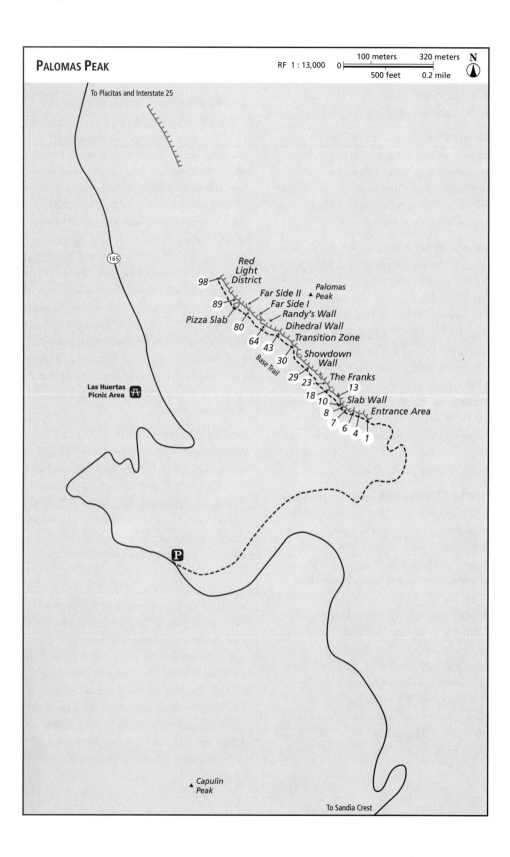

PALOMAS PEAK

RF 1 : 13,000

100 meters   320 meters

0

500 feet   0.2 mile

N

To Placitas and Interstate 25

165

Red
Light
District

98

Far Side II

89

Far Side I

Pizza Slab

80

Randy's Wall

64

Dihedral Wall

43

Transition Zone

30

Showdown
Wall

29

23

13

18

The Franks

10

8

Slab Wall

7

6   4   1

Entrance Area

Base Trail

Palomas
▲ Peak

Las Huertas
Picnic Area

P

Capulin
▲ Peak

To Sandia Crest

Red Light District — Far Side II — Far Side I — Dihedral Wall — Transition Zone — The Franks — Slab Wall

The Entrance

The first sector the access trail reaches is called The Entrance. The Entrance is located on the right end of the cliff where the approach trail reaches the cliff. All routes are described from right to left when viewed from the bottom of the cliff.

1. Double D (5.11d) No topo. A bouldery travesty. Lots of drilled holds. This route is on a short piece of cliff just before the main

Entrance sector. 4 bolts to 2-bolt chain anchor.

2. Entrance Exam (5.10c) No topo. Some looseness near the top. Use caution. Otherwise a good warm-up. 6 bolts to 2-bolt anchor.

3. Sidewinder (5.12a) No topo. A good, long endurance route up the slightly overhanging wall right of a dark cave with a raven's nest. 9 bolts to 2-bolt anchor.

4. Nature of the Beast (5.12a) Excellent pumpfest with a tricky start. 9 bolts to 2-bolt anchor.

5. Drop in the Ocean (5.11c/d) Jam a crack past 4 bolts to a scoop. Diagonal left along the flake after the last bolt to anchors. 8 bolts to 2-bolt anchor. The direct finish (5.12c) finishes at right-hand anchors.

6. Vertical Nothing (5.12a) Edge up a seam, then up and left on the face above The Slab Wall to high anchors. 8 bolts to 2-bolt anchor.

The Slab Wall

"Friends don't let friends climb slabs," says the bumper sticker . . . right. Unless it's this overhanging slab! The Slab Wall is a smooth overhanging wall lined with black streaks.

Many of the cliff's hardest routes are located on this excellent section.

7. Fall From Grace (5.13b/c) Good steep cranking up obviously drilled and chipped holds on the right side of the overhang. 6 bolts to 2-bolt anchor.

8. Turbo Trad (5.13a) The obvious bolted, overhanging, painful hand crack up the center of The Slab. Tape up! 8 bolts to 2-bolt anchor above the lip.

9. Slab City (5.13b) Excellent and recommended. Bernard Moret calls it the "best 5.13 here." Pull up the overhanging seam on the left side of the wall. 9 bolts to 2-bolt anchor.

10. Snake Dance (5.13d/14a) Another good hard one. Short, overhanging, right-facing corner to an overhanging seam. 7 bolts to 2-bolt anchor.

The Franks

The next sector is dubbed The Franks for its supposed resemblance to the limestone in Germany's Frankenjura. The bottom of the cliff is very overhanging, making the route starts very bouldery and difficult. The rest of the cliff above is mostly vertical and hence easier.

11. Sick Man (5.14b) A Tim Fairfield creation. Short, sharp, and dynamic. 4 bolts to 2-bolt anchor.

12. Wooden Jesus (5.14) Starts 3 feet left of *Sick Man*. Crank over the bulge, then crimp upward. 6 bolts to 2-bolt anchor.

13. Love Hate Love (5.12d) Small pockets over a bulge. 4 bolts to 2-bolt anchor.

14. Junkhead (5.12a) More small pockets. 4 bolts to 2-bolt anchor. First bolt is missing.

15. Project (5.13?)

16. Dark Dreams (5.12b) Crux over bulge. 5 bolts to 2-bolt anchor.

17. Entertaining Mike Tyson (5.13b)

Entertaining short route over the low roof. 5 bolts to 2-bolt anchor.

18. Crash Test Dummy (5.11d) Painful pockets up a black streak to anchors below a roof above. Tape up! 4 bolts to 2-bolt anchor.

19. Butthead (5.13+) 4 bolts to 2-bolt anchor.

20. Beavis (5.13a) Short and pumpy over bulge. 5 bolts to 2-bolt anchor.

21. Project (5.13?) No topo. 4 bolts to 2-bolt anchor.

22. Monkey Man (5.12b) No topo. Just left of the overhang. First bolt is chopped. 7 bolts to 2-bolt chain anchor.

An abandoned project with three bolts goes over the big roof between *Monkey Man* and *Funky Junkie*.

23. Funky Junkie (5.11a/b) Interesting and varied climbing up the long face on the left side of The Franks. 6 bolts to 2-bolt chain anchor.

From *Funky Junkie*, hike left 225 feet to the Showdown Wall.

Showdown Wall

24. Gunslinger (5.11d) Layback up the crack on the right side of the face. Crux down low. 5 bolts to 2-bolt chain anchor.

25. Sidekick (5.10c) Not recommended. Follow the left-angling crack system to a loose face. Gear necessary between bolts 1 and 2 to avoid a ground fall. 5 bolts to 2-bolt anchor.

26. Velcro Bootie (5.11a) Start 20 feet left of *Sidekick*. Bulge to steep slab. Crux is at bolt 3. Go left to drop the grade to 5.10c. 5 bolts to 2-bolt chain anchor.

27. Precious (5.11b/c) No topo. Start right of a thick black streak. Pull overhanging wall on sharp pockets past 2 bolts. Continue up the intermittent cracks to slab finish right of a corner. 6 bolts to 2-bolt chain anchor.

28. Sweet Jane (5.12b) No topo. Begin next to small pine trees growing at the base. Stick-clip or boulder 12 feet up to first bolt. Continue up bulging rock above. 7 bolts to 2-bolt anchor.

29. Unknown (5.7) No topo. 75 feet left of #28. Climb a flake to a tree. Bring gear. 2-bolt anchor.

Hike 200 feet left of #29 to the Transition Zone.

Transition Zone

The Transition Zone is exactly that—a broken transition zone in the cliff band. Walk left from the Showdown Wall past a bushy break in the cliff band just before the Transition Zone. Continue up left on the trail to the start of the sector.

30. Stick to Stucco (5.10c) Sharp friction climbing. Edge and smear up a continuous gray slab. 5 bolts to 2-bolt chain anchor.

31. Wavy Gravy (5.8) Popular and fun. Climb the excellent undulating slab left of the left-facing corner. The left-facing corner a good 5.7 gear route.. Going left of the bolts is 5.10. 5 bolts to 2-bolt cold shut anchor.

32. Tutti Frutti (5.11b) Thin edging and smearing up the left side of the gray slab. 5 bolts to 2-bolt anchor.

33. Unknown (5.9) The crack left of *Tutti Frutti*. Bring some gear. Clip bolts 1, 2, and 5 on #32 and lower from its anchors.

34. Rode Hard (5.11c) Recommended route. Climb over broken roofs on the prominent nose left of *Tutti Frutti*. 8 bolts to 2-bolt chain anchor.

35. Put Up Wet (5.11b) Climb broken rock past 1 bolt, then up a steep thin crack to a bolt below a large roof. Turn the roof on the right. TCUs, wires, and 3 bolts. Shares anchors with *Rode Hard*.

36. Big Guns in Cowtown (5.9-) Start 50 feet left of *Put Up Wet*. Climb the laid-back crack to *Pocket Princess*'s anchors. No bolts.

37. Pocket Princess (5.11a) Climb the prow left of *Big Guns in Cowtown*. Technical moves. 5 bolts to 2-bolt anchor.

38. Have Slab Will Travel (5.10c) Stem up a shallow corner to anchors below a large piñon pine. 4 bolts to 2-bolt anchor.

39. Support Your Local Bolter (5.11b) Thin, technical slab route. 4 bolts to 2-bolt anchor shared with *Have Slab Will Travel*.

40. Trigger Happy (5.9) Crack route. Gear placements necessary. Shares anchors with #39 and #38.

41. Factory Direct (5.10c) Climb the short, polished limestone slab to anchors up and left. 5 bolts to 2-bolt anchor.

42. Middleman (5.11b) Over a roof then up a rib to *Factory Direct*'s anchors. Stick-clip bolt 1. 4 bolts to 2-bolt anchor.

The Dihedral Wall

The Dihedral Wall, an extension of Transition Zone, offers some real gems. The large buttress between routes #42 and #43 marks the start of the sector. The cliff is characterized by two large dihedrals and a jumble of loose rock at the base.

43. Unnamed (5.9+) A thin, vegetated crack with a bolt in the choss rock at the bottom. 1 bolt to 2-bolt anchor.

44. Black Panther (5.12b/c) Continuous route diminished by some hold enhancement.

Works up a thin technical slab. 7 bolts to 2-bolt chain anchor.

45. Smoked Salmon (5.10a/b) Climb a left-angling crack system. Belay at the piñon pine at the top. No bolts, no established anchor.

46. Floating World (5.11c) No topo. Rarely climbed. Toprope problem now since all the bolts were chopped.

47. Tina's Rig (5.12b) Work out a line between the triple set of roofs. Drilled-out pockets. 7 bolts to 2-bolt anchor.

48. Green Eggs and Ham (5.10c)
Recommended. Up a perfect dihedral. 6 bolts to 2-bolt anchor.

49. Quickdraw McGraw (5.11c) An area favorite. Left of the dihedral. 6 bolts to 2-bolt anchor.

50. Baba Louie (5.10d) Use the first bolt of *Lucky Boy,* then move right to a left-facing dihedral. 4 bolts to 2-bolt anchor.

51. Lucky Boy (5.11c) Located between two attractive cracks. 5 bolts to 2-bolt anchor.

52. Classic Jam Crack (5.9) Classic Palomas Peak hand crack up a tight corner. Gear placements required. 2-bolt anchor.

Hike 140 feet left of *Classic Jam Crack* to the next sector, Randy's Wall.

Randy's Wall

53. Floating on Moonbeams (5.9+) No topo. Start by a large piñon pine. Climb the right wall of the left-facing dihedral. 4 bolts to 2-bolt anchor.

54. Walking on Sunshine (5.11b) No topo. Excellent climbing. Start the same as *Floating on Moonbeams,* then move left and up a polished face. 4 bolts to 2-bolt chain anchor.

55. Calamity Jane (5.11b/c) Excellent. One of several routes here established in memory of Jane Tennessen, who died in a tragic climbing accident in the Sandias. Start 25 feet left of *Walking on Sunshine*. Climb an attractive steep face left of a left-facing dihedral. 5 bolts to 2-bolt chain anchor.

56. In the Limelight (5.11d) Excellent slab climbing. A left-angling line requiring technical moves and lots of smearing. 5 bolts to 2-bolt cold shut anchor.

57. Behind the Scenes (5.12a) Climb past a small half moon arch to the cold shut anchors for *In the Limelight*. 5 bolts to 2-bolt anchor.

58. Unnamed (5.9-) No topo. Unattractive and seldom climbed. Start 18 feet left of *Behind the Scenes* left of a tall pine tree next to the cliff.

59. Monkey See (5.11c) Steep technical climbing. 5 bolts to 2-bolt anchor.

60. Monkey Do (5.11d) Shares same start and first 2 bolts with *Monkey See*. 5 bolts to 2-bolt anchor.

61. Stemulation (5.11b) Classic stemming problem. Stem up a shallow corner. 6 bolts to 2-bolt anchor.

62. Pretzel Logic (5.11b) Shares bolt and anchors with *Stemulation*. 6 bolts to 2-bolt anchor.

63. Unnamed (5.9) No topo. Start 5 feet left of *Pretzel Logic*. A curving hand crack, then right up a thin crack. No bolts, no established anchor.

64. Kyle's Crack (5.7) Start 4 feet left of #63. Starts as a finger crack and then widens above. Bring large cams. 2-bolt chain anchor.

64.1. Unknown (5.9 R). No topo. Start 40 feet left of *Kyle's Crack*. Climb a ramp to blocks near the top. 3 bolts, no anchors.

Walk left 90 feet to the next route.

65. Fat Lips Thin Smile (5.12c) No topo. A short climb up a white wall with small roofs. 4 bolts to 2-bolt anchor.

The Far Side I

The Far Side I is another 200 feet left from route #65. Walk past a break in the cliff and pass a fallen tree trunk.

66. R.I.P. (5.11d/12a) Start just right of a left-facing corner (#67). A more difficult variation finish goes straight up left of the last 3 bolts. 6 bolts to 3-bolt chain anchor.

67. Unknown (5.8) Off-width crack. Gear placement required.

68. Jane's Addiction (5.12a) Start left of a small cave. 5 bolts to 2-bolt anchor.

68.1. Unknown (?) Climbs the buttress right of the right-facing corner (#69).

69. Unnamed (5.9+) Jam a crack in a dihedral to a 2-bolt cold shut anchor.

70. Surfer Boy and the Shrimp (5.11d) Located to the right of a large chimney. 6 bolts to 2-bolt cold shut anchor.

71. Midnight Rider (5.11c) Good climbing on perfect edges. 5 bolts to 2-bolt chain anchor.

72. Unknown (5.10c) Zigzag hand and fist crack. Carry large cams. Shares anchors with *Midnight Rider.*

73. Dreamer Deceiver (5.12d/13a) No topo. Start 5 feet left of #72. Climb a very thin vertical face along shallow intermittent seams. 5 bolts to 2-bolt chain anchor.

74. Curious George (5.10d) No topo. Classic. 5 bolts protect a thin right-facing corner. 5 bolts to 2-bolt chain anchor.

75. Tigers on Vaseline (5.13c/d) No topo. Thin technical route that features delicate smearing and finger-tip edges. The fifth bolt is missing a hanger. 5 bolts to 2-bolt chain anchor.

76. Ramblin' Man (5.10c/d) No topo. Stem up a tight left-facing corner. Exit right under a roof and follow intermittent cracks to anchors. 5 bolts to 2-bolt chain anchor.

77. Crooked Cross (5.12b/c) No topo. Climb the vertical face to the right of a

dihedral. Easier at the top. 6 bolts to 2-bolt chain anchor.

78. Unnamed (5.10a) No topo. Located 45 feet left of #77. Start in the middle of a face bordered on the left by a chimney system. 1 fixed pin, 1 bolt, gear required. No bolted anchors.

79. Unnamed (5.10b) No topo. 75 feet left of #78. Short southeast-facing wall bordered on the right by a narrow chimney. Climb past 3 bolts to a ledge with a small tree.

The Far Side II

This sector toward the far west end of the cliff band offers lots of popular moderate routes. The lower part of the cliff is somewhat loose. Use caution and climb carefully until you reach more solid rock.

Walk 100 feet left from #79 and drop down, squeezing between the cliff face and a tree to the east end of the Far Side II wall.

80. Chess (5.10b/c) On the left or southeast-facing wall of a large open book. Shares a common start with *Checkers*. Start up a wide section of chossy rock and continue straight to anchors near the cliff top. Fixed stopper and 7 bolts to 2-bolt anchor.

81. Checkers (5.10b) The twin to *Chess*. Shares start, first 2 bolts, fixed stopper, last 2 bolts, and anchors with *Chess*. Go left at top of the choss rock. 7 bolts to 2-bolt anchor.

82. Patchwork (5.10b) 3 bolts protect the lower suspect rock, then past 6 more to anchors nearly at the top of the cliff. 9 bolts to 3-bolt anchor.

83. Lonesome Dove (5.9+) Recommended and popular warm-up route. Start on the face left of a wide crack. Face climb up and left before working back right above a shallow corner. 7 bolts to 2-bolt chain anchor.

84. Knee Jerk Reaction (5.11c) 30 feet left of #83. Climb a rib of unattractive rock and over a scoop to a block that juts out. Go left at the block to anchors near the rim. 8 bolts to 2-bolt chain anchor.

85. Tiger by the Tail (5.9+) Good fun. Climb a shallow left-facing corner system until you can move right onto a steep finishing headwall. 6 bolts to 2-bolt chain anchor.

86. Pussy Whipped (5.8+) One of the easiest routes on the crag. Shares the first 4 bolts of *Tiger by the Tail* but finishes up the left-facing corner. 5 bolts to 2-bolt chain anchor.

87. Uncompleted Project (5.12?) No topo. Bad rock at bottom.

Pizza Slab

88. Fine Line (5.11d) Start below the vertical face right of the Pizza Slab, a huge fallen slab resting against the cliff. Work up a thin crack, then up left over a series of small roofs to the *Main Line* anchors. 6 bolts plus gear at top where it joins #89 to 2-bolt anchor.

89. Main Line (5.9) Great crack climb directly up the right-facing dihedral right of Pizza Slab. 2-bolt chain anchor.

90. Blonde Ambition (5.11c) On the face just left of Pizza Slab. Aesthetic crack and face climbing up a steep slab. Easier if you use the crack. 6 bolts to 2-bolt anchor.

Red Light District

This sector is the farthest west part of the Palomas Peak climbing area. Expect few people, good rock, and great views. This cliff sector is 150 feet left of route #90.

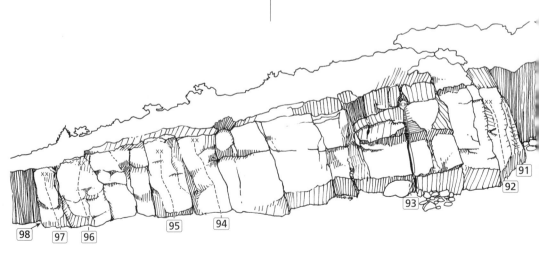

91. Circle K (5.10d) Straight up discontinuous cracks on a buttress. The first bolt is well right of the start. Clip it first before climbing. 4 bolts to 2-bolt chain anchor.

92. X-File (5.10b) Just left of *Circle K*. Lieback a thin crack. Go right at last bolt to anchors. 4 bolts to 2-bolt chain anchor.

93. The Baltzenator (5.11b) Located 60 feet left of *X-File*. Start off broken blocks. Climb an obvious crack over a big roof to an easier finish. Bring a rack of cams. 2-bolt chain anchor.

The next routes are 50 feet left of #93.

94. People Mover (5.6) A good, short beginner lead and the easiest route at Palomas Peak. 4 bolts to 2-bolt chain anchor.

95. Pony Ride (5.9+) Face climb up and left to the crux at bolt 4. 4 bolts to 2-bolt chain anchor.

96. Radio Flyer (5.13a) A pretty sick 5.13 slab! Located 45 feet left of *Pony Ride*. Dimples and smears up a steep slab. 4 bolts to 2-bolt chain anchor.

97. In Pain for Jane (5.12b) Short, technical, painful, and height dependent. Thin face climbing over a bulge, then easier to anchors. 4 bolts to 2-bolt cold shut anchor.

98. WYSIWYG (5.10d) No topo. On a narrow west face left of an arête at the end of the crag. Tricky start. First bolt is right of the obvious line. 4 bolts to 2-bolt cold shut anchor.

SANDIA MOUNTAINS

■ OVERVIEW

The Sandia Mountains, a rugged limestone-capped granite escarpment that towers east of Albuquerque, offers a wealth of adventure climbing on large granite faces. Long approaches, difficult climbing, route-finding decisions, and long descents characterize the area. The routes range in length from one to thirteen pitches. The rock quality of the Sandias varies from poor to good, making route selection paramount for a safe and enjoyable experience. The selections in this guide represent some of the best routes on the escarpment. Gaining familiarity with these routes will provide first-time visitors a basis to explore this complicated area and the knowledge to seek out other more obscure but quality lines.

The Sandia Mountains form an abrupt and rugged skyline for Albuquerque, New Mexico's largest city. Sandia is Spanish for "watermelon." The range's long north-south trending ridge is topped by 10,678-foot Sandia Crest. This lofty point, reached from Albuquerque and Interstate 40 via a 14-mile paved road up Tejano Canyon, overlooks the city's urban sprawl, the broad Rio Grande valley, and distant mountain ranges including the southern tip of the Sangre de Cristo Range above Santa Fe, the Jemez Mountains, and Mount Taylor to the west.

The 14-mile-long crest road winds upward from the dry upland grasslands east of Albuquerque through forests of pine and spruce to the mountain summit. A spur highway, Highway 165, leaves the crest road after 8 miles and drops down Las Huertas Creek to Placitas and the northern foothills of the Sandia range. This highway accesses the Palomas Peak sport climbing area and passes the famed Sandia Man Cave archaeological site. This controversial site, discovered in 1936, dated early man's presence in the New World to 26,000 years ago. Most of the Sandia sierra lies in Cibola National Forest. The spectacular range section north of the crest highway is protected by Sandia Mountain Wilderness Area.

The geology of the Sandia Mountains is quite complex. The large cliffs exposed on the west-facing escarpment are composed of an ancient granite that is an aggregate of quartz, feldspar, and mica. The granite formed during Precambrian times some one to two billion years ago. During the last five to ten million years, massive blocks of the earth's crust slowly lifted along a fault line on the west edge of today's mountains. Thin layers of limestone and shale dating from the Pennsylvanian Period between 250 and 300 million years ago cap the granite atop the range crest. The limestone bands are prominently seen at Palomas Peak on the northeast fringe of the Sandias. The Great Unconformity, a 1.1-billion-year erosive gap of missing geologic history, lies between the granite and limestone.

Climbing in the Sandias requires sound judgment and caution. Objective dangers abound, including loose rock, changeable weather, and lightning. Trails to the cliffs are sometimes complicated affairs that require careful hiking and navigating to reach the crag base. On the routes themselves, climbers need to use traditional skills like route-finding and placing gear for protection and belays to successfully ascend their chosen line. Climbers, especially first-time visitors, should plan on a long day in the mountains when attempting any long Sandia route. The range is not a beginner area. Everyone climbing here should be competent and able to self-rescue should the need arise.

Some of the best routes and rock in the Sandias are found on The Shield, The Needle (sometimes referred to as the Pyramid), Muralla Grande, Torreon, Mexican Breakfast crag, Estrellita, Hole-in-the-Wall, Echo Canyon, and Lower La Cueva Canyon. All of the rock formations are approached either from trails that start at the mountain base northeast of Albuquerque or by driving to the crest summit and descending trails to the cliff bases.

The Shield is approached from both the bottom or the top, with the approach from the top considered the best by far. Either way, it is best to have a car at the top. The Needle, Muralla Grande, Torreon, and Mexican Breakfast are best reached from the top. The La Luz Trail, descending from the crest to Juan Tabo Picnic Area at the western base, provides access to many of the crags on the south end of the mountains. Use this trail for routes in Echo Canyon, Hole-in-the-Wall, and Estrellita. See the individual rock formation descriptions below for specific directions. A recommended map for first-time visitors is the "Sandia Wilderness Area" map available from the Albuquerque Forest Service office and local climbing shops.

Climbing History

Little is known about early climbing in the Sandias. The Shield attracted the most attention with ascents as early as the 1930s. An accident claimed the lives of two climbers here in 1938. The East Saddle of The Needle was ascended in 1944. The period between the 1950s and 1960s saw little recorded activity with the exception of an R. L. Ingraham ascent of The Shield in the mid-1960s. The long approach and wild nature of the crag must have reminded Ingraham of his many classic ascents in the Organ Mountains

to the south. Bob Kyrlack, Jack and LaDonna Kutz, and Larry Kline were also seeking out harder lines in the late 1960s.

The 1970s were the halcyon years of exploration. Standards dramatically rose during this time with many of the classic lines established on The Shield, Muralla Grande, and Torreon. Mike Roybal, one of the most talented and prolific climbers that New Mexico has produced, honed his craft here. Mike teamed up with various partners to establish many of the current classic climbs. Peter Prandoni and Doug Bridgers joined to do many first and second ascents. Both continue to be active in the area climbing scene and pursue high-standard routes. Other 1970s activists include Mark Leonard, Gary Hicks, Carlos Buhler, Paul Horak, Rico Meleski, and Clark Gray.

The Sandias were further explored in the 1980s with the discovery of many new routes and areas. The Techweeny Buttress and adjoining areas in Echo Canyon, featuring upper grade (5.11–5.12) bolt-protected climbs, were developed by Paul Horak, Mark Leonard, Matt Samet, Tom Wezwick, Cayce Weber, Adam Read, Jeff Ash, Dave Dunlap, Bruce Doeren, Wayne Taylor, Steve Verchinski, John Duran, Doug Drumheller, Kathy Kocan, and David Benyak.

Sport climbing has been limited by the area's long-standing traditional ethic and the prohibition on motorized drilling in Sandia Mountain Wilderness Area. In keeping with local ethics, many established sport routes were opened in a quasi-traditional style by placing bolts between gear placements.

In the 1990s and 2000s, many high-quality sport routes, also augmented by gear protection, were opened, adding to the diversity of the Sandia climbing experience. Check out these excellent offerings on Clandestine Cliff, Hole-in-the-Wall buttress, and The Shield. Clandestine Cliff, located just below the crest, features an easy approach, a good range of routes, including *Event Horizon* (5.14a) put up by Nathan Bankroft in August 2003. John Kear's visionary big wall route, *The Promise Land* (V 5.12c) on The Shield, is perhaps the ultimate expression of new routes to come in the future.

Rack and Descent

A standard Sandia rack includes camming units up to 4 inches in size, sets of TCUs, RPs, and Stoppers, extra slings, and ten to twelve quickdraws. The long pitches and belay anchors on Muralla Grande and The Shield eat up gear, making doubles in most sizes mandatory. The few bolts encountered, especially on older routes, are often ¼-inch bolts. Back these up whenever possible. The newer routes are generally bolted with sturdy ⅜-inch bolts. It is useful to climb with two 165-foot ropes, especially if you need to retreat. Water, food, and rain gear are generally necessary on the longer routes. Watch for loose rock, start early, and plan on a long day to hike to the cliff, climb your route, and trek back to the parking lot.

Not all bolts are shown on the topos.

Trip Planning Information

Area description: The Sandia Mountains, towering east of Albuquerque, offer numerous multipitch adventure routes on granite crags in remote wilderness settings.

Location: North-central New Mexico. East of Albuquerque.

Camping: There are no developed campgrounds in the Sandia Mountains. All sites on Sandia Crest are day-use picnic areas only. The nearest developed forest campsites are 50 miles south of Albuquerque on the east side of the mountains. Contact the Mountainair Ranger District for more information. Coronado State Park's campground, next to the Rio Grande in Bernalillo north of Albuquerque, offers showers and is convenient to Highway 165, which travels to the mountain crest.

Climbing season: Late spring to late fall are the best months. Snow depths of 100 inches are recorded annually in the Sandias. July and August are rainy months. Be prepared for possible heavy thunderstorms and lightning. As in any mountain environment, be prepared for changeable weather during any season.

Restrictions and access issues: Sandia Mountain Wilderness Area is administered by Sandia Ranger District of Cibola National Forest. Motorized drilling is not allowed. A seasonal closure protects peregrine falcon nesting sites from March 1 to August 15. The closure area affects all climbing on The Shield, UNM Spire, and Prow, and hiking on Fletcher and Movie Trails. Some routes on The Needle are periodically affected. Call the Sandia Ranger District (505–281–3304) for specific closure information. Fines of up to $5,000 and imprisonment up to six months can be levied for violating closed areas.

Guidebooks: *Hikers and Climbers Guide to the Sandias,* third edition, by Mike Hill, University of New Mexico Press, 1993, is the original and complete guide to the area. *Sandia Rock* by Mick Schein, Sharp End Publishing, 2003, is a good updated guide to the Sandias with some routes not covered here. *Rock Climbing New Mexico & Texas* by Dennis R. Jackson, Falcon Press, 1996. A guide to the Sandias appeared in *Rock and Ice* #43.

Services: Full services in Albuquerque. Restaurants range from fast food to gourmet dining. Lots of cheap motels, too.

Emergency services: Dial 911 for all emergency services in the Albuquerque area. Search and rescue services in Sandia Mountain Wilderness Area are initiated by the New Mexico State Police; dial 911 or (505) 841–9256. Albuquerque hospitals with twenty-four-hour emergency care: Lovelace Medical Center, 5400 Gibson Boulevard SE, (505) 262–7000; Presbyterian Hospital, 1100 Central Avenue SE, (505) 841–1234; University of New Mexico Hospital, 2211 Lomas Boulevard NE, (505) 843–2411; Kindred Hospital, 700 High NE, (505) 242-4444.

Nearby climbing areas: The Cochiti Mesa Crags are 50 miles northwest. White Rock Crags are 90 miles north. Palomas Peak sport area is on the northern end of the Sandias. Gilman Tunnels are 50 miles northwest. Also see the section on Other Albuquerque Areas.

Nearby attractions: Albuquerque is New Mexico's largest city. Founded in 1706, it is rich in history and culture. Visiting Old Town, 2 miles west of downtown off U.S. Highway 40, captures glimpses of this historic past. In this area is the Albuquerque Museum with the largest collection of Spanish Colonial artifacts in the nation. Close by is the New Mexico Museum of Natural History, featuring New Mexico's natural history from the beginning of the earth to modern times plus many hands-on exhibits. Outside attractions include the Rio Grande Nature Center State Park, Rio Grande Zoological Park, Petroglyph National Monument, and Coronado National Monument (ruins). The internationally famous Balloon Fiesta is held annually in October.

Finding the crags: The trails to all described crags begin from Sandia Crest parking area.

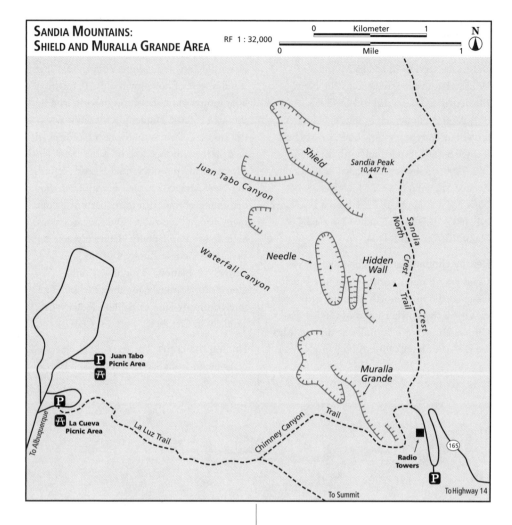

RF 1 : 32,000

Kilometer

Mile

N

Shield

Juan Tabo Canyon

Sandia Peak
10,447 ft.

Waterfall Canyon

Needle

Hidden
Wall

Sandia
North

Sandia Crest Trail

Crest

Juan Tabo
Picnic Area

Muralla
Grande

To Albuquerque

La Cueva
Picnic Area

La Luz Trail

Chimney Canyon

Trail

Radio
Towers

165

To Summit

To Highway 14

To reach the crest from the north or south, turn east onto Highway 165 about 10 miles north of Albuquerque. The road ends 20 miles south at Sandia Crest parking area. Sandia Crest is also reached from the east via Highway 14. Access Highway 14 from the south via I–40. From the north or Santa Fe, follow Interstate 25 to the highway junction north of Albuquerque. Turn west onto Highway 536 at San Antonio, then left at its junction with Highway 165. Refer to each crag's description for trail directions from the main parking area atop Sandia Crest.

The Shield

The Shield offers the area's longest routes (five to thirteen pitches) including *Rainbow Route* (VI 5.9 A4) and *Purple Haze* (VI 5.11 A4+), New Mexico's only Grade VI routes. Due to an area closure between March and August to protect peregrine falcon nest sites, The Shield sees limited climbing activity. Most routes on The Shield, especially the Grade V and VIs, suffer from lack of attention and tend to be loose with antiquated fixed gear. The exceptions are *Purple Haze* and *The*

Promise Land. These recent additions offer the best big wall experience on this formidable face.

Finding the cliff: For routes on the east end of The Shield, the top-down approach is the best option. From the parking area on the crest, walk north through metal gates past the Radio Towers to North Crest Trail heading for North Peak. Hike the trail for about 2 miles until it nears the top of The Shield. Be alert here to take a left fork and follow a climber's trail down through forest and scrub to the top of a gully. (Going onto the top of The Shield reaches the *Knife Edge* route). The trail is cairn-marked and easy to follow.

Rappel for 25 feet from a large tree down a gully to a spot down right of the trail's end. Rappel from here to a spot down right. Stay high and next to the rock below the rappel. Do not go down broken cliffs and forested slopes below. Follow a ramp and ledge system after the rappel for several hundred yards. Locate about 100 feet of fixed lines and some cairns to help navigate to the base of the routes below the east side of the face. Allow about forty-five minutes to descend from the top of The Shield to the cliff base. Follow the obvious descent and scope out the descent to avoid many route-finding problems.

Descent off the cliff top is by hiking south along the crest ridge back to Sandia Crest parking area about forty minutes to the south.

Routes are described from right to left (east to west).

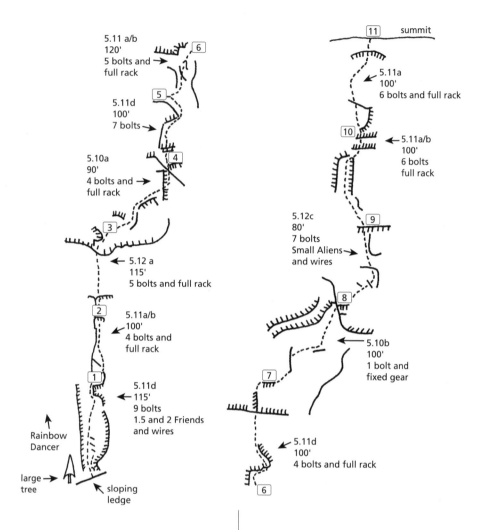

5.11 a/b
120'
5 bolts and →
full rack

6

5

5.11d
100'
7 bolts →

5.10a
90'
4 bolts and →
full rack

4

3

← 5.12 a
115'
5 bolts and full rack

2

5.11a/b
← 100'
4 bolts and
full rack

1

5.11d
← 115'
9 bolts
1.5 and 2 Friends
and wires

Rainbow
Dancer ↑

large →
tree

↖ sloping
ledge

11   summit

5.11a
100'
6 bolts and full rack

10

← 5.11a/b
100'
6 bolts
full rack

5.12c
80'
7 bolts
Small Aliens →
and wires

9

8

← 5.10b
100'
1 bolt and
fixed gear

7

← 5.11d
100'
4 bolts and full rack

6

1. The Promise Land (V 5.12c) This powerful and visionary route is destined for great-
ness. Perhaps the best climbing effort in the
last twenty-five years of New Mexico climbing. First ascent in 2003 by John Kear,
Carolyn Parker, Allan Aiken, and Marc
Beverly. **Pitch 1:** Start on a ramp 10 feet
right of *Rainbow Dancer.* Follow bolts and
dikes straight up. 115 feet. (5.11d) **Pitch 2:**
Move right off the belay and climb dikes and
corner. 100 feet. (5.11a/b) **Pitch 3:** Go
straight up from the belay, avoiding a loose
corner to the left of the bolts to a ledge.

Climb a crack to the roof, then crank
through the roof and right to the belay. 115
feet. (5.12a) **Pitch 4:** Traverse right and up
to a left-facing corner. Leave the corner and
climb up right to a belay. 90 feet. (5.10a)
Pitch 5: Climb straight up through a bulge
and into a remarkable pink quartzite section.
Follow an arching crack and exit left to a
great belay ledge. 100 feet. (5.11d) **Pitch 6:**
Climb up and right on knobs and a funky
face to a belay stance. 120 feet. (5.11a/b)
Pitch 7: Move left off the belay. Layback
and undercling above the belay and follow

bolts straight up. 100 feet. (5.11d) **Pitch 8:** Traverse up and right to exposed layback and undercling moves. Exit a stem-box to the right and gain a belay ledge above. 100 feet. (5.10b) **Pitch 9:** Move right from the belay and follow bolts through the bouldery crux of the climb, then straight up to belay. 80 feet. (5.12c) **Pitch 10:** Climb up left from the belay and follow bolts up. 100 feet. (5.11a/b) **Pitch 11:** Climb up from the belay to a short hand traverse left, then up to the summit. 100 feet. (5.11a) **Rack:** All pitches require some gear to augment lots of bolts and fixed gear. Carry a light rack of wired nuts, TCUs or Aliens, and cams to #2.5 Friend plus a dozen quickdraws and extra slings. **Bivouac:** The first ascent party did not bivouac. A sitting bivy is atop Pitch 5 and a good ledge left of Pitch 8.

2. Rainbow Dancer (V 5.11a) First ascent in 1979 by Peter Prandoni and Doug Bridgers. **Pitch 1:** Start near the top of the ramp below a right-facing overhanging flake and a left-facing corner that meet about 100 feet up. Begin near the flake and move over a bulge to easier moves right into the dihedral. **Pitch 2:** Continue up the dihedral/flake system and belay atop the dihedral on a small ledge. (5.8) **Pitch 3:** Difficult moves (5.10) above lead to a series of steep but featured moves taking the path of least resistance left and up for 100 feet. Belay at the bottom of a good crack. **Pitch 4:** Climb the crack above for 30 feet, then make a difficult traverse across a blank face to the right, ending at the base of a ramp trending up to the right end of the main "Rainbow." **Pitch 5:** From a belay at the top of the ramp, move right and climb a rotten crack to the roof, turning the roof and continuing up increasingly difficult moves to a traverse left, then up and finish on a ledge capped by a large rock. **Pitch 6:** Surmount the rock to gain

access to the face above and climb up to a small roof. Traverse right under the roof, then move up again to a shallow dihedral. The crux moves up the dihedral, then across a slab to the left and belaying slightly higher just right of a small roof. **Pitch 7:** A large red gully is above. Move up then across below the gully and climb the arête right of the gully. **Pitch 8:** Easy climbing leads to the "speed bumps," the large ledges below the summit. Three more easy-to-moderate pitches lead to the top.

3. Rainbow Route (VI 5.9 A4) First ascent in 1973 by Mike Roybal and John Mauldin. Modern gear and better techniques may prompt a reevaluation of the grading for this historic route. Most of the climbing is free with about 100 feet of aid done with nuts and small pitons on the first ascent. A brief description follows. Complete details should be sought from locals before any attempt. **Pitch 1:** Start at the base of the large overhanging right-trending dihedral. A long pitch up the dihedral ends at a bolted belay stance. **Pitch 2:** Continue up the corner to the left to another bolt. Belay on a ledge. **Pitch 3:** Bolt-protected face climbing leads up left to the base of the first "Rainbow." **Pitch 4:** Climb up the corner above to an aid crack through a roof. Above the roof, climb to a belay ledge above. **Pitch 5:** Moderate free climbing leads to 4th-class ledges. Follow these to their high point. **Pitch 6:** Near the top of the ledges is an A1 crack that goes over the first roof/bulge to a bent ¼-inch bolt. Traverse 40 feet left on difficult aid (crux) between the upper and lower sets of roofs. The corner at the end of the traverse offers better protection. Climb the corner to a small belay ledge. **Pitches 7, 8,** and **9:** Continue up the corner 2 to 3 pitches to a large blocky ledge below the "Cyclops," a large roof/cave formation near the top of the

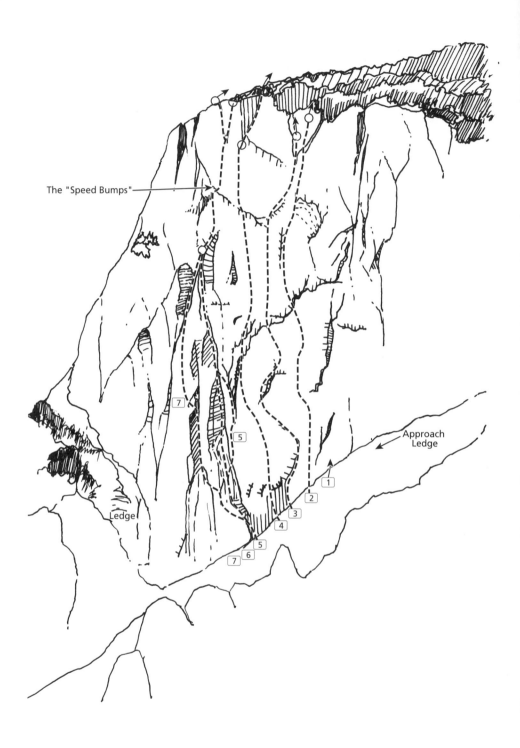

The "Speed Bumps"

Approach Ledge

Ledge

7

5

7

1

2

3

4

5

7 6

face. **Pitches 10** and **11:** 2 more pitches up the corner to the right of the "Cyclops" leads to the top.

4. Purple Haze (VI 5.11 A4+) A stellar modern testpiece put up by John Kear, Davito Hammack, and Eli Lynn in October 1996. **Pitch 1:** Start about 30 feet uphill from the start of *Procrastination* near a large boulder and several aspen trees. Climb a corner with minimal gear. **Pitch 2:** Go left then up past bolts to a right-facing corner and belay above on a ledge. **Pitch 3:** Climb up and right, then left. Aid straight up to a ledge. **Pitch 4:** "The Wild West Show." Traverse left off the ledge and up into a seam. Serious aid using hooks, beaks, rurps, and copperheads to a roof. Belay and bivy just above. **Pitch 5:** "The 9 to 5" pitch. Climb up and left, then aid right and up through roofs to a belay. **Pitch 6:** Climb a steep corner/ramp to a large left-facing corner. **Pitch 7:** Off-width or layback to a major ledge above. **Pitch 8:** Work left then up a 5.9 face to a belay stance. **Pitch 9:** Aid through a bulge and steep corner to an exit left through a roof to a belay stance. **Pitch 10:** Climb a steep corner, then exit left into another corner and follow to the summit. The upper 3 pitches of the route follow *Cowboy's Delight,* a previously existing 3-pitch route that is reached by rappelling from the summit. **Rack:** 4 Lost Arrows, 5 knifeblades, 5 assorted angles, all hooks, rivet hangers, 6 beaks, double set of Friends to #3, 1 each #4 and #5, set of wired nuts, set of RPs, and Copperheads (5-10). **Bivouac:** The first ascent party used portaledges and bivied at the end of pitches 2, 4, and 5. Belays at 4, 5, and 7 have 3 bolts for hanging a ledge. Natural ledges are found at pitches 3 and 7.

The following three routes all share a common start. *Procrastination* is an easier variation of *Chicken Chop Suey.* Start 100 feet left or downhill of the prominent right-leaning corner that is the start of *Rainbow Route.* A 5.9 move with poor protection accesses an easy ramp. *Procrastination* and *Chicken Chop Suey* follow the corner above for 6 pitches. Pitches 3 and 4 of *Chicken Chop Suey* go up the left corner and *Procrastination* up the right corner. Pitches 6 and 7 have loose rock on the ledges. The final pitches go up a large corner left of the "Cyclops," a large roof and cave formation near the top of the face.

Slipping into Darkness continues left on a ramp after the first pitch of #5 and #6. Climb to the base of a ledge/corner about 75 feet left. Follow the corner for 4 pitches to join with #5 and #6 on their seventh pitch. Pitch 4 is the crux lead; originally aided (A2/3), it can be free climbed (5.10c). Pitch 5 also originally involved A2 aid up a thin crack.

A large rack of camming units, including fist-size units, wires, TCUs, runners, and a 165-foot rope, are needed for all the routes. Allow at least 2.5 hours for the approach, a full day of climbing, and 1.5 hours back to the Crest parking lot.

5. Procrastination (IV 5.8+) First ascent in 1970 by Steve Merrill and Steve Schum. Crux is pitch 3. The climbing is mostly 5.7. Usually done in 11 pitches. Quality of rock is fair to good.

6. Chicken Chop Suey (IV 5.9) First ascent in 1973 by Robbie Baker and Charlie Ware. Crux is pitch 4. Quality of rock is fair to good.

7. Slipping Into Darkness (IV 5.10c) First ascent in 1976 by Gary Hicks and Ron Beauchamp. Free climbed in 1977 by Peter Prandoni and Hans Bede. Carry extras in the small and large gear. Quality of rock is good. Some difficult and sustained pitches are found on this route.

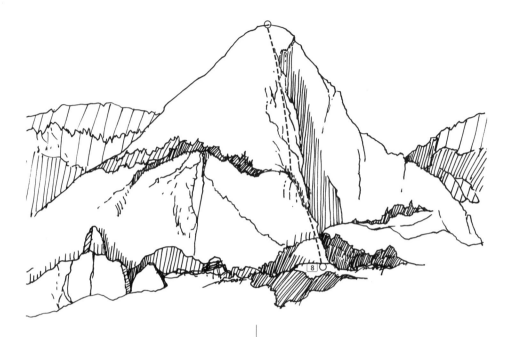

The Needle

The Needle offers the popular 15-pitch *Southwest Ridge* (5.8). A strong party should allow ten to twelve hours to go from car to car to climb this route. The route is mostly moderate climbing with a few sections of 5.8. Climbers should be adept at route-finding, gear placements, and self-rescue on this remote crag.

Finding the cliff: Approach to the base via the Movie Trail or from the Crest parking lot. From the crest, hike right or north through the metal gates past the radio towers to the North Crest Trail. Continue to the Cake and Candle Overlook and bushwhack down the gully below. Allow a couple hours for the approach.

The descent involves descending into a loose gully, then scrambling to easier terrain and back up to the crest.

8. The Southwest Ridge (IV 5.8) 15 pitches. First ascent in 1959 by Reed Cundiff and David Hammack. Start on the west side of the ridge and climb 4th- and/or easy 5th-class rock about 300 feet to a large square trough with a prominent cave above. Climb either side of the trough to the right side of the cave and then up to good ledges. Easy climbing above leads to the first notch on the ridge. Retreat is possible from here via a 150-foot rappel down the east side. From here do many pitches of moderate climbing (occasional 5.8 moves) to the top. Fifth Avenue, a large tree-covered ledge system, is passed at about pitch 10. Retreat is possible here by walking left or north along the ledges. 4 more pitches (2 of 5.8) lead to the summit.

Muralla Grande

The towering walls of Muralla Grande offer some fine adventure routes on good quality rock. Climbing here is reminiscent of shorter Black Canyon of the Gunnison routes in Colorado. The rugged scramble down from the range crest usually commits you to climbing back out because it's a whole lot more pleasant than rock-hopping back to the crest. The recommended route on Muralla Grande is *Warpy Moople* (III 5.9 or 5.10+). The more moderate *Second Coming* (II 5.8) is shorter and almost as good.

Finding the cliff: To approach Muralla Grande, walk north from the parking lot at Sandia Crest through a large metal gate toward the Radio Towers. At the Hang Gliders launch point, look down to the north and you can see most of the approach route to Muralla Grande. Locate an aspen knoll and a large canyon that descends the south side of the cliff.

Walk alongside the buildings on the crest by the parking area and turn left at building 79B. The trail starts here. Follow the trail until it reaches the aspen knoll. This is a good place to leave packs to pick up on the hike out. Go left at the beginning of the knoll and follow a steep trail into Chimney Canyon. At the junction of the south side of Muralla Grande and The Chimney, a large rock formation on the south side of the canyon, bear right and hike to the base of the west face of Muralla Grande. The routes on the crag's south face are all moderate 5.8 to 5.9 lines. Continue around the cliff to the west face and the start of *Warpy Moople*.

Carry a large rack of camming units through 3.5 inches, Stoppers, TCUs, ten to twelve quickdraws, and several slings. A 200-foot rope is handy but not required. As for descent, from the rock summit, scramble off to a path and hike to the aspen grove to retrieve gear and to reach the upper section

of the Chimney Trail. Follow it back up to the crest.

9. Warpy Moople (III 5.9 or 5.10+) First ascent in 1975 by Mike Roybal and Peter Prandoni. **Pitch 1:** Start below and left of a large pine tree under the left side of a large overhang. Climb up and then right around a bulge about 10 feet, then back to left to a large ledge. (5.8) **Pitch 2:** Start with a lay-back undercling to the right and up toward the right, staying away from the left side of the main crack system. Belay on a good ledge about 20 feet under a small roof directly under the main roof system. (5.9) **Pitch 3:** Quality of rock improves on this pitch. Climb up and right to the far right side of the roof, then up right to a good belay ledge. (5.8) This pitch can be combined with pitch 4 if climbing on a 200-foot rope. **Pitch 4:** Climb straight up the corner system on right side of main roof system to a small belay ledge with bolted anchors. **Pitch 5:** Crux pitch. Climbing straight up through the roof is 5.10+ and not generally done. The preferable option (5.9) is to traverse left 20 to 25 feet straight out from the belay, then back to the right to be above the belayer. Climb a dihedral until it ends, then move right to a good ledge with a 2-bolt anchor. **Pitch 6:** Face climb to a fixed pin, then angle right to a large ledge. Climb the crack above the ledge to a sloping grassy ledge. 140 feet. **Pitch 7:** Climb a right-facing corner, then up right for a full rope length. A 200-foot rope gets to the top. **Pitch 8:** A short, easy pitch through a slot to the top and the westernmost part of the aspen knoll behind the summit.

10. The Second Coming (II 5.8) No topo. 4 pitches. First ascent in 1976 by Joe Darriau and Thad Meyerriecks. This route is easy to

locate on the way to *Warpy Moople*. It is located on the south side of Muralla Grande at the end of the descent gully opposite The Chimney, a large rock formation. Look at the top of the cliff and locate three attractive cracks splitting the uppermost section of the wall. The crack on the right is the final lead of 4 pitches. **Pitch 1:** Start on the left side of the slabs at ground level to gain the top of the large tree-covered ledge system. **Pitch 2:** From the very top tree, take the left crack to near the right end of another vegetated ledge. **Pitch 3:** Climb up to the roof and either continue straight up or face climb around the left side. Belay at a bolted anchor. **Pitch 4:** The right-most crack is 5.7, straight up is 5.9.

Torreon

Torreon features a good selection of routes including the difficult Peter Prandoni and Mike Roybal classic *Voodoo Child* (5.12a) and the seven-pitch *Mountain Momma* (5.10c). *Mountain Momma* is one of the most popular routes in the Sandias. Both routes have some fixed gear although both are traditional lines that require skill at route-finding, gear placements, and self-rescue. Some of the best crack and face routes in the range are found here.

Finding the cliff: The approach is relatively easy if the correct gully is located. Remember the top of Torreon is near the range crest and the approach comes from the north, then traverses down and south to the

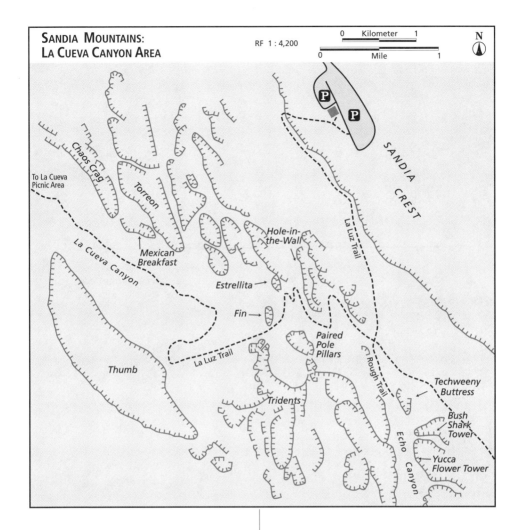

To La Cueva
Picnic Area

Chaos Crag

Torreon

La Cueva Canyon

Mexican
Breakfast

Hole-in-
the-Wall

Estrellita →

Fin →

Thumb

La Luz Trail

Paired
Pole
Pillars

La Luz Trail

SANDIA CREST

Rough Trail

Tridents

Techweeny
Buttress

Bush
Shark
Tower

Echo Canyon

Yucca
Flower Tower

cliff base. Locate the trail on the southern end of the parking area by a gate near some stairs. Go right or north about 150 yards to the second gully. A short downclimb (5.5) on the limestone band next to a dead tree puts you in the gully. Look for an abandoned aspen-log cabin in this area. This is a good place to stash gear for your return. Descend a gully for 500 feet to a saddle on the left near the bottom of the gully. Walk left or south to the base of the west face of Torreon. Allow thirty to forty-five minutes for the approach.

Bring a standard rack of Friends up to 4 inches plus extras in ½-inch to ¾-inch range, a set of Stoppers, ten to twelve quickdraws, some extra slings, and a helmet. A 165-foot rope is fine for climbing. For the descent, gain the top of the cliff and rappel off a tree 100 feet down to a sloping ledge. This requires some traverse tensioning while on rappel. A short fifth-class section leads up and out of the gully behind the formation to the "aspen heap" log cabin. Continue up to Sandia Crest.

11

12

11. Voodoo Child (III 5.12a) First ascent by Doug Bridgers and Peter Prandoni. Start at the toe of the Southwest Buttress. **Pitch 1:** Start about 80 feet left of *Mountain Momma*. Climb a left-facing corner to a small ledge at the top of a pillar. 60 feet. **Pitch 2:** Face climb right then up past 2 bolts. Difficult at the beginning, then easier above. Belay at the hollow corner below some roofs. Pitches 2 and 3 can be combined with a 200-foot rope. **Pitch 3:** A difficult rounded layback (technical crux) brings you to a roof. Undercling left about 12 feet, then climb left of the roof via a strenuous jam crack that leads 100 feet to a belay station with bolts and chains. This is *Mountain Momma*'s 4th pitch belay. **Pitch 4:** Climb a face and crack up and left to a roof. Turn the roof on the right. A short traverse left gets to the base of an overhanging layback and jam crack (the endurance crux). Climb the corner to ledge at top of the fifth pitch of *Mountain Momma*. Continue up the upper pitches of *Mountain Momma* to the summit. Descent is the same as *Mountain Momma*.

12. Mountain Momma (III 5.10c) First ascent in 1977 by Dennis Udall and Dirk Van Winkle. Walk along the base of the west face to the toe of the Southwest Buttress (*Voodoo Child*). *Mountain Momma* follows a large dihedral system for 250 feet before moving left and up corners that lead to the upper face. **Pitch 1:** Start near the south end of the west face below a shallow dihedral system. Face and crack climb to a 2-bolt belay (5.10a). **Pitch 2:** Ascend difficult face climbing (5.10) on questionable rock to a good hand crack on the right. Follow this to an optional belay stance or preferably continue up and left to the top of a buttress below a steep short headwall. Belay at a small ledge with bolts and chains. Rappel descent is possible from here, straight down *Voodoo Child*. **Pitch 3:** Short but difficult. Climb to a fixed piton that protects the crux. Crank past the bulge, then climb the crack above to a belay (5.10c). **Pitch 4:** Face climb around left of the blocks and belay on a large ledge (5.9). **Pitch 5:** Continue up the large crack system and belay in a chimney (5.9). **Pitch 6:** A short, easy pitch ends on a shoulder below the summit. **Descent:** Rappel or downclimb into the notch and then scramble up and left to Sandia Crest.

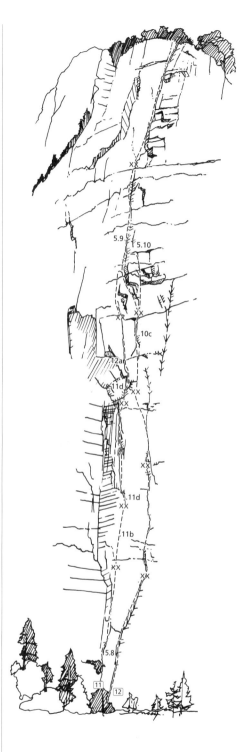

Mexican Breakfast

Directly below Torreon is a small detached formation called Mexican Breakfast. Two recommended routes are found here: *Mexican Breakfast Crack* (5.9) and *Tarantula* (5.10).

Finding the cliff:

Follow directions to the base of Torreon's west face, then continue down to the base of Mexican Breakfast. Alternatively you can approach from Sandia Crest by descending La Luz Trail until you're directly below Torreon. Scramble north to the base of the formation.

13. Mexican Breakfast Crack (5.9)

First ascent in 1974 by Doug Bridgers and Wayne Taylor. **Pitch 1:** Climb an off-size crack on the right side of the formation to a large roof. Traverse under the roof to the right and install a hanging belay on the right-hand end. **Pitch 2:** Either continue up the off-size crack above the roof or traverse right for easier but less protected climbing.

14. Tarantula (5.10) First ascent in 1976 by Peter Prandoni and Jenny McKernan. **Pitch 1:** Climb a thin crack on the face left of *Mexican Breakfast Crack* to the big roof,

then traverse left to an off-size crack. Jam up and over the roof. **Pitch 2:** Easy climbing straight up to the top of the crag.

Echo Canyon

This popular area features some of the easiest approaches in the Sandias. Start near the south end of the gift shop on the Crest Spur Trail #84. Follow the trail down to its termination at its junction with La Luz Trail. La Luz goes right (north) from this point and down to Juan Tabo Picnic Area at the base of the mountain. If you hike south, you reach the top of the tram. The head of Echo Canyon is also near this junction. Hike south down the steep canyon on a rough trail to Techweeny Buttress. This is about ten minutes from the junction.

Techweeny Buttress

15. Cracula (5.8) Recommended. **Pitch 1:** Start on the left end of the formation up a crack to a dihedral to a large ledge. Belay from gear (large cam useful). **Pitch 2:** Climb the wide crack to a small roof, then right via face climbing to another roof. Go right or left at the roof (right is recommended) to the summit.

16. Bojin (5.12b) Begin 10 feet right of *Cracula*. Very difficult face climbing past 6 bolts to a 2-bolt shared anchor.

17. Completely Clueless (5.12a) The center route. Runout to the anchors. 4 bolts to 2-bolt shared anchor.

18. Crankenstein (5.11+) Quality climbing. The most popular line on the crag. 4 bolts to 2-bolt shared anchor.

Bush Shark Tower and the Yucca Flower Tower

On the west-facing slopes south of Echo Canyon are Bush Shark Tower and the Yucca Flower Tower. Both formations have multipitch climbs and are worth visiting. Bush Shark Tower is about fifteen minutes farther down the canyon and Yucca Flower Tower a few minutes farther south. Yucca Flower Tower can also be reached by rappelling from La Luz Trail (going south to the tram). Recommended routes on Bush Shark Tower are *Bush Shark Spire* (5.9) and *Westeron Wynde* (5.9 or 5.10a). *Hammerhead* (5.12a), a new route established in 2003, is just to the right of *Bush Shark Spire.* Bring small gear to augment bolts on this Lee Brinckerhoff pumpfest. The controversial route *Date with Death* is located on a beautiful orange-striped wall close by. This runout route, currently rated 5.12 A0, is likely the hardest climb in the Sandias and is waiting for a first free ascent. Yucca Flower Tower has a good concentration of excellent routes. Recommended routes are *The Great Escape* (5.10), *Rawhide* (5.10c), *Western Justice* (5.11a), and *Squash Blossom* (5.12a).

Hole-in-the-Wall

Hole-in-the-Wall is a long west-facing wall near the top of Upper La Cueva Canyon. The cliff offers some excellent moderate classics as well as hard bolted sport climbs.

Finding the cliff: From Sandia Crest and the road's end, hike down Crest Spur Trail to its junction with La Luz Trail. Turn right here onto La Luz Trail and continue down the

trail past five switchbacks. It's the big obvious cliff to the right (north) of the trail. Turn north onto a climber's path and follow it for 150 feet to the base of the formation. Routes are listed from right to left.

19. Occasional Freshman (5.7) Pitch 1:
Start in a left-facing dihedral. Leave the dihedral and face climb to a ledge just below and right of a chimney. **Pitch 2:** Climb the somewhat loose and poorly protected chimney to a belay on a ledge to the right. **Pitch 3:** Traverse left a short distance on suspect rock, then choose a ridge or gully that leads to the summit.

20. Rastafari (5.11X) Pitch 1: Start 15 feet
left of *Occasional Freshman.* Thin face climbing (crux) to a belay above the last set of roofs. **Pitch 2:** More face climbing (5.10), poorly protected near the top (5.10b X).

21. Insane Clown Posse (5.12d) A difficult
climb put up by John Kear and Carolyn Parker in 2001. 6 bolts to 2-bolt anchor.

22. Sister Sledge (5.11d) A Carolyn Parker
testpiece. 7 bolts to shared anchors with *Insane Clown Posse.*

23. Miss Piggy (5.8) Popular and recom-
mended route. **Pitch 1:** Start at the base of a detached flake left of La Luz Mine entrance. Climb up the middle of a flake to a crack running across a smooth face. Face climb to a right-trending ramp. Belay at #21's anchors. **Pitch 2:** Continue up a dihedral and crack system to the summit.

24. New Shoes (5.11c) 2 pitches. Pitch 1:
Climb either *Insane Clown Posse, Sister Sledge,* or the first pitch of *Miss Piggy* to a 2-bolt anchor. **Pitch 2:** Stiff crack climbing above on a face and crack leads to summit anchors. **Rack:** Bring small gear to augment bolts.

25. Birth of the Cool (5.11a) 2 pitches.
Classic arête climb protected by bolts and fixed pins. **Pitch 1:** Climb either *Insane Clown Posse, Sister Sledge,* or the first pitch of *Miss Piggy* to a 2-bolt anchor. **Pitch 2:** Edge

up the sharp arête, passing several protection bolts to a 2-bolt anchor atop the cliff. Rappel back to the base.

Estrellita

Estrellita, Spanish for "little star," is a small west-facing crag located below Hole-in-the Wall. Its namesake route is one of the most popular routes on the upper mountain.

Finding the cliff: Hike down La Luz Trail, continuing past the turnoff for Hole-in-the Wall. Look for the place where the trail crosses the first major talus field on the left (south). Just below the talus field, exit right from the trail at a switchback that bends to the south. Scramble north on a short trail to the base of the formation. Routes are listed from left to right.

26. Clean Sweep (5.10a) Start left of a right-facing dihedral or go straight up the original route on the bolted face. Work up the dihedral then move right onto the bolt-protected face. 6 bolts and a fixed pin to 2-bolt anchor. **Descent:** Walk off.

27. Beat around the Bush (5.8-) Start 5 feet left of *Estrellita*. Turn the roof above (crux) on the right and continue to anchors for *Estrellita*. **Descent:** Walk off the back.

28. Estrellita (5.8) Classic, excellent, and recommended. Start next to a large aspen tree. Climb a short, 15-foot right-facing corner to a hand crack up a slab. Continue above up a larger right-facing corner to a 2-bolt anchor. **Descent:** Walk off.

Lower La Cueva Canyon

The Lower La Cueva Domes and Gemstone Slabs are easily approached by hiking up La

Cueva Trail from La Cueva Picnic Area at the range base northeast of Albuquerque. At Lower La Cueva Domes, which is not described here, try one-pitch *Mona Feetsa* (5.9) and *Leonardo da Smeari* (5.11a). The Domes are approached from La Cueva Picnic Area. Hike up the canyon until it narrows. Just past the first rocks, follow the first drainage on the south for about 250 yards to some large water-streaked slabs on the west side of the canyon. Not illustrated.

Gemstone Slabs

The Gemstone Slabs, along with some smaller slabs and cliffs, line the southern flank of La Cueva Canyon, a major canyon that rises steeply from the base of the Sandia Mountains to the summit crest. The two Gemstone Slabs offer a selection of easily accessible, fun, and recommended traditional-style routes up cracks, corners, dihedrals, and slabs composed of a firm, excellent granite. This guide describes the best routes on the slabs, although many other routes lace the cliffs.

Gemstone Slab West

Gemstone Slab West is a northwest-facing slab characterized by a series of large, left-facing dihedral systems. Most of the routes link these various dihedrals together and end atop the slabs.

Descent off the slabs is by scrambling down the west side of the formation or preferably by making a double-rope, 150-foot rappel from bolt anchors on the left side of the cliff summit. Routes are described from right to left when facing the cliff.

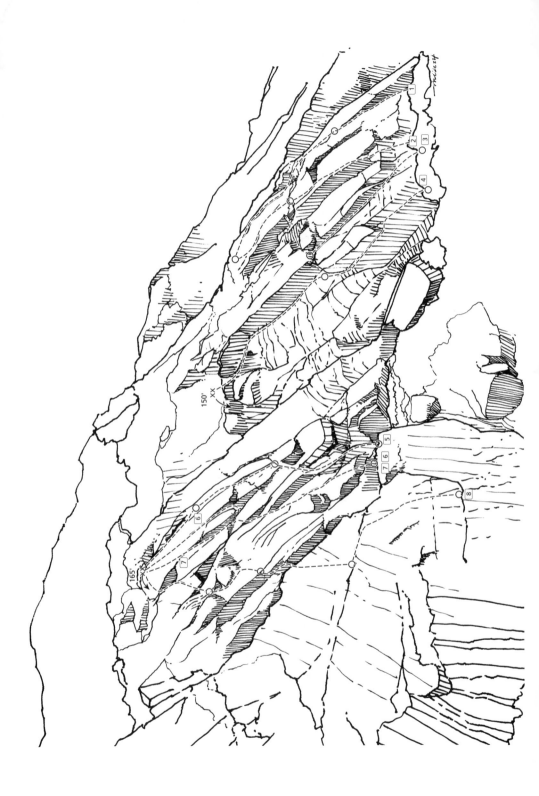

1. Shoots and Ladders (5.9) 2 pitches. Fun climbing up corners and cracks on the far right side of the slab. Start by scrambling up broken rock and bushes to the base of a left-facing dihedral system. **Pitch 1:** Climb the dihedral (5.9), which eases in angle and difficulty to a belay stance. **Pitch 2:** Climb up left along an easy crack and then up a crack in the final slab (5.5) to a belay ledge atop the wall.

2. The Fin (5.9) 2 pitches. **Pitch 1:** Climb up to the left side of a large roof. **Pitch 2:** Friction up a long slab to ledges. Walk off to the right from here.

3. Flail Out (5.9) 1 pitch. Climb the wide crack right of *Gemstone.*

4. Gemstone (5.9-) 2 pitches. Classic and recommended with excellent rock. **Pitch 1:** Layback or otherwise thrutch up a low-angle chimney, then move left and climb a left-facing corner to a good ledge. **Pitch 2:** Crux pitch. Start on the right end of the ledge. Climb a crack, then move left and finish on easy rock to anchors at the top.

4.1. Seamingly Hard (5.10b) No topo. Climb the slab just left of the first pitch of *Gemstone* and belay at the same anchor. This pitch is 5.10a and the second pitch (crux) takes the slab left of *Gemstone*'s second pitch and joins it near the top.

Gemstone Slab East

5. Opal (5.7) 3 pitches. **Pitch 1:** Climb a face below and left of a prominent square roof to a 2-bolt belay on a small ledge. **Pitch 2:** Climb right, then up past some loose flakes and belay from 2 bolts below a small roof. **Pitch 3:** Turn the roof on the right, then run it out on easy climbing to anchors shared by #6 and #8.

6. Sapphire (5.9+) 2 pitches. **Pitch 1:** Climb the first pitch of #7. **Pitch 2:** Downclimb until it is possible to traverse right to an attractive left-facing dihedral. (A belay fashioned from gear can be set up at the bottom of the dihedral on the way up as an alternative to the anchors for #7). Good jams lead up the dihedral to the crux thin crack. Clip 1 bolt on the slab above, then it's runout to the anchors.

7. Emerald City (5.9+) 2 pitches. **Pitch 1:** Climb up a left-facing corner to another slabby section. Friction to a 2-bolt belay. **Pitch 2:** Crux pitch. Go straight up a left-facing corner to a thin crack. Bring lots of small gear. Belay and descend from a 2-bolt anchor.

8. Revenge of the Elderly (5.7) 4 pitches. Start just left of a good-size alcove. **Pitch 1:** Climb past 3 bolts on a slab to a tree belay. **Pitch 2:** Climb to a left-facing corner, then to a cavelike formation and belay. **Pitch 3:** Exit from the rear of the cave and climb up right to an alcove. **Pitch 4:** Friction up a face to a left-facing corner to a slab. Follow twin cracks, then traverse right to anchors for *Emerald City.*

Other Albuquerque Areas

There is an abundant amount of other cliffs in the Albuquerque area that are well worth a visit. The following areas are some suggestions where visiting climbers can hone their skills, get in shape, and meet locals who can suggest other places to further enjoy the bouldering and climbing in this varied wonderland of crags.

The Three Gun Springs climbing area, climbable all year, offers more than twenty bolted routes from 5.8 to 5.12 as well as abundant bouldering. To get there, drive east on I–40 to Carmel. Head north through Monticello Estates to Three Gun Springs Trailhead. Hike about 1 mile north and look for a cluster of large granite boulders on the right.

Good bouldering is found in a designated open space recreational area that runs along the western base of the Sandia Mountains. Excellent biking and running trails are also located here. Tramway Boulevard accesses these areas. Exit onto Tramway Boulevard from I–40 East and turn right or east onto Copper Street. Drive less than a mile to the end of Copper. Hike about 400 yards north on a good trail to the popular U-mound boulders. A short distance north of Copper is Indian School Road. Turn right or east onto Indian School and follow it to its end and a large parking area. Hike past a large water storage tank, then up a canyon past a flood control project to access more good bouldering and short toprope problems.

Near the northern end of Tramway Boulevard is a road that exits east and winds up to La Cueva and Juan Tabo picnic areas. La Luz Trail starts at Juan Tabo area. Good bouldering is found in La Cueva picnic area. Follow signs to both areas.

Big Block is a popular bouldering area with a good selection of nine difficult sport routes. Take I–40 east to the Tierras exit. Turn here and proceed south on Highway 377 for 5 miles to a large road cut on the right. Park and hike a short distance to the easily recognizable, 20-foot-high, detached Big Block.

New Canyon, a small sport area southeast of Albuquerque on the east side of the Manzano Mountains, requires some driving but is interesting with its good selection of difficult sport routes. The problem, however, is that many hangers have been stolen from the bolts and anchors. This situation is fluid so check with locals for the latest beta. To reach New Canyon or Cañon Nuevo from Albuquerque, drive I–40 east to Tijeras. Exit and head south on Highway 337 for about 20 miles to its intersection with Highway 55. Go right, passing through the small towns of Tajique and Torreon, to the village of Manzano. From Manzano drive west on Forest Road 245 for 3 miles. One-half mile past a Forest Service building, turn right and continue for 0.5 mile to the rocks.

SOCORRO CRAGS

■ OVERVIEW

The Socorro Crags climbing area, southwest of Socorro off U.S. Highway 60, consists of numerous cliffs found in rock-walled Box Canyon and on hillsides south of the canyon. The area, considered one of New Mexico's best sport climbing venues, offers lots of moderate and difficult routes as well as out-standing bouldering. The porhyritic andesite rock provides sharp edges and small positive holds on mostly vertical to overhanging faces up to 150 feet high.

Visitors may be disappointed with their initial impression of the area cliffs. It certainly is not one of New Mexico's most attractive cragging areas, but once your hands touch the rock, you realize that this is the real thing. Check out the crags as a destination in itself (you won't be disappointed) or as part of a road trip that includes the Enchanted Tower.

The main area is Socorro Box, a north-draining canyon lined with several excellent cliffs including Fillet à Papillon Wall, Red Wall, and North Wall. Toropers enjoy Waterfall Wall, and boulderers find excellent problems and traverses on low cliffs along the sandy canyon floor.

Waterfall Wall, the canyon's first bolted cliff, rises directly across from the canyon parking area. The face is a popular toprope crag with convenient bolt anchors atop most of the climbs, which range in difficulty from 5.5 to 5.12. The easier routes ascend the right or south end of the cliff, while the left or north end offers harder lines. Some of the routes were originally bolted as leads by Bertrand Gramont. Later he removed the bolt hangers to equip new routes at Enchanted Tower.

Southeast of Waterfall Wall is Fillet à Papillon Wall, a sport climber's nirvana with lots of overhanging bolt-protected routes. One of the best is *Almost Blue* (5.12c) up an obvious black streak on the left side of a cave. Lots of glue was used to reinforce loose holds on this cliff, locally referred to as "Dirt Wall."

The canyon's longest routes ascend Red Wall, a southwest-facing, 150-foot-high cliff on the canyon's east side. The one- and two-pitch routes are mostly bolt-protected, although some also require gear placements.

The Corner Block is a squat triangular-shaped boulder that sits at the west end of Red Wall. Its southwest face offers five face climbing routes that can be led with gear and bolts or toproped. Access the top anchors by scrambling up the back of the block.

North Wall, the farthest north cliff in the canyon and the closest cliff to the high-way, is an excellent northwest-facing wall lined with superb routes that range from 5.7 to 5.13. The cliff is perfect during warm weather since it is usually shaded from the bright New Mexico sun.

The Streambed bouldering area, one of the area's best places to get a wicked pump, lies at the far north end of Box Canyon and just south of the highway bridge. The long low cliff, rising directly from the dry streambed, offers great problems over bulges and roofs as well as sit-down starts and endurance traverses. The landings are usually soft sand and gravel deposited during the latest flash flood to rampage through the canyon.

East Wall, directly north of the parking area on the canyon's west side, yields a small selection of hard bolted lines on the cliff's upper overhanging headwall. *Resurrection Route* (5.12a), an early Gramont testpiece, is recom-mended. The cliff sees relatively little vertical traffic compared to the other area cliffs.

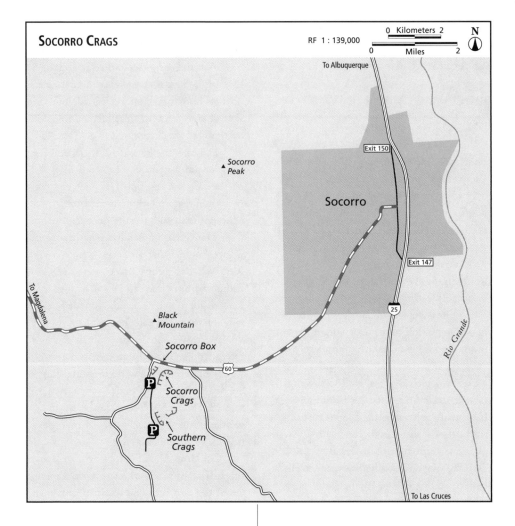

SOCORRO CRAGS

RF 1 : 139,000

0 Kilometers 2

0 Miles 2

N

To Albuquerque

Exit 150

Socorro

Exit 147

25

To Magdalena

Socorro Peak

Black Mountain

Socorro Box

60

P

Socorro Crags

P

Southern Crags

Rio Grande

To Las Cruces

A mile south of Socorro Box are several outstanding crags—Major, Pocket Change, and Alcohol Walls. These south and west-facing crags offer lots of great sport climbing and excellent bouldering in a remote setting. Major Wall has short hard routes up to 5.13d. Uphill and northeast of Major Wall are Pocket Change Wall and Alcohol Wall. Pocket Change Wall has several long excellent climbs up steep rock. Alcohol Wall divides into three sectors—a southwest face, the slabby Southern Prow, and the excellent hidden east face. Southeast of Alcohol Wall is Las Hermanas, the Three Sisters called Angela,

Lucia, and Arniel. Several bolted routes ascend their short faces. For superb bouldering, check out Unbeatable Boulder at the bottom of the grassy valley floor south of the crags. This excellent block offers problems on both slabs and overhung faces, making it a good place to warm up in the morning or cool down after a day of cranking.

Climbing History

The area was developed by Bertrand Gramont, a visiting French geology graduate student at New Mexico Tech, and other locals in the late 1980s. The crags were the first sport climbing venues established in this area of the state. After the subsequent "discovery" and development of Enchanted Tower farther west, the Socorro Crags diminished somewhat in popularity. Its steep walls, however, attracted power climbers like Timmy Fairfield. Some of the early hard routes suffered hold enhancement along with glue, but this practice seems to have faded away. Established during this era and still one of New Mexico's hardest routes, *Keeping Up with the Joneses* (5.13d), is "all natural." Albuquerque climbers including Lance and Alisa Hadfield, Chris Grijalva, Chris Eckstein, and Lewis Rutherford established high standard nonenhanced lines in 1990s and early 2000s, including some of the area's best routes on North Wall. A good time can be had here. Come on down.

Rack and Descent

Most Socorro routes are bolted, although some also require gear to augment widely spaced bolts. A standard rack is a good selection of Stoppers, a set of TCUs, and cams up to 3.5 inches. A 165-foot rope is sufficient for most routes. Descend routes by lowering or rappelling from fixed anchors.

Not all bolts are shown on the topos.

Trip Planning Information

Area description: The Socorro Crags offer bolt-protected sport routes in Socorro Box and on other satellite cliffs.

Location: Central New Mexico. West of Socorro.

Camping: Limited, undeveloped camping convenient to the crags is in the area, including Socorro Box parking lot. Toilet facilities are found across from the Waterfall Wall. Fires are permitted but discouraged. There are no fees, wood, or water. The area is sometimes used for late-night parties, so use caution to avoid problems.

Climbing season: Spring, fall, and winter. High summer temperatures limit climbing time to mornings and evenings. Mild winter temperatures provide for many climbable days.

Restrictions and access issues: The area is administered by the Bureau of Land Management.

Guidebooks: *Rock Climbing New Mexico & Texas* by Dennis R. Jackson, Falcon Press, 1996, details the Box crags. *The Enchanted Tower, Sport Climbing Socorro and Datil, New Mexico* by Salomon Maestas and Matthew A. Jones, 1993, is out of print. *A Climber's Guide to Box Canyon* by Erik Hufnagel and Bertrand Gramont is out of print. This self-published effort may be available from a local.

Services: Socorro offers full visitor services including grocery stores, restaurants, motels, and shops. La Pasadita on Garfield Street serves excellent Mexican entrees at reasonable prices. El Sombrero, 210 Mesquite, serves great Mexican dishes and is maybe Soccoro's best choice. A good place to meet locals and enjoy imported tap beer, music, and live entertainment is the Capitol Bar on the town plaza in Socorro. Coyote Moon, located 5 miles north of Socorro in Lemitar, specializes in vegetarian dishes. The Owl Bar and Cafe in San Antonio, 10 miles south of Socorro on U.S. Highway 380, is famous for green chili cheeseburgers. It's also a convenient stop when visiting Bosque Del Apache Wildlife Refuge.

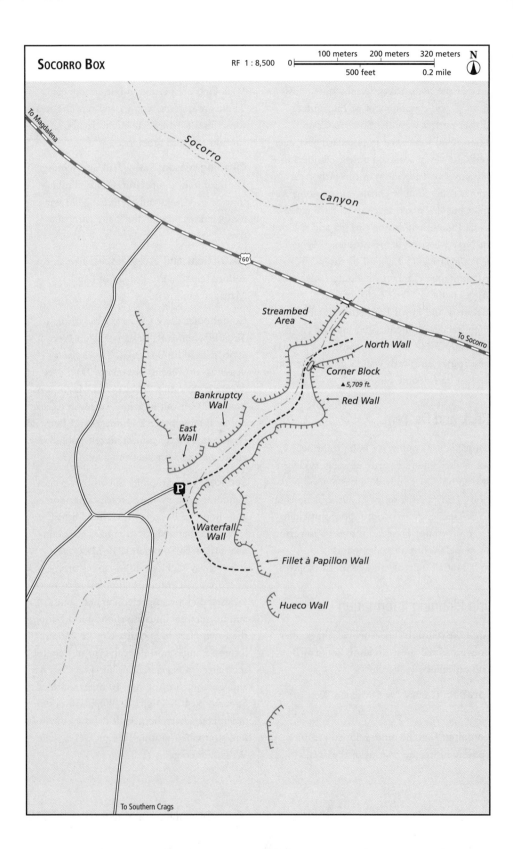

Emergency services: Dial 911 for emergency services in the Socorro area. The nearest telephone is located at Socorro General Hospital. The hospital is on the southwestern edge of town on US 60 as you drive toward the cliffs.

Nearby climbing areas: The Enchanted Tower is 60 miles west.

Finding the crags: The Socorro Box, aka Box Canyon, is located 7.2 miles west of Socorro south of US 60. Turn left onto a dirt road just after crossing a bridge that spans the canyon's north mouth. The crags are visible to the left when crossing the bridge. Drive 0.5 mile on the dirt road, take the first left, and park in the large parking area. A vault toilet, information kiosk, and trailhead to vicinity cliffs are near the lot's north end. Continue 1.1 miles past this left turn to the parking area for Major Wall, Pocket Change Wall, and Alcohol Wall.

The popular toprope Waterfall Wall is east of the parking area. South and uphill is Fillet à Papillon Wall. Red Wall and North Wall are north (down the canyon) on the canyon's east side. The East Wall is on the west side of the canyon just below the parking area. Minor Wall, Major Wall, Alcohol Wall, and Pocket Change Wall are a mile's drive farther south and easy to locate from the small parking area and the trailhead that accesses these areas.

East Wall

This is the first wall encountered on the west side of the canyon when walking north (down the canyon). The rather unattractive crag faces east and sees much less visitation than other crags in the area.

1. Unknown (?) First bolt is high and runout to the anchors. 4 bolts to 2-bolt chain anchor.

2. East Wall's Dirt Ramp Start (5.6 A1) This is the original common start to #5 through #7. The preferable start now is to rap down.

3. Mickey Mouse (5.12a) Start left of the cave passing 2 bolts to reach the 2-bolt anchor above the cave or alternately climb the bottom section of the *Dirt Ramp* and move left at the first bolt. Climb straight up from the belay past 2 bolts and 2 fixed pins to the ridge. No anchor.

4. Resurrection Route (5.12a) Start up the *Dirt Ramp* and bear left at the third bolt. Continue up to the ridge and turn right past two more bolts to the top anchors.

5. One a Day (5.11d) Rappel to mid-height anchors and belay. Go left at first bolt. Finish on the ridge or continue to the top. Gear required, 3 bolts, no anchor.

6. The Luge (5.12c) Climb up then slightly right to anchors at the top. 6 bolts to 2-bolt anchor.

7. Date with Hell (5.12a) Move right from the anchors, clip a bolt, then up and right past 2 more bolts to the ridge. Gear required, no anchor.

Bankruptcy Wall and Above Bankruptcy Wall

Bankruptcy Wall is about 100 feet north (down canyon) of East Wall. Four good 5.10 routes are found here. Routes from left to right are *Bankrupt* (5.10c), *Line of Credit* (5.10a), and *Joint Account,* a direct start to *Line of Credit* (5.10a), and *Layaway Plan* (5.10a).

Above Bankruptcy Wall is the north side of the East Wall. Approach by going up the scree slope between East Wall and

Bankruptcy Wall. *Titanic* (5.9) is on the left. Bolts to gear and a bolted anchor help identify this route. *Oui* (5.10a) is right of *Titanic.* This route has one high bolt and some sketchy gear placement plus bolted anchors. Not illustrated.

Waterfall Wall

Waterfall Wall is a popular toprope area on the east side of the canyon directly opposite the parking area. Good bolt anchors are above most routes. Bring webbing or short pieces of rope to extend your anchors over the cliff edge. The described routes are the original names for the (formerly) bolted routes established on the cliff. Some can be led and some bolts are in place, but don't

count on it. The wall is good for warming up and bouldering.

Access the cliff top by scrambling up the left (north) side. The routes generally get harder when you move from right to left across the cliff. Routes are listed from left to right.

1. Rough Caress (5.12) Sustained and fingery. Over a bulge then up left along the edge of a smooth face.

2. Battle Arms (5.11) Start the same as #1. Bulge to face. Finish up right.

3. Tough Country (5.11a) Overhang to face.

4. 1986 (5.11d) Up a groove to an arête finish.

5. Thumb Nail (5.9) Holds below an arête to a thin corner. Work up left to the top.

6. Highway 60 (5.12) Classic sharp arête.

7. The Chimney (5.6) Good for learning to place gear. Stem up the obvious deep corner cleft.

8. Little Red Wall (5.11a) One of the best routes on the crag. Thin moves up the dark red wall right of the corner.

9. Black Hole (5.7) Up a corner system left of a prow.

10. Crazy Sally (5.10d) Recommended. Over a roof then up a prow.

11. Diamond Clutch (5.7) Fine climb. Left of a dark pour-off streak.

12. Big Horn (5.10d) Over a small roof with a lone

bolt. Crux is grabbing a big horn and cranking over the roof.

13. Nasty Sally (5.10b) Loose start. Climb right of a roof and corner feature.

14. Barite (5.7) Quality checked. May or may not have 2 bolts.

The following six routes are not illustrated but are easy to locate.

15. Little Overhang (5.8) Classic. Up and over the little overhang.

16. Banana Split (5.11)

17. Waterfall (5.6) The face just left of the dry waterfall area.

18. Beginner's Route (5.5) The broken slabby wall right of the waterfall.

19. Waterfall Traverse (V0) Good warm-up bouldering traverse on the wall's right side. Traverse 45 feet from *Waterfall* to the start of *Black Hole* or vice versa.

20. Battle Arms Traverse (V3) Another good and popular bouldering traverse. Begin from the leftmost chalked holds left of *Rough Caress*'s start. Traverse right across the steep face to the start of *Thumb Nail*.

Fillet à Papillon Wall

Fillet à Papillon Wall is located uphill and right of Waterfall Wall. Many routes have glue-reinforced holds. Avoid climbing the fourth bolted line from the right (south) end. This route ends at a 2-bolt anchor and starts with an unsafe bolt placed in a hollow flake. Some routes start with a variation out of the cave near the cliff's left (north) end. Routes are described from right to left.

1. New Kids on the Block (5.10d) Ends on a ledge. 4 bolts to 2-bolt anchor (shared with #2).

2. Little Caterpillar (5.12b) 4 bolts to anchors for #1.

3. Bob Marley Meets Master Ganj (5.11b) Glued flake between bolt 3 and 4. 7 bolts to 2-bolt anchor.

4. Unknown (No rating) Not recommended.

5. If You Can't Do it, Glue It (No rating) A former project. No information available. 8 bolts to 2-bolt anchor.

6. Dreadlock Holiday (No rating) A former project. No information available.

7. Red Tag Sale (5.11b to middle anchors, 5.12b to top) 7 bolts to 2-bolt anchor.

8. Window Shopping (5.12b/c) Starts inside the cave. Use bolts on the right. Traverse

right at top to anchors for #7. 9 bolts to 2-bolt anchor.

9. Fair Trade (5.13b) Link-up of #8 and #10. Starts inside cave. Start up *Window Shopping,* then left across the right cave lip to a bolt over the lip. Finish up *Insider Trading.* 7 bolts to 2-bolt anchor.

10. Insider Trading (5.13c) Start inside the right-hand side of the cave. Crank up and over the lip of the cave and crimp to anchors. 7 bolts to 2-bolt anchor.

11. Sinister Dane (5.13c) Start on far left side of the cave. Climb up right past 3 bolts to a bolt over the lip. 5 more bolts lead to anchors. 8 bolts to 2-bolt anchor.

12. Almost Blue (5.12c) Climb the black streak on the left side of the face. 6 bolts to 1 cold shut anchor.

13. Uncle Fester Gets Sent to Europe (5.12a/b) A long name for a short route. 3 bolts to 2 bolt-anchor.

14. Uncle Fester Gets Sent in Europe (5.12c) Ditto above. Shares third bolt and anchors.

The following route is located about 200 yards north (down the canyon) of the parking area on the canyon's east side.

15. Unknown (5.8) Excellent low-angle climbing up a slabby prow. Climb straight up

to a good ledge. The moves leaving the ledge are the crux. Lower or rappel from a 2-bolt anchor. Best to use a 200-foot rope. 6 bolts to 2-bolt anchor.

Hueco Wall

The Hueco Wall, a face immediately right of Fillet à Papillon Wall, begins just right of Fillet's route #1. The face offers several moderate routes with large huecos. These routes are not illustrated, but they're easy to find. Routes are listed from right to left: *Mr.*

Jibbons (5.6), 3 bolts to 2-bolt anchor; *Unknown* (5.8), 5 bolts to 2-bolt anchor; and *The Throne* (5.9+), start at a cliff-base yucca.

Red Wall

The south-facing Red Wall, located about 300 yards north (down the canyon) from the parking lot on the canyon's east side, is the tallest crag in the canyon. Most of its routes terminate at mid-height and require placing some protection. Descent off the routes is by rappelling or lowering from fixed anchors. Walk off right if you manage to top out on any of the routes. Routes are listed from right to left.

1. Lucid Fairyland (5.10) A short route on the right end of the face. Go right at second bolt. 4 bolts and shared 2-bolt anchor.

2. Unknown (5.8) Same start as #1, then left at second bolt. 4 bolts to 2-bolt anchor.

3. Unknown (5.10) Fun climbing. 6 bolts to 2-bolt anchor.

4. Monkey Business (5.11a) Clip 2 old fixed pins, then pull over a roof protected with gear. 2 bolts to 2-bolt anchor.

5. Unknown (5.10) 2 bolts on the face left of #4. Gear required. Shares anchors with *Monkey Business*. 2 bolts to 2-bolt anchor.

5.1. Phase Dance (5.11a) No topo.

6. Spiderman (5.8) 2 pitches. An area classic with some looseness. It is possible to escape to the left above bolt 3. **Pitch 1:** Face climb (5.8) past 3 bolts to a belay ledge. **Pitch 2:** Work up the face above (5.6) to a cliff-top belay from a bolt.

7. Red Wall (5.7) The cliff's classic climb. Work up the obvious red dihedral using bolts and gear for protection to a large ledge with a 2-bolt belay. You can lower from here or do another good pitch straight up, then trend

right past bolts to finish in a good corner. Watch for loose holds and flakes. Descend by scrambling off the cliff top.

8. Earwig (5.10-) 2 pitches. Fun and crimpy. Start left of a dihedral, then climb past 6 bolts to the anchors for #7. The second pitch goes straight up, then right and up nice corners to the top.

9. The Diagonal (5.9 R) Continuous crack and face climbing with tricky protection. Ground fall potential if you screw up the pro. Shares anchors with #7. 2 bolts and gear to 2-bolt anchor.

9.1. Big Red Roof (5.11a) No topo. Start on *The Diagonal,* then climb straight up to a 2-bolt anchor. (5.10b). **Pitch 2:** Climb up and over the crux roof to anchors just below the top. 1 bolt plus gear to 2-bolt anchor. Descend by rappelling the route.

10. Molotov Cocktail (5.11a) Gear required. 2 bolts plus gear protect a steep face. First bolt is above crux. 2 bolts and gear to 2-bolt anchor.

11. TNT (5.11+) Climb over the bulge past 2 bolts to join *Molotov Cocktail.* 2 bolts and gear to 2-bolt anchor.

12. Gun Powder (5.10c) Protect the seam with gear, then climb up right to *TNT*'s anchors.

13. Hawk's Nest (5.7) Climb the right-trending dihedral to anchors for *TNT.* Continue up, climbing "Klein's Roof" along the way. Go left near the top to a tree anchor.

Corner Block

Corner Block is a large fallen boulder at the cliff base between Red Wall and North Wall on the east side of Box Canyon. Its routes can be led or toproped from a 2-bolt anchor shared by all routes. Access the anchors by climbing the back of the block. Routes are described from right to left.

1. 5.8 Variation (5.8) A variation, like duh, to #2.

2. Nowhere to Go (5.10+) Excellent face climb up the right side of the face. 2 bolts and gear placements to 2-bolt anchor.

CORNER BLOCK

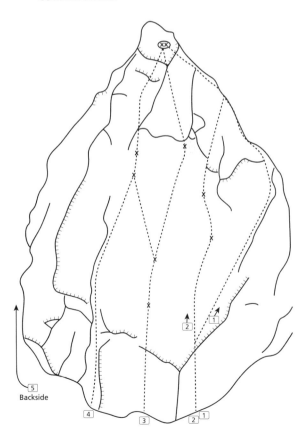

Backside

3. No Bozos (5.11) Good face moves with some laybacks above the top bolt. Bring some wires to protect between the first 2 bolts. 3 bolts to 2-bolt anchor.

4. Last Tango (5.11R) Great face climbing and finger crack. Bring small nuts to protect the runout start. 2-bolt anchor.

5. Pluto (5.9) On the north side of the block. Gear placements, no protection bolts. 2-bolt anchor.

North Wall

The excellent and popular North Wall lies at the far northeast end of the Socorro Box and just south of the highway. The north-facing wall is backside of Red Wall. The wall gets plenty of shade on warm days but is often too cold for comfortable climbing in winter. The wall offers outstanding sport climbing as well as great bouldering in the streambed below.

Access North Wall by parking in the main lot at the southern end of the Box. Hike north down the dry streambed until you're below the cliff. Scramble up easy slopes to the cliff base. Hiking time from car to crag is no more than ten minutes. Routes are described from right to left.

1. Liposuction Massacre (5.10+) Start behind Corner Block. 4 bolts to 2-bolt anchor.

2. The Truth (5.7) Classic and recommended. Start on a slab, then move left past anchors (for #3 and #5) to a crack. No bolts, gear required.

3. Direct on The Truth (5.9) A short difficult crack. Gear required to 2-bolt anchor or continue up *The Truth.*

4. Project (5.13?) A short route with a very steep, bouldery finish.

5. Alarm Arm (5.11+) Short sustained crack. Steep climbing to a 2-bolt anchor. Gear required.

6. Fatty (5.11b) One of Socorro's best for the grade. A bouldery start leads to a great finish.

7. Red Licorice (5.11b) Another great one for the grade. A hard start leads to an easier finish.

8. Bashart (5.12c) A bouldery start to a roof. Avoid grabbing blocks left of the bolts at the top.

9. Maria de la Sangria (5.11+) Climb past fixed pins on a short overhanging face to an anchor.

10. Unknown (5.11) Fixed pins plus bolts protect an overhanging seam to anchors.

11. Looser (5.13a) A hard seam.

12. Grijalva Route (5.12c) A difficult bouldery start with a great steep finish.

13. Project (No rating)

14. Boss Hog (5.12a/b) Climb the left side of the tall middle feature. 7 bolts to 2-bolt anchor.

15. Rock Trooper (5.9) Loose rock. 1 bolt, no anchor.

16. Black Crack (5.10+) No topo. Climb a right-leaning crack. No bolts.

17. Arch of Evil (5.10+) No topo. Start up *Black Crack,* then work left across a large black streak to a bolt. Continue past 1 more bolt to the top and anchors.

18. Jack Be Quick (5.12c) No topo.

19. Grease Mechanic (5.12-) Start left of the black streak. Climb straight up past 5 bolts to shared anchors. Runout.

20. Box Baby (5.10b) No topo. Climb up right to the third bolt of *Grease Mechanic.* Finish on *Grease Mechanic.*

21. Modern Day Contrivances (5.11+) No topo. Start the same as *Box Baby,* then go left at the third bolt of *Grease Mechanic* and pass 2 bolts to shared anchors.

22. Box Frenzy (5.10a) No topo. Start up *Totem.* Climb straight up and move right near the top past 2 bolts to shared anchors.

23. Totem (5.7) Lots of lichen. Climb straight to the top following a crack system. No bolts, no anchor, gear placements required.

24. Tomahawk (5.9) Climb a crack to a roof, then finish up the left-hand crack. No bolts,

no anchor, gear required, including some large Friends.

25. The "Z" Crack (5.8) Interesting but short. No bolts, no anchor, gear placements required.

26. Unknown (5.10c) Good slab climb that could use a lower first bolt.

27. Power House (5.11c)

28. Crystal Ball (5.11b) Technical and difficult with a great finish. Farther left is a good 5.10-.

The Southern Crags

The following crags are located about a mile south of the Socorro Box in the rugged hills east of the narrow dirt access road. See the Finding the crags section above for specific access directions. All the crags are east and

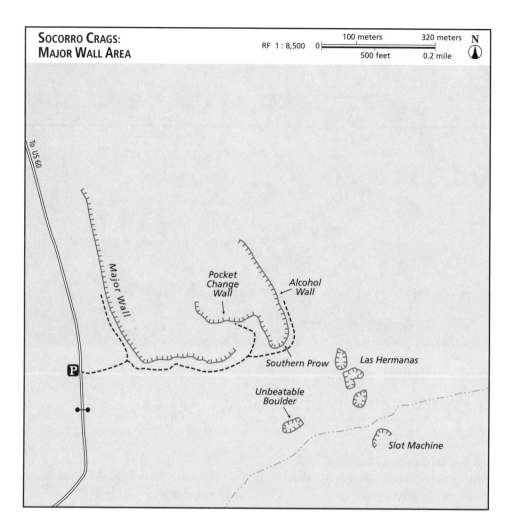

SOCORRO CRAGS:
MAJOR WALL AREA

RF 1 : 8,500

100 meters 320 meters
0 ⊢———————⊣
500 feet 0.2 mile

N

To US 60

Major Wall

Pocket
Change
Wall

Alcohol
Wall

P

Southern Prow

Las Hermanas

Unbeatable
Boulder

Slot Machine

Pocket
Change Wall

Alcohol
Wall South

Major Wall

Southern
Prow

northeast of the road. The west-facing Major Wall, paralleling the road, is the first cliff you will encounter. Alcohol and Pocket Change Walls are farther up the slope east of Major Wall. These crags are all very popular with a wide variety of routes and grades, easy access, and plentiful sun on cool days.

Major Wall

The south-facing Major Wall is a one-minute hike from the small pullout on the access road. All its routes have or share lowering anchors and are well protected with bolts although some require supplemental gear. Routes are listed from left to right.

1. Chingadera (5.10a) The farthest left route on the cliff. Straight up to a bolt, then onto a shelf. Traverse a long distance right here to a bolt shared with *Pinche Verga*. This is the easiest way to clip the second bolt.

2. Pinche Verga (5.12c/d) Direct start to *Chingadera*. You probably don't want to know the English translation of these two route names. 2 bolts to 2-bolt anchor.

3. Zee Wicked Bulge (5.13) A former toprope problem. Start right of a black streak. 5 bolts to 2-bolt anchor.

4. New Unknown (No rating) 6 bolts to 2-bolt anchor.

5. New Unknown (No rating) Shares 4th bolt and anchors with #6. 4 bolts to 2-bolt anchor.

6. New Unknown (No rating) Same start as #7 and same last bolt as #7, then climb up left past 4 more bolts. Shares a 2-bolt anchor with #5.

7. New Unknown (No rating) Same start and shares first bolt of #6, then up right past 3 bolts. Shares a 2-bolt anchor with #8.

8. Unknown (No rating) 4 bolts, shares anchors with #7.

9. Keeping Up with the Joneses (5.13d) One of New Mexico's hardest lines with all natural holds—no chipping. It's also called *Pimp Daddy.* 4 bolts to 2-bolt anchor.

10. Bat out of Hell (5.11d) Up a crack protected by 6 bolts to 2-bolt anchor.

11. The Demon (5.13a) 5 bolts to 2-bolt anchor.

12. Captain Blueberry (5.11a) Joins *Buttress Fly* above a bulge and shares anchors with *Liberace's Anus.* 1 bolt and gear to 2-bolt anchor.

13. Buttress Fly (5.10-) 2 bolts and gear to 2-bolt anchor shared with *Liberace's Anus.*

14. Liberace's Anus (5.9+) Start at the corner of the south face and west face. Finish on the lower-angle slab near the top. It has a long runout that can be protected with gear. 5 bolts to 2-bolt anchor.

15. Prickly Proctologist (5.7+) Shares anchors with *Liberace's Anus.* 5 bolts to 2-bolt anchor.

15.1. The Ramp (5.7) No topo. Gear route. Shares anchors with *Liberace's Anus.*

16. Bananas On Acid (5.12a) Using holds right of third and fourth bolt makes this climb much easier. 4 bolts to 2-bolt anchor. (*Bananas the de la Weenie Way* 5.11c variation: Climb right of bolts then back left to last bolt.)

17. Banana Peel (5.11c) 3 bolts plus gear to 2-bolt anchor.

18. Hurt Me Not (5.12a/b) 2 bolts plus gear to 2-bolt anchor.

19. Bon Bon (5.10a) Gear route. Fun climbing with lots of stemming. No anchor. Walk off or rappel (carefully) from #20.

20. Juckets and Bugs (5.10a) Tricky down low, pumpy up high. 4 bolts to 2-bolt anchor.

The following two routes are in "Dylan's Secret Garden." Try the fine bouldering traverse along the base of the wall here.

21. Milo Mindbender (5.10b) 6 bolts to 2-bolt anchor.

22. Major, Major, Major (5.8) Use first 2 bolts of #21, then right and up past 3 more bolts. Shares anchors with #21. 5 bolts to 2-bolt anchor.

Pocket Change Wall

South-facing Pocket Change Wall, left of Alcohol Wall, is a big piece of stone with several excellent and classic routes. Access it by a trail that runs east from Major Wall and then climbs steeply to the cliff base. Routes are described from left to right.

1. Pocket Change (5.11d) Classic. The final section is runout. 5 bolts to 2-bolt anchor.

2. Route of All Evil (5.11c/d) 1 bolt, then joins #3 for 2 more bolts. Shares anchor with #3. 3 bolts to 2-bolt anchor.

3. The Bowels of Hell (5.11d) 4 bolts to 2-bolt anchor.

4. Payday (5.10-) Pumpy through the roof. Some marginal gear placements supplement the fixed gear. 4 bolts to 2-bolt anchor.

5. Vegetable Massacre (5.11a) Variation of *Payday* using right-sided start. 4 bolts to 2-bolt anchor shared with *Payday*.

6. After the Gold Rush (5.9-) 4 bolts to 2-bolt anchor.

7. Wedding Day (5.10d) 4 bolts to 2-bolt anchor.

Alcohol Wall South

Alcohol Wall South is a mostly south- and west-facing wall that is down and right from

Pocket Change Wall

Alcohol Wall South

Pocket Change Wall. Expect steep stone and some strenuous climbing, especially on the longer pitches.

1. Public Intoxication (5.10d) Gear is necessary before the first bolt and after the second bolt. 2 bolts and gear to 2-bolt anchor.

1.1. Climbing While Intoxicated (5.10b) No topo. Start just right of *Public Intoxication*. Gear plus 2 bolts. Shares anchors with *Public Intoxication*.

2. Brain Cramps (5.12a/b) Through the left side of a roof. Can be toproped from *Spinal Spasms* anchors. 2 bolts and gear to 2-bolt anchor.

3. Spinal Spasms (5.11) Through the right side of a roof. Anchors can be reached from the rappel anchors above and left to set up a toprope. 2 bolts and gear to 2-bolt anchor.

4. Barfly Blues (5.9) Long and fun. Stay out of the chimney to the left. Clip bolt 1 left of the chimney, then step right and climb straight up the face with nice pockets. 7 bolts to 2-bolt anchor.

5. Meat Market (5.10c) Steep and fun. Clip 4 bolts then join *Barfly Blues* and pass 3 more bolts. 7 bolts to 2-bolt anchor.

6. Another Round (5.9) Start around a corner right of the first bolt. Place gear to protect a delicate move left onto a slab below the first bolt. 7 bolts to 2-bolt anchor.

7. Get Shorty (5.11+) Climb the left side of the cave. 5 bolts to 2-bolt anchor.

8. Power Play (5.12-) No topo. Traverse the top of the cave. 6 bolts, shares anchor with #7.

Southern Prow

The Southern Prow is exactly that, a prominent rounded and slabby prow that is located on the southern end of the Alcohol Wall. Routes are described from left to right.

1. Unknown (5.11) Contrived. 4 bolts to 2-bolt anchor.

2. Twisted (5.8+) Clip first bolt of #1, then climb past 3 bolts to a 2-bolt anchor.

3. Just Plain Stupid (5.8) Shares the last bolt and anchors for #2.

Alcohol Wall

Alcohol Wall is an excellent east-facing wall that is hidden from the parking area and the other crags. It offers a selection of excellent routes on perfect stone.

Access the wall by following a climber's path east from the southern base of Major Wall. The trail slowly ascends the steep grass and talus slopes, passes under the Southern Prow and then scrambles uphill to the base of Alcohol Wall. Routes are described from left to right.

Alcohol Wall

Parking Area

1. Anabuse (5.10c) 5 bolts to 2-bolt anchor. A new 5.10c/d route is found just left.

2. Bourbon Street (5.9) 5 bolts to 2-bolt anchor shared with *Anabuse*.

3. Comfortably Numb (5.11c) Fun, crimpy. 6 bolts to 2-bolt anchor.

4. Project. It's resisted many attempts so far.

5. The Jones (5.12b) Shares bolt 4 and anchors with #6. 4 bolts to 2-bolt anchor.

6. Liquid Diet (5.11d) 3 bolts to 2-bolt anchor.

7. Empty Glass (5.11d/.12a) 4 bolts to 2-bolt anchor. A new 5.10d route is located just to the right.

8. B-52 (5.11c) Gear optional before the first bolt. Anchors shared with #9 and #10. 4 bolts to 2-bolt anchor.

9. Stirred Not Shaken
(5.12a) 2 bolts to 2-bolt anchor shared with #8 and #10.

10. Bottoms Up (5.10d) Clip 3 bolts, then climb way left to anchor. 3 bolts to 2-bolt anchor.

11. Cold Turkey
(5.10d/11a) 4 bolts to 2-bolt anchor shared with #12.

12. Delirium Tremens
(5.11b) 4 bolts to 2-bolt anchor shared with #11.

13. Happy Hour (5.10+) No topo. Climb up left to anchors from the fourth bolt. 4 bolts to 2-bolt anchor shared with #12 and #11.

ENCHANTED TOWER

■ OVERVIEW

Central New Mexico is a land of rough mountains, darkened with forests of piñon pine, juniper, ponderosa pine, and fir that tower above broad, dry valleys coated with sagebrush, short grass, and creosote bush. The area's remote mountain ranges, including the Magdelena, Bear, San Mateo, Gallinas, and Datil ranges east of Socorro, are, for the most part, unvisited and unpopulated except for the occasional cowboy in search of grazing cattle, hunters in the autumn, and climbers seeking hidden crags. Rough rock rises above deep canyons and studs steep mountainsides. The Enchanted Tower climbing area hides its vertical treasures within Thompson Canyon in the heart of the Datil Mountains. The area, also known as "Datil" for the nearby village of Datil, is simply one of New Mexico's best and most popular sport climbing areas.

The Enchanted Tower, a 110-foot-high semidetached spire and smaller satellite cliffs, offers more than one hundred excellent sport climbs that range in difficulty from 5.6 to 5.13+. Almost all the routes ascend vertical to overhanging rock using a variety of holds including pockets, huecos, in-cut jugs, and face edges. The routes, particularly on the Tower, are strenuous and pumpy, although good rests are found on most lines. The rock quality is generally good, although a few cliffs are somewhat loose and suspect. The cliffs, a long west-facing band, are composed of welded volcanic tuff. Besides great climbing, other inducements to visit Enchanted Tower are its pleasant mountain surroundings, free camping, and friendly climbing scene.

The climbing area, reached by a one-lane dirt road off U.S. Highway 60 northwest of Datil, divides into several sectors. This guide includes the main, easily accessible sectors above the campground and northwest to the Land Beyond. All the cliffs are easily and quickly reached via climber's paths from pullouts along the access road. Many paths have recently been vastly improved by efforts of the Access Fund, local climbers, and many hours of volunteer labor.

The Enchanted Tower itself is the area centerpiece. It's an abrupt, obvious prow that looms over the camping area and access road. The Tower features long, strenuous routes that range from 5.11 to 5.13. Up right is Rapunzel's Wall, a short cliff featuring moderate lines. Another 100 yards farther south is The Frog Prince with its excellent Training Wall. This short, overhanging wall offers some great 5.12 and 5.13 power climbs.

The cliff band north of the Tower yields several popular walls, including the Sleeping Beauty Wall, Captain Hook's Grotto, Midnight Pumpkin, and the very popular Pogue's Cave Area. Below the cave is the 35-foot-high Ugly Duckling Boulder with fun moderate routes up its south face. The Mother Goose Wall near the long cliff's north end features good bouldering and good moderate routes in the 5.8 to 5.10 range. Easy to find and worth a visit is The Land Beyond, another 1.8 miles farther north of the main cliff sector.

Child of Light, one of New Mexico's hardest routes, rises northwest of the main canyon on the Renaissance Wall. The route works up an overhanging black streak near the wall's center. Glue to reinforce holds and a "prosthetic" edge constructed to replace a broken hold were employed on this Timmy Fairfield creation.

Enchanted Tower is very popular with traveling climbers, despite its relative remoteness, and offers pleasant camping among the

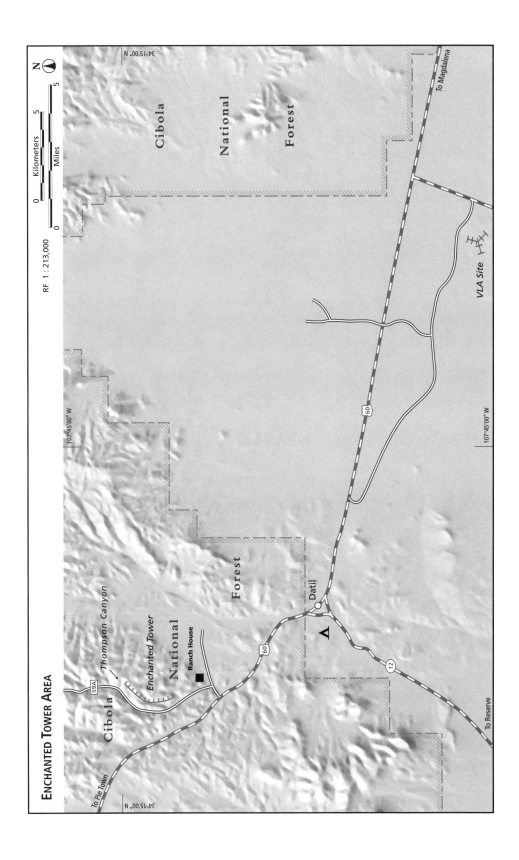

ENCHANTED TOWER AREA

RF 1 : 213,000

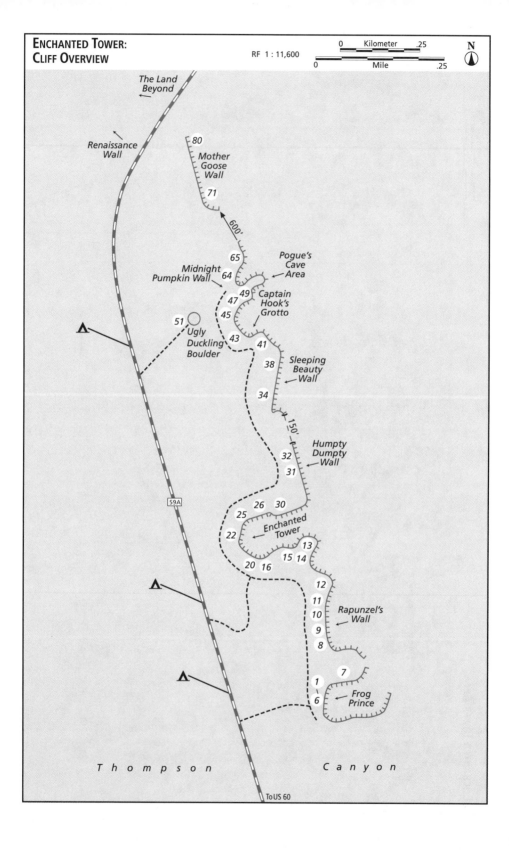

pines on the canyon's flat floor. The trail system has improved over recent years, with better trails and staging areas below popular routes.

Nagging access problems continue to plague the Enchanted Tower area. Visitors, including climbers, hunters, and other users, are asked not to drive in after dark (the interior of the ranch house gets a direct hit from car headlights) and to drive slowly on the dirt road approaching the gate. The gate is generally open or unlocked during the day, and climbers appear to be the most welcome user group.

The canyon lies above 8,000 feet in the rugged Datil Mountains 70 miles west of Socorro. April through October offers the best climbing weather. April and May bring mild, warm days with occasional wind. Summer afternoons are usually hot on the west-facing cliff, with highs in the 80s and low 90s. Plan on rising early in the morning for your daily route quota. Heavy thunderstorms often occur on summer afternoons. Autumn days are great, with highs in the 70s and cold nights. It's possible to climb here in winter, although snow can block and muddy the access road. Only sunny afternoons are climbable. March is good but somewhat unpredictable. Plan on cold nights and warm afternoons. This weather scheme favors the late riser since the west-facing cliffs remain cold until afternoon.

Not all bolts are shown on the topos.

Climbing History

Bertrand Gramont, a visiting French geology graduate student at New Mexico Tech in Socorro, discovered the Enchanted Tower climbing area in 1987. He quickly recognized the canyon's unique climbing possibilities and led a flurry of development. The area was the exclusive domain of Gramont and a small group of New Mexico Tech students until word of the fine climbing reached outsiders. The 1993 publication of a guidebook further opened up the area. Other area activists besides Gramont include Adam Read, John Duran, Jean DeLataillade, Lee Sheftel, and Timmy Fairfield, who bolted and climbed *Child of Light,* the area's hardest route. Road-trippers as well as local climbers continue to visit this remote canyon to enjoy its excellent rock and routes.

Trip Planning Information

Area description: The Enchanted Tower and its satellite crags offer some of New Mexico's best sport routes on steep bolted cliffs composed of coarse volcanic tuff.

Location: West-central New Mexico. About 70 miles west of Socorro and Interstate 25.

Camping: Excellent primitive campsites are found below the crags in Thompson Canyon. The best and most popular sites are among shady ponderosa pines below the Tower. Use established sites whenever possible. Practice low-impact camping. Fires are discouraged to minimize impact. Bring water. Developed BLM sites are at Datil Well Campground 5 miles east of the canyon off US 60 just west of Datil. Water is available here.

Climbing season: Enchanted Tower lies at 8,000 feet. Expect snow and cold temperatures in winter. Late March to early November offer the most climbing days. April, May, September, and October are best. Nights can be very cold.

Restrictions and access issues: The area lies in Cibola National Forest. The initial dirt road is on private property and is the most problematic in terms of access. Please drive slowly and arrive during daylight hours. All visitors, including climbers and hikers, are asked not to drive in after dark since the interior of the house gets a direct beam from headlights. Please consider camping at Datil Well Campground 5 miles east on US 60 if you arrive after dark. Drive slowly on the dirt road approaching the gate. The gate is usually open or unlocked during the day. If the gate is locked, ask climbers at the cliff if they have the current combination number. Climbers appear to be well liked and accepted by the landowners. Please be friendly and respectful in return.

The Forest Service access road is generally accessible to passenger cars. Wet conditions, however, make access difficult. The cliffs are an important nesting site for birds; avoid developing routes or hiking in side canyons that serve as the area's last undisturbed nesting sites. Important nesting months are May through August. Hunting activity is heavy during fall months. Be mindful where you hike and wear bright clothing.

As at other soft-rock sport climbing areas in New Mexico, Enchanted Tower has experienced hold enhancements. The friable rock and sharp edges make this an attractive and easy practice. Beyond the ethical debate lies the specter that these practices will influence future access and management policies. Please act responsibly when visiting.

Guidebooks: *Rock Climbing New Mexico & Texas,* by Dennis R. Jackson, Falcon Press, 1996. *The Enchanted Tower Pockets Full o' Fun* by Eric Fazio-Rhicard and Guy Agee, E Squared Enterprises, 2003. *The Enchanted Tower, Sport Climbing Socorro and Datil, New Mexico* by Sal Maestas and Matthew Jones, 1993, is now out of print.

Services: Datil offers limited services including a restaurant, gas station, and grocery store. Limited motel accommodations are in Datil. Full services are in Socorro. Being self-sufficient is the best way to visit.

Emergency services: The nearest phone is in Datil at the post office a half block north of US 60. The State Police number is (800) 922–9221. Call (505) 773–4600 for an ambulance. The nearest hospital is in Socorro 70 miles east.

Nearby climbing areas: The Socorro Box is 60 miles east. El Malpais Crags are 50 miles north.

Nearby attractions: The Very Large Array, a radio telescope consisting of twenty-seven separate antennas, is located 15 miles east of Datil on US 60. A self-guided tour and visitor center interpret this method of probing the universe. The Mineralogical Museum, located on the New Mexico Tech campus in Socorro, displays more than 12,000 gems and minerals from around the world. Bosque Del Apache National Wildlife Refuge, 14 miles south of Socorro on I–25, is best visited November through mid-February. Snow geese, sandhill cranes, and many ducks winter in this protected habitat. Other attractions include Quebradas Back Country Byway, Kelly ghost town, Gila National Forest, El Malpais National Monument, and the historic village of Magdalena.

Finding the crags: Enchanted Tower is located in Thompson Canyon in Cibola National Forest approximately 7 miles northwest of the village of Datil. From the west, take US 60 from Arizona to Datil. From I–25 in Socorro, turn west onto US 60 on the south side of Socorro. Drive west 62 miles to Datil. From the blinking traffic light in Datil, continue west on US 60 for 5.2 miles to a right turn (north) onto a dirt road. This road is on private property and provides the only access to the forest road that leads to the Enchanted Tower. Drive 0.8 mile to a sharp curve to the left just before a ranch house. This is Forest Road 59A with a sign, THOMPSON CANYON, a short distance into the canyon. Drive 1.8 miles up the one-lane dirt road to Enchanted Tower. The owner has requested visitors arrive before dark when headlights are necessary, to drive slowly, and to leave the gate closed. The road can be impassable after rain or snow.

The Frog Prince

This popular area, including the Training Wall, offers lots of great climbing on The Frog Prince, a prominent jutting buttress south of Enchanted Tower. The west-facing Training Wall has lots of great training routes and link-ups on its steeply overhanging face.

The north face, shaded by a large ponderosa pine, offers three good routes and some short, easy topropes left of the routes. A deep cleft on the south side above a side-canyon has three routes graded 5.10.

The Giant's Molars, not described in this guidebook, is the formation on the south side of the side-canyon south of The Frog Prince. The north-facing cliff, reached by a trail from the road, has five routes. From left to right they are *Gravity Cavity* (5.6) with six bolts; *Unknown* (5.9+) with four bolts; *Unknown* (5.10) with four bolts; *Tooth Fairy* (5.10d) with five bolts; and *Route Canal* (5.10b) with three bolts.

Finding the cliffs: The Frog Prince is 250 feet right or south of Enchanted Tower. Access the area from the climber access trail that starts at the information kiosk located below the Enchanted Tower.

1. White Queen (5.13b/c) Follow a line of bolts up the right side of the Training Wall to

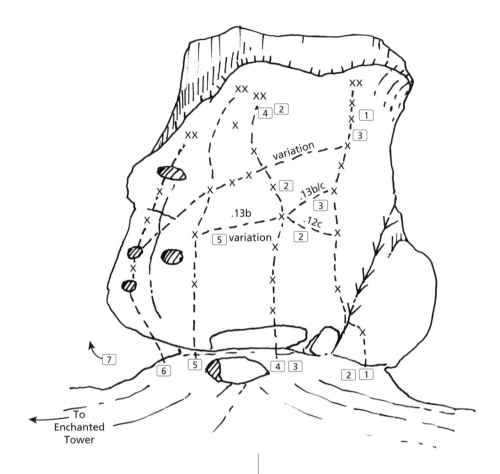

anchors just over the lip. 8 bolts to 2-bolt anchor.

2. White Knight (5.12c/d) Variation of #1. Move left at bolt 3 on *White Queen* and finish up *Through the Looking Glass*. 6 bolts to 2-bolt anchor.

3. Red Queen (5.13b/c) Shares first 4 bolts of *Through the Looking Glass*, then right to finish up *White Queen*. 9 bolts to 2-bolt shared anchor.

4. Through the Looking Glass (5.12c) Good pockets and position. Go left at the fourth bolt of *Red Queen* and up to 2-bolt shared anchor. 6 bolts to 2-bolt anchor.

5. The Frog Prince (aka **Babies**) (5.12a) Short, steep, powerful. Excellent route near the left side of the face. The 8-bolt *Dairy Queen* 5.13b/c variation goes right at bolt 2 and finishes at #1's anchors.

6. Gollum (5.11b/c) Steep jug haul up the left side of wall. Stick clip recommended. 3 bolts to 2-bolt anchor.

7. Blind Man's Bluff (5.11b/c) No topo. Somewhat loose. Located around and up from the left end of the rock near a large pine. 4 bolts to 2-bolt anchor.

Rapunzel's Wall

Rapunzel's Wall is a short 40-foot-high cliff immediately above and right (south) of the Enchanted Tower. The popular area features moderate routes. Routes are described from right to left.

8. Jack's Bean Stalk
(5.7) The tan streak right of *Rapunzel's Revenge*. 4 bolts to 2-bolt anchor.

9. Rapunzel's Revenge (5.8)
Climb a black streak behind a large juniper tree. 4 bolts to 2-bolt anchor.

10. Fee Fi Fo Fum
(5.9) Another streak route. 3 bolts to 2-bolt anchor.

11. The Thorn Bush
(5.10a). Up right side of groove. 4 bolts to 2-bolt anchor.

12. The Blind Prince (5.10a) Fun
climbing up the steep wall right of the groove and above a small cave. Shares anchors with *The Thorn Bush*. 4 bolts to 2-bolt anchor.

The Enchanted Tower

The Enchanted Tower is the area's classic crag with lots of long, strenuous pitches and terrific athletic climbing. A 200-foot rope is necessary for many routes and a 230-foot rope is ideal to reach the ground in one

RAPUNZEL'S WALL

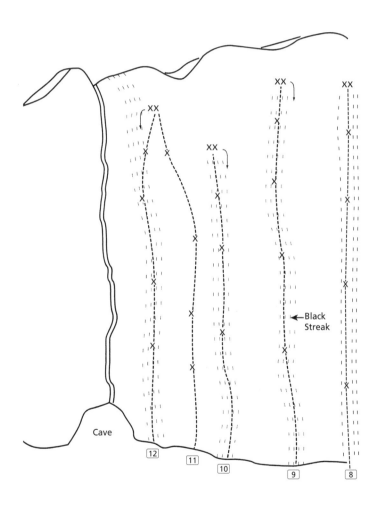

Long
5.10
Runout

18

19

17

16

13

14

15

16

17

19 18

Common Start

rappel for *Ripped Van Winkle, Zee Wicked Witch, The Mad Hatter,* and *Rubber Mission.* The tower is in shade on summer mornings and sunny in the afternoon during the cooler months.

Finding the cliff: Access the tower by following a climber's access trail that begins below the cliff at the information kiosk.

South Face

This is the shorter southeast- and south-facing wall on the right side of the tower. The routes are shorter than on the other faces.

13. Hippogriff (5.11d) The farthest right route. It's somewhat loose but is cleaning up. 8 bolts to 2-bolt anchor.

14. Flotsam and Jetsam (5.12a) Start on a small platform next to a fallen tree. Climb the bulgy wall to anchors. 9 bolts to 2-bolt anchor.

15. Shipwrecked (5.12c) A great pocket climb up the tower's steep southeast-facing wall. The upper headwall is superb and exposed. 9 bolts to 2-bolt anchor.

16. Golden Stairs (5.11b/c) Excellent, classic, and popular. A good warm-up. Most just climb to the lower anchors since the upper section is runout. This route climbs the sunny southeast face up a black streak. Begin near the left side of face just right of the *Goliath* prow. Tricky face climbing leads to bolt 4 and then to the intermediate 2-bolt anchor. Rappel or lower from here or continue to the top on runout but moderate climbing. Rap with two ropes from anchors just below summit. 10 bolts to 2-bolt anchor.

17. Medusa (5.12b) Not as good as the other Tower climbs. Begin up *Golden Stairs.* After 5 bolts, exit up left and climb steep rock to a 2-bolt lowering station. The direct finish along the bolts to the anchors is 5.12c. Most step right to keep the .12b grade. 9 bolts to 2-bolt anchor.

18. Goliath (5.13a/b) A 110-foot-long pitch. One of New Mexico's most beautiful lines. A difficult and continuous directissima up the exposed prow that divides the tower. Start up *Golden Stairs* and ascend the same first pitch as *Ripped Van Winkle* up the right edge of the prow (5.12c) to a midway set of anchors. Voyage up the wildly exposed prow above to anchors just below the cliff top. 17 bolts to 2-bolt anchor. Use a 230-foot rope to climb and lower to the ground or a 200-foot rope to lower to the halfway anchors. **Descent:** Make a two-rope rappel from the upper anchors or lower down to the mid-anchors. Thread those anchors and lower to the ground.

19. Ripped Van Winkle (5.12d) 2 pitches or 1 pitch (230-foot rope). A super classic line near the exposed prow edge. **Pitch 1:** Start up *Golden Stairs* but keep left straight up the prow past 5 bolts to a bolted belay. **Pitch 2:** Go left around the prow onto the west face and follow the right-hand line of bolts just left of the prow to a 2-bolt anchor shared with *Zee Wicked Witch.* **Descent:** Make a two-rope rappel to the ground from here. The route can be done in 1 pitch with a 230-foot rope.

Rapunzel's Wall

25

24 23

22

19
20

21

West Face

The West Face is the overhanging face left of the *Goliath* prow. It's shady on summer mornings and sunny on winter and spring afternoons.

20. Zee Wicked Witch (5.12c) 1 or 2 pitches. Great climb! First ascent by Bertrand Gramont in 1988. This stout line climbs the West Face just left of the obvious *Goliath* prow. The pitch to the first anchors is a quality 5.12a. Start up *Golden Stairs* just right of the prow base but quickly step left onto the right edge of the West Face around the steepening arête. Climb past the right side of a narrow roof and continue up and right to halfway anchors (2 bolts). Continue to the upper anchors by following the right line of bolts (same as *Ripped Van Winkle*). 16 bolts to 2-bolt anchor. Pay attention to rope drag if you do this in 1 long pitch by unclipping the lower bolts and skipping a couple bolts just below the first anchors.

21. Zee Wicked Witch Direct (5.12c/d) This direct start eases congestion on the prow routes by avoiding the popular start to *Golden Stairs*. The moves are not technically hard but make *Zee Wicked Witch* more sustained since it avoids a rest stop. Begin just left of the *Goliath* prow. Crank up some overlaps past 3 bolts before joining *Zee Wicked Witch*. Continue your wicked ways to the top anchors.

22. The Mad Hatter (5.12d/13a) 1 or 2 pitches. Another good climb. Begin left of the prow below some small overlap roofs. Climbing just to the first anchors is a good 5.12c route. **Pitch 1:** Face climb over the small overlaps and then a bigger roof with huecos on its left side. Pull up right on a smooth face to a 2-bolt intermediate anchor. **Pitch 2:** Move up right and then back left. Grab along an obvious overhanging black streak to a 2-bolt anchor at the rim. The route is best done in 1 long pitch with the midway station used for back-cleaning. 15 bolts to 2-bolt anchor.

23. Rubber Mission (5.12b) Begin below the left side of the face. Shares the first bolt with #24. Then climb up right and over a roof to a 2-bolt anchor and a good rest. 6 bolts to 2-bolt anchor. Lower from here or continue up the steep face above to the upper anchors for a *Full Rubber Mission* (5.12b). 12 bolts to 2-bolt anchor.

24. Jabberwocky (5.12b) One of the Tower's best climbs. Sustained, pumpy, and excellent. Begin at the far left side of the West Face. Climb up and over a large roof. Continue up the overhanging wall above to anchors near the cliff top. Stay left of the black streak at the top. 11 bolts to 2-bolt anchor.

North Face

25. Rumplestiltskin (5.11d)
Quality climb. Begin about 15 feet left of *Jabberwocky*. 9 bolts to a 2-bolt anchor.

26. Once Upon a Time
(5.11c) Quality. Begin 5 feet left of *Rumplestiltskin*. Face climbing to an optional intermediate belay station, then up a black streak to anchors. 9 bolts to 2-bolt anchor.

27. Grendel (5.11b/c)
A good introduction to the Tower. Start the same as for *Tinkerbell's Nightmare*. At bolt 3, swing up and right before continuing straight up. 10 bolts to a 2-bolt anchor.

28. Tinkerbell's Nightmare
(5.12b). Recommended. 10 bolts to 2-bolt lowering anchor.

29. Straight on 'til Morning
(5.12d) Start same as *Tinkerbell's Nightmare,* then straight up between *Technowitch* and *Tinkerbell's Nightmare*. 10 bolts to 2-bolt anchor.

30. Technowitch (5.12a)
Farthest left climb on the Tower. The new direct start improves this climb. 8 bolts to 2-bolt anchor.

Humpty Dumpty Wall

This wall, immediately left or north of the Tower's North Face, has three worthwhile routes. Not illustrated.

31. Humpty Dumpty (5.12a)
Right side of wall. 4 bolts to 2-bolt anchor.

32. Bambi (5.11b)
Fun route up steep wall left of #31. 4 bolts. Lower from 1 cold shut and a wired nut.

33. Thumper (5.11c)
4 bolts to 2-bolt anchor.

Sleeping Beauty Wall

Sleeping Beauty Wall, part of the horizontal cliff band, is 150 feet left or north of the Tower and just past an obvious low-angle

break in the cliff. The cliff is shaded in the summer and cold in fall and winter.

34. Cheshire Cat (5.10b) Pockets up the face just right of a black streak. 4 bolts to 3-bolt anchor.

35. Tarred and Feathered (5.10d) A black streak climb. 4 bolts to 2-bolt anchor.

36. Sleeping Beauty (5.11c) Recommended. First route left of a black streak. 5 bolts to 2-bolt anchor.

37. Glass Coffin (5.11a/b) The addition of 1 more bolt has made this climb safer. 4 bolts to 3-bolt anchor.

38. Poison Apple (5.11b) Start by using a crack on the right or coming in from the left. 5 bolts to 2-bolt anchor.

39. Heather's (5.7) A gear route! Climb the left-facing corner. Bring big cams.

40. Prince Valiant (5.9-) Fun climbing. The only route left of the left-facing corner. New enough to be a little crumbly; difficult near the top. 4 bolts to 2-bolt anchor.

41. Sea Hag (5.11c) Around the corner and left of #40. 7 bolts to 2-bolt anchor.

42. Witch's Promise (5.11b) Use pockets up #41's start and then climb up and left. 8 bolts to 2-bolt anchor.

Captain Hook's Grotto

The grotto is a deep bay located left of Sleeping Beauty Wall and above and right of the Ugly Duckling Boulder. Like the other west-facing sectors, it's shady on summer mornings and cold other times of the year.

43. Ruffio (5.12a) Grab small huecos in the second black streak right of an inset dihedral. Watch clipping bolt 3. 4 bolts to 2-bolt anchor.

44. Captain Hook (5.11a) Overhanging face just left of the inset dihedral. Joins #45 and shares anchors. 5 bolts to 2-bolt anchor.

45. Peter Pan Flies Again (5.11b) A direct start to #44. Start on top of chossy rock, then straight up to anchors shared with *Captain Hook*. 5 bolts to 2-bolt anchor.

45.1. Unknown (No rating) A 2004 addition equipped with glue-in bolts. No information available. 8 bolts to 2-bolt anchor.

Midnight Pumpkin Wall

The Midnight Pumpkin Wall is a small buttress located left of Captain Hook's Grotto and above the Ugly Duckling Boulder. It has four short, tricky routes.

46. Unknown (5.10a) No topo. Located around the prow right of *Glass Slipper*. A short 20-foot problem. 4 bolts to 2-bolt anchor.

47. Glass Slipper (5.11d) Climb past a bulging ledge, then up the right-hand black streak. 3 bolts to 2-bolt anchor.

48. Cinderella's Nightmare (5.11c) 4 bolts to 2-bolt anchor shared with #47.

49. Midnight Pumpkin (5.11d) Climb past 2 bolts, one missing a hanger, then up the left black streak. 5 bolts to 2-bolt anchor.

Wire on Stud

Ugly Duckling Boulder

The Ugly Duckling is a huge boulder in the middle of the slope below the cliff band. Its routes are easy and fun. The boulder is 60 feet above the main road near the left (northwest) end of the climbing area. Routes are listed from left to right.

50. Beautiful Swan (5.9+) 3 bolts to 2-bolt anchor.

51. Ugly Duckling (5.9) 3 bolts to 2-bolt anchor.

52. Quackers (5.8) 3 bolts to 2-bolt anchor.

Pogue's Cave Area

Pogue's Cave is a cliff sector located near the left or north end of the main climbing area. The popular cliff offers the area's second largest concentration of routes. All routes, mostly 5.10 and 5.11, are almost all worth climbing.

Finding the cliff: Find the area by hiking up the road from the camping and parking area below the Tower. Find a trail that contours uphill to the cliff base. It can also be accessed by following the cliff-base trail north from Midnight Pumpkin Wall. Routes are described from right to left.

53. Blessed and Blissed (5.12a) Thin and crimpy with a blind move over a bulge. 5 bolts to 2-bolt anchor.

54. Merlin's Mantra (5.11a) 4 bolts to 2-bolt anchor.

55. Ooey Gooey (5.11a) Excellent. 5 bolts to 2-bolt anchor.

56. Prima Donna (5. 10b) Left of *Ooey Gooey.* 5 bolts to 2-bolt anchor.

57. Party Pogues (5.11a) Start in back of a cave and finish up a chimney. 5 bolts to 2-bolt anchor.

58. Pogue's Arête (5.11c) Good climb. Stick-clip the first bolt. Climb the left outside edge of the cave. 3 bolts to 2-bolt anchor (shared with #57).

59. Jeremy Fisher (5.10d) Start just left of the cave. 4 bolts to 2-bolt anchor.

60. The Tale of Jemima Puddleduck (5.11a) Start on the right side of a buttress. Work up right. 5 bolts to 2-bolt anchor.

61. Buzz Light Year (5.11c) Difficult bouldery start. 5 bolts to 2-bolt anchor.

62. Unknown (5.11b/c) A good long route. 10 bolts to 2-bolt anchor.

63. Unknown (5.10b) Watch for loose rock. 8 bolts to 2-bolt anchor.

64. Never Never Land (5.12a) Sustained difficulty up the steep prow. 8 bolts to 2-bolt anchor.

65. Houka (5.11d) Very good. Start just left of #64. A hard start. 7 bolts to 2-bolt anchor.

66. Tweedle Dee (5.11c) Another great route with fun moves. 8 bolts to 2-bolt anchor.

67. Funk Shui (5.11b) Climb up and left over a bulge. 6 bolts to 2-bolt anchor.

68. Tweedle Dum (5.11a) No topo. Begin just right of #67. 7 bolts to 2-bolt anchor.

69. Now and Zen (5.10b) No topo. Near the left-hand side of the face. 5 bolts to 2-bolt anchor. A project is farther left.

70. Project (No rating) No topo.

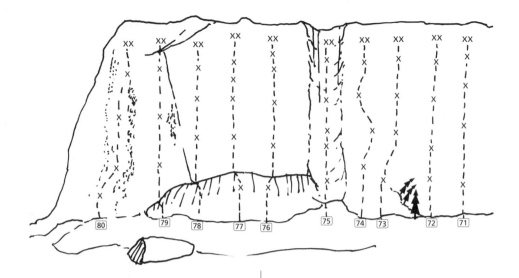

Mother Goose Wall

Mother Goose Wall, approximately 600 feet left of Pogue's Cave, has a mess of fun moderate routes. Routes #71 and #72 are right of a medium-size cedar tree near the right side of the cliff. The rest of the routes are left of the tree. Access it by hiking up the road to a trail that contours up to the cliff base. Hiking time from Enchanted Tower is about fifteen minutes. Routes are described from right to left.

71. Goosey Goosey Gander (5.10b) Right-hand route on the face. 4 bolts to 2-bolt anchor.

72. Mother Goose (5.10c) Stick-clipping the high first bolt is a good idea. Bouldery start. 4 bolts to 2-bolt anchor.

73. What To Do What To Do (5.10a) Another hard start and then moderate above. 4 bolts to 2-bolt anchor.

74. So Many Children (5.10b) Sustained difficulty. 4 bolts to 2-bolt anchor.

75. The Shoe (5.6) The area's easiest climb. Straight up the black slabby trough. 5 bolts to 2-bolt anchor.

76. Old Woman (5.8) Start 12 feet left of #75. 5 bolts to 2-bolt anchor.

77. Black Sheep (5.8) Good clean fun. 5 bolts to 2-bolt anchor.

78. Big Good Wolf (5.7) 3 bolts to 2-bolt anchor.

79. Geese Make Good Sleeping Bags (5.7) Located near the cliff's left side. 3 bolts to 2-bolt anchor.

80. Big Bad Wolf (5.6) Another easy one. 4 bolts to 2-bolt anchor.

The Land Beyond

This fun area is far up the canyon from the Enchanted Tower, but it's well worth visiting with lots of good but mostly hard routes. The crag, just off the road, has east, south, and west faces, offering either sun or shade depending on the weather. The West Face routes are recommended.

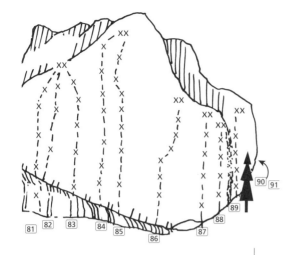

88. Lucky Number (5.12a) 4 bolts to 2-bolt anchor.

89. Hoggle (5.10a) A pumpy warm-up on the face's far right side. 4 bolts to 2-bolt anchor.

South Face

90. American Psycho (5.12d) No topo. Quality crank. 5 bolts to 2-bolt anchor.

91. Yo la Tango (5.11d) No topo. 5 bolts to 2-bolt anchor.

East Face

92. Alice Does Wonderland (5.12) 4 bolts to 2-bolt anchor.

93. Lord of the Rings (5.11d) 4 bolts to 2-bolt anchor.

94. Where the Thrush Knocks (5.11d) Climb straight up over a bulge or move right at bolt 3 to finish on #95. 6 bolts to 2-bolt anchor.

Finding the cliff: Drive 1.8 miles up the canyon road from the Tower. The crag is on the left side of the canyon 0.3 mile past a windmill. Routes are listed left to right.

West Face

81. Beagle (5.11a/b) 5 bolts to 2-bolt anchor.

82. Smeagol (5.11c) Use first bolt of #81, then up right. 4 bolts to 2-bolt anchor.

83. Gandolf (5.12a) Recommended. 5 bolts to 2-bolt anchor. Shares anchors with *Beagle* and *Smeagol*.

84. Servant of the Secret Fire (5.12b) Excellent. Go right at top to anchors for *Something Lethal*. 7 bolts to 2-bolt anchor.

85. Something Lethal (5.12b) Great route. 7 bolts to 2-bolt anchor.

86. Incredible Journey (5.12b/c) Perhaps the best route on the rock. 6 bolts to 2-bolt anchor.

87. Mr. Baggins (5.11d/.12a) 6 bolts to 2-bolt anchor.

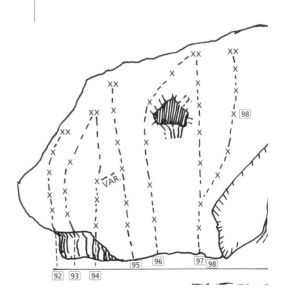

95. Soft Start (5.10d) 5 bolts to 2-bolt anchor. A hanger on the anchor may be missing.

96. Smaug (5.10c) 5 bolts to 2-bolt anchor (shared with *Frodo*).

97. Frodo (5.11c) 6 bolts to 2-bolt anchor.

98. Black Arrow (5.11a) Start up *Frodo* but veer right at bolt 2. 7 bolts to 2-bolt anchor.

Renaissance Wall

The Renaissance Wall on the west side of the canyon is a large south-facing cliff with few routes. Two routes along with a few projects are found on the cliff's somewhat friable stone. The best route is *Child of Light*, a powerful, bouldery line up a black streak. Projects are to the right and left of the *Child*; all are

crimpy and continuous and are still works in progress.

Finding the cliff: The wall is 0.5 mile up the canyon from the Enchanted Tower. Hike up the road to a left fork that leads toward the prominent wall. Scramble up to the base of the wall.

99. Child of Light (5.13c/d) One of New Mexico's hardest routes. Established by Timmy Fairfield. Powerful, painful pocket pulling up an obvious overhanging black streak in the middle of the face. Stick-clip the first bolt or two. Some manufactured holds. 6 bolts to 2-bolt anchor.

100. Unknown (5.13a) No topo. Located well to the right of *Child of Light* in a black streak. 5 bolts.

MENTMORE CRAGS

■ OVERVIEW

The Mentmore Crags, just west of Gallup near the New Mexico and Arizona border, are a welcome addition to western New Mexico climbing. The region, part of the Colorado Plateau, is blanketed by an abundance of sandstone, most of which is unclimbable because it is either soft and featureless or on Indian reservation lands. The horizontal cliff bands at Mentmore are an exception. The rock, part of the Mesa Verde Formation, is composed of a hard, metamorphosed sandstone that is eminently climbable and offers enjoyable climbing adventures easily accessed from Interstate 40.

The city of Gallup, just east of the climbing area, purchased the cliffs and surrounding land in 2003 and designated the area as an open-space city park. The area, a former dump site with years of accumulated litter and garbage, was cleaned up through the efforts of community volunteers. Future plans call for improving the access road, parking area, and trails to the crags. Currently the area is used primarily by city recreational and social programs and a small contingent of local climbers. Climbers traveling by on I–40, however, are both welcomed and encouraged to stop and sample Mentmore's excellent bouldering, challenging routes, and free camping.

The climbing is up vertical cliffs that range from 40 to 70 feet in height. The climbing area is divided into two sectors: The Original Area and The New Area. The southeast-facing Original Area cliff, lying on the west side of the broad wash opposite the parking area, offers vertical, pleasant climbing on positive holds along with a few great crack routes. The west-facing New Area, south of the parking area, has lots more vertical climbing on a long excellent cliff band. Most lines at both cliffs are safely protected with ample bolts and lowering anchors or can be easily toproped. Some faces have sturdy bolt anchors atop the cliff to facilitate toproping nonbolted lines. Throughout the area are also some very fine crack climbs that require gear placements for a safe ascent.

Climbing History

Mentmore, a relative latecomer to the New Mexico climbing scene, began with route development in 1999 at The Original Area. Members of the small Gallup climbing community responsible for the routes at The Original Area include Michael Laplante, Pat Estes, Marvin Seale, Don Tamminga, and Scott Halliday. The New Area, a great addition to the area crags, was developed by Scott Halliday, partnered by his wife, Amy, and Jim Smith. Michael Laplante wrote the area's first guidebook, now out of print, bringing the area to the attention of outside climbers.

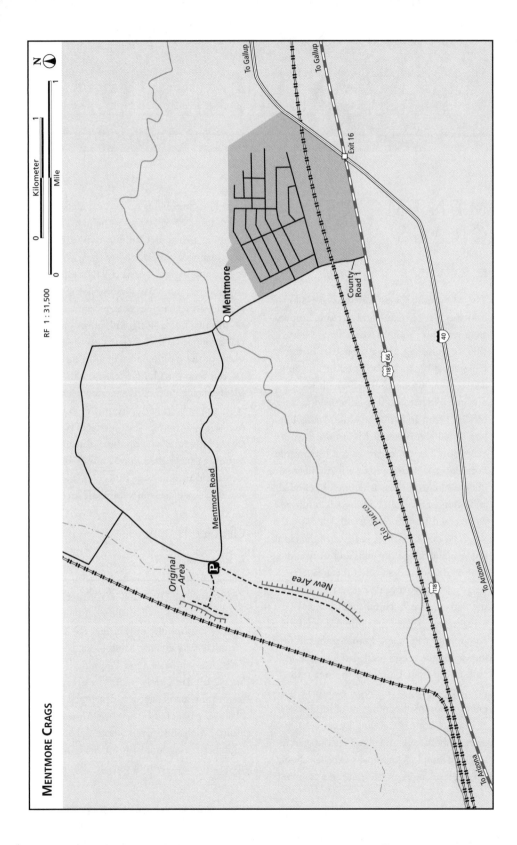

MENTMORE CRAGS

Rack and Descent

A dozen quickdraws and a 150-foot rope get you up and down all the sport routes. A small rack with cams up to 4 inches protects the crack routes. Descent off all routes is by lowering or rappelling from bolt anchors or scrambling off.

Trip Planning Information

Area description: Metamorphosed sandstone cliffs north of I–40 offer a fun selection of one-pitch bolted routes as well as crack climbs.

Location: Western New Mexico. Mentmore is just west of Gallup and about 16 miles east of the New Mexico/Arizona border.

Camping: Free, undeveloped camping is available close to the parking area. Developed fee sites are found about 15 miles east off I–40 at Red Rocks State Park (505–722–3829). Take exit 26 and then drive east on Historic U.S. Highway 66. Lots of cheap motels are in Gallup if you don't want to camp.

Climbing season: Climbing is possible year-round except on colder winter days or the hottest summer days. The area's relatively high elevation keeps temperatures cooler than other desert areas. Autumn is excellent with pleasant warm days. Spring can be windy and cold.

Restrictions and access issues: The Mentmore Crags are owned and operated as a city park by the city of Gallup. No climbing or access restrictions are currently in place. Legal access to The Original Area is via a trail that crosses a deep arroyo from The New Area. Driving on the road next to the railroad track and parking next to The Original Area cliffs is illegal and should be avoided.

Guidebooks: The area's original guide, *Mentmore Climbing Mecca* by Michael Laplante, is out of print and unavailable.

Services: Full services, including motels, Mexican restaurants, and groceries, are found in Gallup.

Emergency services: Dial 911. The nearest hospital is Rehoboth McKinley Christian Health Care Services, 1901 Red Rock Drive, Gallup (east end of town), (505) 863–7000.

Nearby climbing areas: Some other climbing areas are being developed in the Gallup area. The big west-facing Hogback that I–40 slices through offers a selection of easy beginner routes. Some decent bouldering is found at several sites near the Hogback including The Barnyard, The Bull Ring, and Todd's Boulder. Just east of Gallup and north of Red Rock State Park is a two-pitch route up Church Rock, a tall spire seen from the interstate. Other secret climbing areas are found on sandstone cliffs east and west of Gallup. Ask locals for updated beta and directions. *The Gallup Guide* by Peter Tempest and Bob Rosebrough details these climbing areas as well as area hiking and mountain biking trails. The El Malpais area including *Crack of Heraclitus* is 50 miles east.

Nearby attractions: There is ample hiking, mountain biking, road biking, and cross-country skiing in the immediate Gallup area. *The Gallup Guide,* a local publication available in Gallup, is a great resource for visiting outdoor enthusiasts. The 262,000-acre El Malpais National Monument, 50 miles east, is a rough land of lava flows, lava tube caves, cinder cones, great hiking trails, and Chain of Craters Back Country Byway. El Morro National Monument with Spanish inscriptions, Anasazi ruins, and sandstone cliffs is to the south. Within Gallup is Red Rock Museum, highlighting the area's native cultures; Navajo Code Talkers Room; and Rex Museum, highlighting the railroad and mining history of Gallup. Northwest of Gallup is Window Rock, capital of the Navajo Nation.

Finding the crag: From either east or west I–40, take exit 16 on the west side of Gallup. Turn west onto US 66 and drive 0.3 mile, passing several large truck stops along the way. Turn right onto McKinley County Road 1. Continue 0.9 mile to Mentmore Road and turn left (west). Drive 0.2 mile to a gate on your right at a sharp right curve. Go through the gate and drive a short distance to the parking area.

The New Area cliff is south of the parking area. The access trail to the obvious cliff band begins on the south side of the parking lot. The trail to The Original Area cliff starts at the parking area and heads northwest across a large arroyo to the cliff. Hiking time is five minutes.

The Original Area

The 50-foot-high, southeast-facing Original Area cliff has more than thirty-five quality routes. Most lines are well-bolted sport routes along with a few good crack climbs. Vertical climbing on positive solid holds is normal. All routes have 2-bolt lowering anchors and can be toproped. Access the cliff top from the right (east) end to set up topropes. Routes are listed from left to right.

1. Mr. Moto (5.8) Wide crack 10 feet left of the fence. Gear route.

2. I'm Just a Little Hoppy Bunny (5.10b) Start 5 feet left of the fence by a painted peace symbol. 5 bolts to 2-bolt anchor.

3. Redemption (5.10d/11a) Wide crack route that is seldom climbed.

4. The Demon Within (5.12a) Short and hard. Anchors are on a large ledge below the top.

5. Duuuuuuuude!! (5.10d) 6 bolts to 2-bolt anchor.

6. Leaning Slab (5.3) The easiest route on the cliff.

The next 70-foot-long cliff section has many high-ball boulder problems.

7. Shin of My Skin (5.10d) Start behind a freestanding boulder. Climb over the large roof at the top. 4 bolts to 2-bolt anchor.

8. Pillow Roof (5.11a/b) Start 18 feet right of *Shin of My Skin*. 6 bolts to 2-bolt anchor.

9. No Identity But a Title (5.10c/d) 4 bolts to 2-bolt anchor.

10. Looking for Daniel (5.8) Good route. 6 bolts to 2-bolt anchor.

11. Pseudo-Supercrack (5.9+) Start inside a cave. Good handjams up a crack lead to a ledge and easier climbing above. Gear route.

12. Stick Your Fist Here (5.8) Off-width crack. Gear route.

13. Hookymaster (5.10b) Start 5 feet right of *Stick Your Fist Here.* 6 bolts to 2-bolt anchor.

14. Muy Enfermo (5.10c) Excellent—the must-do route at Mentmore Original. First bolt is above "love" graffiti. 7 bolts to 2-bolt anchor.

15. Stuck in Puberty (5.11b) Sport route. Straight up the left side of an arête, then move right to join *D.D.M.*

16. D.D.M. (5.10b) Good sport climb. The right side of the arête.

17. M3G (My Three Girls) (5.11c) Sport route. Start 5 feet right of *D.D.M.*

18. Fetis Envy (5.8) Off-width crack. Gear route.

19. Razors from Heaven (5.10d) Very sharp hold above the first bolt. 7 bolts to 2-bolt anchor.

A toprope problem with bolt anchors is 12 feet right of #19.

20. Joe's Crack (5.8) One of the best cracks here. Gear route.

21. From CZ With Love (5. 11b/c) Start 15 feet right of *Joe's Crack*. 5 bolts to 2-bolt anchor.

22. Rapture (5.10a) Start at "Bennie Silva" graffiti. Climb up and over a bulge. Reachy. Shares anchor with #21. 5 bolts to 2-bolt anchor.

Two toprope problems with bolt anchors is 3 feet right of #22.

23. Big Blobs of Love (5.8) Climb the corner and arête. 5 bolts to 2-bolt anchor.

24. Tres Amigos (5.11a) No topo. Not recommended. Just left of #25. Steep and pumpy. Difficult stemming to a ledge. Slightly easier climbing left or right of the bolts above the ledge.

25. May Cause Health Problems (5.8) Great crack climb. Gear route. It's been led with one piece but you can also sew it up.

26. Not Suitable for Pregnant Women (5.11a) Abundantly bolted. Crux at the roof.

A toprope route with bolt anchors is between #26 and #27.

27. Magnum cum Masochist (5.10a) Boulder up to a ledge below a peace symbol.

28. STD (Short Tenuous Deckability) (5.7) The crack system to the right of the peace symbol. Gear route.

29. The Inner Sanctum (5.10a) Excellent route. The first route established at Mentmore Original. 5 bolts to 2-bolt anchor.

30. Reggae's Route (5.10c/d) Start left of a curving crack system (*The Why Crack*). This is one of the few pocket climbs here. Runout to the anchors.

31. The Why Crack (5.7) Gear route.

32. Phalanx (5.10a) Finger crack with ample opportunities to place pro.

33. Smegma Deluxe (5.11d) Start 25 feet right of *Phalanx*. Sustained and pumpy. Finding hidden holds keeps this climb at its grade.

34. Piled High (5.9 R/X) Difficult climbing on the right-most crack coming out of a roof. Gear route.

35. Rob's an A (5.11b) Excellent climbing. Boulder out the roof to a large clipping hold for the first bolt. 4 bolts to 2-bolt anchor.

The New Area

The New Area crag offers lots of good quality and recommended routes on a long west-facing cliff band conveniently located a short distance south of the parking area. Lots of good bouldering is also found in the immediate area. Routes are listed from left to right.

1. Breakfast at Denny's (5.10a) Start 10 feet right of a large gully. 4 bolts to 2-bolt anchor. These anchors are set well back on the cliff top, so bring long slings.

2. High Stepping (5.10a) Start just left of an off-width crack. 3 bolts to 2-bolt anchor.

3. Unknown (5.9+) Off-width crack with no anchors. Easy walk-off.

4. Five O'clock Shadow (5.10a) No topo. Located in the "Corridor," a narrow slot between the main cliff and the huge

detached "Monolith." Start about 20 feet right of the off-width crack.

5. Marvin Bolted Line (5.10b/c) No topo. Located in the "Corridor" on the "Monolith." A left-trending bolt line near the formation's center. 7 bolts to 2-bolt anchor.

6. Pumping Beauty (5.10c/d) No topo. The left-most route in the "Corridor" on the "Monolith." You must top out to get to the anchors. 6 bolts to 2-bolt anchor.

The wall right of the "Monolith," bracketed by an arête on the left and a hand and finger crack on the right, is under development.

7. Flakes Don't Fail Me Now (5.10b) Area classic. Start up a tenuous flake at ground level, then turn left onto the wall. 7 bolts to 2-bolt anchor.

8. Sink or Swim (5.11b) The route's start has interesting moves that resemble a swimming stroke. 7 bolts to 2-bolt anchor.

9. Unknown (5.9) Crack with chain anchors.

10. On the Edge (5.11c) Classic arête climb. 5 bolts to 2-bolt anchor.

11. Stolen Dream (5.11a) Highly recommended. First bolt is high. 4 bolts to 2-bolt anchor.

12. Unknown (5.11) Finger crack. Usually toproped from a 2-bolt anchor.

13. Purchase Agreement (5.8) Beautiful route. Established the day the area became a city park. Located above and behind a large boulder. 5 bolts to 2-bolt anchor.

14. Betty's Redemption (5.8) Excellent climbing. Betty's own route after being a belay slave. 4 bolts to 2-bolt anchor.

15. Heave Ho (5.11+) Wildly overhanging and a terrific climb. The last route on the cliff. 4 bolts to 2-bolt anchor.

EL MALPAIS NATIONAL MONUMENT

■ OVERVIEW

El Malpais National Monument, south of Grants and Interstate 40 in western New Mexico, is a landscape of cinder cones and foreboding black lava flows. This stunning natural area is well worth visiting even if you aren't climbing. It offers dramatic scenery, great hiking across the *malpais* or lava flows, and good camping. These flows stand in sharp contrast to a pale roadside cliff composed of Zuni sandstone in the east side of the monument. *Crack of Heraclitus,* an obvious and excellent two-pitch traditional climb, jams up one of these cliffs. This New Mexico testpiece, while remote from other climbing areas, is one of the best multipitch crack climbs in the state. The crack involves a diverse variety of jams, including thin fingertip jams protected with TCUs, hand jams, off-width moves, laybacking, and a roof problem. The soft sandstone is very climbable and protects well with modern-day cams. A successful ascent requires a big rack, good technique, and staying centered.

Climbing History

Earl Wiggins, surely one of the best crack climbers of all time, and Ken Sims attempted the route in March of 1977. In April of the same year, Dave Baltz and Andy Embick made the first ascent of the line, rating it 5.10 A1 after using aid to bypass the difficult moves in the thin crack at the start of the route. Baltz returned with Paul Horak in July 1977 and freed the line, rating it 5.11c/d. Mike Head joined the duo a short time later

for the second free ascent. One month later, crack masters Doug Bridgers, Peter Prandoni, and Ken Trout made the third free ascent. Ken Sims, partnered by New Hampshire climber Albert Dow, returned in early 1979 to lead all of the pitches free. All parties during this time climbed to the top for a three-pitch climb. Now parties can descend from anchors (three drilled angles) at the left end of the large roof near the summit.

Currently, the route is generally unknown and seldom attempted except by crack aficionados from around New Mexico and Colorado. Crowds are never an issue. Several other easier quality crack routes farther down the road in "The Narrows" add to the adventure.

Rack and Descent

Bring a big rack for *Crack of Heraclitus* that includes multiple TCUs and double sets of Friends or their equivalent through #4 Camalots. Descend by rappelling from a three-bolt anchor 160 feet to the ground (two 165-foot ropes required) or continue up loose rock to the cliff top.

Trip Planning Information

Area description: Several crack climbs, including two-pitch *Crack of Heraclitus,* are located on a roadside 200-foot-high Zuni sandstone cliff.

Location: Western New Mexico. The cliff is in El Malpais National Monument about 13 miles south of Grants and I–40.

Camping: No camping in the immediate area. Developed campsites are found farther south on Highway 117 toward La Ventana Arch. Do not camp on Acoma Indian Reservation land to the east.

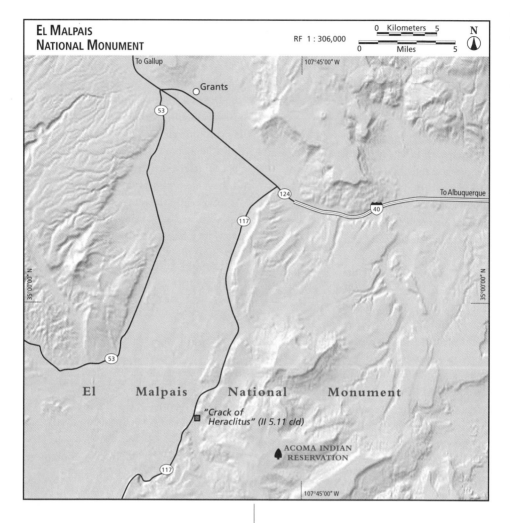

EL MALPAIS
NATIONAL MONUMENT

RF 1 : 306,000

0 Kilometers 5

0 Miles 5

N

To Gallup

107°45'00" W

Grants

53

124

To Albuquerque

117

40

35°00'00" N

35°00'00" N

53

El   Malpais   National   Monument

"Crack of
Heraclitus" (II 5.11 c/d)

ACOMA INDIAN
RESERVATION

117

107°45'00" W

Climbing season: Spring, summer, and fall are best for climbing although it is possible to climb on mild winter days.

Restrictions and access issues: The route is just barely on public land in El Malpais National Monument. Written permission to enter adjoining Acoma Pueblo land to the east is required.

Nearby climbing areas: Mentmore is 50 miles west near Gallup. Enchanted Tower lies 50 miles south off Highway 117 near Datil.

Nearby attractions: El Malpais National Monument (505–287–7911) includes the scenic drive Chain of Craters Back Country Byway and ancient hiking trails used by the Anasazi and other early inhabitants. To the east is Acoma Pueblo (800–747–0181 or 505–469–1052), one of the most unusual and beautiful pueblos in New Mexico. El Morro National Monument offers great scenery, inscriptions from early Spanish explorers, Anasazi ruins, camping, and hiking.

Finding the crag: *Crack of Heraclitus* is located in El Malpais National Monument about 13 miles south of Grants. From Albuquerque drive west on I–40 about 70 miles to exit 89. Turn left (south) onto Highway 117 and drive 13.2 miles to the imposing *Crack of Heraclitus* on the left (east) side of the road. Park about 100 yards past the cliff at a narrow gated road that marks an entrance to Acoma Pueblo land. Walk back up the road to the cliff.

1. Crack of Heraclitus (II 5.11c/d) 2 pitches. **Pitch 1:** Climb a thin vertical crack 25 feet to a small roof. This is the crux. Turn the roof on its left and then jam a finger to hand crack into a short pod and belay. **Pitch 2:** Continue jamming straight up the hand and fist crack above, passing another roof (5.10) to a huge roof below the summit. Face climb left under the roof on surprisingly moderate climbing to a three-drilled-angle belay anchor. **Descent:** Either rappel 160 feet (two ropes) to the ground from the anchors or finish to the top on lesser quality rock and walk off.

SOUTHERN NEW MEXICO

THE TUNNEL

■ OVERVIEW

The mountains east of Alamogordo in south-central New Mexico are seamed with long bands of limestone, most of which are undeveloped by climbers. The best and most accessible area is The Tunnel. This area, with two long, easily accessible cliff bands, offers a superb selection of both challenging and pleasing routes. The Tunnel, like most limestone crags, is laced with difficult routes graded between 5.8 and 5.14. Most of the climbing is in the 5.11+ to 5.12+ range, making it an ideal winter venue for accomplished and strong sport climbers.

The Tunnel climbing area, named after a nearby tunnel on U.S. Highway 82, is composed of two distinct cliff bands separated by deep Fresnal Canyon. Both are easily accessed and visible from the spacious parking area just before the highway tunnel. The north-facing Shady Side/Midtown area is a long roadside cliff that looms above the south side of the highway. Since it's usually shaded, it's best climbed during the warmer months. Perfect winter climbing is found at the Sunny Side and The Dig, an excellent and sunny, south-facing cliff on the north flank of Fresnal Canyon. The Sunny Side Right and Far Side offer positive in-cut holds along with the more prevalent slopers that characterize much of the climbing. The Shady Side

offers fifty-one routes while another twenty-five lines ascend the Sunny Side.

The climbing tends to be on vertical to overhanging faces, using a variety of holds including crimps, edges, sidepulls, occasional pockets, and unique sloping holds. The steep routes at the Sunny Side tend to be endurance jug-haul routes. Many climbs start with tricky boulder problems to the first bolt, which is deliberately placed high to minimize visual impact. A stick clip is recommended for both sectors to protect the opening moves. All routes are one pitch in length, and most hangers are camouflaged.

The usual safety concerns are found at The Tunnel. It's impossible to set up topropes at both crags without first climbing the route. Avoid trying to set up a toprope from above the cliffs since few anchors are found and rock fall is a real danger. New route development, particularly on the Far Side and near the tunnel itself, has been avoided because of the highway's proximity below the cliff. A few lines still remain to be done, but essentially the crags are fully developed. It's a good idea to check with locals before you establish any new route.

The tumbling creek in the deep canyon below Sunny Side is a popular recreation site with locals for swimming and sunbathing. Use extra caution for their safety, even in cooler months, by not trundling rocks down the hillside below the cliff. The harsh Chihuahuan Desert environment features lots

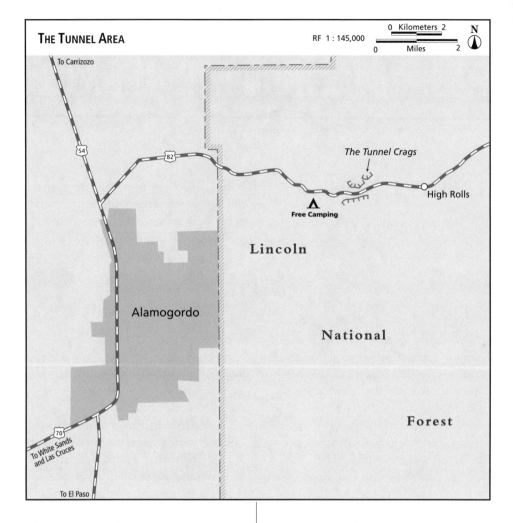

RF 1 : 145,000

0   Kilometers   2

0   Miles   2

N

To Carrizozo

54

82

The Tunnel Crags

High Rolls

Free Camping

Lincoln

Alamogordo

National

Forest

70

To White Sands
and Las Cruces

To El Paso

of the usual desert hazards. Rattlesnakes and excessive heat, often over 100 degrees, are common in the warm summer months. Flash floods are rare but also present a significant danger, particularly on the Shady Side Left. Avoid this area before and during hard rains. Be prepared to clean dirt off routes (use only a toothbrush) after rain storms or for the first seasonal ascents.

Climbing History

Some old pitons and aid gear speak of early climbers visiting this roadside crag. *Junk Yard*

Dog and perhaps the crack to the left of *Side Straddle Hop* reportedly were climbed in the mid-1970s.

John Hymer, an Alamogordo native, is the driving force behind the development of sport routes at The Tunnel. Starting in the late 1980s and partnered with his wife, Tracey, and friends Ed Denton, Dave Head, and Jason Spier, John is responsible for bolting and climbing about 75 percent of the area's routes. Many of these routes were boldly drilled on the lead with the aid of hooks. The first bolted line established was *Runaway Truck* in 1988.

Other route developers include Chris Grijalva (*Pip-Squeak, Big Bad Love, Blue Velvet, Something Profound, Gluttony, Down in the Hole*), Ed Denton (*Ed's Route, Ed's Other Route*), Lance Hadfield (*Up from Below*), Ed and Rich Strang and Luke Lazer (*Cinco Trinta, NIMBY*), Michael Gillet (*Side Straddle Hop, Sweet Christine*), and John Gogas (*Scot*). *Scot* is considered by some climbers to be the best 5.12a in New Mexico.

Rack and Descent

A dozen quickdraws and one 165-foot rope is the only rack needed for all the sport routes unless the route description indicates a longer rope is necessary to safely lower off.

Descent off all routes is by lowering from two bolts equalized by a short chain. It is best to toprope off your own carabiners to reduce wear on the anchor hangers and to rappel whenever possible rather than lower from bolt anchors.

Not all bolts are shown on the topos.

Trip Planning Information

Area description: The Tunnel crags offer many difficult sport routes from 5.8 to 5.14 on two quality limestone cliff bands in Fresnal Canyon.

Location: Southern New Mexico in Lincoln National Forest. The cliffs are about 10 miles northeast of Alamogordo alongside US 82.

Camping: Ample undeveloped, primitive campsites are available in Lincoln National Forest. The two nearest sites are Dry Canyon, 1.5 miles west of Tunnel Vista parking area, and along West Side Road about 1.5 miles east of the parking area. A more attractive choice in summer is to continue east on US 82 toward Cloudcroft and turn right at mile marker 9, then right onto Karr Canyon Road. Continue approximately 3.5 miles to the campsites. Developed sites near Cloudcroft cost between $8.00 and $11.00. Showers are available for $3.00. Reservations can be made by calling (877) 444–6777 or go online at www.reserveusa.com. There is a thirty-day limit for primitive camping and fourteen days at developed sites. A full-service KOA (505–437–3003) is in Alamogordo. Showers for $1.50 are available at the Family Recreation Center (505–439–4142) in Alamogordo.

Climbing season: It is possible to climb year-round at The Tunnel. The north-facing routes of the Shady Side are best in the spring, summer, and fall, while the south-facing Sunny Side is best in winter. Summers can be brutally hot.

Restrictions and access issues: There are currently no U.S. Forest Service restrictions on climbing at The Tunnel area. The proximity of many important prehistoric archaeological sites requires visitors to exercise extra care and precautions while climbing here. Stay on paths while hiking to and from the crags and do not violate federal antiquities laws by disturbing or removing any artifact. Local climbers have worked with the Forest Service to keep the area accessible to climbers and have honored a commitment to respect it by keeping a low profile and minimizing visual impact. Please do your part to keep this excellent climbing area open.

Guidebooks: None. *Rock and Ice* #116 featured a mini-guide by developer John Hymer.

Services: All services are available in Alamogordo and in Cloudcroft. High Rolls has limited services, including a gas station and convenience store.

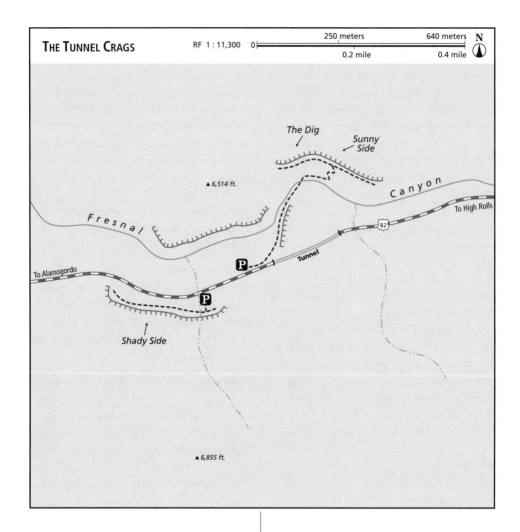

THE TUNNEL CRAGS

RF 1 : 11,300

250 meters   640 meters   N

0   0.2 mile   0.4 mile

The Dig

Sunny Side

▲ 6,514 ft.

Canyon

Fresnal

82

To High Rolls

Tunnel

P

P

To Alamogordo

Shady Side

▲ 6,855 ft.

Emergency services: Call 911 for assistance. The nearest phone is in High Rolls. The nearest hospital is on North Scenic Drive in Alamogordo.

Nearby climbing areas: The Organ Mountains, Doña Ana Mountains, the Rough and Ready Hills, and Hueco Tanks State Historical Park.

Nearby attractions: White Sands National Monument, New Mexico Museum of Space History, Clyde Tombaugh Imax Dome Theater, Alameda Park and Zoo, Oliver Lee State Park, Three Rivers Petroglyph Site, the Malpais-Valley of Fires State Park, National Solar Observatory, Holloman Air Force Base, White Sands Missile Range Museum, and Trinity Site (open two days a year, check with Alamogordo Chamber of Commerce).

Finding the crags: Just north of Alamogordo, turn east from U.S. Highway 54/70 onto US 82 and drive toward Cloudcroft. Drive 7 miles and park on the north (left) side of the highway in the paved Tunnel Vista parking area. Parking spaces are limited, so an early start is advisable on weekends. Weekend parking is a problem.

The other option is to park across the high-way in a small dirt area below the Shady Side/Midtown area. Long-term parking in nearby emergency pullouts is prohibited.

To reach the Shady Side/Midtown area, cross the highway to a small dirt parking area. Cross a rock-retaining wall adjacent to the parking area and walk directly toward the base of the short steep cliff below the main cliff band. A well-used trail goes left (east) and switchbacks uphill to the base of *Pip-Squeak*. A good cliff-base path goes right from here to access all routes. Please avoid the steep eroding path to the right.

The Dig and Sunny Side cliffs are visible to the northeast from the paved parking lot. They are one rock layer higher and east of the layer at creek level directly across from the parking area. Walk up the highway shoulder toward the tunnel and locate a support for a large pipe running parallel to the road's left side that is marked 99 with spray paint. Leave the highway here and follow a good path that gradually descends below a cliff band to the creek in the canyon bottom. Continue along the creek a short distance and cross it below a 20-foot waterfall. Scramble over some short

cliff bands and continue up the path above the creek for about 100 yards. A steep path switchbacks up the slope to the cliff base at route #4. Go left along the cliff-base path for all but three of the Sunny Side routes and all of The Dig routes. Hiking time from car to cliff is fifteen minutes.

Shady Side

The Shady Side is the long, obvious cliff band above the south side of the highway. The cliff is divided for convenience into several sectors. The left side is the Shady Side. The middle section is Midtown. And the far right side is the Far Side Left and Right. All routes are accessed from a cliff-base trail. Routes are listed from left to right.

1. Pip-Squeak (5.13a) 6 bolts to 3-bolt anchor.

2. Project (5.14?) 8 bolts to 2-bolt anchor.

3. Doug (5.13b) 5 bolts to 2-bolt anchor.

4. Oktoberfest (5.13b) 6 bolts to 2-bolt anchor.

5. Big Bad Love (5.13c) 8 bolts to 2-bolt anchor.

6. Rebecca (5.13a) 8 bolts to 2-bolt anchor.

7. George (5.12c) 8 bolts to 2-bolt anchor.

8. Jerk Off (5.13a) 3 bolts to 2-bolt anchor.

9. Julie (5.12c) 5 bolts to 2-bolt anchor.

10. Scott (5.12a) 7 bolts to 2-bolt anchor.

11. Hanging Meatloaf (5.12d) 7 bolts to 2-bolt anchor.

12. RURP Crack (5.11b) Not recommended. Gear, one bolt, no anchors.

13. Tunnel Visions (5.12a) Start on #12 placing gear, finish on #14, lower from cold shuts after the roof. Seldom done. 4 bolts to 2-bolt anchor.

14. HIVD (5.12b) 6 bolts to 2-bolt anchor.

15. Gromit (5.12c) Shares anchors with *HIVD*. 6 bolts to 2-bolt anchor.

16. Abby (5.12a) 7 bolts to 2-bolt anchor.

17. Butch (5.11c) 8 bolts to 2-bolt anchor.

18. Bandit (5.11) 5 bolts to 2-bolt anchor.

19. Budro (5.11b) 6 bolts to 2-bolt anchor.

20. Project (No rating) No topo.

Midtown

21. Cliff Nazi (5.9) 6 bolts to 2-bolt anchor.

22. Side Straddle Hop (5.8) 5 bolts to 2-bolt anchor.

23. Squeeze (5.11c) 6 bolts to 2-bolt anchor.

24. Warm Up (5.9) 7 bolts to 2-bolt anchor.

25. The Arête (5.12b) 7 bolts to 2-bolt anchor.

26. Lech (5.12a) 7 bolts to 2-bolt anchor.

27. Sloopy (5.11c) 7 bolts to 2-bolt anchor.

28. Efflorescence (5.12c) 9 bolts to 2-bolt anchor.

29. Blue Velvet (5.12b) 5 bolts to 2-bolt anchor.

30. Project

31. The Roof (5.12b) Height dependent. 6 bolts to 2-bolt anchor.

32. Cletus (5.12d) 6 bolts to 2-bolt anchor.

33. The Pillar of Pummel (5.12a) 7 bolts to 2-bolt anchor.

34. Guchi (5.13a) 5 bolts to 2-bolt anchor.

35. Moce (5.12d) 6 bolts to 2-bolt anchor.

36. Cracker Jack (5.10d) Gear route. Crack.

37. El Nino (5.11b) 4 bolts to 2-bolt anchor.

38. Junk Yard Dog (5.7) Gear route. Chimney. An early trad route by Kenny Hanson.

39. Pokey (5.11a) 5 bolts to 2-bolt anchor.

40. The Tree Route (5.11d) 5 bolts to 2-bolt anchor.

41. The Corner (5.12a) 6 bolts to 2-bolt anchor.

42. Rational Expectation (5.12a) 5 bolts to 2-bolt anchor.

Far Side Left

43. The Block (5.13b) Approximately 200 feet right of #42 behind a large, freestanding block. No topo. 5 bolts to 2-bolt anchor.

Far Side Right

44. The Dihedral (5.12b) 5 bolts to 2-bolt anchor.

45. Ed's Other Route (5.11a) 5 bolts to 2-bolt anchor.

46. Birthday (5.11d) 5 bolts to 2-bolt anchor.

47. Ed's Route (5.11a) 6 bolts to 2-bolt anchor.

48. Slice (5.11b) 5 bolts to 2-bolt anchor.

49. Sweet Christine (5.8) 4 bolts to 2-bolt anchor.

50. Runaway Truck (5.9) No topo. 4 bolts to 2-bolt anchor.

51. Escape Ramp (5.7) No topo. Gear route. Belay from large cams. Descend gully to the left.

Sunny Side

The Sunny Side is the broad cliff band on the opposite side of the canyon from the parking area. It's divided into two sectors: the

The Dig

Sunny Side

Sunny Side on the right and The Dig on the left. Routes are described from right to left.

1. Burn Baby Burn (5.11b) Start 25 feet right of *Melanoma*. 5 bolts to 2-bolt anchor.

2. Dehydration (5.10d) 5 bolts to 2-bolt anchor.

3. Biggus Diccus (5.12d) 8 bolts to 2-bolt anchor.

4. Melanoma (5.12d) An excellent and recommended area testpiece. The first route installed on the Sunny Side. 6 bolts to 2-bolt anchor.

5. Sunspot (5.12c) Popular and excellent. 8 bolts to 2-bolt anchor.

6. The Nimby Factor (5.13a) 8 bolts to 2-bolt anchor.

7. Jump Start (5.12a) 8 bolts to 2-bolt anchor.

8. Sun Burn (5.12a) One of the "must do" climbs. 7 bolts to 2-bolt anchor.

9. Cinco Trinta (5.13a) 7 bolts to 2-bolt anchor.

10. Heat Stroke (5.11c) Highly recommended. Perhaps the most climbed route on the cliff. Go right at third bolt. Shares anchors with *Cinco Trinta*. 6 bolts to 2-bolt anchor.

11. Heat Stroke Straight Up (5.12b) 7 bolts to 2-bolt anchor.

12. MLK (5.13a) 6 bolts to 2-bolt anchor.

13. Right Dihedral (5.11d) 60 feet left of #12. 7 bolts to 2-bolt anchor.

14. Left Dihedral (5.12a) Shares first 2 bolts with #13. 7 bolts to 2-bolt anchor.

15. Project (No rating) 4 bolts to 2-bolt anchor.

16. Project (No rating) No topo. 5 bolts to 2-bolt anchor.

17. The 5.14 (5.14a) No topo. 100 feet left of #16. End of Sunny Side routes. 4 bolts to 2-bolt anchor.

The Dig

18. The Dig (5.10d) No topo. Located 120 feet left of #17 just after the path at the base of the cliff starts downhill. 8 bolts to 2-bolt anchor.

19. La Primera (5.11d) No topo. 7 bolts to 2-bolt anchor.

20. Project (5.13d?) Located 45 feet left of #19. 7 bolts to 2-bolt anchor.

21. Up from Below (5.13c) Shares anchor with #20. 7 bolts to 2-bolt anchor.

22. Down in a Hole (5.13b) 8 bolts to 2-bolt anchor.

23. Gluttony (5.12d) 7 bolts to 2-bolt anchor.

24. Something Profound (5.12c) 7 bolts to 2-bolt anchor.

25. 2001 (5.12a) 7 bolts to 2-bolt anchor.

PERCHA CREEK CRAG

■ O V E R V I E W

Percha Creek Crag, west of Interstate 25 in southern New Mexico, is an off-the-beaten path climbing area. It's well worth visiting if you're passing through the area or otherwise want a couple days of fun climbing. The south-facing crag features fun crack routes and some partially bolted face routes on andesite, a volcanic rock. The roadside crag, lying in a desert canyon carved by Percha Creek, is between 70 and 100 feet high, and route grades are from 5.7 to 5.10d. Rock quality ranges from fair to excellent.

The climbing is an interesting mix of steep face climbing using pocket holds and long continuous crack systems that require good jamming technique. Traditional climbing skills that include placing secure cams and nuts are necessary since even the bolted routes require gear to supplement the sparse bolts.

Percha Creek is an excellent winter, spring, and autumn climbing area. It is usually very hot during the summer. All climbs receive direct sun, so plan accordingly by bringing plenty of water.

Climbing History

Las Cruces climbers, with some help from northern friends, developed the Percha Creek Crag in the 1990s. Climbers active in the area include Chris Kessler, Grady Viramontes, Karl Kiser, C. Wedick, and Kelly and Susan Elverum. Look for more routes to be developed in the near future as the area has an abundance of unclimbed rock.

Rack and Descent

A standard rack for Percha Creek includes sets of wires, TCUs, and camming units up to 3 inches. A 200-foot rope is necessary for some routes (#11–13) and a 165-foot rope suffices for climbing and lowering on the rest. Descent off all routes is by lowering or rappelling from fixed bolt anchors.

Toproping is an option, although you will have to lead an adjacent line to sling the TR. It is almost impossible as well as dangerous to attempt to set up topropes from the cliff top.

Not all bolts are shown on the topos.

Trip Planning Information

Area description: Percha Creek is a 100-foot-high andesite crag that features traditional routes up crack systems.

Location: Southern New Mexico. The crag is 20 miles east of I–25 alongside Highway 152.

Camping: A small, developed, and free campground is found in the small village of Kingston (no services) about 6 miles west of the Percha Creek Bridge parking area. Drive through Kingston to the pavement's end; continue straight ahead on a dirt forest road a short distance to good sites on the road's left side. Other pleasant, primitive, and free camping is in Gila National Forest.

Climbing season: The cliff's south-facing aspect makes it a good choice in the spring, late fall, and on warmer winter days. High summer temperatures, which are usually in the 90s and 100s, preclude climbing on most days.

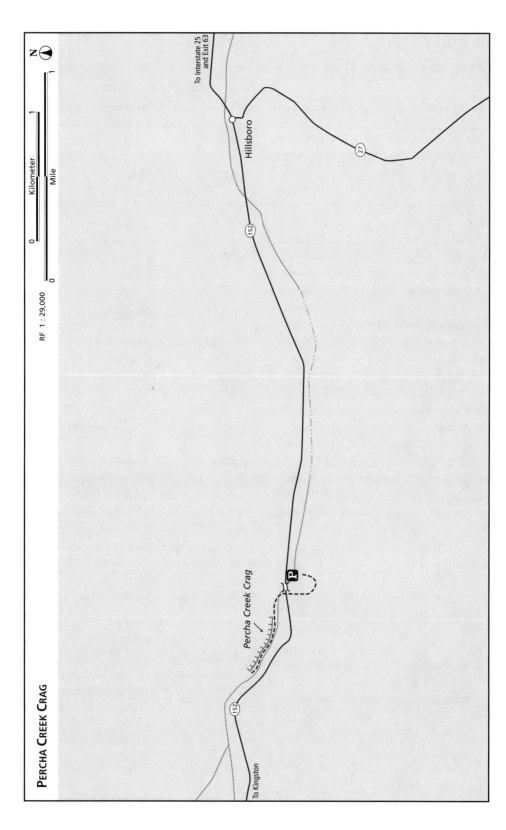

Services: Limited services in Hillsboro. Complete visitor services are found in Truth or Consequences 30 miles to the northeast off I–25.

Emergency services: Call 911. None in the immediate area. Nearest medical facilities are in Truth or Consequences.

Nearby climbing areas: None nearby. The Organ Mountains and Doña Ana Mountains are about 75 miles southeast.

Nearby attractions: Gila National Forest offers many recreational opportunities for hiking, camping, mountain biking, and back-packing. The Gila Wilderness Area, the first established wilderness area in the United States, is 75 miles to the west. The area offers superb outdoor experiences. The Lake Valley Back Country Byway is a scenic drive across Lake Valley to the south. Fishing is found in the Rio Grande east of the crag as well as at Elephant Butte State Park.

Finding the crag: From I–25, turn west (right from the north, left from the south) onto Highway 152 toward Hillsboro and Silver City. Drive through Hillsboro and continue 2.2 miles from the intersection of Highway 27 on the west side of Hillsboro to a parking lot at the Old Percha Creek Bridge on the left. Kingston and camping areas are another 6.5 miles farther west along Highway 152. From the parking area, jump over a stone wall and walk down a steep trail to the creek. The trail begins near the east end of the bridge. Once in the creek, turn right, and after passing under the new bridge, hike west up the stream 500 feet to the main climbing area. Allow five to ten minutes for this easy hiking approach. Routes are listed from right to left.

1. Unknown (5.11) No topo. Start about 80 feet from the new highway bridge below a large roof about 10 feet off the ground. Climb out the right side of the roof, then up a crack system to a 2-bolt anchor. No bolts.

2. Unknown (5.11) No topo. Located about 300 feet from the bridge. Climb a slab protected by 1 bolt to a difficult bolt-protected move over a roof. 2 bolts to 2-bolt anchor.

3. Duck Soup (5.10a/b) Quality climb. This is the first route in the main climbing area and the only route totally protected by bolts. Start 10 feet left of a tree growing 12 feet up the cliff. Negotiate mud and a small pond hazard before getting to the first holds so your shoes are dry when you start. Technical moves, thin climbing, and small pockets. 4 bolts to 2-bolt anchor.

4. El Loco Solo (5.8+ X) Climb a bulging face and arête right of *Grady's Route*. Seldom done. Use *Grady's Route*'s anchors.

5. Grady's Route (5.10a/b) Recommended. Slightly runout and difficult to protect. Climb the steep west-facing wall just right of *Dihedral 1*. Toprope this route by redirecting the rope from *Dihedral 1*'s anchors. No bolts. 2-bolt shared anchor.

6. Dihedral 1 (5.9) Quality climb but difficult for the grade. Small gear protects a flared dihedral down low. No bolts. 2-bolt anchor.

7. Burning the Candle at both Ends (5.8 R) Worth climbing. Can be toproped from *Dihedral 1*'s anchors. Climb the crack just left of *Dihedral 1*. Difficult and hard to protect at the bottom. No bolts. 2-bolt anchor shared with *Dihedral 1*.

8. Meanderneath You (5.11-) Start on a smooth face 45 feet left of *Dihedral 1*. Bolts protect face moves to a large ledge with a cactus. Above is runout and hard-to-protect climbing to the anchors. Using the corners drops the grade. 4 bolts to 2-bolt anchor.

9. Project Routes #10 to #12 are clustered around a large alder tree and dead snag at the cliff base.

10. Worth the Wade (5.7) Quality route. Start 6 feet right of a large alder tree. Climb a west-facing wall past 2 bolts to a right-facing corner. Gear placements protect the corner to anchors off left at the top. 2 bolts to 2-bolt anchor.

11. Wade for Me (5.9) Excellent. Use the first 2 bolts of *Worth the Wade,* then move left and climb straight up past 3 bolts to anchors. 5 bolts to 2-bolt anchor.

12. Dihedral 2 (5.8-5.10+) Recommended. Start next to a large alder tree and climb straight up the flaring dihedral above. The rock is inferior in this section, requiring careful and thoughtful movements. At the dihedral's top, you have four options. Descend from anchors (good option). Go straight up the left-facing crack above (least desirable option). Climb the face between the two corners (good climbing but it's best to toprope this thin, hard-to-protect section). Or traverse left and climb a right-facing corner to the *Nutcracker* anchors (the best option). 100 feet. No bolts. 2-bolt anchor.

13. Nutcracker (5.10) Good route. Start at an inset dihedral 12 feet left of the large alder tree. Climb straight up the dihedral, passing a large roof on the right. Finish up an attractive 40-foot right-facing finger crack. Some suspect rock and badly protected sections down low add to the route's challenge. 100 feet. No bolts. 2-bolt anchor.

14. Unknown (No rating) Start the same as *Nutcracker,* then left at about 35 feet to a crack system directly under a 2-bolt anchor. Not much is known about this route. Looks difficult to lead and rock quality is inferior.

15. Just Your Style

(5.10) Stellar route with varied climbing and good protection. Start up fractured rock 45 feet left of the large alder tree. Jam straight up a hand and finger crack. Finish in a wide right-facing corner. No bolts. 2-bolt anchor.

16. Rolling Stones Gather No Mas

(5.10+) Start on the face just left of *Just Your Style*. Climbing the face keeps the grade at 5.10+. Gear required above the fourth bolt. Use anchors for *Just Your Style*. 4 bolts to 2-bolt shared anchor.

17. Unnamed (5.8)

Start right of a broken roof system above white rock. Climb the crack of your choice to a spacious square ledge about two-thirds of the way up. Finish up an easy crack to anchors. No bolts. 2-bolt anchor.

THE
ROUGH AND
READY HILLS

■ O V E R V I E W

The Rough and Ready Hills, one of New Mexico's newer climbing areas, is a beautifully situated crag in a remote desert setting northwest of Las Cruces. Besides good climbing, the cliff offers immense views of desert ranges as far away as Texas and Mexico. The crag, ranging from 45 to 90 feet high, is composed of flow-banded rhyolite and rhyolite tuff. Although some of the rock is unsuited for climbing, for the most part the cliff is solid and offers safe and enjoyable routes.

Climbing History

Students from nearby New Mexico State University in Las Cruces began developing the crag in 2000 by establishing *First Move* and *The Paw*. The cliff was ignored until 2003, when Mickey Hazelwood, then a graduate student at New Mexico State University, jump-started the crag's development. Hazelwood, helped by Scott Jones and Tom Sterrett, hand-drilled most of the bolt holes from a fixed rope and opened many of the cliff's best lines, including *Reddi-Wip, Rough Rider,* and *Brangus by the Horns*. During this time Dave Lucas established many fine moderate climbs at the North End. He and Barak Shemai teamed up to retrobolt *Unnamed Arête,* with the blessing of the local climbing community, and establish *Halitosis Monkey*. A few new routes are still left to do, but the area is nearly complete.

Rack and Descent

The routes are well bolted with beefy ⅜-inch Fixe and Rawl placements in solid rock. All routes have or share two-bolt anchors.

Some routes require supplemental gear, so bring a good rack to the crag and scope your proposed line before climbing. A 165-foot rope gets you up and down most routes. Descend by lowering or rappelling from fixed anchors. Please use your own carabiners and quickdraws to toprope routes and rappel through the lowest chain link when finished with the route.

Trip Planning Information

Area description: The Rough and Ready Hills are a small range of volcanic hills with sport and mixed routes in a desert setting.

Location: Southern New Mexico. The area is approximately 15 miles west of Las Cruces on West Mesa of the Mesilla Valleys.

Camping: No developed camping sites in the immediate area. See the Organ Mountains section in the next chapter for area camping information.

Climbing season: The crag faces east-northeast. Climbing is possible year-round. Hot summer days are best in the afternoons, and winter visits are best in the morning.

Restrictions and access issues: The crags are on land administered by the BLM.

Guidebooks: *Lookin' Rough, But Feelin' Ready: A Guide to Climbs in the Rough and Ready Hills, NM* by Mickey Hazelwood is a self-published guide that may be available in Las Cruces.

Nearby climbing areas: City of Rocks State Park, Doña Ana Mountains, and Organ Mountains. Hueco Tanks in Texas.

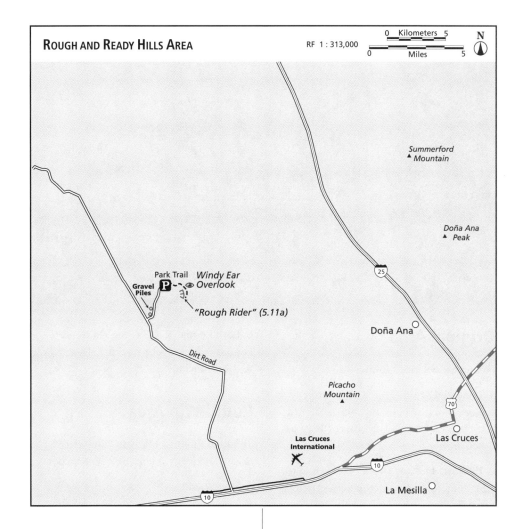

ROUGH AND READY HILLS AREA

RF 1 : 313,000

0 Kilometers 5

0 Miles 5

N

Summerford
▲ Mountain

Doña Ana
▲ Peak

25

Park Trail *Windy Ear*
Gravel   P ◉ *Overlook*
Piles

"Rough Rider" (5.11a)

Doña Ana ○

Dirt Road

Picacho
Mountain
▲

70

Las Cruces
International
✈

Las Cruces ○

10

La Mesilla ○

10

Nearby attractions: The Old Butterfield Overland Stage Trail traveled through the pass just south of the microwave tower. Also see the Organ Mountains section in the next chapter for more area information.

Finding the crag: From Las Cruces, take Interstate 10 west to the Las Cruces Airport exit. Go right from the exit and take an immediate left onto a frontage road that parallels I–10. After a few miles, turn right toward Corralitos Ranch. After driving through a pass between an observatory and

microwave tower, look for a small road on the right just after the DIP and WATCH FOR WATER signs. Go right on this road, which leads to two large gravel piles. Follow this rough road past the piles to a parking area and trailhead. It is approximately 13 miles from the Corralitos Ranch exit to the parking lot. A well-marked trail leads from the parking area to the crag base. Allow fifteen minutes for hiking.

Stay alert on Corralitos Ranch Road to avoid hitting cattle and slow-moving pickups.

Original Area

Routes are described from left to right.

1. Unnamed Arête (5.11d/.12a) Formerly a toprope problem, but now bolted. Climb a steep, blunt arête to a large flake. 7 bolts to 2-bolt anchor.

2. Halitosis Monkey (5.10c) It's been called "the shortest climb with the longest history." Steep face to a slab finish. 3 bolts to 2-bolt anchor.

3. First Move (5.8) Fun climbing with pockets and face holds.

4. V 5 Project (No rating) Shares the first 3 bolts with #3, then finishes up right to 2 more bolts and chain anchors. The route is unfinished and loose at the top. 5 bolts to 2-bolt anchor.

5. The Paw (5.11) Good face climbing with a tough, thin finish. Crux is the final moves getting to the anchor. 5 bolts to 2-bolt anchor.

6. Born Ready (5.10a) Chossy at the very bottom but good face climbing above. 4 bolts to 2-bolt anchor.

Reddi-Wip Area

7. Rough Rider (5.11a) Fun climb! Steep, reachy, and juggy. 5 bolts to 2-bolt anchor.

8. Fingerbang (5.10b) Use anchor for *Reddi-Wip* and a fixed nut at top of a crack for a directional if you're toproping. Don't remove the nut please. 6 bolts and small- to mid-size cams for crack at the top.

9. Reddi-Wip (5.10c) Neo-classic! Pockets and face holds through a mid-height bulge. 7 bolts to 2-bolt anchor.

10. Brangus by the Horns (5.11b) Take the Brangus by the horns for the overhanging crux start, then easier climbing to a 5.10 upper face. 7 bolts and cam between second and third bolts to 2-bolt anchor.

11. Brangus Muffins (5.12a) This is the connect-a-crux variation for #10 and #12.

Climb past the first 2 bolts of #10, place a piece, climb up and right to the second bolt of #12, and finish at #12's anchor.

12. Excrement Adventure aka Paleo and Sierra's Excrement Adventure (5.12a)
Climb the lower face (5.10) to a steep, sustained 5.11+ headwall. Use an extended shoulder-length sling on the bolt below the roof or back clean. 8 bolts and small- to mid-size cams (for crack between first and second bolts) to 2-bolt anchor.

13. Blood, Sweat, & Steers (5.9) Finally slabbin' comes to the R&Rs. Good climb. 6 bolts to 2-bolt anchor.

Jungle Gym Area

14. Well-disciplined Monkey (5.11c/d) A steep, powerful start to easier, pocketed upper face. After third bolt follow left line of bolts. 6 bolts to 2-bolt anchor.

15. Unruly Macaque (5.11c/d) Shares #14's start, then follow the right line of bolts. Can be done two ways—after the third bolt, climb past 3 more bolts to a 2-bolt chain anchor or clip the next 2 bolts, angle up left to last bolt on #14, and finish to #14's anchor. Both are slightly more sustained than #14. 6 bolts to 2-bolt anchor.

16. Monkey Grip (5.11d) Project. Start right of the arête. Climb past 4 bolts, then join #15 to 2-bolt anchor.

North End Routes

17. Southern Fried (5.10b/c) Moves just like down home. Follow the bolts up left across a steep slab to an overhanging crux finish. 5 bolts to 2-bolt anchor.

18. Don't Have a Cow (5.7). Easy climbing up a short, blocky face. Make the climb more difficult by staying on the arête. 5 bolts to 2-bolt anchor.

19. Dances with Brangi (5.9+) A short face climb with a nice roof. 4 bolts to 2-bolt anchor.

20. Under the Bull (5.9) Start same as #19, then traverse up right under the roof. Turn it at its right end and finish at #19's anchor. 4 bolts to 2-bolt anchor.

21. Golden Brangus (5.10c) Climb the arête and face through the roof and finish at #19's anchor. Clip the last bolt on #20 to shorten the runout to the anchor. 3 bolts to 2-bolt anchor.

22. Windy Gap Overlook (5.9) Nice climbing. Climb a featured slab with various easy starts to bolt 1, place gear in a horizontal crack below a roof, place gear in the crack above the roof, climb past 2 more bolts to a chain anchor. Take time to enjoy the view from the rests and the anchor. 3 bolts and small- to mid-size cams to 2-bolt anchor.

THE ORGAN MOUNTAINS

■ OVERVIEW

Adventure climbing in a pure traditional sense is what visiting rock climbers can expect to find in southern New Mexico's rugged Organ Mountains. A flashlight or headlamp is always carried by experienced Organ climbers in anticipation of the usual late return due to the rugged, forced-march approaches, long multipitch routes, and devious scrambling descents that are the hallmarks of climbing in this complex mountain range.

The Organ Mountains, a 20-mile-long ridge of spires and rough peaks, forms an immense, ragged skyline above Las Cruces and the Rio Grande valley. The Organs, topped by 9,012-foot Organ Needle, stretch south from 5,719-foot-high San Augustin Pass to the Franklin Mountains on the Texas border. The range, an uplifted fault block, rears almost 5,000 feet above the surrounding lowland valleys. Granite composes most of the Organs, although snatches of sedimentary and volcanic rocks appear on its lower elevation fringes. A lot of mining took place in the northern part of the range in the latter half of the nineteenth century, yielding rich deposits of lead, silver, gold, zinc, and copper.

This wild, desolate range, once an enclave of the fierce Apache Indians, was originally named *La Sierra de la Soledad,* or "Mountains of Solitude," by the Spanish who trekked past the range along El Camino Real en route to Santa Fe. The rugged demeanor of the Organ Mountains still maintains its solitude and wilderness character. Despite its proximity to Las Cruces, no roads, save U.S. Highway 70 over San Augustin Pass, and few trails cross the lofty range. The Wheeler Survey, which explored the sierra in the 1870s, described them as "lofty, rugged, and inaccessible." This description still rings true today.

Climbing History

The first recorded climb in the Organs was in 1904, when two college students from Las Cruces scaled Organ Needle, the range high point, and planted a flag on the summit. German rocket scientists, brought to nearby Fort Bliss after World War II, initiated the first exploration of the Organ Mountains in the late 1940s. These early pioneers, brought to New Mexico to work as rocket scientists after the fall of Germany, were driven by the mountaineer's tradition of reaching the summits of the sierra's many granite spires. Local climbers banded together in 1955 to form the Tularosa Climbing Club, which later became The Southwest Mountaineers. This intrepid group of explorers managed to ascend technical routes on almost every Organ peak. Later efforts concentrated on the more difficult faces found in canyons and on rugged slopes on the range's west side. Difficult routes were established on The Wedge, Southern Comfort Wall, The Citadel, and The Tooth. The famed Yosemite climber Royal Robbins, stationed at Fort Bliss in the 1950s, partnered with P. Rogowski and pushed a direct route with lots of aid up the South Face of The Wedge. Dick Ingraham in his early guidebook to the Organs called it " . . . the most difficult route in the Organs."

Dick Ingraham and Paul Wohlt pioneered many classic routes up almost every peak and rock face, setting bold and high standards for future climbers. Jim Graham, Ed Ward, Mark Motes, Karl Kiser, Paul Seibert, and Glen Banks are longtime local activists responsible for establishing many routes. Jim Graham in particular led an effort to replace many old and rusty ¼-inch bolts on the more popular Organ climbs.

The new millennium ushered in significant route development, notably on Organ Needle and Minerva's Temple. The Lesser Spire, with a relatively short approach and good steep stone, has also seen some activity with several new routes and one project under way. Jim Graham, John Kear, and Carolyn Parker have been active in the area. To reach the Lesser Spire, continue past Southern Comfort Wall to the next canyon. Turn up the canyon heading for the Lesser Spire located on the left side of the canyon. Orp is on the right side. About 150 yards below the canyon's top is *Mixed Nuts and Raisins* (5.10/c). Look for a large tree at the bottom of a dihedral. Start just right of the dihedral in a hand crack. Two more pitches in a vegetated crack lead to rap anchors. A little farther up the canyon is a project that needs one more pitch to be completed. The four existing pitches are well worth climbing. The first pitch has a fixed wire about 20 feet up and a bolt at about 50 feet. The 5.11b/c crux of the route is just past this bolt. Rappel from slings at the top of the fourth pitch.

The dramatic east face of Organ Needle (IV 5.10) was ascended via a beautiful twelve-pitch effort by John Hymer, Jason Spier, and Dave Head in the summer of 2001. Hymer, Spier, and Head also teamed up for another impressive line on the east side, climbing twelve pitches up the Northeast Buttress of Minerva's Temple (IV 5.12c) after ten days of effort on hot days in 2000. Also on Minerva's Temple, the Southeast Face (IV 5.11d A1) was ascended in seven days by Hymer and Head during the summer of 2002. This route links with the Northeast Buttress at its tenth pitch to finish up a beautiful, exposed knife-edge ridge.

Written approach directions to these new routes is almost impossible. Getting to the base of these climbs requires both physical and mental effort. To start it's best to talk with locals and reference Dr. Dick Ingraham's book, *A Climbing Guide to the Organ Mountains,* available from the Zuhl Library at New Mexico State University and online at www.nmsu.edu. Follow directions to *The Marathon Route* on Organ Needle to find routes on the Needle.

Except for a small local climbing community, the Organs see very little climbing activity. Trails to the cliffs are obscure and require careful hiking and navigating across a rugged desert landscape of cliffs, couloirs, scree slopes, hillsides guarded with cacti and yucca, and a maze of small canyons. Once on the rocks, climbers must utilize many of the traditional rock climbing skills for a successful and safe outing. On all but the shorter, modern climbs, creative gear placements and route-finding skills are necessary.

Proper preparation and the ability to self-rescue is also required. Any Organ emergency that requires outside assistance is usually an involved and difficult affair. The routes in the Organ Mountains are not underrated. Many older lines often carry a sandbag rating. Use caution when climbing here, and always err on the side of your own good judgment to remain alive. The Organs are not a good beginner area. Even the easy and moderate routes require good climbing skills, and many are long multipitch lines that require expertise in placing protection and setting up belay and rappel stations.

Climbers should be prepared for a long day whenever venturing into the Organs, particularly if you're a first-time visitor. The crags, the access trails, and the descent routes all take time to locate. Lots of water is a must in this arid climate. A good starting point is

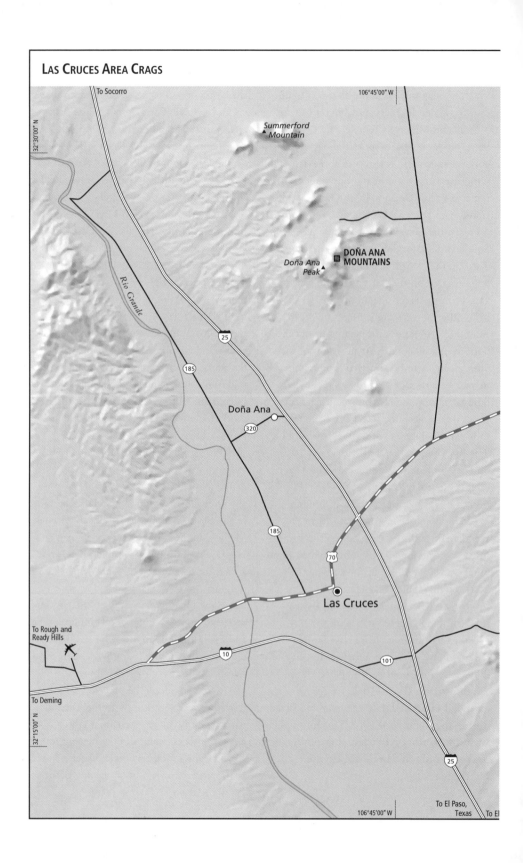

LAS CRUCES AREA CRAGS

To Socorro

106°45'00" W

N 32°00'00"

Summerford Mountain

DOÑA ANA MOUNTAINS

Doña Ana Peak

Rio Grande

25

185

Doña Ana

320

185

70

Las Cruces

To Rough and Ready Hills

To Deming

32°15'00" N

10

101

25

106°45'00" W

To El Paso, Texas

To El

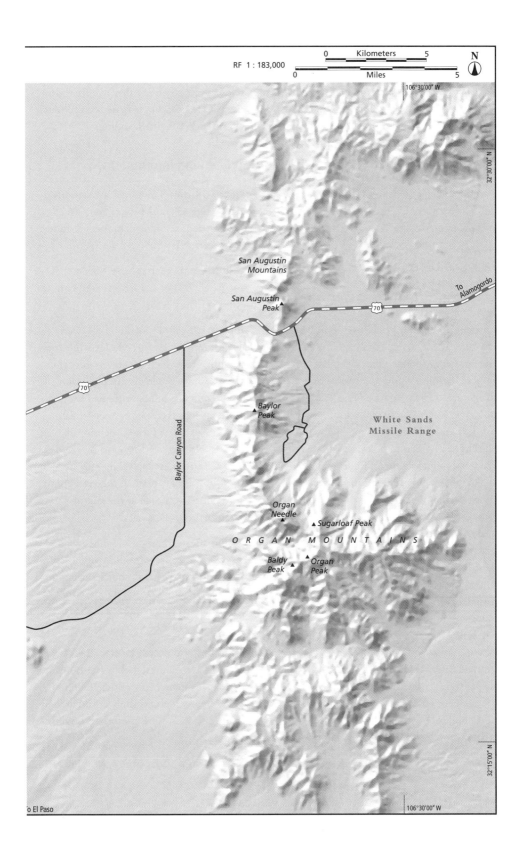

two quarts per person per day. Hot weather may require more water. Don't plan on finding any water out in the mountains, and if any is located, purify it before drinking. Other Organ essentials include a headlamp for the often necessary night descent. A space blanket, extra clothes, and food make forced bivouacs more tolerable. You should be able to avoid any epics on the described routes if you start early, climb efficiently, and monitor the remaining daylight.

Rack and Descent

An Organ rack is usually big. Carry a wide variety of gear including sets of RPs, wired Stoppers, TCUs, and Friends or equivalent-size cams. If you bring extra cams, it's best to carry more mid-range units. Bring lots of slings of various lengths and twelve to fifteen quickdraws. Bring extra webbing to back up old rappel slings. Use extreme caution whenever you are climbing or rappelling with existing fixed gear and bolts as your anchors. Many old ¼-inch bolts are found, although some rappel stations are retrofitted with newer ⅜-inch bolts and chains. Fixed pitons come loose over time, and old bolts tend to weaken from rust and exposure to the area's extreme weather conditions. Many Organ climbers use British double-rope technique on multipitch routes, especially the older classics, to alleviate rope drag on long, circuitous pitches. Lastly, bring and wear a helmet here. The Organs are filled with loose, tottering rocks and blocks that are easily knocked off by lead climbers or even by a trailing rope.

Descent off Organ routes is either by rappelling from existing bolt and piton anchors on the cliff or more usually by scrambling, downclimbing, and rappelling off the backside of the mountain. Double ropes are needed on many rappels. It's a good idea to scout out the descent route before climbing your route to ensure that you have a notion of the descent's general terrain. Watch for loose rock when descending.

Trip Planning Information

Area description: The Organ Mountains, a rugged range of granite spires and faces, offers excellent traditional, multipitch routes in a wilderness setting.

Location: South-central New Mexico. Immediately east of Las Cruces and 40 miles north of El Paso, Texas.

Camping: Any level spot along the access roads to the Topp Hut or Modoc Mine serve as primitive campsites. Wherever you camp, bring your own water, do not build fires, haul out all trash, and bury human waste. Aguirre Springs Recreation Area on San Augustin Pass offers fifty-six developed campsites. No water. Restrooms on site. Fees and time restrictions apply. The only drinking water in the entire area is at the Cox Visitor Center on the west side at the end of Dripping Springs Road.

Climbing season: Year-round. The range rarely receives snow, but routes with a southern exposure are the best choice during the colder winter months. Summer days are hot and dry. Early-morning starts and shady north faces are best bets.

Restrictions and access issues: The Organ Mountains are administered by the Bureau of Land Management. Most of the climbing areas are in a wilderness study area. The only current restriction is no motorized bolting.

Guidebooks: *Rock Climbing New Mexico & Texas* by Dennis R. Jackson, Falcon Press,

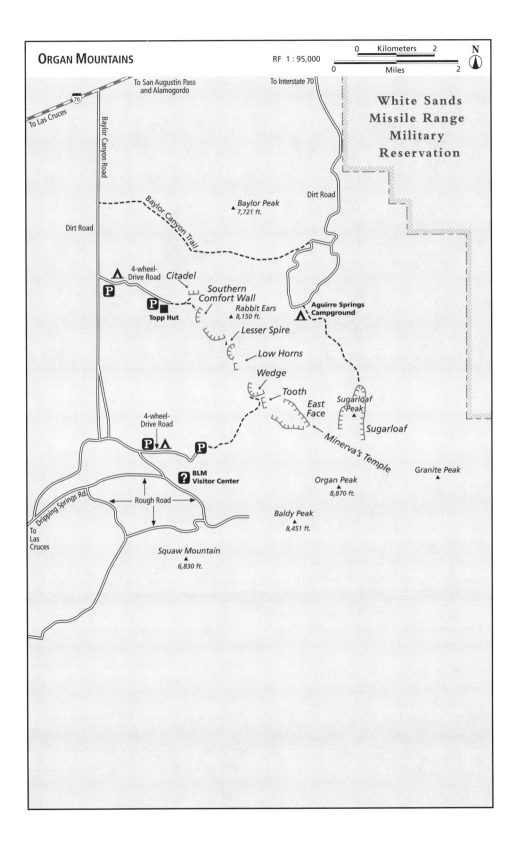

The Citadel · Southern Comfort Wall · The Tooth · Topp Hut

1996. *A Climbing Guide to the Organ Mountains* by Dick Ingraham, a local climbing pioneer who has been compiling information on the area since the early 1960s. The guide is available at the New Mexico State University library. *Rock and Ice* #48 featured a guide to the Organ and Doña Ana Mountains.

Services: Food, fuel, and lodging are readily available in Las Cruces, one of New Mexico's largest cities. The Mesilla Valley Kitchen is a local favorite and good spot to meet other climbers. Also try Nopalitos and My Brothers Place. La Posta de Mesilla in nearby Mesilla is a local favorite. High Desert Brewing offers microbrews.

Emergency services: Call 911. Hospitals are Memorial Medical Center, 2450 South Telshor (505–521–8641 or 505–521–2286, twenty-four-hour emergency number), and Mesilla Valley Hospital, 3751 Del Rey Boulevard, (505–382–3500). New Mexico State Police (505–524–6111).

Nearby climbing areas: Bishops Gap bouldering area is south of Las Cruces. The Rough and Ready Hills are northwest of the airport. Farther away are City of Rocks State Park and Percha Creek Crag to the west, The Tunnel near Alamogordo to the east, and Hueco Tanks State Historical Park southeast by El Paso, Texas.

Nearby attractions: Las Cruces is rich in history. Nearby Mesilla served as the Confederate capital of the Territory of Arizona. The Gadsden Purchase, clarifying the boundary of the United States and Mexico, was signed here in 1853. The Gadsden Museum presents a history of the purchase plus displays of Native American and Civil War artifacts. Billy the Kid was tried for murder in Mesilla and escaped the jail. Nearby Fort Selden State Monument is a frontier fort established in 1865. The "Buffalo Soldiers" were stationed here. White Sands National Monument is approximately 45 miles northeast. The border city of Cuidad de Juarez is a short drive south on Interstate 25.

Finding the crags: Climbing is found on both the east and west sides of the mountains. Good climbing on the east side is on Sugarloaf and Organ Needle. Sugarloaf is a prominent 800-foot white granite slab visible from the east side of San Augustin Pass.

The range's west flank, visible from Las Cruces, offers most of the climbing. Popular crags include The Citadel, Southern Comfort Wall, The Tooth, and The Wedge.

Trailheads for The Citadel and Southern Comfort Wall start from Topp Hut Road, and the trailhead for The Tooth and The Wedge start from Modoc Mine Road. Both roads, neither of which are signed, are accessed from Baylor Canyon Road, which parallels the Organ's west side. Baylor Canyon Road is accessed from U.S. Highway 70 about 10 miles east of its junction with I–25. This is just west of the village of Organ. Baylor Canyon Road is also accessed by University Avenue on the east side of Las Cruces. Drive about 7 miles east on University Avenue to a well-marked left turn for Baylor Canyon Road. Refer to each crag's description for specific access directions. Routes are described from left to right.

The Citadel

The Citadel, a 400-foot-high crag perched on the west side of the Organ Mountains, offers a good selection of moderate climbs on its north face. Some routes go to the summit, but most parties choose to descend after one or two pitches. Many of the original ¼-inch bolts have been replaced with ⅜-inch bolts, and new descent anchors have been added. Caution is advised when relying on the occasional ¼-inch bolt you might

find. *Glad We Came* (5.9), a one-pitch bolt-protected face climb, and *Wish You Were Here* (5.9) are area classics. Equally recommended are *Hercamur Snurd* (5.10) and *Finger Zinger* (5.10b/c), a bolt-protected, classic face climb. Many choose to climb only the first two pitches of *Hercamur Snurd* (5.10-) and rappel from a two-bolt anchor.

Finding the cliff: The approach is relatively easy to this fine crag. Follow the above directions to Baylor Canyon Road. If approaching from the east or west via US 70, turn south (right from the west, left from the east) onto Baylor Canyon Road just west of the village of Organ and drive 3.7 miles to a left turn onto Topp Hut Road. This is just past the sixth cattle guard. This very rough road eventually reaches Topp Hut, but few will choose to drive that far. Several pullouts are handy for parking when you call it quits, then continue walking to the Topp Hut, a rock building.

Continue walking the road past the hut for nearly a mile to a fork in the road. Take the left fork and hike a short distance to an abandoned mine. The trail to The Citadel starts above the mine tailings. Find it above and left of the mine. This moderate trail heads into Rabbit Ears Canyon. To climb *Glad We Came* and *Hercamur Snurd* requires bushwhacking up the canyon to the east side of the crag and then backtracking across slopes to the routes. Allow one hour for this hiking approach.

1. Glad We Came (5.9) No topo. 1 pitch. Excellent climb and highly recommended. The arête on the northeast corner of the rock. A #3 Friend protects the bottom moves up to 8 bolts to descent anchors.

2. Wish You Were Here (5.9) No topo. 2 or more pitches. **Pitch 1:** Start in the dihedral right of *Glad We Came*. Traverse left near the

top and belay from #1's anchors. Descend from here or traverse right to a roof to a 2-bolt anchor. **Pitch 2:** Face climbing (5.11) to a right-facing corner and a belay over a roof. From here, 2 moderate pitches reach the summit. Most parties descend after pitch 1, although a fine route can be pieced together to the summit by the accomplished climber.

3. Hercamur Snurd (5.10-) 2 pitches. Located about 150 yards right of *Glad We Came*. **Pitch 1:** Traverse left on mossy rock left of a gully onto a face. Climb steeply up poor-looking rock protected by bolts (5.10-) to a fixed anchor. **Pitch 2:** Face climb (5.9) past a bolt and a fixed piton, then work left via an awkward crack (5.10) to a rappel station.

4. The Whole Banana (5.10) Difficult face climbing leads to a crack. Belay on a good ledge.

5. Murray's Crack (5.8) Carry large Friends.

6. Tugboat (5.10) Toprope route.

7. Finger Zinger (5.10b/c) Classic Organ face climbing. Located near the west end of the crag. Excellent bolt-protected face and edge climb to fixed rappel anchors. Rappel from here or continue to the top via the *West Ridge* (5.6).

8. Anticipation (5.9 R) Runout near the bottom.

9. West Ridge (5.6) Adventure climbing to the summit.

10. The Nose (5.9-) No topo. Rappel from *Finger Zinger*'s anchors or continue up *West Ridge*.

Southern Comfort Wall

Southern Comfort Wall, featuring a relatively easy approach and a smattering of good routes, is worth a visit. The crag is popular with locals, especially during the winter and late fall months.

Finding the cliff: To find the trail to Southern Comfort Wall, follow the above directions to the left turn to the abandoned mine above Topp Hut. Stay right on the main road until you reach a large white road cut. Leave the road here and slog up the slope on a well-defined trail to the base of a cliff. Southern Comfort Wall finally becomes visible after a short traverse up and right to the cliff's left-hand end. Allow an hour for this approach.

11. Irish Cream (5.10+) No topo. 2 pitches. About 80 feet left of *Black Velvet* near the left end of the crag. **Pitch 1:** Up a right-leaning, discontinuous hand crack (#3 and #4 Friends very helpful) to a belay stance in a crack. **Pitch 2:** Climb right past a fixed pin (5.10), then up past 1 bolt and some unprotected 5.9 face climbing to a 2-bolt rappel anchor. Make a two-rope 165-foot rappel back to the ground. Several 5.7 and 5.8 routes are to the left of *Irish Cream*.

12. Lowenbrau Light (5.7) 2 pitches. Start at a large oak tree at the base of #13. **Pitch 1:** Climb a left-facing corner system. Belay below a short left-slanting crack. **Pitch 2:** Face climb left or up the crack until the crack bends right. Move up left from here and either belay and do a short third pitch or, depending on the length of your rope, go for the top. Scramble right to fixed rappel anchors on the central wall for a two-rope (165-foot) rappel to the base.

13. Black Velvet (5.9) 2 pitches. The prominent left-facing corner. **Pitch 1:** Start at the
large oak tree. Climb a short 5.6 section up
right to reach the left-facing corner. Belay at
a stance in the corner above a short, blocky
vertical section. **Pitch 2:** Climb the corner
until it bends right (5.9). Three choices from
here: 1. Face climb (5.9) straight up past 2
bolts to the top. 2. Go right to a crack that
traverses left under a large roof (5.7) and
belay. 3. Continue traversing right (5.2) to
anchors. If a belay is installed, one more
rope-length of moderate climbing to the
right reaches rappel anchors for the central
wall. Descent from all variations is by a
double-rope (165-foot) rappel from fixed
anchors on the central wall.

14. Margaritaville (5.10-) 2 pitches. **Pitch
1:** Up a left-facing corner (5.10-) right of
Black Velvet to a bolted belay. **Pitch 2:**
Continue straight up (5.9) to a belay.

Descent: Traverse right to rappel anchors for
the central wall.

15. Hangover (5.11 R) 2 pitches. About 200
feet right of *Black Velvet*. **Pitch 1:** Climb a
thin, short crack, then face climb up left
(5.10- R) to a belay below an overhanging
finger crack. **Pitch 2:** Tricky climbing up
right (5.11) via thin crack and face climbing,
then up right to a 4th-class section that leads
to the top.

15.1. DWI (5.10-) No topo. This is a good
single-pitch route uphill from #15. Follow
bolts left, then turn a roof and follow discontinuous cracks up and right. Clip a bolt, then
straight up to fixed anchors. Gear, bolts, and a
2-bolt anchor. The route just uphill from
DWI is *DT's* (5.10+/.11- R/X). This scary
route was successfully led by Mike Head and
Mark Motes but is now usually toproped
from *DWT's* anchors.

The Tooth

The Tooth offers long quality routes. The requisite long, steep approach ends at the best granite in the area. Locals agree that The Tooth offers the best climbing on the range's west side.

Finding the cliff: To reach The Tooth follow directions to Baylor Canyon Road, accessed by driving east on University Avenue on the south end of Las Cruces. After about 7 miles, turn left (north) onto Baylor Canyon Road and drive approximately 0.5 mile to a right turn to the east onto Modoc Mine Road. Follow this road past the mine, through a gate, and park above the mine. This is a hideously rough road, and you may choose not to drive all of it.

Find the trail above the mine by walking right or east by southeast down the road and then up a steep hill. At the hilltop the trail begins. Hike east on a short section of tire tracks and then continue around the hillside to a large gully. Follow the trail across the large gully and then up to the base of The Tooth. Continue up the large gully to the base of the crag. Allow at least one hour for the approach. Plan for a trip of up to ten hours car to car.

A Tooth rack is a single set of camming units up to #3 Friend and a good selection of wired nuts. Any ¼-inch bolts found here are more than twenty-five years old, so use caution and back them up whenever possible. Retrobolting efforts are under way to replace these bolts. To descend, rappel from fixed anchors just below the summit.

16. Tooth Fairy (III 5.10) 5 pitches. A super, highly recommended route. **Pitch 1:** Start on low-angle slabs near the left (northern) edge of the rock. Climb a crack toward a large triangular roof. After clipping the first bolt (ignore bolts going left), traverse about 20 feet right and belay at the right end of

the roof. 1 bolt and gear placements are here. **Pitch 2:** Turn
the roof and climb a crack
(5.9) past a bush, past a tree
with rappel anchors, to another
tree and belay. **Pitch 3:** Face
climb left to a ¼-inch bolt,
then up left to a finger crack
(5.10). Belay at a 4-bolt anchor
left of the slot where the crack
widens. This is the crux pitch.
Pitch 4: Climb a short crack
(5.7) past a bush to a belay
ledge. Alternately, face climb
(5.9) left past 2 protection bolts
to the same belay ledge. **Pitch
5:** Crack and face climbing
lead to anchors below the
summit. Rappel from here.
Descent: Multiple double
rope (165-foot) rappels down
the route.

17. Tooth or Consequences

(III 5.10a/b) 6 pitches. This is
the best route in the Organs
and one of New Mexico's best
rock adventures. **Pitches 1** and
2: Same as the first 2 pitches of
Tooth Fairy. Some prefer to
belay at the first tree. **Pitch 3:**
Traverse left onto the face, then
up left (5.10a/b) with widely
spaced bolt protection to a
bolted belay station. An airy,
exposed, and exciting pitch.
Pitch 4: Step right to a crack,
climb over blocks, then face
climb left near the formation's
north edge (5.9+). Move back right to a 2-
bolt belay. **Pitch 5:** Face climb past 2 bolts
and a fixed pin to a crack and belay on a
ledge. **Pitch 6:** Climb either a 5.7 crack on

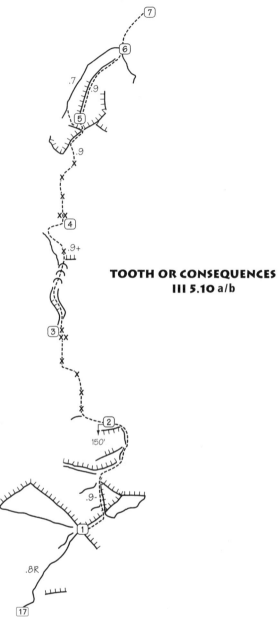

**TOOTH OR CONSEQUENCES
III 5.10 a/b**

the left or a 5.9 crack on the right to a belay
stance and rap anchors below the summit
shared by all three routes. **Descent:** Rappel
the route or *Tooth Fairy* with double 165-
foot ropes.

18. Tooth Extraction (III 5.10) 5 pitches. Highly recommended. **Pitches 1** and **2:** Same as the first two pitches of *Tooth Fairy.* Move right along a ledge at the end of pitch 2 and establish a belay. **Pitch 3:** Climb a right-trending, grass-filled crack, then face climb right (5.9-) below a small roof to the base of a large left-facing dihedral system that angles up left. **Pitch 4:** Face climbing (5.10) leads up the dihedral to a belay on a sloping ledge. **Pitch 5:** Continue up a hand crack in the dihedral (5.9) to a ledge. Go left about 15 feet to an off-width crack (look for a hand crack in the back) to rappel anchors shared by all three routes. **Descent:** Multiple two-rope (165-foot) rappels down *Tooth Fairy.*

The Wedge

The Wedge is a sharp peak at the southern end of a long row of serrated pinnacles and needle peaks in the central Organs. R. L. Ingraham, in his original Organ guidebook, calls this magnificent formation "the jewel of the Organs." The Wedge's most spectacular formation is its dramatic arrowhead-shaped, 1,000-foot-high South Face, which dominates the range when viewed from Las Cruces.

The South Face offers several classic routes that are seldom climbed because of the difficulty in reaching the face as well as the serious nature of climbing in this wilderness area. Any adventure climber well-versed in traditional climbing should seek out these routes to recapture the spirit of exploration and discovery that is part of the Organ's early climbing history. Ask knowledgeable locals for specific information on the following routes as well as newer ones, or better yet, tag along with them on a Wedge adventure. Just remember your headlamp!

The following information for The Wedge classics is gleaned from Ingraham's old guidebook to the Organs. Seek out the guide for more detailed directions and some specific climbing beta. Not illustrated.

Finding the cliff: To find The Wedge, follow the above directions to The Tooth. From the base of The Tooth, keep north (left) of the next large gully. The Wedge is above and to the left. Allow at least 1.5 hours for the approach march. Descent is by rappelling down the east face.

19. West Ridge (5.7) 5 pitches. An Organ classic put up by Royal Robbins and friends in the early 1950s. This excellent climb ascends the obvious West Ridge of The Wedge. R. L. Ingraham calls it " . . . a smooth knifeblade when viewed from the west." To find the start requires bushwhacking and scrambling past some small pinnacles below the ridge to a saddle. Traverse into a narrow gully between West Ridge and Lost Peak to the north. Climb the gully and then a roofed chimney. Squeeze through a hole through the roof and climb onto the West Ridge between two obvious parallel grooves. Rope up here. **Pitch 1:** Climb left of the grooves to a good belay on the First Shoulder. A ledge system descends right from here onto the South Face to the prominent Green Band. **Pitch 2:** The crux and "an ingenious exercise in route-finding." Work up a jam crack on the left side of the ridge to a delicate step right onto the ridge. Climb to a bucket, then up vertical rock to a handhold atop a flake, which Ingraham notes, " . . . removes all doubt as to the essential benevolence of the Great Belayer." Belay above on the Second Shoulder. **Pitch 3:** Climb a slanting ramp on the south side of the ridge to the Great Shoulder. *Diagonal Route* joins here. **Pitch 4:** Climb a crack on the South Face to an niche. Chimney past the niche to a belay. **Pitch 5:** Continue up the ridge "on small holds over moderately inclined rock" to easy scrambling to the summit.

20. Diagonal Route (5.9+) Classic and recommended. Ingraham calls this an "airy, beautiful route" up the tremendous exposed slabs of the South Face. It was originally climbed using a "shillelagh," a term for a Scottish golf club, but in this case referring to a "stout piece of green wood about 2 inches thick and 2 feet long." It was wedged into a crack above a roof high on the route and used as a handhold to "muscle up over the overhang." Very exciting stuff!

To find the start, scramble right from the pine at the base of the wall until you're halfway between the pine and a pass on Organ Ridge and below a crack system that angles up left. Begin by climbing a flake to a belay ledge with a tree. Climb an exposed ramp that leads to the east end of the Green Band. Pass the Band and continue up left to the left side of the upper face. Jam a crack up a slab to the famous Shillelagh Overhang. Thrutch over the crack that splits the roof and climb straight up to a rightward traverse to the base of the Great Overhang and a belay. Next is the exposed crux pitch. Move around a corner to a niche beneath the overhang. Aid off a bolt on the right wall or free climb over the roof to a narrow shelf above the lip. Work left up the steep face to the West Ridge and continue up the ridge to the summit.

21. Robbins Route aka **Direct Route** (5.9+) This classic route was put up by Royal Robbins and P. Rogowski in the early 1950s while Royal was stationed at Fort Bliss. It was originally done with mixed free and aid

climbing but later free climbed. The route begins at a big pine tree at the base of the South Face. Climb steep slabs, following left-angling crack systems. Above is a series of overhanging roof systems. The route heads up and right through overhangs and bulges and reaches the Green Band at 500 feet. The first ascent party bivouacked here. Work through overhanging rock above a pine on the right side of the Green Band to steep rock on the eastern facet of the wall. Finish up a wide crack system to the summit.

Sugarloaf

Every visiting climber's Organ experience is rounded out with an ascent of one of Sugarloaf's long slab routes. Located on the east side of the Organ Mountains, the sweeping lines of this 900-foot granite formation have lured climbers for more than forty years. The original lines up the northern and southern slabs, in keeping with mountaineering tradition, were ascended to the summit. Today these lines provide long moderate climbs and are regularly enjoyed by locals and area visitors. The steeper sections in the middle of the face offer less opportunities for natural protection and waited until the 1970s for ascents. Some of the original ¼-inch bolts have been replaced by ⅜-inch bolts. Climbers can still expect many old ¼-inch bolts that protect long runouts on difficult face climbing. Exercise caution and discretion whenever you rely on these ancient bolts, and back them up whenever possible, especially at belays.

Allow eight to ten hours to hike and climb from car to car for this remote formation, although the *North Face* was soloed in a remarkable two hours and forty-five minutes, car to car, by John Hymer from

Alamogordo. The hiking approach takes 1 to 1.5 hours, with a similar time for the return. Once on the summit, allow yourself at least an hour to get back to your pack at the cliff base.

The ten-pitch *The Left Eyebrow* (5.7) and seven-pitch *The Right Eyebrow* (5.7) are recommended moderate climbs to the summit. *Science Friction* (5.11), with three pitches, can be combined with *The Left Eyebrow* for a great nine-pitch route to the summit. On all routes be prepared for a long climbing day. Expect widely spaced protection and many route-finding decisions. It also takes time to figure out the descent route.

A Sugarloaf rack includes ten quick-draws, an assortment of slings, small wired Stoppers and RPs, and nuts and Friends up to fist-size. It's a good idea to bring two ropes; otherwise, a single 200-foot cord works fine.

The best way to descend from Sugarloaf's summit is from the south saddle. It is possible to rappel down the east side but not recommended. To descend from the summit, walk south along the ridge line to a 2-bolt anchor. Roping up for the ridge may be desirable. Rappel with two ropes for 150 feet to the ground. There are intermediate anchors to make two one-rope rappels. Once you are on the ground, a short scramble west leads to another bolt anchor. Rappel down a short slab and follow an obscure trail along the west side of Sugarloaf to the base of the slabs.

Finding the crag: Access to Sugarloaf is via US 70, which connects Las Cruces and Alamogordo. From Las Cruces drive east on US 70 approximately 14 miles to Aguirre Springs Recreation Area exit located on the east side of San Augustin Pass. This exit is 55 miles from Alamogordo to the east. Drive 6 miles south to the campground. The BLM campground opens at 8:00 A.M., so if you want an early start, plan on camping the night before. Deposit a $3.00 day-use fee at a self-pay station, located near the first group campsite on the one-way loop road. The Sugarloaf trailhead is located at the second "group area" approximately 0.4 mile beyond the pay station.

South of the large canopy at the parking lot's southeast corner is a wooden turnstile gate. This is where the Sugarloaf trail begins. From the parking lot, Sugarloaf is obscured by a large hill to the south. Walk through the gate and across a streambed. Cross the high hill along its northeast base. Follow this trail for about an hour. The trail, although obscure when crossing rock slabs, is easy to follow until you are close to Sugarloaf's base. If you encounter a fence, you are on the lower trail and should turn back. After an hour of hiking, the trail passes a campsite. This is a good place to leave some water for the walk out. A few minutes past the camp, the trail forks. Take the obscure left fork and traverse up and left toward the obvious base of Sugarloaf. Aim for a large roof system close to the base near the middle of the face. *Science Friction* and *The Left Eyebrow* start left of this feature. Watch out for rattlesnakes along the entire trail. Allow 1 to 1.5 hours of hiking to approach Sugarloaf.

Routes are described from left to right.

22. North Face (IV 5.6+) 14 pitches. The + is the original rating. Great route with lots of moderate climbing and runouts up to 60 feet long. Start near the lowest or north end of the formation, well below and left of the prominent roof system close to the ground. Pitch 1 climbs past a roof with trees at both sides of it. A fixed pin protects the easy roof. Continue up right for 5 pitches of moderate

2 Rappels

150'

-11

140'

25   26

24

22   23

climbing to a belay below a band of roofs. Trend up right over the roofs onto the upper slabs, which you climb for 7 or 8 more pitches to the summit.

23. The Left Eyebrow (IV 5.7) 10 pitches.

Start below and left of the prominent roof system that is close to the ground. **Pitch 1:** Face climb to a right-facing crack to a tree on its left end. Two more trees are on the right side. Climb a short right-facing corner up left to another tree and belay. **Pitch 2:** Face climb left, then up a crack past a bush to a belay (5.6). **Pitch 3:** Crack climb up right, then work up left to a belay. **Pitch 4:** Face climb past a bush and belay at the end of a roof system. **Pitch 5:** Face climb right to a tree and belay. **Pitch 6:** Angle right and up into a left-facing corner. 4 more pitches (with many choices and options for easy climbing and belay stances) lead up to the

summit. Look for a 2-bolt belay at the end of pitch 8.

24. Science Friction (I or III 5.11) 3 to 10

pitches. An Organ classic and highly recommended. It's a Grade III route if it's combined with the upper pitches of #23. **Pitch 1:** Start in short right-angling cracks below and left of the prominent roof system close to the ground. Face and crack climb (5.10) past 2 fixed pins. Face climb left past 2 bolts to a belay stance. **Pitch 2:** Move right, then face climb past 3 bolts and 1 fixed pin (5.10-). It is 140 feet to the ground from here. **Pitch 3:** Face climb straight up (5.11) past a bolt (a 5.9- face climbing variation to the left circumvents this short hard section) and into a crack system with a fixed piton. Move up right to a belay stance. A two-rope rappel reaches the ground from here. But after climbing this far, you might as well keep climbing toward the summit. The upper pitches are fun and the summit view is outstanding. **Pitch 4:** Face climb right, then up to the tree at the end of pitch #5 of *The Left Eyebrow*. To continue to the top, follow the above #23 route description starting with pitch 6 of *The Left Eyebrow*.

25. The Right Eyebrow

(III 5.7) 7 to 8 pitches. Start on the right side of the prominent roof system close to the ground. **Pitches 1** and **2:** 2 pitches of face climbing end at the top center of the prominent roof system. **Pitch 3:** Climb a left-facing corner. **Pitch 4:** Crux lead. Start in a right-facing corner, then up a left-facing corner to its end. **Pitch 5:** Face climb up left to a right-facing corner. **Pitches 6** and **7:** Face climb up easy slabs to the summit.

26. Flea Tree Dihedral

(III 5.8) 6 pitches. Starts right of *The Right Eyebrow*. Climb a dihedral system for 4 or 5 pitches to the "lonesome pine" on the right skyline. 2 more pitches of moderate slab climbing lead to the top.

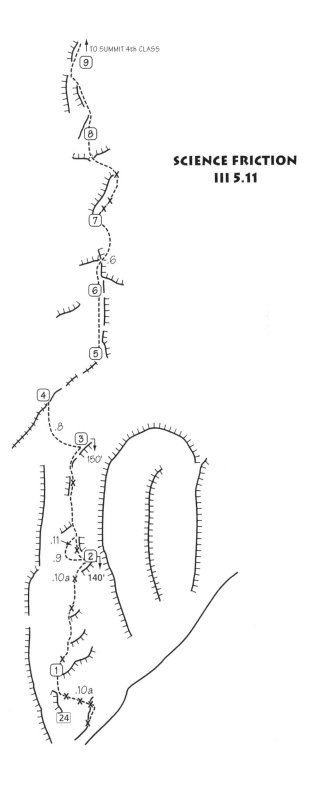

**SCIENCE FRICTION
III 5.11**

DOÑA ANA MOUNTAINS

■ OVERVIEW

Coarse outcrops of porphyritic desert granite scatter throughout the rugged Doña Ana Mountains in southern New Mexico, providing pockets of excellent climbing. This small range, north of Las Cruces, is topped by 5,835-foot-high Doña Ana Peak. The range, the peak, and the nearby town of Doña Ana were named for Doña Ana (Lady Ann) Robledo, a seventeenth-century resident. The Doña Ana Mountains, like the neighboring Organ Mountains, is a superb off-the-beaten-track area that yields good climbing in a wild desert setting. Numerous one- to three-pitch traditional routes scale the range's rock cliffs, while several lines ascend Checkerboard Wall, a 500-foot-high crag on the north flank of Doña Ana Peak. The face is grooved with slicing cracks that give it a huge checkerboard appearance. Besides its easily accessible routes, the range also offers great bouldering on blocks along the area's dirt roads.

As of the summer of 2004, portions of the Doña Ana Mountains, including The Columns, have been closed to climbing.

The Doña Ana crags offer lots of adventure climbing. There are few sport routes in the entire area. Traditional climbing skills and competence at placing gear, setting up belays, route-finding on devious faces, and self-rescue are all necessary to have a safe and successful ascent in the Doña Anas. Use caution on all routes and watch for sandbag ratings. Loose rock and blocks are found on most routes and on the cliff tops. Rattlesnakes are also common here, especially in the warmer months. Keep an eye and ear out for them when crossing talus fields and hiking rocky slopes. Remember, if you are bitten by a snake, seek medical help immediately. Do not apply ice or a tourniquet or cut the bite area and attempt to suck the poison out.

The Doña Ana Mountains bask in the same mild climate as the adjoining Organ Mountains as well as Hueco Tanks farther south near El Paso, Texas. Autumn, winter, and spring are the best times to visit. Expect warm days and cool nights. Winter nights can drop as much as 50 degrees below the daytime high temperature. Snowfall is usually light and rare. Expect windy afternoons in spring. Summers are very hot, with daily highs in the 90s and low 100s. Get an early start, climb in the morning coolness, and look for shade. Carry plenty of water to the crags; at least two quarts a person daily is a good starting point. Don't expect to find any water.

Climbing History

Little recorded history exists of early climbing in the Doña Ana Mountains, although Dick Ingraham and Anuta made the first ascent of the Checkerboard Wall in 1964. Later local climbers established numerous routes on the range crags. Jim Graham was active, replacing some of the old ¼-inch bolts with new beefy ⅜-inch bolts.

Rack and Descent

Bolts placed on the lead by first-ascent parties are found at some belay and rappel stations. Use any old ¼-inch bolts with extreme caution. Always back them up with gear if possible, particularly at belays.

All routes require gear placements. A rack of camming units up to 4 inches along with a set of Stoppers and an assortment of quickdraws, runners, and a 165-foot rope is adequate for most routes. Descent is usually by rappel from fixed anchors. Be prepared

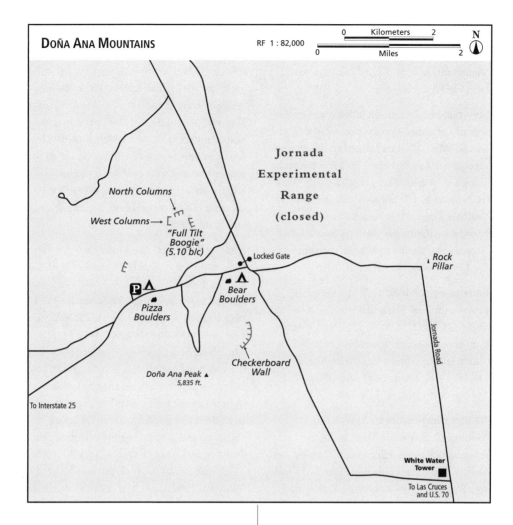

Jornada
Experimental
Range
(closed)

North Columns

West Columns →

"Full Tilt
Boogie"
(5.10 b/c)

Locked Gate

Rock
Pillar

P

Bear
Boulders

Pizza
Boulders

Checkerboard
Wall

Doña Ana Peak ▲
5,835 ft.

To Interstate 25

Jornada Road

White Water
Tower ■

To Las Cruces
and U.S. 70

to fashion your own rappel anchors on some routes.

Trip Planning Information

Area description: The Doña Ana Mountains, rising above the desert north of Las Cruces, yields excellent bouldering and routes on rough granite outcrops in a wild setting.

Location: Southern New Mexico. North of Las Cruces.

Camping: Undeveloped free camping is available at the Bear Boulders and the Pizza Boulders just off the access road. Fires are discouraged. Bring water. Please practice minimum impact camping to protect this fragile area.

Climbing season: Climbing is possible year-round in the Doña Ana Mountains. Fall, winter, and spring are best. High summer temperatures and occasional cold winter days can limit climbing opportunities. Expect wind in the spring.

Guidebooks: *Rock Climbing New Mexico & Texas* by Dennis R. Jackson, Falcon Press, 1996.

Restrictions and access issues: As of the summer of 2004, portions of the Doña Ana Mountains, including The Columns, have been closed to climbing.

Services: Food, fuel, and lodging are available in Las Cruces, population 62,000. The Mesilla Valley Kitchen located in the Arroyo Plaza, 2001 East Lohman, is a local favorite and good spot to meet other climbers. Also try Nopalitos, 310 South Mesquite, and My Brothers Place at 334 South Main. Specialty beers at the Old West Brewery located on Avenida De Mesilla in Mesilla just south of Las Cruces is worth the short drive.

Emergency services: Call 911 for emergency assistance. Memorial Medical Center, (505) 521–8641 or (505) 521–2286 (twenty-four-hour emergency number) is at 2450 South Telshor. Mesilla Valley Hospital, 3751 Del Rey Boulevard, (505) 382–3500. New Mexico State Police, (505) 524–6111.

Nearby climbing areas: The Organ Mountains are a short drive south, the Rough and Ready Hills about 20 miles west. Hueco Tanks State Historical Park is 75 miles southeast. City of Rocks State Park is 80 miles west, and Percha Creek Crag is 80 miles northwest.

Nearby attractions: Founded in 1848, Las Cruces and the surrounding area is rich in history. Nearby Mesilla served as the Confederate capital of the Territory of Arizona. The Gadsden Purchase, clarifying the western boundary of the United States and Mexico, was signed here in 1853. The Gadsden Museum presents a history of the purchase plus displays of Native American and Civil War artifacts. Billy the Kid, one of the West's most notorious miscreants, was tried for murder in Mesilla and escaped the jail. Fort Selden State Monument is a frontier fort established in 1865 about 12 miles north on Interstate 25. The famous black "Buffalo Soldiers" were stationed here. White Sands National Monument is 45 miles northeast near Alamogordo via U.S. Highway 70. The Mexican border city of Cuidad de Juarez is a short drive south on I–25. Visitors should inquire about entry requirements before entering old Mexico, although generally a visit is simple.

Finding the crags: The Doña Ana Mountains are east of I–25 and north of Las Cruces. Exit I–25 onto US 70/82 and head east toward Alamogordo. Turn north or left after about 3 miles onto Jornada Road. Signs here say JORNADA EXPERIMENTAL STATION. Also look for a large white water tower on the northeast corner and a Shell gas station. Drive 6.4 miles north on the road to USDA signs by a rock pillar; turn left (west) here. Bear Boulders is a left turn at 1.9 miles. Camping and bouldering opportunities are found here. The turn to the Pizza Boulders is 3.5 miles from the rock pillars. This area is located 1.2 miles south on a fairly rough dirt road. Southeast of the boulders is the popular Checkerboard Wall, a thirty-minute hike southeast.

Bear Boulders

Because of their ease of access and good bouldering, this is where locals are generally introduced to the Doña Ana Mountains. One large boulder and several smaller ones are located here. A toprope can be rigged on the largest boulder by slinging the top. A bolt on the top helps direct your rope. Not illustrated.

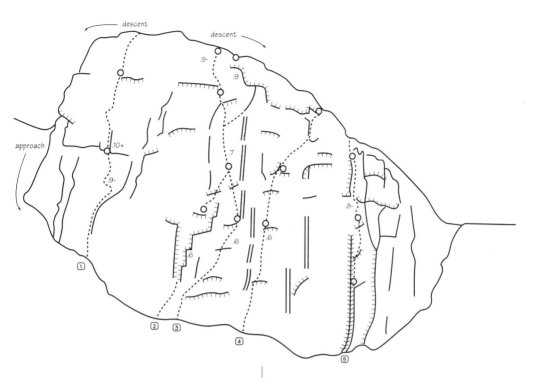

Checkerboard Wall

The Checkerboard is a 500-foot-high east-facing cliff with routes that range in difficulty from 5.6 to 5.10+. This popular area is very good in the mild winter. Bring a standard rack for these three-pitch routes and a 165-foot rope. Expect long runouts on easy and moderate climbing, with crux moves on the summit overhangs.

Finding the cliff: Approach by parking at Pizza Boulders and walking southeast. Allow thirty minutes to reach the cliff base. Descend to the south or north depending on which end you are climbing on. A new bolted line (not described here) has recently been installed, which may make descending easier. Routes are described left to right.

1. Worth the Effort (5.10+) 3 pitches up the left side of the wall. **Pitch 1:** Works up a right-leaning crack past some bushes. Face climb up left (5.9-) to an intermittent crack system and belay on a small ledge below an obvious roof. **Pitch 2:** Pull over the roof and follow an off-width crack (5.10+) to runout face climbing. Belay on a ledge up right. **Pitch 3:** Climb easy rock to the summit.

2. Unnamed (5.9-) 4 pitches. Start well right and downhill from #1 in a right-facing crack just right of a left-facing crack. **Pitch 1:** Easy climbing (5.6) ends on a ledge. **Pitch 2:** Start in a crack, then face climb above a ledge to another ledge and belay. **Pitch 3:** Face and crack climb (5.7) past a ledge, then face climb to under a roof. Belay by bushes. **Pitch 4:** Crack and face climbing lead to the top. Crux pitch.

3. Circus Finish (5.9) 4 pitches. Start on a ledge right of #2. **Pitch 1:** Face climb (5.6) to a belay on a ledge. **Pitch 2:** Face climb to the left of a large crack past a ledge to the top of the second pitch of #2. **Pitch 3:** Face and crack climb (5.7) to a ledge, then right and up to a ledge below a left-facing crack.

Pitch 4: Crux pitch. Climb the crack and roof system to the top.

4. Punch in the Nose (5.7) 3 pitches. Start on a ledge right of the large cracks. **Pitch 1:** Face climbing and cracks (5.6) lead to a ledge belay. **Pitch 2:** Discontinuous cracks lead to a belay on a ledge. **Pitch 3:** Face climb right, then up a large crack to the top. A 5.9 variation goes up a shallow right-facing dihedral on the left

5. Knight's Move (5.8) 3 pitches. Start in a right-facing corner left of trees. **Pitch 1:** Climb the corner to a ledge belay. **Pitch 2:** Continue up the corner, then right via a ledge to face climbing that ends on a sloping ledge. **Pitch 3:** Climb a short crack, then face climb (5.8-) to a right-facing corner. Belay at the top of the corner.

The Columns

As of the summer of 2004, The Columns has been closed to climbing. The land is part of the Chihuahuan Desert Rangeland Research center, owned by New Mexico State University and run by the Department of Animal and Range Sciences, which is part of the College of Agriculture and Home Economics. The closure is in effect so that research in the area will not be compromised. Hopefully this situation will change in the future. Check with Rick Kieser at the NMSU Office of Real Estate prior to planning a visit for the latest access information. In case the ban is lifted, here is a brief description of The Columns. In the meantime, please respect the closure.

The Best (5.10-) is an excellent route on the Southwest Face. Left of this route are several more good routes, including a short finger crack (5.10+) and a steep face that has not been free climbed to date. Additional routes are on the West Face. *Crack 5* (5.9) is a hand and fist crack on the left. *Crack 4* (5.10-) goes up the roof in the center. *Baskin Robbins* (5.8) climbs the prominent dihedral on the right.

Other Doña Ana Areas

Local consensus says that the area's best route is *Full Tilt Boogie* (5.10b/c). To get there, continue past Bear Boulders 0.6 mile to a right turn through a gate. Continue on the road until it leaves the power line and hike west. This is about a half mile before the left turn to The Columns. Look for a 50-foot vertical crack that leans left for another 50 feet near the top. The route is visible from the road. The area's original sport climb, *Anorexic* (5.11), climbs the face below and then through *Full Tilt Boogie*. Descend to the east. Not illustrated.

SITTING BULL FALLS

■ OVERVIEW

Sitting Bull Falls, a small limestone cliff hidden in a canyon on the northeast flank of the Guadalupe Mountains, continues to be a popular New Mexico sport climbing area. It's a remote crag, far from any other climbing area, but is nonetheless well worth a visit. The area was named after an American Indian chief, but not Sitting Bull, the famous Sioux war chief. This Sitting Bull was chief of a small band that lived in the area in the 1880s. The falls were named after him after he led a group of ranchers on a merry chase after stealing some of their horses and cattle.

The crag is divided into two sectors separated by a bulging prow topped with a cave. The overhanging Bighorn Wall on the right side features a selection of difficult and pumpy routes that are mostly 5.12. The Rosebud Wall on the left offers shorter, more moderate routes in the 5.10 and 5.11 range.

The 80-foot-high north-facing cliff is composed of tufa or travertine, a limestone formed in freshwater. The spongelike rock is riddled with many pockets and holes that result from calcification around organic material like algae, small plants, and trees. The organic material was deposited, rotted, and then weathered, leaving pockets from monodoigts to potholes large enough to rest inside. The limestone's relative softness helped erode it into a scooped-out, arching, cavelike cliff that overhangs as much as 40 feet in 80 vertical feet.

Climbing History

The area has been historically used by local cavers for rappelling and ascending practice.

John Gogas, along with other climbers, visited Sitting Bull Falls in the early 1980s but rejected the area as a climbing locale because of the lack of protection possibilities. After gaining experience on Texas crags, Gogas returned with his soon-to-be-wife, Carol, and Eric Isaacson on Memorial Day 1992. Thinking they had proper permission from the U.S. Forest Service, they began developing the cliff. The "permission" as it turned out was granted by unauthorized personnel. The painted hangers, glue-in Petzl anchors, and low-key approach, however, went unnoticed until the summer of 1995 when all development, although not climbing, was suspended pending a Forest Service Environmental Assessment of the area. Subsequent meetings between Gogas and Forest Service personnel paved the way for area management to include climbing as a legitimate recreational activity. Please read and adhere to all climbing rules and regulations to keep this excellent area open.

Rack and Descent

Rack for all routes is ten to fifteen quickdraws and a 165-foot rope. Descent is from lowering anchors at each route's end.

Trip Planning Information

Area description: Sitting Bull Falls offers excellent sport climbing routes on a 50- to 80-foot-high tufa limestone cliff.

Location: Southeastern New Mexico. In the mountains west of Artesia and Carlsbad.

Camping: The crag is located at the picnic area at Sitting Bull Falls. Camping is not allowed in the immediate area. Undeveloped sites, with no facilities or water, are located along the road several miles northeast of the

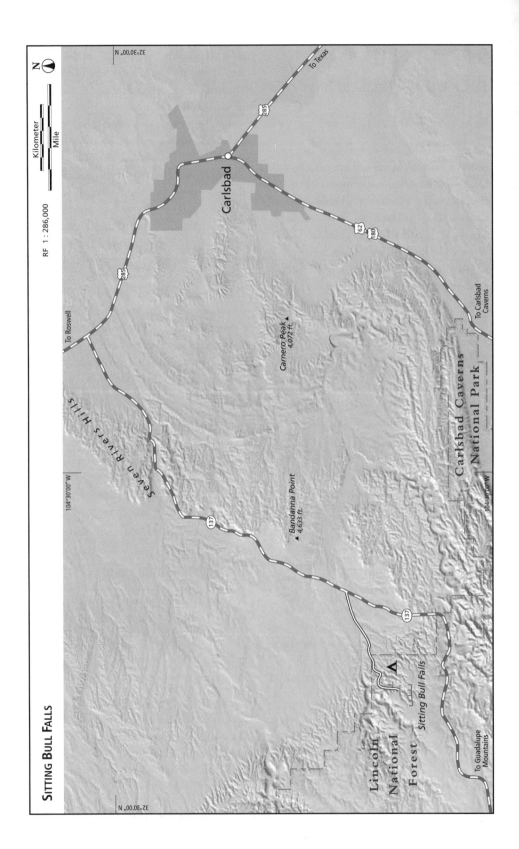

Sitting Bull Falls

RF 1 : 286,000

N

Kilometer

Mile

To Roswell

Seven Rivers Hills

Carlsbad

To Texas

285

285

62
180

Carnero Peak
4,072 ft.

Bandanna Point
4,633 ft.

137

137

Lincoln
National
Forest

Sitting Bull Falls

To Guadalupe
Mountains

Carlsbad Caverns
National Park

To Carlsbad
Caverns

32°30'00" N

32°30'00" N

104°30'00" W

104°00'00" W

picnic area. Practice clean, primitive camping and leave little evidence of your visit. Use existing fire rings and campsites. Water and restrooms are available at the picnic area. Be self-sufficient when visiting as it is a long distance to any amenities.

Climbing season: Climbing is best in early spring to late fall. Summer temperatures in this desert climate can limit climbing, although the north-facing cliff can occasionally be bearable on hot days. Climbing is possible on all but the coldest winter days. Check the Carlsbad temperatures for an idea of daily highs and lows.

Restrictions and access issues: The area, in Lincoln National Forest, is managed by the U.S. Forest Service. It is first and foremost a picnic area. After somewhat of a rough start, the area is open to climbing with the following stipulations and restrictions: Climbing is limited to the one wall behind the restrooms; all other areas are off-limits. The area will not accommodate more routes, so leave your drills at home. Citations and fines will be issued to violators. The extreme right end of the cliff is a bat nursing area and closed to climbing and other disturbing activities. Periodic closures of some of the routes just to the left of this area to protect the bat habitat may be necessary in the future. The area's environmental assessment calls for closing the current trail and building a new one. Local climbers are committed to helping with trail maintenance and trash cleanup. All climbers are encouraged to aid this effort. Climbers may wish to call Guadalupe Ranger District (505–885–4181) for conditions and possible closures before visiting.

Guidebooks: *Rock Climbing New Mexico & Texas* by Dennis R. Jackson, Falcon Press, 1996.

Services: None nearby. Carlsbad, approximately an hour east and south, offers all services. Artesia, approximately one hour northeast, also offers full services.

Emergency services: Call 911 if possible. No emergency services are nearby. The closest are in Carlsbad. Getting emergency assistance here is a time-consuming process. It would be easiest to self-evacuate the patient and drive Highway 137 to U.S. Highway 285 and then south to Carlsbad and emergency facilities. Call New Mexico State Police (505–524–6111) for emergencies.

Nearby climbing areas: Hueco Tanks is 190 miles to the southwest in north Texas. The Tunnel near Alamogordo is a great sport climbing area.

Nearby attractions: Carlsbad Caverns National Park lies 50 miles directly south. Guadalupe National Park, south in Texas, offers excellent hiking, camping, and exploring.

Finding the crag: From 24 miles south of Artesia and 12 miles north of Carlsbad, exit from US 285 onto Highway 137. Drive southwest on paved Highway 137 for about 20 miles. Look for the main highway to trend left past several right turns to ranches and drill sites to a signed right turn to Sitting Bull Falls. Follow dirt Eddy County Road 409 about 8 more miles until the road ends at Sitting Bull Recreation Area. The cliff band is seen from the end of the road and the restrooms at the picnic area. A five-minute hike leads directly to the cliff's left side. Routes are described from left to right.

The Rosebud Wall

1. The Brit Route (5.11b) The least popular climb on the crag. Start just right of the cave-like formation on the left end of the cliff.

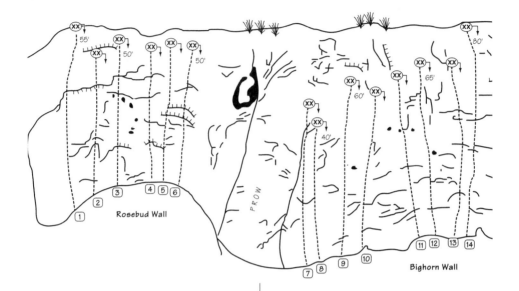

Rosebud Wall

PROW

Bighorn Wall

2. Firewalker (5.10b) Excellent.

3. Wounded Knee (5.10a) A good introduction to Sitting Bull Falls.

4. Six Little Indians (5.10c) Quality. Difficult at top.

5. Big Medicine (5.11c) Recommended. Tricky finish.

6. Sweat Lodge (5.11b) Quality climbing.

The Bighorn Wall

The following routes are located on the Bighorn Wall on the same cliff band about 40 feet right of *Sweat Lodge*.

7. Smoke Signals (5.11b) Quality. Another good warm-up for the harder routes to the right.

8. Ghost Dancers (5.12a) Excellent. Short and fingery.

9. Counting Coup (5.12b) A runner-up for the best 5.12b route in New Mexico.

10. Eagles Aren't Crows (5.12c/d) Great route. Not as steep as #11, but thinner.

11. Tribal War (5.12c/d) An area favorite. Similar to #12 with easier crux and harder climbing to the anchors.

12. Broken Arrows (5.12d) Recommended. Pumpy climbing leads to a powerful crux, then easy cruising to the anchors.

13. Kootenai Cruiser (5.13d) Start 30 feet right of #12. A V9 boulder problem followed by a burly dyno, then pumpy 5.12a/b to the anchors. Get ready for big air time if you miss the dyno.

14. Custer's Last Stand (5.13b) Quality moves.

CITY OF ROCKS STATE PARK

■ OVERVIEW

City of Rocks State Park, a secluded jumble of boulders in arid southwestern New Mexico, is a virtually undiscovered bouldering paradise. The off-the-beaten-track area sees little serious activity, although there is serious potential for hundreds of boulder problems. Lots of 10- to 30-foot-high boulders and rock formations, composed of ash-flow tuff or ignimbrites, cover this 680-acre parkland. The strangely shaped rocks, part of the Kneeling Nun tuff formation that erupted 34.9 million years ago, are the result of nearby volcanic activity. The erosive sculpting by wind and water produced edges, huecos, and cracks similar to the rock at Hueco Tanks and Enchanted Tower. While City of Rocks doesn't offer the diversity and outstanding quality of Hueco Tanks, the lack of crowds, pleasant camping among the rocks, and the potential for personal statements on untried problems make it an attractive alternative.

Bob Murray is City of Rocks's most prolific boulderer. Murray, long one of the West's best boulderers, left his mark here as well as at Hueco Tanks. He considers the City one of the best bouldering areas he explored and developed while living in Tucson in the 1980s. Murray often wrapped the boulder summits at the City with long lengths of webbing and worked out the hard moves while protected by a Gibbs ascender. Writing about City of Rocks in *Stone Crusade,* John Sherman notes that " . . . there's always the feeling that when you're doing something hard, it probably isn't a first ascent. Still, 100 Thimbles wait to be done by someone with chrome-moly nerves and freon-filled veins."

Unlike Hueco Tanks, no guidebook or named and rated problems are found at City of Rocks. It's best for the adventurous boulderer to roam the area and search out what looks good. A network of roads and trails lace the park, allowing easy access to every area. A few suggestions include the boulders above campsites on the east side of the one-way road and at The Suburb, a boulder grouping at the far northwest end of the park. Some excellent boulders and problems rise above the few campsites in this sector.

Rack and Descent

Most of the park's bouldering is on sharp edges and flakes, with occasional problems that jam or layback up cracks. Many problems are quite painful to the fingertips. Descent off many boulders is problematic. Sometimes it's easiest to downclimb a desperate problem to a point where it's possible to launch onto your crash pad. Others require trailing a tied-off rope up and rapping down the backside. Remember to bring bouldering ethics with you. Don't chip, alter, or file holds. Not only is this illegal, but it is also cheating and destroys the area's future for hard bouldering. A crash pad and a spotter help avoid injuries.

Trip Planning Information

Area description: City of Rocks offers hundreds of boulders scattered across a rolling plain in an arid desert environment.

Location: Southwestern New Mexico, 27 miles north of Deming and Interstate 10.

Camping: City of Rocks State Park keeps a tidy, well-maintained fifty-two-site campground year-round. Most sites sit among the boulders. Just camp and climb. An added plus

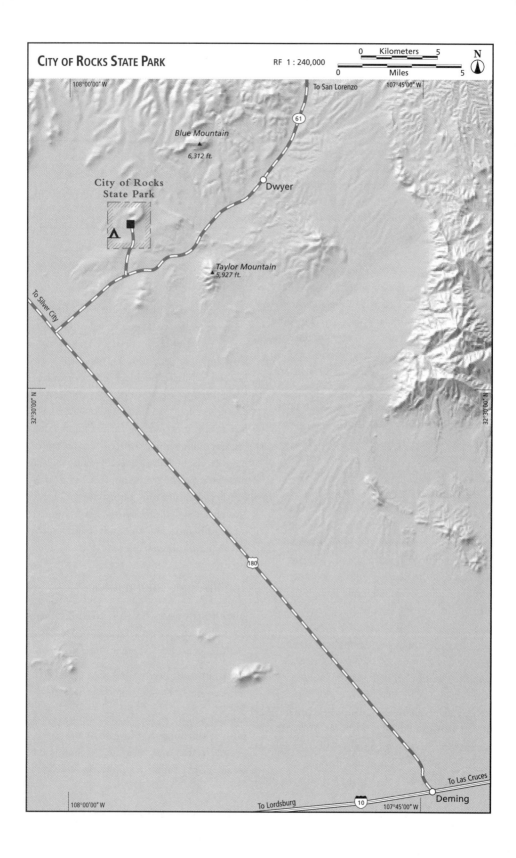

CITY OF ROCKS STATE PARK

RF 1 : 240,000

Kilometers

N

108°00'00" W

To San Lorenzo

107°45'00" W

61

Blue Mountain
▲
6,312 ft.

City of Rocks
State Park

Dwyer

Taylor Mountain
▲ 5,927 ft.

To Silver City

32°30'00" N

32°30'00" N

180

To Lordsburg

To Las Cruces

10

108°00'00" W

107°45'00" W

Deming

are showers and drinking water. Fees and time limits apply. Campsites at The Suburb on the north end of the park are usually deserted.

Climbing season: Year-round. The best seasons are spring, fall, and winter. Hot summer temperatures are normally in excess of 90 degrees. At an elevation of 5,200 feet, occasional cold winter days may restrict opportunities. Expect windy days, particularly in spring, at this exposed area.

Restrictions and access issues: Rock defacement and bolting are the primary concerns of park personnel. Both are illegal. Rescuing stranded visitors on the boulders is a park problem. Determine descent routes prior to starting out, and have a rope available to lower or rap off with the assistance of an anchored belayer. Park officials want climbers to use chalk sparingly to avoid unsightly marks on the rocks. If climber visitation and use increases, the possibility of additional restrictions exists. Also pick up your trash, walk on existing trails, and leave no evidence of your visit.

Services: All services in Deming, Silver City, and Las Cruces. Fuel and a convenience store are in Hurley, 18 miles north on U.S. Highway 180.

Emergency services: For all park incidents, contact the rangers at the visitor center. Emergency medical services are available in Deming, 28 miles south on US 180, and in Silver City, 34 miles north on US 180.

Nearby climbing areas: City of Rocks is relatively isolated from other climbing areas. The closest are Organ Mountains and Doña Ana Mountains, 60 miles southeast; Hueco Tanks, 130 miles southeast; and Enchanted Tower, 190 miles north. Nearby areas in Arizona include Cochise Stronghold.

Nearby attractions: Gila Cliff Dwellings National Monument, Gila Wilderness Area, Gila National Forest, Pancho Villa State Park, Rock Hound State Park, Deming Luna Mimbres Museum, and Columbus Historical Museum are all close to City of Rocks. Outdoor fun in this beautiful area includes hiking, backpacking, fishing, hot springs, and white-water boating. The Great American Duck Race with attendant festivities is held every year in Deming on the fourth weekend in August. A privately owned hot spring, located approximately 2 miles south of the park on Highway 61, is sometimes open.

Finding the boulders: From Las Cruces or Arizona, take I–10 to Deming. Turn right or north onto US 180 for 23 miles, then turn right onto Highway 61 for 3 miles. Turn left or north at a sign to City of Rocks State Park and drive 2 miles to the visitor center.

From Albuquerque and Santa Fe take Interstate 25 south and exit west at the Hillsboro exit onto Highway 152 12 miles south of Truth or Consequences. Drive west on Highway 152 for 51 miles. This highway section is steep, hilly, and winding; allow lots of time for driving. Turn south onto Highway 61 at San Lorenzo and drive 23 miles southwest to City of Rocks State Park.

A fee is charged to enter and use the park. A one-way loop drive circles the park. Find whatever boulders you like, park, and climb. Not illustrated.

APPENDIX A:
HEART OF STONE ROCK

Heart of Stone Rock, a beautiful and historic crag, has been closed to climbing since 2004. Tucked into a narrow canyon, this rock once offered a small selection of three-pitch routes on a 350-foot-high granite crag rising above the twisting Arroyo Seco Creek in the mountains of northwest Taos. Climbs included *Heart of Stone* and *The Edwin Terrell Memorial Route* variation (5.11) and *Laid Back Limey* (5.9+).

A smaller version of nearby Questa Dome, Heart of Stone Rock yielded excellent climbing on surprisingly solid granite. First-time visitors must have been intimidated by the lack of protection and the initial impression of poor rock quality. Early Taos climbers, however, were undeterred and established several multipitch routes in bold traditional style. Most of this activity occurred in the late 1970s and early 1980s. Development then slowed, except for Ken Sims's fine one-pitch variation to *Heart of Stone*. This variation was named for Edwin Terrell, a talented Santa Fe climber who was tragically killed while climbing Makalu. Both routes were somewhat unobvious affairs that ascended a variety of edges, pockets, flakes, and cracks. Climbers had to be adept at route-finding and willing to run it out on sparsely protected sections.

Although Heart of Stone Rock is currently closed to climbing, Jay Foley and other local activists have been working with the Land Grant owners to resolve the issues preventing access to this beautiful and historic crag. Please honor the closure until resolution and accord are reached. If, and when, the crag reopens to climbing, check with locals for new access information.

Don't confuse Heart of Stone Rock with nearby El Salto, which is made up of some of the large granite formations north and west of the crag. Climbed by early Taos climbers, several 5.7 routes were established on the original El Salto that looked like exciting affairs. El Salto is also on private land and is closed to climbing.

APPENDIX B: FURTHER READING

A Climber's Guide to Box Canyon, Erik Hufnagel and Bertrand Gramont, self-published.

A Climbing Guide to the Organ Mountains, R. L. Ingraham, c. 1960, self-published.

The Enchanted Tower, Pockets Full O'Fun: A Climber's Guidebook to the Enchanted Tower, Datil, New Mexico, Eric Fazio-Rhicard and Guy Agee, Esquared Enterprises, 2003.

The Enchanted Tower, Sport Climbing Socorro and Datil, New Mexico, Sal Maestas and Matthew Jones, New Mexico Institute of Mining and Technology, 1993.

Hikers and Climbing Guide to the Sandias, third edition, Mike Hill, University of New Mexico Press, 1993.

Lookin' Rough, But Feelin' Ready: A Guide to Climbs in the Rough and Ready Hills, NM, Mickey Hazelwood, self-published, 2004.

Mentmore Climbing Mecca, Michael Laplante, Big Wall Productions, 2001.

Rock Climbing New Mexico & Texas, Dennis R. Jackson, Falcon Press, 1996.

Sandia Rock, Mike Schein, Sharp End Publishing, 2003.

Sport Climbing in New Mexico, North, Randal Jett and Matt Samet, 1991.

Sport Climbing in New Mexico, South, Randal Jett and Matt Samet, 1991.

Taos Rock III, Cayce Weber and Ed Jaramillo, self-published, 1991.

Taos Rock: Climbs and Boulders of Northern New Mexico, Jay Foley, Sharp End Publishing, 2005.

APPENDIX C: RATING SYSTEM COMPARISON CHART

YDS	British	French	Australian
5.3	VD 3b	2	11
5.4	HVD 3c	3	12
5.5	MS/S/HS 4a	4a	12/13
5.6	HS/S 4a	4b	13
5.7	HS/VS 4b/4c	4c	14/15
5.8	HVS 4c/5a	5a	16
5.9	HVS 5a	5b	17/18
5.10a	E1 5a/5b	5c	18/19
5.10b	E1/E2 5b/5c	6a	19/20
5.10c	E2/E3 5b/5c	6a	+20/21
5.10d	E3 5c/6a	6b	21/22
5.11a	E3/E4 5c/6a	6b	+22/23
5.11b	E4/E5 6a/6b	6c	23/24
5.11c	E4/E5 6a/6b	6c	+24
5.11d	E4/E5 6a/6b	7a	25
5.12a	E5 6b/6c	7a	+25/26
5.12b	E5/E6 6b/6c	7b	26
5.12c	E5/E6 6b/6c/7a	7b	+26/27
5.12d	E6/E7 6c/7a	7c	27
5.13a	E6/E7 6c/7a	7c	+28
5.13b	E7 7a	8a	29
5.13c	E7 7a	8a	+30/31
5.13d	E8 7a	8b	31/32
5.14a	E8 7a	8b	+32/33
5.14b	E9 7a	8c	33
5.14c	E9 7b	8c	+33

APPENDIX D:
GOVERNMENT AGENCIES AND
CLIMBING ASSOCIATIONS

Access Fund
P.O. Box 17010
Boulder, CO 80308
(303) 545–6772
www.accessfund.org

Albuquerque BLM Field Office
435 Montano Road NE
Albuquerque, NM 87107-4935
(505) 761–8700
www.nm.blm.gov/aufo_home.html

Bandelier National Monument
HCR 1, Box 1, Suite 15
Ls Alamos, NM 87544
(505) 672–0343
www.nps.gov/band/

Carlsbad BLM Field Office
620 East Greene Street
Carlsbad, NM 88220
(505) 234–5972
www.nm.blm.gov/cfo/cfo_home.html

Carson National Forest
208 Cruz Alta Road
Taos, NM 87571
(505) 521–1922
www.fs.fed.us/r3/cibola/

Cibola National Forest
2113 Osuna Road NE, Suite A
Albuquerque, NM 87113
(505) 346–3900
www.fs.fed.us/r3/cibola/

Cimarron Canyon State Park
P.O. Box 185
Eagle Nest, NM 87719
(505) 377–6271
www.nmparks.com

City of Rocks State Park
P.O. Box 50
Faywood, NM 88034
(505) 536–2800
www.nmparks.com

El Malpais National Monument
123 Roosevelt Street
Grants, NM 87020
(505) 285–4641
www.nps.gov/elma

Farmington BLM Field Office
1235 La Plata Highway, Suite A
Farmington, NM 87401
(505) 599–8900
www.nm.blm.gov/ffo/ffo_home.html

Gila National Forest
3005 East Camino del Bosque
Silver City, NM 88061
(505) 388–8201
www2.srs.fs.fed.us/r3/gila/

Las Cruces BLM Field Office
1800 Marquess Street
Las Cruces, NM 88005-3370
(505) 525–4300
www.nm.blm.gov/lcfo/lcfo_home.html

Lincoln National Forest
1101 New York Avenue
Alamogordo, NM 88310
(505) 434–7200
www.fs.fed.us/r3/lincoln/

New Mexico CRAG (Climbers
Resource and Advocacy Group)
www.nmcrag.org

Rocky Mountain Field Institute
1520 Alamo Drive
Colorado Springs, CO 87903
(719) 471–7736
www.rmfi.org

Santa Fe BLM Field Office
1474 Rodeo Road
Santa Fe, NM 87505
(505) 438–7542
www.nm.blm.gov/field_offices

Santa Fe National Forest
1474 Rodeo Road
Santa Fe, NM 87505
(505) 438–7840
www.fs.fed.us/r3/sfe/

Socorro BLM Field Office
198 Neel Avenue NW
Socorro, NM 87801–4648
(505) 835–0412
www.nm.blm.gov/sfo/sfo_home.html

Sugarite Canyon State Park
HCR 63, Box 386
Raton, NM 87740
(505) 445–5607
www.emnrd.state.nm.us/nmparks

Taos BLM Field Office
226 Cruz Alta Road
Taos, NM 87571–5983
(505) 758–8851
www.nm.blm.gov/tafo/tafo_home.html

Wild Rivers National Recreation Area
Taos BLM Field Office
226 Cruz Alta Road
Taos, NM 87571–5983
(505) 758–8851
www.nm.blm.gov/tafo/tafo_home.html

ROUTES BY
RATING INDEX

INDEX

Formations, walls, and crags are in roman. Routes are in italics (*route name* followed by rating and page number). Routes starting with "A" or "The" are alphabetized by the second word.

ABOUT THE AUTHOR

Dennis Jackson (Taos, New Mexico) is a professional guide and outdoor educator. He is a member of the professional staff of the Rocky Mountain Field Institute and the Kent Mountain Adventure Center and is president of Challenge Designs, an outdoor consulting and instructional company.